Glimpses of Freedom

 Cornell University

May Adadol Ingawanij and Benjamin McKay, editors

Glimpses of Freedom

Independent Cinema in Southeast Asia

SOUTHEAST ASIA PROGRAM PUBLICATIONS
Southeast Asia Program
Cornell University
Ithaca, New York
2012

Cornell Southeast Asia Program Publications
640 Stewart Avenue, Ithaca, NY 14850-3857

Studies on Southeast Asia No. 55

Printed in the United States of America

ISBN: hc 978-0-87727-785-9
ISBN: pb 978-0-87727-755-2

Cover: designed by Mo Viele.
Cover image: from Chris Chong Chan Fui's film, *Block B*, photo by Pang Khee Teck.

For Benjamin McKay (1964–2010) and Alexis A. Tioseco (1981–2009)
with enduring affection and gratitude.

TABLE OF CONTENTS

INTRODUCTION:
DIALECTICS OF INDEPENDENCE

May Adadol Ingawanij

Since the late 1990s, the word "independent" has been resurfacing to demarcate a certain sphere of cinematic practice in Southeast Asia. As a vitalizing if vague signpost, this term is being variously iterated by local filmmakers and critics, and taken up by transnational sites that mediate the international circulation of contemporary films and videos from the region.[1] The starting point for this book is the concurrence of these factors: the seemingly simultaneous surfacing of independent cinema as aesthetic and social practice, and discursive category, in all of the archipelagic and in a number of the mainland Southeast Asian countries, and the seemingly new global profile of films and filmmakers of a few of them. The deliberate hesitancy of this description draws attention to two basic questions for a book of this sort. The first is how to approach independent cinema or film culture as a regional phenomenon. In other words, on what ground do we undertake the methodological labor of identifying commonality, mapping regional flows or movements, and positing comparability? The other question concerns the productivity, effects, and contradictions engendered here by the encounter between the local and the transnational. This question seems especially relevant when analyzing the contexts and forms of cinematic articulation and film cultural practice, and thinking through the ambivalence of gesturing to the "new," or the "emerging," as the basis for endowing the cinemas of the periphery with aesthetic, critical, or commercial value.[2]

---

[1] Such references are, for instance, the "I-Sinema" manifesto in Indonesia in the late 1990s. See Ekky Imanjaya, "Idealism versus Commercialism in Indonesian Cinema: A Neverending Battle?" *Rumah Film*, March 17, 2009, http://old.rumahfilm.org/artikel/artikel_neverending_7.htm. The Pusan International Film Festival has recently featured special programs: "Mabuhay Pinoy Indi-Cinema" (2009) and "Three Colors of New Malaysian Cinema" (2007). There were, of course, practices of independent cinema in Southeast Asia prior to this contemporary period, the most outstanding of which were the Filipino new wave of the 1970s and 1980s, hence the choice of the word "resurfacing."

[2] See Dina Iordanova, David Martin-Jones, and Bélen Vidal's discussion of the usage of the term "peripheral cinema" in the post-cold war period, where they define it as a cinema that

In preparing their contribution to this collection, the writers were asked to respond to the following questions:

- How have local independent cinemas risen to visibility? What preconditions were necessary?

- What discursive effects do the terms "independent" or "indie" engender in relation to the film, video, filmmaker, group, or institution in question? In what sense are signifiers of this nature relevant to the work or phenomenon discussed?

- Apart from the issues of production (funding, work methods) and text (form, narrative, style), what other terrains of cinematic practice must be taken into consideration? How do issues of diffusion and spectatorship apply to practices of independent cinema in Southeast Asia, especially if we think in terms of the more expansive notion of "independent film culture" rather than independent filmmaking as such?

Readers will quickly realize that the contributors to this book do not uniformly adopt the epistemology of the academic essay. As editors, we made the decision to let contributors shape their responses to some of our questions in a mode of writing or dialogue most appropriate to their own experiential and practical engagement with cinema in contemporary Southeast Asia. There is an important point, to be returned to later, concerning the relationship between the various modes of writing encompassed in this book and practices of independent film culture in the region. But before we reach that point, this introductory chapter will first identify three conceptual frames that place the contributions within a connective field.

The task of defining independent cinema is one of identifying discernible (practical, formal, and discursive) tendencies, as well as delineating generative networks. This line of inquiry leads to further questions: in what sense can we speak of independent cinema as independent from certain structures of dominance, exploitation, or repression? Should we not rather pay analytic attention to identifying constitutive dependencies within shifting networks? For example, scholars of the comparable phenomenon of post-Tiananmen independent Chinese cinema have proposed shifting the terms of analysis to "in dependence," signaling the need to trace the network of transnational market forces and foreign sites and institutions that enable Chinese filmmakers and artists to produce works outside the structure of state-controlled funding, distribution, and exhibition.[3]

The conceptual frames developed in this introduction lend themselves to certain comparisons with Geoff King and Chris Berry's respective outlinings of the conjunctures of independent cinema in the United States and China during the 1990s and early 2000s. King defines American independent cinema as that shaped by

---

also emphasizes dynamic interrelationships among multiple peripheral locations around and beyond the centers of power. Dina Iordanova, David Martin-Jones, and Bélen Vidal, "Introduction: A Peripheral View of World Cinema," in *Cinema at the Periphery*, ed. Dina Iordanova, David Martin-Jones, and Bélen Vidal (Detroit, MI: Wayne State University Press, 2010), pp. 1–19.

[3] Paul Pickowicz and Yingjin Zhang, "Preface," in *From Underground to Independent: Alternative Film Culture in Contemporary China*, ed. Paul Pickowicz and Yingjin Zhang (Lanham, MD: Rowman and Littlefield Publishers, 2006), p. ix.

varying combinations of the following structural factors: the filmmaker's placement in relation to the Hollywood-led industry; formal and aesthetic markers that differentiate a film from the classical Hollywood style; and the film or filmmaker's relation to the broader social, cultural, or political landscape.[4] In comparison with the private-sector orientation of King's framework, Berry's analysis identifies the state as one structure in the "three-legged system" within which Chinese independent filmmakers have to operate, the other two "legs" being the globalized market economy and foreign arts or cinema institutions.[5] Highlighting the state in the analytic frame is likewise necessary in the case of Southeast Asia. As many of the chapters indicate, state economic aspirations and censorship do play a decisive role in shaping the independent cinematic terrains in question. Both King and Berry shift from discussing economic and other structural factors to identifying aesthetic patterns and formal strategies associated with independent practices in the United States and China, such as, for instance, the adoption of the observational documentary style among Chinese independent filmmakers, or the eschewing of dramatic action by US indie auteurs, such as Jim Jarmusch. A comparable framing of Southeast Asian practices should also aim to highlight how the combination of state controls and/or inducements, economic and cultural globalization, technological change, and local political ruptures create aesthetic tendencies and formal strategies, as well as encouraging certain modes of spectatorship.

Each overarching frame proposed below therefore highlights a key determinant of independent cinema in contemporary Southeast Asia, whose combination with other structural and contingent factors creates definitional tendencies as well as contradictory consequences. These frames are: 1) Production, namely the place of the filmmaker within relations of production shaped by state power, globalized capital, transnational cultural networks, and digitalization; 2) Diffusion, which refers to the often unpredictable circulation of moving images, critical discourses, or cinephilic expressions in local, underground, national, or transnational contexts; 3) The national, or the problematic of relating cinematic experience—spectatorial responses to narrative construction and sensory stimulation in a variety of screen environments—to the invocation of freedom and the possibility of an alternative future within a shared territory.

PLACE IN PRODUCTION

Although production conditions are locally variable, it is still useful to identify some common parameters constituting the range of possibilities within the region. A spectacular factor across Southeast Asia is the opening up of national territories to the digital media market, a transformation whose infrastructural activation is contingent on political calculations (see chapters by Eloisa May P. Hernandez and Hassan Abd Muthalib). On the back of this change comes the appearance of a market feature most contributors to this book identify as a crucial condition for independent filmmaking and other accompanying activities of dissemination: the affordability and accessibility of digital technologies of production, post-production, and

---

[4] Geoff King, *American Independent Cinema* (London: I. B. Tauris, 2005).

[5] Chris Berry, "Independently Chinese: Duan Jinchuang, Jiang Yue, and Chinese Documentary," in *From Underground to Independent: Alternative Film Culture in Contemporary China*, pp. 109–22.

circulation, often facilitated by piracy. The second structural factor concerns state responses to neoliberal economic globalization via efforts to capitalize culture, efforts that intensified as a consequence of the 1997 Asian economic crisis. The Singapore state's recent cultural policies under the rubric of a "creative economy" rhetoric are the clearest example of a shift of this sort.[6] A comparable rhetoric—though one that was not implemented with equal intensity—was a striking feature of the first phase of Thaksin Shinawatra's premiership in Siam (2001–04). The third factor is the expansion of the global film festival network and its associated channels for film funding. As Marijke de Valck summarizes, during the 1970s, programmers of major European film festivals, such a those in Berlin and Venice, began to showcase the "discovery" of peripheral cinema, a shift in programming that rapidly expanded in the ensuing decade.[7] This shift became augmented by film funding initiatives aimed at achieving greater global coverage than did the previous model of European co-productions for films shot in Europe. In the 1990s, the emergence of Asia-oriented festivals, or the reorientation of existing "second tier" festivals toward the Asia-Pacific, further intensified this trend with targeted (production and distribution) funding opportunities for filmmakers based in the region.

The practices and roles adopted by independent filmmakers in this structured network range from artisanal practices to negotiated dependencies. An example of a filmmaker working in the artisanal mode is Martyn See, who makes documentaries about opposition politicians in Singapore. Aiming to create a social record for the future and a probe of the contradictions of current censorship practices by the Singapore media authority, See constructs his films from his own archive of footage and interviews (see Vinita Ramani's chapter). Insofar as the filmmaker emphasizes making his documentaries available for public viewing via channels that tend to elude effective censorship, the term "oppositional" is an appropriate characterization of the intention driving his production and dissemination activities. Examples of another type of artisanal practice more fittingly described as "underground" can be found in Chalida Uabumrungjit's discussion of Thai short films and documentaries that attempt to subvert social taboos. Such works have been routinely screened at the Thai Short Film and Video Festival since its inception in 1997, but, as my chapter discusses, during the past decade the festival itself has been operating quite comfortably under the radar of the cultural authority.

The accessibility of digital video devices has given strong impetus to the amateur or "do-it-yourself" (DIY) mode of practice across the region.[8] This point is widely acknowledged by those who write about contemporary Southeast Asian cinema. However, rather than merely underlining low- or no-cost budgeting—and associated low- to no-budget production scales—the DIY phenomenon prompts us to open a more interesting vista by reevaluating the aesthetic and pedagogical worth of works displaying the "amateurism" of low production values. In this respect, there is a close correlation between conceptualizing DIY filmmaking as an act of aesthetic

---

[6] Kenneth Paul Tan, *Cinema and Television in Singapore: Resistance in One Dimension* (Leiden: Brill, 2008); Lee Weng Choy, "Authenticity, Reflexivity, and Spectacle; or, The Rise of New Asia is not the End of the World," *Positions: East Asia Cultures Critique* 12,3 (Winter 2004): 643–66.

[7] Marijke de Valck, *Film Festivals: From European Geopolitics to Global Cinephilia* (Amsterdam: Amsterdam University Press, 2007).

[8] Gaik Cheng Khoo, "Just-Do-It-(yourself): Independent Filmmaking in Malaysia," *Inter-Asia Cultural Studies* 8,2 (June 2007): 227–47.

liberation and the artistic embrace of amateurism as an inherent part of formal experimentation.[9] However, it is not always possible to draw a hard and fast line between the amateur as experimental artist and the artist as freelancer in the media or film industry. Artists such as John Torres (see his chapter), or Thailand's outstanding videomaker and soundman Paisit Punpreuksachat, shift as circumstances demand between mainstream commissions and filmic experimentation on an artisanal scale. Yet, as much as DIY experiments are personal expressions, they simultaneously function as commentaries on the limitations of the industrial–commercial setting. In his chapter, Hassan Muthalib discusses how the Malay-centric nature of racial representation on the public screens in Malaysia has impelled "fourth-generation Indian Malaysian filmmakers" to seek alternative channels of financing and exhibition for their personal films—works that narrate or allegorize experiences of marginality in one's homeland.

Parallel to the artistic invocation of the artisanal mode is the proliferation of filmmaking workshops organized by big and small arts bodies and social-issue campaign groups, the overwhelming majority of which utilize DV (digital video) and other digital equipment. Like those artists who emphasize the worth of amateurism as a process of experimentation, these workshops stake their claim to pedagogical value on the process of teaching (mostly young) people to make films, an affirmative response to digital's so-called "democratization" of filmmaking (see Jan Uhde and Yvonne Ng Uhde's chapter, and May Adadol Ingawanij's chapter).

While the above categories address filmmaking practices that do not, on the whole, aim to partake in some form of economic transaction, filmmakers who are capable of accessing the convoluted network of global art cinema have to handle a more complex kind of interdependence. Transnational co-production channels are made available to "auteurs" or "emerging" filmmakers at film festivals, in particular those festivals that have been cultivating an image of expertise in Asia-Pacific cinema. Rotterdam and Pusan, for instance, have interlinked film market events. Each year during the festival period, filmmakers are selected to pitch their projects to an international array of potential funders at CineMart (Rotterdam) and the Pusan Promotion Plan. Supplementary funding takes the form of prestigious schemes affiliated with major film festivals, as well as the older channel of grants from cultural and governmental institutions outside Southeast Asia.[10]

The obvious strength of transnational funding is that it can help filmmakers gain independence from restrictive financial arrangements offered by state agencies in their home countries (if these funding opportunities do indeed exist on a substantive scale) or by domestic film industries. Apichatpong Weerasethakul's freedom to structure his feature films the way he does is partly due to his ability to secure funding almost entirely from foreign sources. (Whether he can show his works in their intended form on cinema screens in his home country is another matter.) As Muthalib and Gaik Cheng Khoo's chapters indicate in the case of Malaysia, multiethnic and multilingual feature films struggle to secure industrial and state

---

[9] Apichatpong Weerasethakul, David Teh, Benedict Anderson, and May Adadol Ingawanij, "Conversations," in *The More Things Change: The Fifth Bangkok Experimental Film Festival*, catalogue for festival, March 25–30, 2008 (Bangkok: Project 304 and Kick the Machine, 2008), pp. 23–53.

[10] On this point, see also Sylvie E. Blum-Reid's article on French funding for cultural cinema and its impact on the work method of Cambodian-French filmmaker Rithy Panh. "Khmer Memories or Filming with Cambodia," in *Inter-Asia Cultural Studies* 4,1 (2003): 126–38.

funding in their domestic contexts, fostering thereby the tendency of practitioners of the "little cinema" to finance themselves or to look for support abroad. At the same time, the economics of global art cinema heightens certain interdependencies between filmmakers and film festivals. Festivals feed off the glamour of stars and auteurs and also the fetish of the new—the quickening cycle of discovering forms and faces from remote places. Meanwhile, peripheral filmmakers rely on festivals for building profiles for themselves. They make this choice not only because critically acclaimed screenings on the film festival circuit may enhance a completed film's prospects for international distribution. Increasingly, the situation seems to be that upcoming filmmakers must quickly establish their presence on the circuit just to increase their chances of completing their first or second feature.

The link between the early career of filmmakers from Southeast Asia and such initiatives as CineMart, Pusan's Asia Cinema Fund, or Berlin's Talent Campus figure as useful empirical case studies in this regard. Further research in this vein, looking into the terms of relations between the cluster of prestigious film festivals largely situated in Europe, the handful of professional programmers who work across festivals, and the multitude of filmmakers from peripheral territories, promises to tell us much about current world cinema. Such an investigation would raise questions about the politics of cultural labor in a context of neoliberal globalization, as well as narrower questions concerning film economics. For instance, we might want to ask what surplus values are extracted from the participation of "emerging" filmmakers in festival marketplaces and training/networking events or from their receipt of festival prizes and funds. From another methodological angle, ethnographic and sociological research into the "festival experience" of independent filmmakers from Southeast Asia should tell us quite a bit about the potentials and the contradictions of film festivals as sites of cross-cultural mediation.[11] At the same time, the historian of film poetics may want to ask how the mutual entanglement of filmmakers and the film festival network fosters certain narrative, stylistic, or aesthetic tendencies (see Khoo's chapter).

The case of Vietnam adds further complications to the question of transnational interdependence. As Mariam Lam's chapter shows, "transnational" funding after *đổi mới*[12] encompasses the investing of diasporic capital in genre films that aim to position themselves as blockbusters within and outside Vietnam. Yet such films are "independent" insofar as they are shot in Vietnam by local or diasporic filmmakers, but do not rely on state funding. The definition of independent filmmaking being explored in this context is in some ways comparable to the one that Augustin Sotto identifies in relation to the Filipino B-movies made during the 1960s.[13] Whereas these filmmakers operated outside of the production sphere of the dominant (but declining) private studios, independent creators of contemporary Vietnam cinema are producing mass commercial films alongside the residual state-studio structure. However, given that the state-run sector itself has been moving towards attracting greater private capital for film funding, a fascinating issue here concerns the extent to

---

[11] Bill Nichols, "Discovering Form, Inferring Meaning: New Cinemas and the Film Festival Circuit," *Film Quarterly* 47,3 (Spring 1994): 16–30.

[12] *Đổi mới* refers to the program of economic reform initiated by Vietnam's Communist Party in 1986. Its aim was to encourage the transition to a market economy while maintaining the existing structure of political control.

[13] Augustin Sotto, "Philippines: A Brief History of Philippine Cinema," in *Film in Southeast Asia: Views from the Region*, ed. David Hanan (Hanoi: SEAPAVAA, 2001), pp. 47–48.

which diaspora-driven independent filmmaking constitutes an "alternative" to the shifting structure of state-controlled funding, distribution, and filmic representation.

Another relevant factor in analyzing the independent production terrain in Southeast Asia is the involvement of industrial or state funds and agencies in practices whose point of emergence had previously been within underground, experimental, or amateur settings. One example is the appearance in the Philippines of what looks like a micro-industry, in which subsidiary production houses owned by media corporations fund low-budget auteur films (see Alexis A. Tioseco's chapter). This can certainly be seen as one instance of the industrial capitalization of independent production for a niche market.[14] What is also interesting to note in the Philippine case is the way media corporations mirror the production and exhibition practices of the independent scene in their involvement with "alternative" production, as demonstrated in the example of the Cinema One Originals festival and its attendant grant scheme (see Hernandez's chapter). Meanwhile, in Singapore, it is the state's "creative economy" investment that is creating contradictory opportunity structures. Jan Uhde and Yvonne Ng Uhde's chapter on The Substation, the leading independent cinema and arts venue in Singapore (and indeed in Southeast Asia), indicates that the success and relative longevity of this institution is partly due to its skillful navigation of state-funding channels and selective collaboration with national arts institutions. In Thailand's case, an interesting recent development concerns the cultural authorities' appropriation of the convention of independent filmmaking for the reproduction of spectacular royalism. Since the 2006 coup, Thai state agencies such as the Office of Contemporary Art and Culture have been commissioning short films and filmmaking competitions commemorating the birthday of the ailing Rama IX. This can be seen as an effort to channel the appeal of vitality associated with the artisanal/amateur creative process to the performance of royalist propaganda (see my chapter).

DIFFUSION: PUBLICNESS, PIRACY

The ambition to show films and videos in public settings forces both filmmakers and organizers of independent film events to contend with the repressive force of state power. Of the countries in Southeast Asia, only Timor-Leste does not practice film censorship (see Angie Bexley's chapter). Elsewhere censorship laws are actively, if erratically, applied. The most well known of recent cases is the censoring of Apichatpong's *Syndromes and a Century* (2006) in Thailand, a decision implicitly linked to the fractious aftermath of the 2006 coup (see Benedict Anderson's chapter). Likewise, the works of Amir Muhammad and Lav Diaz have been banned in Malaysia and the Philippines, respectively.

The publicness of cinema is at stake in both acts of state censorship and the screening of films and videos that subvert or undermine official discourse. As Anderson's and Ramani's chapters exemplify, cultural authorities, or those conservative groups that put pressure on the authorities to censor a given film, tend to articulate the threat of a film or film screening event in terms of its transgression of (dominant) national identity and national security. These articulations usually rest

---

[14] Michael Z. Newman, "Indie Culture: In Pursuit of the Authentic Autonomous Alternative," *Cinema Journal* 48,3 (Spring 2009): 16–34.

on a conception of cinema's power that acknowledges and emphasizes the mimetic potency and mobile visibility of films. In this logic, film is potent because its imputed power to stimulate imitative behavior wields excessive influence over the young and the susceptible masses. Secondly, film and video are media that transcend state borders and solicit the global gaze, and therefore must be kept within the parameter of sanctioned national representation.

We can note here, too, another dimension whereby film's photographic ontology implies a potency and, in some circumstances, a threat to anxious efforts to sustain the reductive surface of official nationalist spectacles. Filmic images are simultaneously iconic and indexical. They narrate stories, reflect certain dimensions of collective or individual existence, or figure certain dreamworlds and fantasies, but film images do more than signify; after all, such images bear physical traces of the moment of their recording.[15] In the subsequent moment of projection, these images index physical presence at a specific moment of time ("this was now"). In other words, filmic images give a negative imprint or appearance of reality, even while they fulfill the function of conveying information, signifying ideas, or propelling associations. This uncertain boundary between the filmic/photographic image as trace and as connotation complicates the question of how films reflect or represent reality, or how they work objectified conditions into textual form. Considering Benjamin McKay's intricate tracing of the "dreamed community" of liberal, multiethnic, and egalitarian Malaysia projected by Yasmin Ahmad's film trilogy (*Sepet* [2005], *Gubra* [2006], *Muksin* [2007]), we might say that the affective power of these films comes from precisely the ambiguity between the image as index (of the immediacy of everyday experience in a recognizable place in the country) and as fantasy or untimely figuration (of the promise of a liberated Malaysia-to-come).[16] After *Sepet* and *Gubra* were released, the *uncanny* resemblance of the enframed images to the real Malaysia panicked reactionary factions into branding these films as "cultural pollutants," both because they transgressed the official image of Islamic Malaysia and were potential instigators of mimetic behavior. Regarding a similar case, Benedict Anderson speculates on a dynamic that may have surreptitiously heightened the anxiety of the Thai moral guardians who called for the censorship of *Syndromes and a Century*: the ambiguity between filmic traces of acts of pleasure (indexical images of a young man dressed up as a monk playing a guitar, a middle-aged woman playing a doctor pouring herself a drink, a young man playing a doctor canoodling with a girl) and visible representations of generalized social types (bad Thai monks, irresponsible Thai doctors).

Given the profound changes in cinema spectatorship in this digital era, a key question concerns the spatial contexts of screening that state forces, or other forces of cultural authority in Southeast Asia, perceive as part of cinema, or more precisely, as constituting the public space of cinema. Chris Chong's chapter, a dialogue with John Badalu, the founder of the Q! Film Festival (Q!FF), refers to the decisive implication of this queer festival's decision to screen films on DVD (Digital Video Disc) free of

---

[15] Laura Mulvey, *Death 24x a Second: Stillness and the Moving Image* (London: Reaktion Books, 2006); Siegfried Kracauer, *Theory of Film: The Redemption of Physical Reality* (Princeton, NJ: Princeton University Press, 1997).

[16] For a reading beautifully sensitive to the spiritual grounding of Yasmin Ahmad's films, see Amir Muhammad, *Yasmin Ahmad's Films* (Petaling Jaya: Matahari Books, 2009).

charge. By screening on DVD, and at venues other than commercial cinemas, thus falling outside the legal definition of an official film festival, Q!FF is able to bypass the censorship board's vetting of (celluloid) prints prior to their screening in cinemas. While this would seem to indicate one instance where new technologies of exhibition can play a part in enhancing cinema's publicness by making these films more widely accessible than the law would allow, we might also want to pay attention to how the authorities themselves are adapting their understanding of the public space of cinema in the light of digitalization. For instance, under what circumstances do such alternative venues as shophouses, bars, or galleries—venues that uniformly rely on digital projection and that resemble, to some extent, the locations of early cinema's itinerant, mobile screenings because of their ephemeral characteristics and libertarian atmosphere—brush up against censorship and surveillance in each locality?

On a more abstract plane is the question of what accounts for cinema's status as an alternative public sphere, one of the key concerns of cinema theorizing and historicizing. Addressing the historical context of early cinema in the United States, Miriam Hansen identifies film's circulation in the market sphere, along with its reproducibility (its exhibition value, which exceeds its "cultic value" or "aura," in Walter Benjamin's terms), as the major structural conditions endowing the spaces of film exhibition with the potential to generate horizons of intersubjective recognition.[17] This theory of spectatorship emphasizes the potential of cinema to constitute a shared public horizon that recognizes experiences elsewhere denied. In other words, the embodied potency and communicability of film (in its cognitive, sensorial, and affective dimensions), combined with its technological capacity and historical conditions of exhibition, carry the potential to configure symbolic public spheres that recognize experiences ignored or rendered invisible in official spheres of exchange and representation. It is in this sense that cinema implies the possibility of iterating *alternative* public spheres, and does so even (or especially) in places characterized by the absence or malfunction of institutionalized civil society.[18] Cinema's promise of a radically different future—in other words, cinema as the public space for rehearsing desired futures, disinterring forgotten ones, and for projecting social collectivities to come—no doubt plays a large part in energizing the present organization of film screening and filmmaking events by independent groups in Southeast Asia. As Chris Chong and John Badalu's dialogue richly describes, the visibility of film festivals and their communitarian air tend to generate the kind of atmosphere conducive to registering the possibility of collective recognition of marginalized groups, and to performing democratic discursive exchange in the "liminal" space of civic inclusiveness that festivals can sometimes evoke.

While publicness in the above sense is premised on film viewing in a collective space and situation, there is no denying that, with digitalization, viewing practices in Southeast Asia have become an immensely fertile ground for reflecting on twenty-first century spectatorship and cinephilia. All manner of films are commonly viewed on small (computer, television) screens in private or semi-public contexts. The paucity of commercial art cinema circuits and cinematheques, or institutionalized

---

[17] Miriam Hansen, *Babel and Babylon: Spectatorship in American Silent Film* (Cambridge, MA: Harvard University Press, 1991).

[18] Stephanie Hemelryk Donald, *Public Secrets, Public Spaces: Cinema and Civility in China* (Lanham, MD: Rowman and Littlefield Publishers, 2000).

courses in film history and appreciation, and the absence of local, moderately priced DVD labels for art or independent films, together propel those hungry for expansion of their filmic horizons to seek out pirated modes of dissemination (see Tilman Baumgärtel's chapter). The norm of filmic experience, especially among cinephiles in Southeast Asia, is typical of the "performance" model of spectatorship recently proposed by the film theorist Francesco Casetti.[19] What Casetti calls the relocation of filmic experience, which began to emerge from the videotape era, is facilitated by new technologies of diffusion and situates itself in relation to a transformed media environment. But crucially, the proliferation of film consumption sites and screen contexts in the contemporary period signals a new culture with which cinema must engage, characterized by the equation of identity with expressivity and the need for the relational engagement of social subjects amid the fragmentation of pre-established social networks. Consequently, in Casetti's theorization, spectatorship has become more personalized, yet also more active: "[the spectator] is asked not only to see, but also to do."[20] The viewers' experience of films increasingly involves the activities of selection, recomposition, and intervention in the text of the film rather than theatrical attendance for a portion of time. This personalized, elective mode of spectatorship is both expressive of identity and part of the process of constructing social networks via acts of discussion, exchange, and sharing.

The key issue raised by situating empirical viewing practices in Southeast Asia in relation to this performance model of spectatorship is the extent to which piracy constitutes a requisite condition for these practices. In Baumgärtel's description, pirated DVDs facilitate both institutional film education and provide an opportunity for autodidacts to immerse themselves in a range of critical and creative activities. His article speculates that the next generation of independent filmmakers will now emerge from the rank of cinephiles dependent on watching pirated films, and who are accustomed to multiple contexts of film viewing, rather than those filmmakers who enjoy the economic privilege of making educational pilgrimages to Europe or North America. The shift from film viewing to filmmaking of cinephiles of the "piracy generation" is the expressive consequence of their piracy-facilitated viewing. From another vantage point, the "fiction" proposed by John Torres imagines a scenario whereby, through collaboration with vendors of pirated DVDs in the Philippines, an independent filmmaker such as himself could intervene in the piracy network to create a context of engagement between his work and an elusive constituency of intended viewers. Given the problem of distributing independent films within the country to which the filmmaker belongs, perhaps there is a way to sublate the piracy mode of diffusion so that an alternative Filipino film can meet Filipino viewers in a relocated network that, in this case, happens to have a strong affinity with culturally rooted modes of social interaction and personal consumption.

THE NATIONAL QUESTION

As globalization became a major theoretical focus across the disciplines from the late 1980s, the idea of national cinema as an analytic object and basis of empirical description came increasingly under question. Critics have pointed to the fallacy of

---

[19] Franscesco Casetti, "Filmic Experience," *Screen* 50,1 (Spring 2009): 56–66.

[20] Ibid., p. 63.

describing a film funded by international investors through various co-production deals as the product of a single national territory. In terms of film exhibition, the argument against prioritizing the nation-state as a boundary of analysis calls attention to the historically transnational character of film exhibition, as well as the affinity of the medium with cross-cultural spectatorship due to its mobility and sensorial/affective mode of communication. Certain writers have also cautioned against the careless projection of national identity as the representational content of a given film, arguing that this sort of interpretation actually fosters the homogenizing tendency of dominant nationalist discourses and the power of official nationalism to delegitimize the political and cultural claims of marginal groups.

We can acknowledge the necessity of critiquing anachronistic or mystifying articulations of the idea of national cinema while recognizing that cinema and the national continue to intersect in consequential ways. Paul Willemen points to the "ironic situation" whereby films that give perceptible forms to determinate experiences within national territories and address the complex causal links between present realities and concrete socio-historical formations do so as dependent cinema—their production process dependent in many cases on transnational capital or official institutions of the nation-state.[21] The relationship between festival-connected structures of funding and independent films in Southeast Asia demonstrates the continuing relevance of this ironical argument. Furthermore, the category "national cinema" remains active as a mode of classification and program presentation among film festivals across the globe, despite the inevitably misleading nature of such an interpellation. This has led a number of film scholars to adopt the term "national cinema effect" to highlight the discursive consequence of this type of "discovery" convention of festival programming, whereby a handful of films, often from an unfamiliar territory, are made to stand as representative of the entirety of film production within that given territory.[22] Given the importance of the film festival circuit for peripheral filmmakers, the classifier of "national cinema" remains relevant in this sense as a programming convention that mediates the international display of independent films and videos produced in Southeast Asia.

As narrativizing text and visual media, film and video have the capacity to give figurative form to imagined communities. They form part of cultural struggles through their mediating capacity to represent collective identities, dreams, anxieties, and desires in ways corresponding to differing political positions and conflicting ideological persuasions. Wimal Dissanayake's summary of the connection between nationalism and cinema in Asia makes a broad distinction among three modes of articulating cinema and the national. He argues that "hegemonic" films reproduce the idea of the essentializing nation-state and its unitary apparatus. In comparison, "critical" films attack the restrictive tendencies of the nation-state and may substitute for official nationalism alternative horizons of identification, such as regionalism. Thirdly, Dissanayake defines "oppositional" films as those that seek to expose the repressive dimensions of the nation-state apparatus, addressing in particular

---

[21] Paul Willemen, "The National," in *Looks and Frictions: Essays in Cultural Studies and Film Theory* (London: British Film Institute, 1994), p. 212.

[22] Bliss Cua Lim, *Translating Time: Cinema, the Fantastic, and Temporal Critique* (Durham, NC: Duke University Press, 2009), pp. 182–89.

collusions between global capital and postcoloniality.[23] In her chapter, Angie Bexley discusses some of the ways in which this broad distinction applies to hegemonic and counter-hegemonic cinematic representations of the political relationship between Indonesia and Timor-Leste. Bexley highlights cinema's capacity both to serve the colonizer's myth concerning threats to national security and to shed light on the unfinished imperative of justice in Timor-Leste after independence. More interesting still, according to Bexley, is the mobilization of the documentary mode by the younger generation of Timorese in the nation's postcolonial period. Documentary making is one of the channels by which members of the generation that grew up during the period of Indonesian occupation (1975–99) are beginning to give expressive form to their sense of national belonging. This process involves a degree of inter-generational conflict: the generation that came of age towards the end of Indonesia's occupation differs from the generation of leaders that had struggled for independence from Portugal in the early 1970s over the issue of the rightful terms of reconciliation with Indonesia.

Although the question concerning cinema and national projection/identification is often conceived in reflectionist terms, whereby visible aspects on the screen are identified as analogous representations of shared identity or social/political burden in the external world, it is important to recognize that film and video do not just communicate through specularized representation. Certain works may still imply a "national" horizon of spectatorship, even if they do not emphasize the formal labor of exposition and representation, preferring instead to address spectators through the construction of fragmentary, sensuous, or disjunctive forms. In other words, the intersubjective richness of a given film or video may be contingent upon the way certain of its sensuous, non-signifying, spectral elements resonate with people's shared experiences or evoke collective traumas and repressed memories.[24] Hence, when we think through the relationship between the national and cinema, it is important to stress the connection between aesthetics and the dynamic of spectatorial address: how certain works contain signifying or sensuous elements that evoke shared horizons of experience. A good example in this regard is Apichatpong's rhythmic, aurally seductive film poem, *The Anthem* (2006), widely shown internationally and ostensibly described as a short film, designed to be played in cinemas before the start of any feature as a form of ritual blessing for the film to follow. In Siam, *The Anthem*'s playful tone and deadpan allusion to the ritual of standing to attention while the royal anthem is played before the start of all films in commercial cinemas lends itself to subversive (national–popular) spectatorial pleasure. To "get" the film immediately, to laugh and discuss with people nearby whether we should express our identification by standing or imitating the aerobics movement of the bodies displayed on the screen during *The Anthem*'s brief running time, is to partake in a fleeting moment of subverting official (royalist) nationalist interpellation, and, at the same time, to register the possibility of channeling the energy of shared bodily perception toward collective liberation for an alternative future.

---

[23] Wimal Dissanayake, "Introduction: Nationhood, History, and Cinema: Reflections on the Asian Scene," in *Colonialism and Nationalism in Asian Cinema*, ed. Wimal Dissanayake (Bloomington and Indianapolis, IN: Indiana University Press, 1994), pp. ix–xxix.

[24] Jeffrey Skoller, *Shadows, Specters, Shards: Making History in Avant-Garde Film* (Minneapolis, MN: University of Minnesota Press, 2005).

The issue of how certain films or videos address (rather than represent) the national through seemingly opaque textual elements, or through formal designs that play on sensuous perception more than by emphasizing diegetic comprehension, is highly relevant to independent films and videos produced in Southeast Asia. This practice can partly be linked to the existence of censorship, insofar as censorship heightens the suggestive potential of formal strategies premised on the fragmentary, the allusive, or on the inclusion of recalcitrant details—surface appearances that invite allegorical readings. Moreover, since independent Southeast Asian films tend to circulate in local and international contexts among viewers highly differentiated in terms of their cinematic awareness and contextual knowledge, one of the most fascinating questions regarding the spectatorship of these films concerns the way the combination of textual transparency and opacity affects the range of possible audience experiences embodied in differing viewing contexts. Discussing the international circulation of New Hong Kong Cinema during the 1980s, Linda Chui-han Lai refers to "enigmatization," or the prevalence of a bifurcated textual design, whereby aspects of a particular film were legible to those who shared a certain cultural history, while "outsiders" could still comprehend that same film on other levels.[25] In his chapter on Apichatpong's *Tropical Malady* (2004), Benedict Anderson complicates an insider/outsider dichotomy of this sort by speculating on the subversive opacity of this film for Thai urban bourgeois spectators. *Tropical Malady's* experimental aestheticization of the animistic lifeworld—a mode of spectrality long sedimented in the region we now call Southeast Asia—constitutes a "difficulty" for members of the audience who have materially benefited from the originary claim of sovereign Thainess and the teleological projection of official nationalism. Those spectators who rely on and accept the nation's hegemony are detached from the spheres of socio-cultural existence in which animism's magical power may be mobilized against the dominant myth of nation. Since Apichatpong's film plays on such animistic power, we might say that the sensorial charge and temporal duration evoked by his aesthetics threatens to remain an "enigmatic" source of anxiety for Siam's urban elites.

Film's aesthetic capacity to address multiple viewing constituencies would seem to complicate the theory of interpretation that posits the national as a necessary frame of reference for interpreting films from the global south. (The limiting case of this position is the one exemplified by Fredric Jameson's proposal that Third World literary works in the multinational capitalist era must necessarily be read as national allegories.) Gaik Khoo's auteurist close reading of the films and videos of Chinese Malaysian independent filmmaker James Lee presents just this challenge to the critical approach that tends to read independent Malaysian films within the paradigm of the "national (race) problem." In Khoo's interpretation, the presentation of alienated urban characters in Lee's works is analogous to the fundamental alienation of modern subjects of capitalism, and to this extent Lee's films and videos bear universal, rather than localized, characteristics.

Yet the persistence of the tropes of haunting, excavation, and ruins across the works of some of the most outstanding filmmakers in Southeast Asia today would suggest the continuing validity or utility of national allegory as a major interpretive frame (if not an overdetermined structure as such). Alexis Tioseco's highly personal reflection on the works of the Filipino filmmakers Lav Diaz and Raya Martin can be

---

[25] Lim, *Translating Time: Cinema, the Fantastic, and Temporal Critique*, p. 176.

productive situated in this frame, especially insofar as Tioseco intuitively foregrounds their experiments with cinema's representation of time and, despite the appearances of reality indexed on the screen, the filmic image's ontological grounding in absence. The ghosts of the nation's past constitute a common point of departure for both Diaz and Martin. While the latter's works are preoccupied with mobilizing the sensuous plasticity of film and video to bring fragmented details or the repressed underside of the nation's history into embodied, imaginative contact with amnesiac present-day viewers, Diaz is concerned with finding an adequate cinematic form with which to represent mass immiseration in the contemporary period. His epics have as their historical referents the betrayal of the Filipino people—anti-imperialism's promise of freedom gone awry—in this postcolonial period. Eschewing the dramatic convention of political films that offer wishful moral solutions to circumstances beyond the characters' own making, Diaz's epics are structured by gaps, ellipses, stases, delays, and spectral disruptions to the fiction of homogenous, empty time. His aesthetics, which extend the duration of the images and interactions pictured on screen far beyond the commercial convention of the ninety-minute film, are exacting in their demand for attention. This quality endows the experience of watching his films with the weight of bearing witness to social suffering and—as Tioseco so movingly writes when describing the tenderness with which Diaz sees the body of actor Ronnie Lazaro—to endurance.

A final word about the naming of each of the sections in this book: Action, Reflection, and Advocacy. Given the ephemeral nature of alternative cultural spheres in Southeast Asia, including the sphere of independent cinema, the chapters in the first part of this volume highlight the necessity of documenting pioneering action through writing in some detail about the activities and testimonies of those who undertook the unprecedented step of making independent films and videos or establishing alternative contexts for screening and disseminating such works. The second section of the book then features critical reflections on various aspects of the phenomena of independent cinema in Southeast Asia, and here we find more explicitly analytic work that attempts to define, classify, and clarify the question of independence, not least to draw attention to relevant determinants of existing practices and to account for agencies of transformation. Chapters in the last section of the book demonstrate how writing about independent cinema in Southeast Asia effectively asserts the value of certain films, sites, or practices that are unfamiliar to most people, or that are overlooked and undervalued. In contributing to what is often described as this "young field," each of these approaches to writing about cinema remains vital and often requires the writer to wear different hats for different contexts (critic, cultural activist, researcher)—but none is sufficient on its own.

PART I

ACTION

VOICES OF THE FOURTH GENERATION OF MALAYSIAN–INDIAN FILMMAKERS

Hassan Abd Muthalib

I do not see myself as a fourth-generation Indian. I am a Malaysian first and foremost. The Indian part is merely an ethnic detail. I do not come from India, have not been to India, have nothing in common with Indians from India. I see myself as a first-generation Malaysian.[1]

Cinema in Malaysia began as Malay cinema, and for about seventy years used nothing but the Malay language. The screen stories were drawn from the Malay world, both past and present, with most of those stories depicted by ethnic and migrant Malay actors and actresses.[2] If any other race was cast, those actors would be relegated to being the comedy relief. The irony, however, is that Malay cinema was started and given shape by Chinese entrepreneurs and Indian directors who mostly came from outside the country. The industry eventually became Malay-based and Malay-owned. Chinese and Indian involvement became restrained and was finally relegated to the same role that the Malays had played at the beginning—that of providing support and production assistance.[3]

Many generations of Indians came from India and Sri Lanka, some voluntarily, while others were being brought in by the British colonialists as laborers to work in the rubber estates and to build roads. These workers, part of the first generation of non-Malays, arrived towards the end of the 1800s. The second generation came during the 1930s and 1940s. Some from this group married into the local population, but ties to the old country remained strong, as these arrivals' parents and relatives still resided there. Almost everyone included in the third generation was born in

---

[1] Arivind Abraham, independent filmmaker, wrote this in an email to me in 2007.

[2] Hassan Abd Muthalib and Wong Tuck Cheong, "Gentle Winds of Change," in *Being and Becoming: The Cinemas of Asia*, ed. Aruna Vasudev, Latika Padgaonkar, and Rashmi Doraiswamy (New Delhi: MacMillan India, 2002), p. 301.

[3] Over the last decade a number of Malaysian Chinese-owned companies have emerged, among them Metrowealth Pictures, Red Films, and Dahuang Pictures. Metrowealth Pictures has been the most successful, making films only for a Malay audience.

Malaysia. Proficient in the Malay language due to compulsory education, third-generation non-Malays assimilated easily and became a part of the local milieu.

Malaysia's contemporary film industry is a polyglot mix of film workers, with ethnic Malays working alongside Chinese, Indians, Eurasians, and others who have made Malaysia their home for several generations. Many of them have either film-school training or a formal education in related disciplines, such as theater or animation. Some of the film-school graduates have managed to gain a foothold in mainstream cinema. Those who do not have film-school degrees, however, do not have access to the same film-industry opportunities, and have subsequently turned to digital media that have partially democratized filmmaking.[4] In fact, it was the accessibility of digital technology that activated the independent filmmaking group dubbed "The Little Cinema of Malaysia" (or simply "The Little Cinema," which is described later in detail). Included in this group are some fourth-generation Indian filmmakers, an upwardly mobile, energetic, and articulate cohort of youths eager to test out their storytelling skills. Unlike their predecessors in the industry, these young filmmakers express their concerns about their individual communities in their film narratives. As a result, a discernible movement is beginning to emerge in their works. Almost every one of their feature-film narratives subtly voices the problems faced by their communities. At the same time, their films raise questions about non-Malays' identity and place in a multiracial Malaysia. A similar but also subtle articulation has already emerged in Malaysian-Chinese independent films.[5]

INDIANS AND EARLY MALAYSIAN CINEMA

Indians have played a prominent role in Malaysian cinema right from the beginning. Malaysia's first film, *Leila Majnun* (Lovestruck Leila, 1933), was directed by Bhimsingh S. Rajhans (B. S. Rajhans), a director from India, and was produced by Motilal Chemical, a Bombay-based company. After the Second World War, Indian directors and other personnel were brought in from India to restart the Malaysian film industry. Prominent among these newcomers were Rajhans, Phani Majumdar, Dhiresh Ghosh, V. Girimaji, and B. N. Rao. Rajhans directed *Seruan Merdeka* (The Call to Liberty, 1946), the first and only film to show multiracial collaboration on screen. The film depicts Malays fighting alongside the Chinese against the Japanese aggressors during World War Two. This generation of Indian filmmakers had no ties to the country. They were directors for hire and were entirely dependent on the locals, for example, on their employers (the Chinese entrepreneurs) for their salary, and on the support staff (the Malays) for production assistance. The employees were salaried staff and were provided living quarters by their employers and even a bonus upon the successful completion of a film.

These directors' contracts specified that they were to also write scripts. The majority of the stories they came up with were adaptations of India's Hindi or Tamil movies. And so their films, at the early stages, looked similar to those from their home country. The stories (screenplays) were written in English and then translated

---

[4] Gaik Cheng Khoo, "Just-Do-It-(Yourself): Independent Filmmaking in Malaysia," *Inter-Asia Cultural Studies* 8,2 (June 2007): 227–47.

[5] In particular, in the works of Ho Yuhang: *Min* (2003), *Sanctuary* (2004), *Rain Dogs* (2006), and *At the End of Daybreak* (2009); James Lee: *Room to Let* (2002), *The Beautiful Washing Machine* (2004), and *Before We Fall in Love Again* (2006); Khoo Eng Yow: *The Birdhouse* (2007); Tan Chui Mui: *Love Conquers All* (2006); Yeo Joon Han: *Sell-Out!* (2008); and Chris Chong: *Karaoke* (2009).

to Malay by the locals.[6] The first interracial love story, *Selamat Tinggal Kekaseh-ku* (Goodbye, My Love, 1955), was directed by Lakshamanan Krishnan (L. Krishnan). Based on the classic Indian story "Devdas," it depicts a Malay madly in love with a Chinese girl. The legendary Malay film director Teuku Zakaria Teuku Nyak Puteh, better known as P. Ramlee, also experimented with an interracial love story, in *Gerimis* (Drizzle, 1968), in which the hero falls in love with an Indian girl. But both films were in Malay and were aimed at the predominantly ethnic-Malay audience. Interestingly, among the first Indian directors were three who were Malaysian-born: L. Krishnan, K. M. Basker, and S. Ramanathan. Their familiarity with the local culture can be seen in the films that they wrote or directed. Krishnan told me that he would keenly observe the customs and traditions of the Malays whenever he was invited into their houses.[7] Krishnan, in particular, can be singled out as the first director who was to shape the acting skills of the versatile P. Ramlee (the "P" standing for "Puteh," his father's name). Prior to his involvement, acting styles were typically in the *bangsawan* (Malay opera) manner—highly stylized and clichéd. These three Indian directors, knowingly or unknowingly, sowed the early seeds of a more realistic form of Malay cinema that would be reflected in the films of directors like P. Ramlee, Muhammad Amin Ihsan (M. Amin), and Hussein Haniff.

Indian films made in Malaysia have always been in Tamil, due to the fact that the majority of Indian immigrants came from South India, where Tamil is the major dialect. In 1966, Muban (Mohamed Baharuddin), a Tamil-speaking Indian-Muslim, made the first Tamil movie in the horror genre, *Retta Peyiee* (Blood of the Vampire, 1968). Sivaji Rajah, one of the actors in the film, said that Baharuddin subsequently left to resettle in India, and nothing has been heard of him since.[8] M. Raj produced and directed a Malay film (his only one), *Melati Putih* (White Flower, 1984), an adaptation of the successful Indian film *Pathinaru Vayathinile* (At the Age of Sixteen, Bharathiraja, 1977).

Among the filmmakers with Indian ancestry, the most successful film entrepreneur is Pansha Nalliah, who belongs to the third generation. He produced and directed the Tamil-language *Naan Oru Malaysian* (I Am a Malaysian, 1991), which had a limited run of screenings in theaters. In 1996, he wrote and directed a Malay movie, *Suami, Isteri dan ...* (Husband, Wife, and ...), which is a word-for-word adaptation of another popular Indian movie, *Mouna Geethangal* (The Music of Love, Bhagyaraj, 1981).[9] Another filmmaker, Mohan Sunderaj (S. Mohan), a graduate from a film school in India, began his career as a cinematographer making movies and television commercials. He has since directed a feature, *The Deadly Disciple* (2001), which is in English and Malay. A. Razak Mohaideen, a film academic at the Faculty of Artistic and Creative Technology, Universiti Teknologi MARA Malaysia, has become the most prolific and successful Indian-Muslim film director. He mostly uses actors from Penang, the majority of them being of mixed Malay/Indian-Muslim parentage. He has dabbled in a number of genres, and though his films have been consistently panned by critics, almost all of them have gone on to be box-office successes.

---

[6] Abd Muthalib and Wong, "Gentle Winds of Change," p. 302.

[7] Personal interview with Dato' L. Krishnan in Kuala Lumpur in September 2006.

[8] Personal interview with Shivaji Rajah in Kuala Lumpur in October 2006.

[9] It needs to be noted that, even as late as the 1990s, Indian film producers still looked to India for their film stories, due to the dearth of quality scripts in Malaysia.

Malaysia's first short animated film, *Hikayat Sang Kancil* (Legend of the Mouse Deer, 1978), was made by Anandam Xavier, a Malaysian-Indian set designer working at Filem Negara Malaysia, the government-owned documentary film studio.[10] The film is an adaptation of the well-known story of a mouse deer and how it cleverly outwits menacing characters. Subsequently, I was one of the first filmmakers to make animated shorts and public-service spots for television.[11] I also wrote and directed Malaysia's first animated feature-length film, *Silat Legenda* (Legendary Silat Warriors, 1998). In its prologue, the film refers to the well-known heroes of old Malacca who are already rooted in popular memory. The story then moves to the twenty-first century, and explores the theme of Malay religious and cultural identity and its survival in the midst of profound change.

In general, the third-generation of Indian filmmakers catered to a Malay audience by featuring only Malay stories, issues, and characters. None of the films they made was directed at the Indian communities in Malaysia. These young filmmakers' sensibilities were mainstream and pragmatic: they sought to entertain as well as to make a profit, as, for most of them, life in Malaysia was all about survival. Most of these young filmmakers lived with their parents, who had come from India. For the great majority of the immigrants, life in the old country was one of poverty and deprivation. The young filmmakers were aware of their parents' suffering and hard work, and Malaysia had been good to them: many had attended university and were well off, and most had adapted easily to the local (Malay) culture. Born on or before Malaysia gained its independence in 1957, they considered themselves to be a part of the country and were proud to have contributed to its development.[12] It is significant that these filmmakers have never expressed any dissatisfaction with conditions facing the Indians in any of their writings. But (major) changes were in the offing, and it was to be left to the fourth generation of Indian filmmakers—those born after the country attained independence, who didn't know firsthand about the struggles of those filmmakers who came before them—to strike out in a direction never taken before. Ironically, many of these filmmakers were to be formally trained in filmmaking by their predecessors (including by me). Not having had to struggle in the industry like those of us from the third generation, and, most importantly, coming to the industry at the same time that the digital revolution was cresting, the fourth-generation filmmakers were able to be brash, self-confident, and assertive. Here was a new Malaysian generation that, unlike its predecessors, had no baggage to carry and wanted its voice to be heard.

---

[10] Abd Muthalib and Wong, "Gentle Winds of Change," p. 324.

[11] I am an Indian-Muslim of Tamil-speaking parents who has, because of my active involvement in the industry, been recognized as an animation pioneer. See John A. Lent, "Development of Malaysian Animation from the Perspective of Pioneer Animator Hassan Muthalib," *Asian Cinema* 14,1 (Spring/Summer 2003): 107–15.

[12] This is the subject of Amir Muhammad's documentary *Lelaki Komunis Terakhir* (The Last Communist, 2006), which was subsequently banned by the Malaysian censor board for allegedly glorifying Chin Peng, the head of the Malayan Communist Party in the 1950s. In reality, the documentary explores the contributions of the Chinese and Indians in pre-Independence Malaysia.

FOURTH-GENERATION INDIAN FILMMAKERS

The year 2000 was to be a turning point for Malaysian cinema—and for filmmakers who are fourth-generation Malaysian-Indian.[13] In that year, Amir Muhammad (himself of Malay-Indian parentage) made a digital feature, *Lips to Lips,* that was to have a profound effect on Malaysian cinema. It was this film that led to the birth of what has been termed by the late Dr. Anuar Nor Arai as The Little Cinema of Malaysia.[14] The name denotes works by those independent filmmakers of various races who are developing alongside the mainstream filmmakers. The Little Cinema group is insistent upon developing a socially and politically conscious audience. These filmmakers reject the mainstream approach and concentrate instead on what Madhava M. Prasad calls "realist/artistic products which correspond to a certain conception of true cinema."[15] This group is aware of and influenced by the works of great filmmakers like Satyajit Ray, Michaelangelo Antonioni, Hou Hsiao-Hsien, and Tsai Ming-Liang. Like these masters, Little Cinema members aspire to bring realism to their works as a reaction to the crass commercialism of mainstream Malaysian cinema. It is no surprise, then, that The Little Cinema's image of nation would never be consonant with the national ideology, and, as a result, most of its gritty, realistic representations (mainly of the exploited, the dispossessed, and the alienated) have, unsurprisingly, irked the authorities.

The term "independent" requires some explanation. In the United States, it used to identify filmmakers in the mid-1960s who were not part of the studio system, and particularly those who had "final cut," in other words, maintained control over how the final film would look. In Malaysia, there are four corporations involved in filmmaking that function like film studios. They provide funding, production assistance, and are involved in the actual making, marketing, and distribution of the films. Filmmakers operating outside those four corporations are considered "independents," that is to say, they fund their productions themselves through loans, and then they have to find resources to finance the films' marketing and distribution. As a result, filmmaking for independents involves much greater financial risk than it does for the corporations.

For The Little Cinema members, being independent and having the final cut is what matters most. They are determined that their works must come out the way they intend them to look. Their anti-mainstream and anti-establishment approach, however, doesn't translate into profits, and independent producers shy away from their films. The only way for Little Cinema members to make movies, then, is to fund themselves. The mainstream cinema filmmakers use high-end equipment, mostly shoot on 35mm film, and work with large crews and budgets of anywhere between US$280,000 to US$600,000 per film, which includes amounts for promotion and marketing. By comparison, The Little Cinema's filmmakers' projects are made for anywhere between US$4,000 to US$40,000, with a minimal crew (that often includes

---

[13] Ironically, it was the government that provided the impetus. When Dr. Mahathir Mohammad became the nation's fourth prime minister, he immediately set into motion the aggressive promotion of the use of digital technology.

[14] Dr. Anuar Nor Arai was a film lecturer, director, and critic. See Hassan Abd Muthalib, "Voices of Malaysian Cinema," in *Goethe in Malaysia, Malaysia in Goethe* (Kuala Lumpur: Goethe-Institut Malaysia, 2008).

[15] Madhava M. Prasad, *Ideology of the Hindi Film: A Historical Construction* (New Delhi: Oxford India, 2000), p. 14.

the filmmaker's friends and family), and mainly rely on the Internet's social media sites for promotion and distribution. To keep costs low, the director frequently writes the script, edits the film, and sometimes manages the production as well.

The "independent" movement has also been defined as being "underground, low budget, non-profit oriented, guerrilla filmmaking, and made without consideration of being screened in the censor-ridden mainstream cinemas."[16] The term "The Little Cinema" is, therefore, appropriate to describe independent filmmakers in Malaysia. Being part of The Little Cinema, in another sense, also allows filmmakers to "pay their dues" before making an entry into the mainstream market, if that is the path they choose.

The Little Cinema is notable for its ethnic and linguistic diversity as compared to mainstream cinema (which is totally Malay in cast and language). This diversity is also seen in the ideas, issues, and narratives that Little Cinema filmmakers bring to the screen. As a consequence, a true "face" of Malaysia—and a Malaysian cinema in the true sense of the word—is beginning to emerge. However, this has not pleased the National Film Development Corporation (Perbadanan Pembangunan Filem Nasional, FINAS), which has been trying for years to market mainstream Malaysian films to an international audience.[17] Not a single mainstream film has made it overseas commercially thus far. Only U-Wei Hajisaari, with his *Kaki Bakar* (The Arsonist, 1995, which screened at the Cannes Film Festival), is internationally known, being one of only two Malaysian films mentioned in the annual *Time Out* anthologies (the other being Amir Muhammad's *The Big Durian,* 2003, which screened at the Sundance Film Festival). Since 2003, the films of the late Yasmin Ahmad, James Lee, and Ho Yuhang have become known to an international audience and been distributed commercially. In a few short years, The Little Cinema has made its presence felt in major festivals around the world, with commercial screenings and sales on DVD, including through Amazon.com.[18]

The shorts and features of the Fourth Generation Indian filmmakers constitute a potpourri of stories. Though the majority of the films are in Tamil and feature mainly Indian characters, a few are about Malays and make full use of the Malay language. But it is through independent feature films that a "voice" is emerging: it is the voice of filmmakers who, unlike the earlier generation of Indians, will not bear their conditions silently anymore. Born about four decades after Malaysia gained its independence, these filmmaker have never known the hardships faced by their parents and grandparents. Many have attended college and hold comfortable jobs. As a consequence, their films are not about the struggle to make a living, but about the frustrations the Indian community continues to face in receiving equal treatment in the areas of economy, education, and politics. These filmmakers are aware that the toil and sweat of their forefathers helped to shape the country, and they do not want to be treated as second-class citizens.

---

[16] Khoo, "Just-Do-It-(Yourself): Independent Filmmaking in Malaysia," p. 228.

[17] In fact, there were attempts recently by Malaysian embassies to block the screenings of some of the works by directors associated with The Little Cinema group, as such works were deemed "not suitable"—obviously, because they were not in the national language and many depicted scenarios that were less than complimentary (meaning, not officially sanctioned).

[18] At the 2006 Pusan International Film Festival, one of the festival directors commented that all the directors preferred supporting The Little Cinema's works, as Malaysian mainstream films were "not convincing."

Among the films that articulate these concerns are *Chemman Chaalai* (The Gravel Road, Deepak Kumaran Menon, 2005), *Chalanggai* (Dancing Bells, Deepak Kumaran Menon, 2007), *Aandal* (The Prostitute, Santosh Kesavan, 2005), *Uyir* (The Soul, Premnath Pillai, 2004), *Ethirkaalam* (The Future, Kumaresan Chinniah, 2006), *Sweet Dreams* (Shunmugham Karuppannan, 2006), *S'kali* (All Together, Arivind Abraham, 2006), *Pensil* (Pencil), and *Jomlah C.I.U.M.*(Come, Find an Identity for Malaysia, 2009), both by M. Subash Abdullah (as a word, the initials "C.I.U.M." denote the Malay word for "kiss"; they actually stand for "Cari Identiti Untuk Malaysia," or "Find an Identity for Malaysia"). Two other films are *5:15* (Arivind Abraham, 2009), and *The Joshua Tapes* (Arivind Abraham and Benjy Lim, 2010). All of the above films were shot digitally, with only *Ethirkaalam* being transferred to film. *Sweet Dreams* went to video compact disc (VCD), while the other films were shown commercially in digital cinemas.

Shanta goes home after her dream of attending the university is shattered.
From Deepak Kumaran Menon's *Chemman Chaalai*

Deepak Kumaran Menon's *Chemman Chaalai* is the only Indian film that has had wide international exposure.[19] It generated interest in the print media and was featured in the *International Herald Tribune* and at Variety.com, among others.[20] The

[19] *Chemman Chaalai* premiered in 2005 at the thirty-fourth Rotterdam International Film Festival and the forty-eighth San Francisco International Film Festival, and was in competition at the Bangkok International Film Festival. Among the awards it has garnered is a Special Jury Prize at the twenty-seventh Nantes Festival of Three Continents, in France. See this article by David Walsh stemming from the film's screening in San Francisco: David Walsh, "What Should be Encouraged: San Francisco International Film Festival 2005—Part 1," *World Socialist Website*, May 10, 2005, http://wsws.org/articles/2005/may2005/sff1-m10.shtml, accessed on May 3, 2011.

[20] Lim Li Min, "A Lens on the Malaysian Margins," *International Herald Tribune*, April 5, 2005, http://groups.yahoo.com/group/beritamalaysia/message/76819, accessed on May 3, 2011; and Dennis Harvey, "The Gravel Road," Variety.com, May 17, 2005, www.variety.com/review/VE1117927157?refcatid=31, accessed on July 25, 2011.

film is about Indians working as rubber-tree tappers—a profession that has for decades been associated with poverty, exploitation, and deprivation. *Chemman Chaalai* depicts the conditions of second- and third-generation Indian rubber tappers in the 1960s, told through the story of Shantha, a young girl who is set on leaving the misery of the rubber estate to pursue a university education at a time when higher education for women was unheard of.

Like *Chemman Chaalai,* Menon's *Chalanggai* was selected to screen at festivals abroad.[21] *Chalanggai* is quite different from *Chemman Chaalai* in terms of its setting and stylistics, but both films articulate the same issues. While *Chemman Chaalai* makes use of long takes and is paced slowly, with its cinematography bordering on the lyrical, *Chalanggai*'s visual look is gritty. Its fast-paced editing moves the story forward quickly. Set within bustling Kuala Lumpur, the film portrays the trials and tribulations of family members whose paterfamilias has deserted them. *Chalanggai*'s landscape is urban (the town of Brickfields), while *Chemman Chaalai*'s is a calm and "tranquil" rubber estate (in the southern part of the Malaysian Peninsula). These are two different landscapes, but both function in the films' diegesis as milieus from which the two families cannot escape. The families' "entrapment" is, in effect, a metaphor for the wider sense of entrapment experienced by the Indians (and Chinese), even after Malaysia gained independence.

Family (or the lack of it) is articulated differently in *Ethikalaam,* directed by Kumaresan Chinniah (C. Kumaresan). Aimed at a specifically Indian audience, the film fully uses narrative and stylistic conventions prevalent in 1990-era films from South India. Featuring two groups of university students that are antagonistic towards each other, the film shows stereotypical stand-offs, song-and-dance sequences, and the ubiquitous happy ending found in Tamil films. The film was a celebration of Indian youths today and about how they are influenced by popular culture, in particular, by the films of South India. That focus, however, is not meant to be negative, as the happy ending suggests that even though society may appear to look down upon them, today's youths are able eventually to solve their own problems, without always being dependent upon their parents. *Uyir,* directed by Premnath Pillai, is a horror movie liberally spiced with comedic elements. A group of Indian students experience weird happenings at an abandoned bungalow. A Hindu priest (who turns out not to be a priest at all) ends up as the students' savior by casting out the demons in the bungalow. *Uyir* appears to be a take on the Hollywood-studio film *The Blair Witch Project,* skillfully employing MTV-type stylistics. It was a hit with the Indian audience.

Four films in particular—*Aandal, Sweet Dreams, Chalanggai,* and *S'kali*—are worth examining in detail, as a common thread runs through their narratives, articulating frustrations and issues about the Indian community that have never before been addressed intelligently through mainstream films made in Malaysia.

Aandal

Aandal (2005), by Santhosh Kesavan, is based on a true story. It is not concerned with issues of Indians being treated as second-class citizens. Kesavan's criticism is aimed at another segment of Indian society. *Aandal* is an indictment of today's young

---

[21] *Chalanggai* premiered in 2007 at Rotterdam (winning a Special Mention) and was subsequently selected for the Bangkok International Film Festival, Pusan, and the Hong Kong International Film Festival.

Indians who have forgotten or are unaware of the trials and tribulations of the first generation and who have subsequently lost touch with their roots. The story begins with images of the supposedly real Aandal remembering her past (a technique often used in Tamil films). The opening titles are then fast-cut to an upbeat song, accompanied by striking visuals of the city that signify physical development at the expense of personal development. The film then introduces us to the young Aandal, an Indian girl from a rubber estate. Longing to escape from the drudgery of her family's life, she is lured to the city by a young, handsome Indian pimp, Suresh, who marries her and then forces her into prostitution. With the help of Dr. James (one of her clients, who is trapped in an unhappy marriage), and her landlady, an old woman called Asha (who has her own problems), Aandal finally manages to escape and, with her infant daughter, is able to rebuild her broken life. The final shots of the film shows Aandal happily raising aloft her baby, Gayatri, but the stylistics indicate that her troubles may not yet be over. In this sequence, Aandal and Gayatri are first seen from behind a wire fence. This scene is juxtaposed with three more shots, all shot in backlight with the two in silhouette against a contrasting background of the sea. All these elements function as ominous indicators of an uncertain future, if not for Aandal, then for her daughter, and raise the question: Will Gayatri take the same road as her mother? In a sense, the ambiguity of the ending represents the unresolved problems of the Indian community.

In another sense, however, *Aandal* offers a positive resolution. Amongst the bad, there are also good people. The heroine, Aandal, was able to break free with the help of sympathetic adults who had lived hard lives themselves. Though we are not told whether Dr. James and Asha managed to solve their own problems, we feel that Aandal's release from her misery helped both Dr. James and Asha to live better lives as a result.

As in *Chemman Chaalai,* only Indians are visible throughout *Aandal.* Malay is spoken, but with a Chinese accent, and it is spoken by an Indian named Towkay, who has been brought up by Chinese—one example of an identity crisis that further compounds the social and political problems faced by Indians. At the end, the pimp's cohort, Guna, gets beaten to a pulp by Suresh, who is portrayed as a handsome, well-built young man. Kesavan's camera at times intensifies Suresh's on-screen image to the level of that of a Bollywood star, in effect, raising the question: What has happened to the young Indians in Malaysia? They have what it takes, but why must they stoop to such low levels? Is it because this country does not offer them a better way out?[22]

A reading of the deep structure of the film's narrative and setting reveals the director's feelings about the fate of Indians in Malaysia. Harsh conditions presented by their origins, with life beginning in the rubber estates, may have been tolerated by earlier immigrants, but it is unbearable to the youths (the next generation). So the young people are lured by promises of a better life in the city (the government's call to be involved in the nation's development), but urban life proves to be even worse (they are cheated of what they were promised). Even a professional like the doctor faces misfortune. The Indians have to make to do with the life that they have and keep on hoping that conditions will improve for the next generation. Such

---

[22] Tan Chui Mui's *Love Conquers All* also features a Chinese pimp who deludes the female protagonist and then tricks her into becoming a prostitute.

articulations can also be seen in the films of Chinese filmmakers like James Lee, Ho Yuhang, and Tan Chui Mui.[23]

Sweet Dreams

Sweet Dreams (2006) is about a successful young television newscaster, Jeeva, who decides to buy a house through a middleman called "Goodwill" Bala. But soon Jeeva's nightmare begins. He and a friend, Elango, get conned out of all their money by Bala, a smooth-talking Indian. Bala convinces them that a bribe is necessary to expedite matters, and then Bala disappears with their money. Elango and his friend then get deeper into trouble when they hire Indian gangsters to trace Bala, but Bala is found dead (obviously killed by a disgruntled customer). The naïve youths end up getting cheated by the gangsters, too, thereby losing even more money in the process. At the end of the film, Jeeva and Elango have still not managed to get back their money, but they realize that they have learned a good lesson and become wiser in the process.

The director, Karuppannan, uses a playful, parodic style for this film. With his very first shot, he makes a reference to mainstream Indian cinema, leading the audience to think that *Sweet Dreams* is going to be another typical Indian movie. Jeeva and a sari-clad girl are seen dancing to a song in slow motion, but it turns out to be a dream that Jeeva is having. The scene encapsulates the theme of the film: his dream will soon turn into a nightmare. He wakes up and smiles, and looks at the numerous photos he has pasted on the wall of the popular Bollywood actress Aishwarya Rai, and of his own dream house. This introductory scene is, in effect, Karuppannan's wry comment on the role the media play in promoting "dreams" to the consumer.[24] Another song appears later in the movie, but this time it is treated in a hilarious and creative manner—again parodying Tamil movies. Jeeva is in his car, having lost all his savings to Bala. He plays a selection from a disc, but it is a happy song. Nonplussed for a moment, he then searches for and finds a sad song. He replays the sad melody again and again, trying hard to restrain himself, but then he sobs, giving free rein to his emotions. Karuppannan's adeptness at subverting audience expectations is again apparent when he introduces the name of a Malay into the film through main characters, who identify this Malay as the person who had received bribes for selling the house, but subsequently discover him to be a fictitious intermediary invented by the Indian con man.[25]

Karuppannan stresses the role of family, referring back to how important family ties were in the old country. *Sweet Dreams* also points out how important religion is in the lives of Indians, and how this is not appreciated by young Indians today. Without any attempt at moralizing, the film contrasts two Indian families and shows how differently they react to the difficult situation in which the youths find

---

[23] For further elaboration on this point, see Pusan's recent publication on new Malaysian cinema. Mina Oak, ed., *Three Colors of New Malaysian Cinema* (Pusan: 12th Pusan International Film Festival, 2007).

[24] Interestingly, representations of the media (mainly television) appear in almost every film that came out of The Little Cinema and are always treated negatively, apparently as an indictment of mainstream media's effects on the minds of Malaysians who allegedly tend to believe everything that is broadcast to them.

[25] Perhaps Karuppannan is alluding to the widely held belief that some Malays (who make up the majority of the staff at agencies (both public and private) are on the take and that Indians (and other non-Malays) simply have to live with the situation in order to get things done.

themselves. Jeeva's family stands by him even though he has gone against their wishes by resisting an arranged marriage. They calmly accept his predicament, and Jeeva's brother offers him money, even though he is hard-pressed himself. Karuppannan visually portrays Jeeva's family as being religious, in contrast to Elango's father, who brooks no excuses and derides both Elango and Jeeva for their mistake. He refuses to see that all Elango wanted was just a house of his own. Like Santosh Kesavan, Karuppannan uses dramatic irony to depict the negative paths taken by the antagonists in *Sweet Dreams,* both young and old. Their fathers and forefathers worked hard and struggled to make a dollar honestly, but why have their descendants sunk to such levels by resorting to paying bribes and taking short cuts towards achieving their dreams?

The film speaks of serious issues that concern Indians and is thus aimed at an Indian as well as a general audience. For Karuppannan, life is what you make of it. Pieces must be picked up, and the journey must be continued. And to press home his point, he has Elango remarking to Jeeva, "sometimes the best may not really be good enough. It is better to go with what you have." This perhaps denotes the director's own view of life in general: that it is better to take the middle path and be satisfied with what one already has. By bringing the theme of family into the picture, the director depicts Jeeva as one who has strong roots in a family that accepts both the good and the bad. Elango's family, on the other hand, appears to have lost its sense of direction and harangues him for having been conned. We know Jeeva has learned his lesson and that he will not make the same mistake twice, but Elango's future is uncertain.

Chalanggai

Malaysia's official New Economic Policy, formulated in 1971, was meant to eradicate poverty among the races and to restructure Malaysian society so that the various races were not identified with particular economic activities. (Traditionally, the Malays were identified with agriculture and fishing, the Indians with rubber-tree tapping, and the Chinese with business.) That policy, however, is seen to have benefited the Malays the most. In *Chalanggai* (2007), Deepak Kumaran Menon obliquely refers to this development in one scene where a Malay government officer arrives in his gleaming Mercedes Benz from Putrajaya (the seat of political power). He wants to park his car temporarily at the car wash where the protagonist, Siva, works. Siva asks the official whether he has ever been to Brickfields. He answers in the negative, but nonchalantly says he has been to KL Sentral, an ultra-modern transit rail and taxi station, which is on the opposite side of the road from Brickfields. In another scene, an old Chinese man repairs the bicycle of Siva's little sister, Uma, and, as he does so, he plaintively sings a Chinese song: "I am devoted to you, I am sincere, but where are you?" With these scenes, the filmmaker comments on the apathy of the ruling elite (in particular, the Malays) who have not tried to understand the problems faced by the other races. In his lament, "… but where are you?," the Chinese man bemoans the (literal) absence of the Malay politicians who should be sensitive to his community's needs.

Similarly, in *Aandal,* the absence of Malays in the film signifies their lack of interest in Indian problems. In *Sweet Dreams,* too, no Malays are shown. A Malay officer, supposedly on the take, is mentioned but never portrayed, signifying the negative image of Malays (i.e., many are on the take). But like the directors of *Aandal* and *S'kali,* Menon ends *Chalangaai* on a positive note. Uma wants to learn the

Bharathanatyam, the classical Indian dance, and is finally presented with the required dancing bells to tie round her ankles. We then see the guru teaching her and other students the dance. Menon's choice of actor to play the guru is a Malay, Ramli Ibrahim, himself a national icon. In the context of the story, the choice is significant. In a dialectical sequence of affectionate images, Menon fills the frame with the guru and his student dancers, suggesting that the only way to understand another race is to understand their culture—and this is what the Malays need to do to appreciate the problems of the Indians.

Uma and her mother watch the dance guru.
From Deepak Kumaran Menon's *Chalanggai*

S'kali

If Menon, Kesavan, and Karuppannan are subtle and use subtexts to express their frustrations about their place in the country, Arivind Abraham takes the opposite tack. *S'Kali* (2006) is about five young people of different races: Ravin (Indian), Bahir (Malay), Sze Huey and Tzao (both Chinese), and Tehmina (Eurasian). They are close friends and are frequently seen together in coffee shops, at their homes, and on the beach, sharing thoughts and feelings about themselves and their country. Their optimism that things will change soon turns into pessimism over the course of the film. The inequalities, prejudices, and biases created by "the system" begin to surface in their relationships with each other. Ravin and Sze Huey are in love, but are of different races (and of different colors, too). The director, Abraham, graphically shows this in a close shot of Sze Huey's hand folded over Ravin's hand. Her fair skin is in stark contrast to Ravin's dark skin, signifying that "color" is not a problem for them. The director is, in a sense, alluding to the problems of inter-racial and inter-religious relationships in Malaysia—relationships that have become sensitive topics (particularly when it involves Muslims). Tzao has a different problem. He has gained top marks in his examinations, but is unable to enter a local university due to the quota system (one that favors Malays, and is enshrined in the

Malaysian Constitution). Bahir's examination results are inferior to Tzao's, yet Tzao ruefully admits that Bahir won't have a problem securing a place in a local government-sponsored university since he is Malay. Tzao does not want to leave Malaysia, but decides, reluctantly, to leave his friends and go overseas. Bahir likes Tehmina, but he, too, realizes that their being of different races and religions will cause problems as they try to negotiate Malay society. Tehmina is an alcoholic, a condition brought about by problems in her family, but Bahir loves her and tries to help. Tehmina ends up dying in an accident. The circumstances that led to the accident could have been prevented by her friends, and that realization further traumatizes them. But her death also brings the friends closer together. They accept the fact that life is also about facing unhappiness. At the end of the film, the friends are back in their usual coffee shop, but now they are subdued—a reflection of their newly attained maturity. Abraham's camera slowly moves from the friends to the smiling ghost of Tehmina, who happily observes them and seems glad that they are still "all together" (*s'kali*).

The story is obviously inspired by a scene from Yasmin Ahmad's first feature film, *Sepet* (Slit-Eyed, 2005), where unequal educational opportunities in Malaysia are hinted at, alongside the problems associated with interracial love.[26] (See Benjamin McKay's chapter in this collection, which discusses her films.) The death at the end of *Sepet* of the Chinese male protagonist, Jason, parallels the death of Tehmina in *S'kali*. Perhaps, like Yasmin Ahmad, Abraham is raising the following question: Do we have to wait for a death to occur before we start to see things clearly?

Abraham's second feature, *5:15,* made in 2009, is, literally, a dark story about a present-day Malaysia that has been overrun by an unknown, evil force. As has become the norm in Malaysia, the real nature of what is happening—or why—is not revealed in the official news (on the radio, in the case of the film), and so the characters in the story try to make sense of what is transpiring outside their house. Everything is in darkness due to a power outage. The tension exhibited by the characters is conveyed in monochrome images, shot in a subjective manner, with quirky camerawork. At the end, the characters find that the monster—or monsters— is inside their house. Abraham continues to assert, via his films, that the real problem facing the country is not the imagined threat from outside, but comes from within. In *The Joshua Tapes* (2010), which he co-directed with Benjy Lim, Abraham goes back to his multiracial theme. Three friends—Malay, Chinese, and Indian—go on a road trip to the coast. We are not told why at the beginning, and only towards the end do we learn that the trip is to scatter the ashes of their good friend, Joshua. On the way, they argue with each other, and their personal problems almost destroy their relationships. Ultimately, they come together and, solemnly, standing in a boat on the open sea, scatter the ashes of their good friend Joshua (whom we never see alive, but who was captured in a videotape sequence shown as part of the film). As in *S'kali,* the death of a companion brings these friends of different races together. In a sense, the film is saying that everyone has problems, but death will ultimately embrace us all. Why do we then need to quarrel and segregate ourselves from one another while living?

---

[26] The late Yasmin Ahmad makes a brief appearance in *S'kali* as herself, offering words of wisdom to Ravin. Yasmin was highly respected by filmmakers associated with The Little Cinema, as she had been their strongest supporter—sometimes providing funds, sometimes playing the role of executive producer, and sometimes appearing as an actor in The Little Cinema films.

Arivind Abraham emphatically calls himself "a first-generation Malaysian." And in *S'kali* and *The Joshua Tapes,* he proclaims a brave new world, heralding a new generation, one that feels no qualms about rejecting the prejudices, inequalities, and artificialities that have become entrenched in Malaysian society. Abraham shows this through Bahir's comment in *S'Kali*, when he says he wants the music he is creating to be different and not like "the stupid reality TV show singers" (the current Malaysian craze). The friends even condemn the local band *Alleycats,* a national icon, and they also take a potshot at the only film school in the country (a government-run institution), asking Ravin if that's where he wants to study. Later Ravin, in frustration, says he wants to leave the country because he is sick of fighting the system and fighting "with people who won't make concessions" (a reference to Malay hegemony and chauvinism). These articulations of the characters are, in reality, a reflection of the frustrations of Abraham and other young people like him, the new generation of Malaysians who are not being given a chance to change things for the better.[27]

CONCLUSION

Deepak Kumaran Menon and Arivind Abraham are members of The Little Cinema of Malaysia, while Sandosh Kesavan, Kumaresan Chinniah, and Shunmugham Karuppannan are independent filmmakers with mainstream sensibilities. But all of them, including the Chinese members of The Little Cinema, are expressing their feelings and frustrations in a manner never seen in almost eighty years of Malay(sian) cinema. Over the last decade, Chinese filmmakers like Ho Yuhang, Tan Chui Mui, James Lee, Khoo Eng Yow, Yeo Joon Han, and Chris Chong have been very subtly questioning the place of Chinese (and Indians) as second-class citizens in today's Malaysia. Their films invariably show characters at the fringes of society who are disenfranchised or alienated, and who are powerless to chart the direction of their lives. Power is shown to lie in the hands of the state, with the parties entrusted to look after the welfare of the ethnic communities being conspicuously absent. The filmmakers are also critical of those from among their ethnic communities who have become successful. In one scene in Tan Chui Mui's *Love Conquers All,* a Chinese professional "examines" the body of the young girl who has had to prostitute herself to save her boyfriend. The client, portrayed as a successful Chinese, regards her disdainfully as nothing more than a product to be used and then discarded. On whom can the young Chinese of today look for support if those who have succeeded are not helping others to also succeed? In a style reminiscent of Antonioni, Tan sums it all up towards the end of the film. The girl realizes that she has been tricked into being a prostitute. She lies on the road, and then in a jump cut we see her walk as if she were in a daze. She stands, looking out over the South China Sea—in the direction that her forefathers had taken to travel to this land in search of fortune. What would they think if they knew what had befallen their offspring, the generation that was supposed to build on the successes of the

---

[27] This frustration is not just expressed by the non-Malays. Mansor Puteh, a graduate of Columbia University, expresses the same sentiments in his post-modernist feature, *Seman* (The Lost Hero, 1987). In the film, the protagonist opens a crumpled piece of paper on which is written the word *merdeka* (independence). Through this, Mansor Puteh raises the question, "Have we *really* achieved Independence?"

previous one, but which is now reduced to the level of whores? It is the kind of rumination that overlaps with the articulations of the Indian filmmakers.

The subjects and issues raised by the fourth-generation Indian filmmakers actually reflect the dilemmas that they themselves face as non-Malay filmmakers in Malaysia. Opting to make their films mostly in Tamil (or in English, as with *S'kali* and *The Joshua Tapes*), they have fallen afoul of the outdated 1981 National Film Development Corporation Act, which decrees that all Malaysian films must be 70 percent in the national language, Malay. (Only recently has this restriction been lifted, due to the increase in the production of mainstream Chinese movies). *Chemman Chaalai, Aandal, S'kali,* and *The Joshua Tapes* ended up being screened in Malaysian cinemas under the rubric "International Film"! The filmmakers, therefore, were not eligible for the 25 percent entertainment tax rebate that local film producers receive as an incentive for them to continue making films. The situation appears to be an anomaly, as the government, in its efforts to promote tourism, has adopted the slogan "Malaysia, Truly Asia." This appears to be an empty phrase—a blurb for tourists. And all this in spite of the fact that *Chemman Chaalai* and a number of The Little Cinema's films have raised the Malaysian flag at numerous festivals around the world. On the other hand, not a single mainstream film has made it to a major festival overseas for competition, even though a lot of Malaysian taxpayers' money has been spent to support production of these works over the years.[28]

It appears that in these filmmakers' case, life truly reflects the narratives in their films, and vice versa. They, like their films' protagonists, will continue to be strangers in their own country. The positive aspect of this state of affairs is that their angst might encourage them to continue their struggle, as it is from such tension and conflict that great narratives arise. And it is possible that the seeds planted by the fourth-generation Indian filmmakers will enable the fifth generation to, perhaps, ultimately claim their rightful place in Malaysia. It may be that the fifth-generation Indian filmmakers will then not be known as such, but as second-generation Malaysians, echoing Arivind Abraham's emphatic and heartfelt declaration quoted at the beginning of this chapter. Like a true film hero, Abraham is optimistic that change will ultimately take place. In a scene in *S'kali*, he has Tzao telling Bahir that he will return from his studies overseas because people like Bahir make him hopeful that things will change. For these young, idealistic filmmakers, the battle has not been lost. It has just begun, and the fourth-generation Indian filmmakers' voice—or the first-generation Malaysian filmmakers'—is the clarion call.

SELECTED FILMOGRAPHY

5:15 (Arivind Abraham, 2009)
Aandal (Sandosh Kesavan, 2005)
At the End of Daybreak (Ho Yuhang, 2009)
Before We Fall in Love Again (James Lee, 2006)
Chalanggai (Deepak Kumaran Menon, 2007)

---

[28] The Ministry of Information, Communications, and Culture, which oversees the film industry, has a program to support films that promote the arts and culture of the country. As a consequence, troupes of dancers accompany screenings of selected films overseas, at considerable cost. However, none of these state-selected films has been critically acclaimed even in Malaysia, and they all have failed to get commercial screenings overseas.

Chemman Chaalai (Deepak Kumaran Menon, 2004)
Ethirkaalam (C. Kumaresan, 2006)
Gerimis (P. Ramlee, 1968)
Hikayat Sang Kancil (Anandam Xavier, 1978)
Karaoke (Chris Chong, 2009)
Leila Majnun (B. S. Rajhans, 1933)
Lips to Lips (Amir Muhammad, 2000)
Love Conquers All (Tan Chui Mui, 2006)
Melati Puteh (M. Raj, 1984)
Min (Ho Yuhang, 2003)
Naan Oru Malaysian (Pansha, 1991)
Rain Dogs (Ho Yuhang, 2006)
Rette Payiee (M. Baharuddin, 1968)
Room to Let (James Lee, 2002)
Sanctuary (Ho Yuhang, 2004)
Selamat Tinggal Kekaseh-ku (L. Krishnan, 1955)
Sell-Out! (Yeo Joon Han, 2008)
Seman (Mansor Puteh, 1987)
Sepet (Yasmin Ahmad, 2004)
Seruan Merdeka (B. S. Rajhans, 1946)
Silat Legenda (Hassan Abd Muthalib, 1998)
S'kali (Arivind Abraham, 2006)
Sweet Dreams (K. Shunmugham, 2006)
The Beautiful Washing Machine (James Lee, 2004)
The Birdhouse (Khoo Eng Yow, 2007)
The Deadly Disciple (S. Mohan, 2001)
The Joshua Tapes (Arivind Abraham and Benjy Lim, 2010)
The Last Communist (Amir Muhammad, 2006)
Uyir (Premnath Pillai, 2004)

DISSENT ISN'T DISLOYALTY: IN CONVERSATION WITH MARTYN SEE

Vinita Ramani Mohan

HOURS BEFORE THE VOTES CAME IN

It was about 10:00 PM on a Saturday, and I was stationed, together with a group of journalists, outside the office of the Singapore Democratic Party (SDP), one of the four major political parties in Singapore that contest in the country's general elections. It was a typically humid night in Singapore, and the threat of a thunderstorm loomed, but you could not quite tell if it would pour down with rain or if the storm would pass. Considering it was polling night for the general elections in 2006, most of us were not just wondering which way the weather was going to swing.

For once, though, there was a spirit of camaraderie amongst us journalists that extended beyond the usual tacit agreement to share information. Some of us had been working non-stop for eleven days, attending rallies organized by the various political parties in the lead-up to polling day, May 6. Skeptics may say that Singapore elections are hardly anything to get excited about, given that only one political party, namely the People's Action Party (PAP), and its three prime ministers, have been at the nation's helm since independence in 1965.

But something about this year felt different. Rumors had been flying that it could be a clean sweep for the PAP—a devastating outcome if the prediction proved true, given that only two incumbent opposition Members of Parliament (MP), from the Singapore Democratic Alliance and the Worker's Party, had provided the tiniest hint of opposition voices over two decades, which was otherwise lacking.[1] When it was finally announced that the opposition MPs had retained their seats, there was a gleeful cacophony. Hands were thrust in the air. Motorists who drove by sounded their horns and waved in solidarity. Worker's Party and Singapore Democratic Alliance flags were swung by jubilant supporters in vans that sped by late at night, and incoming news from the radios we had pressed to our ears indicated that, while

---

[1] The Singapore Democratic Alliance's Chiam See Tong has been a Member of Parliament for over twenty years and the Worker's Party's Low Thia Kiang has been a Member of Parliament since 1991. The SDP has never held a seat in Parliament.

nothing had really changed in Singapore, *something* had. For a moment, we felt no fear. We, the media, did not censor ourselves, and Singaporeans had become just a little more brave.

Singapore writer, blogger, and activist Alex Au's photos of opposition rallies were sufficient evidence in that regard: hundreds and thousands of Singaporeans, often described as being uninvolved in their neighbor's affairs, and even more so in the nation's, had trawled through a muddy field in the rain just to hear members of the Worker's Party during one of its rallies before polling day. Singaporean bloggers had meticulously chronicled these events and, more importantly, expressed their own views on the Internet, prompting the Ministry of Information, Communication, and the Arts (MICA) to wonder whether there was some way to curb the bloggers. There was a perceptible change in civil-society consciousness in Singapore. As Dana Lam aptly put it, it was a "rare sign of an active citizenry mobilizing for no more than a chance to hear what the opposition has to say. The result is a palpable, even infectious, excitement that spills over from the virtual space onto the concrete pavements."[2]

Something about that moment resonates when I think of the Singaporean filmmaker Martyn See. Small-framed, guarded, and reticent for the most part, See nonetheless displays a quiet passion and curiosity for the state of politics and free speech in Singapore. His three short documentaries follow a similar stylistic approach, juxtaposing talking heads, footage of rarely seen protests in Singapore, and inter-titles to contextualize Singapore's recent history and the protagonists he feels have been conveniently erased out of the "official" picture. His is the kind of action and expression of views that should be shown on the evening news, but will never see the light of day in contemporary Singapore. The approach taken is more akin to the agitprop footage a burgeoning group of Singaporeans are cataloguing with digital video cameras in what can only be seen as a growing tradition of civil-society journalism in the country.

No surprises, then, that Martyn See has the peculiar distinction of being the only filmmaker in Singapore whose two short documentary films, namely *Singapore Rebel* (2005) and *Zahari's 17 Years* (2006), have been banned by the Board of Film Censors. See was informed that he could be levied a fine of up to 100,000 SGD and/or a prison sentence not exceeding two years for possession or distribution of the films. Needless to say, no license was ever granted to exhibit those films, automatically making it untenable to screen the films at any venue in Singapore. Unsurprisingly, See decided not to release his third documentary film, *Speakers Cornered* (2006), in Singapore, choosing instead to submit it to festivals in Taiwan and Malaysia.[3]

Nonetheless, why the ruckus over a small filmmaker releasing low-budget short films that are hardly the kind of blockbuster Hollywood fare the majority of Singaporeans enjoy watching? After all, even without a ban, the films do not have the kind of commercial appeal that would cause them to be distributed or shown in Singapore's massive cineplexes.

---

[2] Dana Lam, *Days of Being Wild: GE2006 Walking the Line with the Opposition* (Singapore: Ethos Books, 2006), p. 19.

[3] See's films have been shown at numerous international film festivals, including the Toronto Singapore Film Festival. See www.tsff.org/www/images/yt_st_article.pdf (viewed on June 20, 2011) for more on the festival and the 2007 program.

Imagine, if you will, watching a production of Tom Stoppard's 1966 play, *Rosencrantz and Guildenstern Are Dead*, that existentialist tragicomedy which turns Shakespeare's *Hamlet* on its head by giving lead roles to the peripheral characters Rosencrantz and Guildenstern. By turning everything upside down, Stoppard allows us to consider the internal conflicts, the exercise of free will (or the lack thereof), and the internal confusion of characters we would otherwise never notice. See's films are a little bit like that. They are a snapshot of political rumblings in Singapore, and they attempt, in however rudimentary or truncated a manner, to consider the *personae non gratae* in the "play" that captures Singapore's history. Doing this apparently rubs the government the wrong way.

Ironically, See has accepted the reaction to his films with the same kind of steely pragmatism that characterizes the status quo in Singapore. It is a lesson well learned. To him, practical resolve is the only way to go on doing what he does: documenting the lives of individuals whom he feels have taken on the state. See wants to tell their story, to show a different diary of (to) the nation.[4]

NO POLITICAL FILMS, PLEASE, WE'RE SINGAPOREANS

See, a long-time film editor, made his debut film *Singapore Rebel* in 2005. As is required in Singapore, he submitted it to the Board of Film Censors (BFC) under the Media Development Authority (MDA), which subsequently banned it because it was deemed to be a "party political film" under Section 2 of the Films Act.[5] While writers posted opinions about this decision on their blogs, the ban hardly caused what one could call a public stir in Singapore. Instead, the incident was covered by international media and human rights watchdogs abroad.[6]

The film is about Dr. Chee Soon Juan. Dr. Chee, a trained neuropsychologist, joined the SDP in 1992 and later took over as its secretary-general, counting figures like Mahatma Gandhi and Martin Luther King, Jr., as sources of his inspiration. The intrepid academic-turned-political-activist has been convicted for offences under the Public Entertainments and Meetings Act, which lays out clear rules regarding obtaining a permit for speaking in public and holding rallies—rules that Dr. Chee has frequently attempted to challenge, while also questioning the legitimacy of the ruling government.

In particular, Dr. Chee has taken on Lee Kuan Yew, ostensibly the "father" of the nation and one of the founding members of the PAP. Lee led Singapore to independence in 1959 and remained the prime minister until 1990, when he was succeeded by Goh Chock Tong. Now a government "minister mentor," Lee once famously said: "Everybody knows that in my bag I have a hatchet, and a very sharp

---

[4] *Diary of a Nation* was a television series about the history of Singapore. It was produced in 1990 by what was then known as the Singapore Broadcasting Corporation (SBC). SBC is now known as MediaCorp, and is 100 percent owned by Temasek Holdings, the Singapore government's wholly owned investment arm.

[5] The Singapore Films Act can be found in its entirety at http://statutes.agc.gov.sg/non_version/cgi-bin/cgi_retrieve.pl?actno=REVED-107&doctitle=FILMS%20ACT%0A&date=latest&method=part (accessed May 10, 2011).

[6] Ron Brownlow, "Banned, But Not Broken," *Taipei Times*, October 6, 2006, available at www.taipeitimes.com/News/feat/archives/2006/10/06/2003330692 (accessed May 10, 2011). *Index on Censorship*, "Filmmaker Faces Political Ban," May 11, 2005 (no longer available online).

one. You take me on, I take my hatchet, we meet in the cul-de-sac."[7] Chee no doubt felt the blade when both Lee and Goh sued him for defamation in 2001. Since Dr. Chee failed to pay the damages, totaling 500,000 SGD, the supreme court declared him bankrupt, thereby effectively barring him from standing for elections. Clearly, See's films deal with issues that are contentious, controversial and sensitive.

Singapore Rebel is a 27-minute short film with a three-minute opening sequence of generic and fast-cut shots of Singapore's central business district and shopping malls, while a voice-over narrates a series of stereotypical statistics about the nation. Those data cover the usual terrain that most news wire agency reports about Singapore include when discussing the economic success of that anomalous "little red dot on the map." Indeed, although Singapore has far outperformed its Southeast Asian neighbors economically, it continues to be perceived with guarded cynicism by some outsiders and citizens alike for its lack of political and social freedom.

The film then takes us to an apartment above an innocuous shop, where Dr. Chee works and lives with his wife and three children. An informal question-and-answer interview allows See to craft a vignette of the man and his forays into politics. See's journalistic-style narrative allows the key moments to speak for themselves. Archival footage shot by See is edited into the film, including Dr. Chee's attempts in 2002 to get a "people against poverty" May Day rally going outside the grounds of the Istana (office of the president of Singapore). The film provides a gentler and more nuanced perspective of Dr. Chee than what Singaporeans are generally exposed to through the country's mainstream mass media.

In many ways, the 28-minute short *Speakers Cornered* continues from where *Rebel* ends. The film is divided into eighteen parts (I to XVIII), with each part introduced via inter-titles that capture the most significant exchange or event typifying the moment recorded on camera. The film's context is the IMF–World Bank Meetings that took place in Singapore from September 15 to 20, 2006.

In all, twenty-six or so NGOs, as well as two reporters from *The Epoch Times,* were barred from entering Singapore for the meetings. Those who wished to engage in any direct protest action were—for all intents and purposes—"assigned" a space in the Singapore Convention Center measuring roughly eight by eight meters (twenty-six by twenty-six feet), sectioned off with red and green tape. Given that it was a relatively snug fit in the otherwise enormous convention center, where up to 24,000 delegates were scheduled to congregate, the designated "protest" space was predictably underutilized during the meetings.[8]

Dr. Chee, his sister Chee Siok Chin (also a SDP member), as well as a number of other party members and supporters decided to organize a march to "empower Singaporeans" on September 16, 2006, which would have its starting point at the

---

[7] This ubiquitous quote is also on See's website, http://singaporerebel.blogspot. com/2008/08/democracy-justice-equality-peace.html (accessed May 10, 2011).

[8] There is a lot of writing and reports on the IMF–World Bank Meetings held in Singapore in September 2006, all of which is available on the Internet. A comprehensive summary of the event, which includes no mention of the protests or problems, can be found at: http://en.wikipedia.org/wiki/Singapore_2006 (accessed May 10, 2011). Alternate reports can be found at www.twnside.org.sg/title2/finance/twninfofinance007.htm (accessed May 10, 2011); at Indymedia's site at www.indymedia.org/en/2006/09/846454.shtml (accessed May 10, 2011); and http://en.epochtimes.com/news/6-9-15/45978.html (accessed May 10, 2011).

Hong Lim Park Speakers Corner.[9] Beginning at 11:00 AM on that day, See catalogued the events that unraveled as the Chee siblings attempted to speak or march and were subsequently halted by a phalanx of police officers. The police attempted everything from establishing human barricades to "calm negotiation" in order to prevent the rally or any other similar events from taking place.

In this documentary, which is shot in a style that resembles news footage, filmmaker See is featured interviewing protestors as well as the police assigned to control them. See asks police officers why they, too, are filming the march (for archival purposes?), what their duty for the day is, and whether they have a warrant to arrest either Dr. Chee or his sister. The questions posed are neither overtly biased in favor of the Chees nor provocative, and See remains behind the camera throughout.[10] Shot over three days, the film captures the mood of exhaustion and frustration experienced by the people who form the main focus of the film. But for all the activity and dynamism of the event, See's film succeeds in portraying the irony of how little could be accomplished throughout the three days, given that the authorities quite literally restricted any movement. While the film at first viewing appears to be a dispassionate catalogue of a series of events, See's focus on Chee and the Singapore Democratic Party is in itself an indicator of his continuous fascination with, and political support for, the few individuals who exercise the very rights that are categorically denied to Singaporeans—namely, the right to protest and speak about sensitive political issues in the public domain. Claiming allegiance with an opposition party is something Singaporeans rarely do publicly, and certainly not outside of the hustings period when rallies enable citizens to show passionate support for a party other than the PAP. With these films, See also makes it evident that he unequivocally supports the SDP and Chee's cause.

In his next documentary, *Zahari's 17 Years,* See shifts his focus to Said Zahari, a former political detainee now living in Malaysia, who was swept up as part of the mass arrests conducted in 1963, code-named Operation Cold Store. Ostensibly detained for his involvement with Partai Rakyat (People's Party), which wanted to forge a leftist alternative to the direction taken by the PAP and its leader, Lee Kuan Yew, Said was detained without trial for seventeen years.[11] In popular memory, he is probably best remembered as the dynamic journalist-turned-editor of the anti-colonial Malay-language newspaper *Utusan Melayu*, which was published in the tumultuous 1950s and 1960s.

In *Zahari's 17 Years,* See once again maintains his simple, straightforward style, allowing Zahari to speak in the comfort of his home library. Zahari recalls key political moments, such as the night he joined the Partai Rakyat and was elected as its leader, as well as his contention with the term "communist" that was applied to

---

[9] This would not be the first time that Dr. Chee had attempted to use the space, set up in 2000, to raise issues he felt were pertinent to the social and political landscape of Singapore. His previous attempt to speak at the venue in 2002 about religious issues led to a 3,000 SGD fine. The Ministry for Home Affairs detailed the rules on the Speakers Corner here: http://www2.mha.gov.sg/mha/detailed.jsp?artid=416&type=4&root=0&parent=0&cat=0&mode=arc (on file with the author).

[10] I raised this point with the filmmaker when I interviewed him, and his response was: "I was inspired by the US TV series *Cops*—documenting the exchanges between civilians and uniformed officers in a nonjudgmental manner, dispensing with the need to embellish it with narration or music." From an interview, via email, with Martyn See, February 7, 2007.

[11] Said Zahari, *Dark Clouds at Dawn: A Political Memoir* (Kuala Lumpur: INSAN, 2001).

him following his arrest and detention. See allows personal recollections to coalesce with or weave in and out of the political musings, humanizing a man who is not widely known in Singapore, as See himself admits (see the interview that follows). The interview See documented on film is interspersed with shots of archival photos and microfilmed documents from political events of the 1960s—a period when, as most Singaporeans will recall, an anti-colonial struggle shriveled to become an ideological battle between the People's Action Party and leftist parties, such as the Barisan Socialis (Socialist Front), a contest to see who would ultimately rule the nation.

The documentary was dealt with in more or less the same manner as his previous short films. Soon after See submitted it to the BFC in April 2007, a media release was issued stating that the film gives "a false and distorted portrayal of [Zahari's] detention ... [which] could undermine public confidence in the Government" and was therefore prohibited under Section 35(1) of the Films Act.[12] Interestingly, the government media release emphasizes Zahari's "past involvement in communist united front activities against the interests of Singapore" and that he was a "security threat to the country."

This is where Martyn See has chosen to locate himself—in the fractious turf where the dominant power decides how history will be written, but where the stubborn shadows of the erased narratives nevertheless remain somewhat visible. Despite police investigations, confiscated video equipment, and excessive media attention, See is determined somehow to persevere. In early 2007, I met him on several occasions at local coffee shops in Singapore, and we eventually sat down over dinner one night for our most extensive interview. Always soft-spoken and often dead-pan when he loosens up, See still considers himself a humble video editor, with an incorrigible desire just to find out what life is like for the outsider or the marginalized individual in Singapore.

THE CONVERSATION

Vinita Ramani Mohan (VRM): How long have you been making films and when did you start?

Martyn See (MS): I've been working as an editor for more than ten years, but I didn't make my own film until *Singapore Rebel* in 2005. I didn't set out to be a filmmaker; I was pretty happy editing other people's stuff. Then I sort of decided to film Chee Soon Juan when he was arrested at the Istana during May Day of 2002.[13] I kept that footage, and I looked at it again and again and thought, good God, this is the sort of footage you need to show. So I decided to construct a short film around the ten-minute footage that I had. I decided to interview him and basically track his life as a politician. That's how *Singapore Rebel* came about.

---

[12] "Press Release on Prohibition of the Film *Zahari's 17 Years*," Singapore Government Media Release, April 10, 2007.

[13] On Labour Day, May 1, 2002, Dr. Chee staged a rally in front of Istana, the official residence and office of the president of Singapore. Dr. Chee was arrested after he ignored a police officer's warning to leave. Dr. Chee had earlier applied for a license to hold the rally, but the application was denied. He was later charged with trespassing and for attempting to hold a rally without a license.

VRM: What aspects of your personal life, travels, and experiences came into play and led you to explore what is documented and what is not documented?

MS: I think my biggest complaint about Singaporeans [concerns] their apathy toward any kind of political or social issues; and, secondly, their tremendous amount of fear of the government and of authority, which I think is extremely unhealthy for the building of any kind of civic consciousness. So I felt compelled to document that, because we all know the climate of fear exists, but somehow we don't talk about it. But my problem is, how do you use the medium of film to express the fear and the apathy that Singaporeans feel? So, I guess by showing them reality as it exists—such as the arrest of opposition politicians, interviews with an ex-political detainee—it jolts people's consciousness, and perhaps they could leave the screening thinking about their role as active citizens in Singapore. I wanted to get people interested in political issues. That's why I began *Singapore Rebel* with a three-minute montage cut to a punk song by the band Opposition Party. It was admittedly a cheap shot for getting people's attention to a politically themed film.

VRM: What sort of response was there to *Singapore Rebel* when people saw it?

MS: *Singapore Rebel* is on Google Video, registering over 20,000 hits, and it's on YouTube (more than 200,000 hits), as well. I don't really read the comments, so I don't really know how Singaporeans feel about this film.

VRM: In terms of the reach and impact your films can have, on one hand you're saying you don't really look at comments, and at the same time you are acknowledging that what is prompting you to do this is the desire to raise civic consciousness, to want people to take some kind of an interest, even in a completely nonpartisan sense. So, are you curious at all to know whether your films can *have* that kind of impact?

MS: Yeah, eventually I'd like to have a proper screening in Singapore where we can actually sit down and discuss the film and what it means. But that's out of the question, because it's been banned and my tapes are still with the police. So, I mean, I can't get much feedback if it's banned and people tend not to leave too many comments on the Internet.

VRM: What about the response abroad, or the trajectory of response it got abroad?

MS: I didn't get many comments from abroad, either. I think the reason why the foreign festivals screened it in the first place was only because it was banned. I don't think they were really interested in Singapore issues. So I think *Singapore Rebel* took off only because the government banned it, not because of the allure of its subject matter.

VRM: Was that disappointing or frustrating?

MS: No, it wasn't. When I made the film, I expected less than a hundred people to turn up to watch it in a small room at the Goethe Institute in Singapore—that is, if they had passed it—and I would have been happy with that. So, the fact that they banned it and festivals came knocking on my door to want to screen it is already a huge achievement, way beyond what I had anticipated.

VRM: Going back to this idea of gaining legitimacy abroad, as a "banned filmmaker," and being held in high esteem by human rights film festivals and so on—does this put you in a dilemma, this way of being represented and then having that legitimization questioned when you are here in Singapore?

MS: I used to wonder why Singaporeans don't take to local music, and also why local art or any kind of local works are not appreciated by Singaporeans. I've come to realize that it's the same all over much of Asia. Some Asian artists have to get international recognition before their own people will take to their work. So it's something that I've begun to reconcile with; I just live with it.

VRM: Why is it like that, from your perspective? Why is it that we frequently sit up and notice something *after* it has been applauded or hailed or championed by the "West"?

MS: Sometimes the insular proclivities of the local audience force artists, particularly those who are attempting to break new ground, to the sidelines. Then the artist takes his work abroad, finds acclaim, and re-imports it back home to find a new audience! It's not just confined to the arts or film or music. The phenomenon happens with politicians and activists just the same. If you get recognition abroad for the political or social or human rights work you do, it enhances your work locally. Aung San Suu Kyi is still alive because the international community is fighting for her release. The junta could have poisoned her in prison had it not been for international scrutiny. So, I can understand, in that aspect, where someone like Chee is coming from. If you are a prisoner, surely you can't be pleading to the prison warden to free you. You have to get people outside of prison to speak on your behalf.

VRM: Again, what were the seeds of your documentary, *Zahari's 17 Years*, and in relation to that, what has your exposure to history been like in Singapore?

MS: While I was in Malaysia for the screening of *Singapore Rebel*, some Malaysians suggested there that maybe I should approach Said Zahari. I found out from them, the Malaysians, that he is actually Singaporean and that he was a political detainee for seventeen years.[14] So, when I came back, I read his book *Dark Clouds at Dawn: A Political Memoir,* and I decided to do a film on him. One of my motivations for making *Singapore Rebel* was also to open up a space for filmmakers to attempt to do politically themed films. By the investigation and through the banning of *Rebel*, I think the space was closed. I think a lot of filmmakers were fearful of attempting to go into that area, so I decided to make *Zahari's 17 Years* just to prove to them that you should actually do it and that you shouldn't pull back because of what's happening to me.

---

[14] See's film was shown at the 2005 Freedom Film Festival, held in Kuala Lumpur, Malaysia.

VRM: So it was much more of an organic process, in that the screening of one film led you toward the possibilities of making the other? It wasn't so much that you made a conscious decision to do documentaries focusing on politics or activists?

MS: I already had a deep interest in political detainees, but there wasn't much being written about political detention in Singapore apart from former Solicitor-General Francis Seow's *To Catch a Tartar*,[15] Chee Soon Juan's *To Be Free*,[16] and a couple of documents on the Internet about the 1987 Marxist arrests.[17] So I wanted to find out more. After reading Zahari's book, I realized that he is probably the only ex-detainee who doesn't have any inhibitions about speaking out.

VRM: Even then, in terms of social and personal memory, "speaking out" is still a process of selectively speaking; we always tend to remember things in vignettes or portions, not as some "objective print-out" of a document with all the pages included and all the data filled in. So, what do you think about documenting acts of remembering, especially by people recalling their detention and imprisonment? What have you discovered in terms of what memories they hold onto, what they repeat and reiterate, what they tend to (or choose to) forget?

MS: A common thread among Singapore dissidents is their preoccupation with Lee Kuan Yew, which I find quite peculiar. Whenever they talk about Singapore and its restrictions and repression, inevitably Lee Kuan Yew comes up. For example, with Zahari, I asked him general questions, but somehow Lee Kuan Yew always came up in his answers! So does Chee, when you speak to him [Chee] privately. It's like a psychological chess match between them and Lee—both sides figuring out each other's moves.

And another thing is that these ex-detainees, even though they were jailed a long time ago, they remember every little detail of what they went through in jail, especially in the first few days of detention. They remember the interrogation; they remember the cell. So, it's almost like the recollection of their detention experience is frozen in time.

VRM: On the theme of preoccupations and memories, we had this interesting incident at the Asia Research Institute [National University of Singapore] where Malaysian filmmaker Amir Muhammad screened his latest documentary, *Apa Khabar Orang Kampung* [Village People Radio Show, 2007], in which he interviews ex-communists [formerly with the Malayan Communist Party], now living in southern Thailand. Most were nostalgic about the anti-colonial freedom struggle, but never really identified themselves as "communists" through all the interviews. Some members of the audience reacted strongly to this. They felt these communists were

---

[15] Francis T. Seow, *To Catch a Tartar: A Dissident in Lee Kuan Yew's Prison* (New Haven, CT: Yale University Southeast Asian Studies Monograph Series, 1994).

[16] Chee Soon Juan, *To Be Free: Stories from Asia's Struggle against Oppression* (Melbourne: Monash Asia Institute, 1998).

[17] Under the code name Operation Spectrum, the Internal Security Department (ISD) used its Internal Security Act (ISA) to arrest and detain twenty-two Roman Catholic church members and social activists for allegedly being members of a Marxist conspiracy to overthrow the PAP-ruled government. The arrests were conducted in two waves, the first on May 21, 1987, and the second on June 20, 1987.

refusing to acknowledge *what* they were, that they were not being honest. In other words, when some people see what they understand to be "political documentaries" or "politically themed" documentaries, they want confessions and testimonies. People seem to want the truth, and documentaries that touch on history or politics are particularly burdened with this responsibility.

MS: I'm surprised by these comments if they are coming from people who lived through those years. There is a huge difference between Amir's *Village People Radio Show*, the documentary *I love Malaya*, and *Zahari's 17 Years*.[18] I don't think any of the exiles featured in Amir's film and in *I Love Malaya* ever denied that they were communists or that atrocities were committed for their cause to oust the colonial powers; but let's not forget that there were also atrocities committed by the colonial authorities.

Now *Zahari's 17 Years* is totally different. You're talking about someone who took part in what he considered was legitimate political activity for only three hours. On the night he decided to take up leadership of a Malay opposition party, he was arrested. So, to place Zahari in the same category as the ex-communists who are living in Betong, Thailand, who were obviously members of the Malayan Communist Party, is problematic. I always remember what Lim Chin Siong said in one of his interviews right before he died.[19] According to Lim, the label "communist" was slapped by the PAP on anybody who was on the other side of the fence, be it the Chinese-educated, be it union leaders, be it student leaders, be it leaders of the Barisan Socialis, which had split from the PAP. If that is true, we have to be mindful of these labels, and we can't just tar everyone with the same "communist" brush.[20]

The fact that he [Zahari] endured seventeen years in prison just to prove to the authorities that he wasn't going to recant or sign any confession that he was a communist, that itself for me is proof enough. However, is Said Zahari a fellow traveler or a sympathizer of the communist party? I would say yes. But is he a communist, a card-carrying member of the Communist Party? No. There really is no reason to detain anyone for seventeen years without charge or trial, especially when Singapore had attained independence in 1965. A lot of what Zahari said on film is revelatory from the historical perspective, so I decided to leave it in, all forty-nine minutes of it.

---

[18] For further information on *Village People Radio Show,* see Amir Muhammad's archived blog http://lastcommunist.blogspot.com/ (accessed May 10, 2011). Ironically, both *Singapore Rebel* and *Zahari's 17 Years* have been shown in Malaysia, but are banned in Singapore. Conversely, Amir Muhammad's films *The Last Communist* and *Village People Radio Show* were both shown at the Singapore International Film Festival (in 2006 and 2007, respectively), but are banned in Malaysia. The film *I Love Malaya* was made by a group of Singaporean filmmakers: Ho Choon Hiong, Chan Kah Mei, Wang Eng Eng, and Eunice Lau. For more details, see www.ilove malaya.com/synopsis.html (accessed May 10, 2011).

[19] Lim Chin Siong is seen as one of the key players in Singapore's political history. He joined the PAP in 1954 and was a famous Hokkien orator, trade union leader, and activist. He was arrested for instigating the well-known 1955 labor strike riots. In 1961, he split from the PAP to form the Barisan Socialis Party. He was one of the political activists to be rounded up as part of Operation Cold Store on February 2, 1963, and was not released until 1969.

[20] In a post-interview communication, Martyn See referenced these statements by referring to Hussin Mutalib's *Parties and Politics: A Study of Opposition Parties and the PAP in Singapore* (Singapore: Eastern Universities Press, 2003).

VRM: The nature of your films being what they are, they have an immediate quality to them. They are comprehensive; they are concentrated on a certain juncture in history and give a fairly clear overview of the political reality in Singapore. Your films seem like they are being made for posterity's sake. Why that choice?

MS: It was definitely a conscious choice on two counts. One, I didn't want to get into trouble for making a subjective political film. That's one reason why I kept my subject relatively objective: so that they [the films] can be credible references for political historians as well as film buffs. Secondly, I don't want to watch a film where the director has his hands all over it, such as through overuse of voice-over narration. So I tried to avoid that. At the same time, I've been accused, or I've been asked why I didn't interview the authorities in *Singapore Rebel,* or why I didn't show the government's point of view in my interview with Zahari. Again, it's a valid point—

VRM: Do you really think that's a valid point? It's valid insofar as it's the diplomatic thing to say, but why is a documentary filmmaker—an independent one at that— obliged to represent "all" points of view? Surely you're not making an educational film, and even then, when are "all" the points of view represented?

MS: Well, I think it makes for a stronger film when opposing dynamics of any issue are investigated before the filmmaker slams home his message in the end, especially when they are cause-driven, such as in Michael Moore's films.[21] But I don't see myself making agitprop. For me, in the time that I have being a one-man show, there's not much I can do in exploring both sides of the story. Also, for forty years we've been subjected to the mainstream media telling us one side of the story. So I think it's about time the other side gets heard. If you think it's not objective enough, then you can read *The Straits Times* and you can watch Channel News Asia and then form your own conclusions.

VRM: At the same time it's ironic that as far as the legal bind you were in goes, you have made something that is deemed a "political film" under the Films Act, something that is seen to be "partisan."[22]

MS: Yes, "partisan, political bias, with biased references," yes!

VRM: You're going to get this kind of rhetoric thrown at you. That aside, there *is* something of you in it, there has to be. The very fact that these are the people you decided to look at shows a conscious decision on your part. Whatever you might see as "civil society" in Singapore, or other forms of activism in the country, nascent or

---

[21] Michael Moore is an American filmmaker and author. His documentary films include *Fahrenheit 9/11, Capitalism: A Love Story, Bowling for Columbine* (which won an Academy Award in 2002 for Best Documentary Feature), and *SiCKO*. He has written a number of books on American foreign policy, corporate crime, America's relationship to the Middle East, and elections in the United States.

[22] Singapore statutes online can be found in their entirety at http://statutes.agc.gov.sg/ (accessed May 10, 2011). The change to the Films Act regarding films with political content was first made in 1998. See www.singapore-window.org/80227wp.htm (accessed May 10, 2011).

otherwise, those things were not the things that stood out for you. You chose certain things that did resonate for you, and the protagonists were Chee and Zahari for your films, so there is something of you in it. And what is that?

MS: I have this natural affinity to empathize with the guy who I feel is being bullied. I'd like to know how they survive, how they fight the odds. So I've always been interested in those kinds of people. So for me, people like Chee, Zahari—being ostracized by the very people [Singaporeans] whom they feel they are fighting for or have fought for, to me, they are worthy stories.

VRM: What's the interest there for you?

MS: Anyone in Singapore who dares to stage some kind of an open protest, expecting arrests, must have deep convictions about their cause. It's a rare commodity in Singapore. So, by getting to know them or filming them, I hope that, perhaps, some of their courage will rub off on me.

VRM: Has that happened so far?

MS: Unconsciously it has. The fact that I made *Zahari* even though I was under police investigation probably confirms it.

VRM: But what is that fear of authority about? Have you experienced that?

MS: It's the fear of being put under surveillance by the authorities, the fear that maybe you'll lose your job or not get a place in the National University of Singapore, the fear that perhaps your family members may face some sort of harassment from government bodies. A lot of it is unfounded, imaginary. But at the same time it's something that we need to acknowledge. By acknowledging that it exists, it's one way of working toward overcoming it. There's still ways to try to talk about this fear, either on film or on websites or podcasts.

VRM: And as far as being open, despite that fear, was Zahari open to the idea of your film, to even talking?

MS: Yes. I think I would be much more comfortable interviewing dissidents who are open to talking about it. The majority of the dissidents in and out of Singapore are pretty reluctant to talk. You probably have to coax them, and I don't want to do that. Zahari had already published a book by the time I interviewed him, so he was already very open to speaking out.

VRM: What aspects of Zahari's recollections stand out to you in all the footage that you shot?

MS: For me, it's how they were arrested, the knocks on the door at midnight, the blindfolding, being driven in a Black Maria, the first hours of interrogation, and just the entire shock and trauma of it all. For me, it's something that I find very compelling to document, and my problem is, how do you document it without getting actors and actresses to play the parts, to recreate the scenes? I was tempted, in the case of *Zahari's 17 Years*, to intersperse his interview with recreations of the scenes, getting actors to play the part. But that is also another problem, because it may just dilute his experience, or it may distort his experience if it wasn't done well. So I decided to stay with him. To recreate the scenes would take a lot of logistical planning. I've been a production assistant in feature films, and it's not something I enjoy doing. It's pretty dehumanizing to work in a crew with a hundred extras. The whole filmmaking experience for me is personal. But if you have to work in a huge crew, you lose that personal touch.

VRM: It's almost as though you are saying filmmaking can be a therapeutic or cathartic process for the filmmaker and, given the opportunity, you play witness or "writer" to record the recurrent memories of people who've undergone experiences we only comprehend in theory. Do you think such films would in the future be accepted as an alternative discourse on history and the nation or nationalism? Not just for Singapore, but when such films are made in any country? You are not an ethnographer or social anthropologist shooting ethnographic films; but you are documenting nonetheless. Do you think it will find a space within educational institutions or other places where it can be discussed and used as a way of thinking about history differently? Or again, is it too early for that?

MS: Films are the best medium to record history. Someone wrote recently that he was unable to find locally recorded images of old Bugis Street, where transvestites had cruised the alleyways. The only footage available is from *Saint Jack*, as shot through the eyes of a visiting Peter Bogdanovich who had to deceive the Singapore authorities with a dummy script. Singaporeans have to start documenting Singaporean places and people.

POSTSCRIPT

The impact of social-media platforms and video-sharing websites on See's work is undeniable. Singapore-based websites like The Online Citizen and The Temasek Review provide updates on legislation pertaining to his films and at times post video links to his latest works. To date (2010), *Singapore Rebel* has been seen by over 253,000 viewers on either YouTube or Google Video. Similarly, *Zahari's 17 Years* has over four thousand hits on YouTube and Google Video, and continues to be freely available online, though it remains banned. From the time of its release in late 2006, *Speakers Cornered* has been freely available online to be viewed by Singaporeans and foreigners alike.

What remains a recurrently fascinating factor is the manner in which See uses these tools to respond to legislative changes or suggestions of liberalization by the MDA. In essence, See tests what Singaporeans commonly refer to as the "out of bound (or OB) markers." A case in point is *Speakers Cornered*. Having chosen to make the short freely available online, a strategy supplemented by screenings at international film festivals and global media coverage, See did not need to submit the film for a rating. However, around November 2007, the MDA—in a move widely seen as an awkward attempt to raise the institution's "hip" factor—released a rap video on YouTube to show how "in tune" with the trends of the day it was.[23] In a move that appeared to be tongue-in-cheek, See responded by choosing to submit his short for a rating in December of that year.[24] In April 2008, the film passed with an NC-16 rating.[25] That year, See's shortest film to date, *Nation Builders* (14.14 minutes), which catalogues the lives of the elderly and poor in Singapore, also passed with a NC-16 rating, almost a year after it was made. Interestingly, the film had been made available on See's website for a year prior to that, yet raised no protest from the authorities.

The year 2009 was marked by further announcements regarding changes to the Films Act. In March, the MDA stated in its website that "Recognizing Singaporeans' desire, in particular that of the young, for greater space in society for political discourse," certain films would be classified as "party political films and made available to the public."[26] Changing its tack somewhat, the MDA at the same time set up a Political Films Consultative Committee, headed by Richard Magnus, a retired senior district judge and chairman of the Casino Regulatory Authority of Singapore. The seven-member panel, composed of academics and heads of private organizations in the media, legal, and film industries, has been presented as an independent body to advise the MDA on what films pass the test.[27] Commenting on these changes to the press in May 2009, See indicated that he would submit *Singapore Rebel* for a rating.[28] On September 11, 2009, the MDA lifted the ban and passed the film with an M-18 rating instead, making it the first film under the new rules and amendments to be reviewed and rated.

That the decision came four years after the film's release is virtually immaterial. See continues to maintain that the only reason to resubmit films for a rating is to

---

[23] The video can be viewed online at www.youtube.com/watch?v=qjLw28UVWEU (accessed May 10, 2011). Online comments about the video can be found at the bottom of Neumann's article: A. Lin Neumann, "Singapore Raps," *Asia Sentinel*, November 26, 2007, www.asiasentinel.com/index.php?option=com_content&task=view&id=899&Itemid=31 (last viewed on May 10, 2011).

[24] This is a speculative point on my part: it is as though See is saying, if the MDA is, indeed, as liberal as the rap video seeks to project, then perhaps it would take a similarly liberal and open-minded approach to rating my films.

[25] *The Online Citizen*, "Breaking News: MDA Approves Martyn See's Film for Screening," April 16, 2008, http://theonlinecitizen.com/2008/04/breaking-news-mda-approves-martyn-sees-film-for-screening/ (accessed May 10, 2011).

[26] See Political Films Consultative Committee (PFCC) at www.mda.gov.sg/Public/Consultation/Pages/PFCC.aspx (accessed May 10, 2011). Also see Reuters, "Singapore Eases Law on Political Films," March 23, 2009, www.reuters.com/article/idUSTRE52M29320090323 (accessed May 10, 2011).

[27] A more detailed discussion of the amendments to the Films Act goes beyond the parameters of this article, although they merit a thorough examination, given their implications for both See and other filmmakers. However, See responded astutely to the amendments to the Films Act by providing on his website a section-by-section breakdown of what the act actually means for filmmakers (see: http://singaporerebel.blogspot.com/2009/03/new-restrictions-to-films-act.html, accessed on June 15, 2011). See: Seelan Palay, "New Restrictions to Films Act Introduced under the Guise of Liberalization (Singapore)," *EngageMedia*, April 29, 2010, available at www.engagemedia.org/Members/Seelan/news/new-restrictions-to-films-act-introduced-under-the-guise-of-liberalization-singapore/view (accessed May 10, 2011).

[28] Pearl Forss, "Independent Committee Formed to Assess Political Films," *Channel News Asia*, May 26, 2009, www.channelnewsasia.com/stories/singaporelocalnews/view/431959/1/.html (accessed May 10, 2011).

create a space for other filmmakers to engage legitimately in investigative, exploratory filmmaking about the Singaporean political and historical landscape. A film that remains banned does little to encourage such aspirations. Additionally, See's decision to resubmit his older films obliges the review committee to engage with the work and for the amendments to the Films Act to be enacted. Simply put, it clarifies the legislative landscape, or at least reveals the ambiguities and loopholes that are still inherent in the statute.

In this regard, the legislative landscape has remained murky at best, its actors engaged in a somewhat equivocal one-step-forward, two-steps-back dance. While the revised ratings and admissibility of both *Speakers Cornered* and *Singapore Rebel* might have filled some observers with cautious optimism, that sentiment was short-lived. On November 14, 2009, See attended a book launch at the Alumni Medical Centre. The book in question was *The Fajar Generation*,[29] which documents the activities of the University of Malaya Socialist Club (USC) to advance the anti-colonial, democracy, and social-justice movement in Singapore in the 1950s and 1960s. See video recorded the speech by Dr. Lim Hock Siew, a founding member of Singapore's PAP. (Lim had been arrested in 1963 under Operation Cold Store, one of the nation's largest security operations, launched that year to round up over a hundred left-wing politicians and trade unionists. Dr. Lim was released in 1982, nineteen years after his detention.)

Soon after the speech was delivered, See uploaded his video on YouTube. Then, nearly eight months after it had been in circulation, the MDA banned the video recording and seized all copies of the film from See.[30] Speaking again to the media on the ban, See stated that *The Fajar Generation* is available for purchase in Singapore; Dr. Lim had been interviewed by the press; and the event itself had not been banned, making the ban of the video recording perplexing at best. This certainly continues to highlight the lack of clarity on what is deemed permissible and what is not.[31] See had also submitted the film to the committee, taking into account that the amendments to Section 33 of the Films Act would allow for a video recording of a public event that does not violate any laws. However, like *Zahari's 17 Years*, the video recording of Dr. Lim Hock Siew's speech was banned under Section 35(1) of the Films Act, which gives See the rather dubious status of being the only filmmaker to have had two films banned under this section of the act. Section 35(1) accords the minister full discretionary powers to prohibit the possession and distribution of a film that is deemed to be "contrary to the public interest." Section 35(1) throws a spanner in the works by both complicating and even negating the amendments to other sections of the act. The essential message being conveyed by the MDA in banning two films about historically relevant political figures is that "official" history cannot and should not be rewritten; this is what is ultimately "contrary to the public interest."

In conclusion, two things remain interesting in this regard. First, such discretionary power is not beyond being challenged. In a separate case involving the

---

[29] Poh Soo Kai, Tan Jing Quee, and Koh Kay Yew, *The Fajar Generation: The University Socialist Club and the Politics of Postwar Malaya and Singapore* (Malaysia: SIRD, 2010).

[30] While See has ceased all distribution of the film, it has since re-appeared on YouTube at www.youtube.com/watch?v=8nEyfVOKrPo and is also available at vimeo.com/13292596 (both web pages accessed on May 10, 2011).

[31] Cassandra Chew, "Ban on Video Recording of Lim Hock Siew Speech," *The Straits Times*, July 13, 2010.

use of discretionary power, the Court of Appeal of Singapore held that power does have "legal limits" and that, ultimately, the courts "should be able to examine the exercise of discretionary power."[32] One wonders, then, whether the courts at any juncture will exercise this right, or whether See will have to wait another three to four years before the bans on both his films are lifted. However, the second and final point renders this question somewhat irrelevant, and this concerns the Internet. Occasional public events with a small turnout do not draw significant attention and may occur only once for a particular purpose; they are temporally and spatially limited. By comparison, a video recording of such an event may potentially reach hundreds of thousands of people via the Internet, with no regard to national boundaries. On video-sharing websites such as YouTube and Google Video, films exist in a seemingly perpetual loop, so that Said Zahari and Dr. Lim speak again and again, testifying to their experiences and recollecting, documenting, and uttering a different history of Singapore, one that challenges the official, state-sanctioned version. As it stands, the regulation of such a domain remains difficult at best. It is this perpetuation, this looping of an alternative discourse that filmmakers such as Martyn See contribute to by stripping the visual medium to its most essential function—to act as a witness and a documenter.[33]

SELECTED FILMOGRAPHY

All films are by Martyn See:
Singapore Rebel (2005); Available on Google Video
    http://video.google.com/videoplay?docid=-8057768553173785296
    (accessed May 10, 2011)
Zahari's 17 Years (2006)
Speakers Cornered (2006)

---

[32] *The MINDEF Legal Counsel*, "A Guide to Making Administrative Decisions in the SAF," April 2005 (on file with the author).

[33] Because of their basic relevance to the discussion, references not cited in the text are included here. All of these are by Chee Soon Juan: *Dare to Change: An Alternative Vision for Singapore* (Singapore: Singapore Democratic Party, 1994); *Singapore, My Home Too* (no publisher detail: 1995); *Your Future, My Faith, Our Freedom: A Democratic Blueprint for Singapore* (Singapore: Singapore Open Centre, 2001); *The Power of Courage: Effecting Political Change in Singapore through Nonviolence* (no publisher detail: 2005). See also Han Fook Kwang, Fernandez Warren, and Tan Sumiko, *Lee Kuan Yew: The Man and His Ideas* (Singapore: Times Editions, 1998).

THE AGE OF THAI INDEPENDENCE: LOOKING BACK ON THE FIRST DECADE OF THE SHORT FILM

Chalida Uabumrungjit

I often think that the reason why so many Thais underestimate the importance of being independent must have some connection with the "we've never been colonized" myth. When it comes to the question of what constitutes a "Thai independent film," the answer is not easy to come by and the situation is constantly changing.

Contemporary writings on independent films, dated roughly since the 1990s,[1] usually relate the definition of "independent" to various aspects of the filmmaking process. This might refer to a mode of production that does not conform to the industrial assembly line model exemplified by the Hollywood studio system,[2] or filmic content that tries not to duplicate ubiquitous, mass-market cinema products. That definition usually describes a film that will be made on a limited budget because financing from large film companies will not be available. But what happens when we try to apply those criteria for "independent film" to the Thai context?

If we look at the mode of Thai film production from a historical point of view, we would have to admit that the Thai film industry has never really been managed systematically, like the Hollywood dream factory (which profited in its heyday through the rationalization of labor). Although there were two so-called film studios in Thailand before World War II, Sri Krung Sound Film and Thai Film Company, the concept of the studio as such was never fully developed in Thailand. Perhaps the lifespan of those pioneering companies was too short.[3] After WWII, Thai film production shifted from 35mm to 16mm because of the shortage of 35mm stock. Correspondingly, the mode of production that developed became something of a precedent for today's do-it-yourself (DIY) filmmakers. From the late 1940s, 16mm

---

[1] Anchalee Chaiworaporn, "Patibatkarn nang nok rabob" [Operation Indie Film], *Thai Film Quarterly* 1,2 (July–September 1998): 2–24.

[2] David Bordwell, Janet Staiger, and Kristin Thompson, *The Classical Hollywood Cinema: Film Style and Mode of Production to 1960* (London: Routledge, 1985).

[3] Sri Krung opened in 1934 and closed in 1942. The Thai Film Company, which operated between 1936 and 1938, made only five films.

filmmaking, which was already popular among amateur filmmakers, actually became the core of the Thai film industry.[4] The cost of 16mm production was much cheaper than the expense of making films with 35mm stock, so anybody with a small budget could still enter the "industry." And flock to it they did. A sort of household industry developed, in which the husband was the director and the wife the producer. Alternatively, whoever wanted to be credited as a film producer could hire a crew, buy the film stock, and just start producing his or her own films. These filmmakers would themselves tour their own films, since, in most cases, they could make only a few copies of any one film for circulation around the country. This compares to the distribution approach of many Thai independent filmmakers today. However, the intended audience for films produced during the 16mm-period differed greatly from that of contemporary independent films. Those older films were solely aimed for the entertainment of a mass audience.

Srikrung Film Studio

Things started to change around the mid-1970s, when distribution companies became influential in the production of feature films. Most filmmakers became employees of the film-distribution companies. During this period, there were still many films being made independently (in the sense of being self-financed), but filmmakers needed the big companies to help them distribute their films. Since the cinema business was monopolized by only a few large companies, it was up to these

---

[4] Wimonrat Aroonrojsuriya, "Phapphayon thai nai yuk 16mm (2490–2515)" [Thai Films during the 16mm Period (1947–72)], *Thai Film Foundation*, July 9, 2004, available at www.thaifilm.com/articleDetail. asp?id=10.

large companies' distribution agents to decide which films, or what genre of films, would actually be shown in movie theaters. There was very little chance that a film made outside this framework would make it into the cinemas for public screenings. Consequently, even if someone dared to make a nonconventional film at his or her own expense, he or she would still have come up against the problem of where to show the film. Such restricted access to theaters was probably one factor leading to what might be called the "un-independent" mindset.

In some countries, independent films are often produced as a way to voice opposition to the state or other authoritarian bodies, but that motivation is not so much the case in Thailand. Even during the period of intense student activism, which resulted in the mass uprising against Thailand's military dictators in 1973, cinema did not play much of a role in the movement itself. Jiranan Pitpreecha, one of the student leaders at that time, once explained to me that filmmaking was then regarded as a luxury, and the technology for making films was not convenient to the activists. After the brutal massacre of students and other protestors around Bangkok's Thammasat University in October 1976, Thai citizens became fearful and turned silent. People thereafter were careful about expressing themselves, and this fear affected filmmakers, as well.

Two outstanding films were made during that period of political crisis and cultural revolt, however, and together they gave birth to the category of oppositional independent Thai film. *The Struggle of Hara Factory Workers* (1976) is a documentary in the style film historians call direct cinema.[5] It was made on Kodak Super-8 film by Jon Ungpakorn, a former senator and social activist. This was probably the only film he ever made. He obtained the money to buy the camera from his father, Puey Ungpakorn, who, in 1976, was the rector of Thammasat University. In the film, Jon Ungpakorn simply provides the (mostly female) employees of the Hara jeans factory the opportunity to speak for themselves on camera. *The Struggle of Hara Factory Workers* illustrates the workers' problems and the reasons for their fight, letting the workers explain directly to the audience the working and living conditions that led to these employees' demand for better wages. The documentary was shown at many factories, and encouraged the collective uprising of other factory workers.

Tongpan (1977, from the Isan Film Collective) is another example of the oppositional independent film. It is a reenactment of a seminar organized at Thammasat University to consider the case for building a dam in Thailand's northeast region. Tongpan, an impoverished farmer, leaves his dying wife to join the intellectuals and bureaucrats at the seminar in Bangkok. He finally realizes that these elites, who have no real understanding of his hardships, cannot solve his problems, so he goes back home only to find that his wife has died. Completed just after the 1976 massacre, *Tongpan* was immediately banned, but nevertheless managed to circulate around universities for many years.

There is also another aspect of filmmaking that exists outside the industry, namely, the home-movie or the amateur film, which has not always been considered part of cinema. This kind of filmmaking has long been the hobby of Thai elites, ever since the 1900s, when cinema was introduced to Siam. In 1930, King Rama VII initiated the Amateur Cinema Association, whose members were the royal family

---

[5] Jack C. Ellis and Betsy A. McLane, *A New History of Documentary Film* (New York, NY: The Continuum International Publishing Group, 2008).

and society's elites.[6] They made films, which were only to be screened among themselves, as an activity of the association. In this respect, filmmaking was a luxury and a diversion for well-off people. It is not until recently that some amateur films have progressed beyond being the product of personal leisure to become, instead, personal statements intended for an audience beyond the filmmaker's circle of family and friends.

Given the history presented here, it seems that the practices we now describe as characteristic of independent filmmaking have long existed in Thailand. The *consciousness* of the need to be independent, however, has only been developing gradually over the past ten years.

SCREENINGS BEYOND THE SCREEN

One of the challenges of making films outside the commercial circuit has been, and remains, the difficulty of finding a place to exhibit the film. At the beginning of the 1990s, there were a few places that screened so-called art films, but, in practice, this did not go beyond showing foreign films at cultural institutes such as the Alliance Française and the Goethe Institute. Where could Thai independent films be shown (and watched)? There were, of course, some small, university-based film clubs that featured a number of student shorts every now and then, but the general public was usually unaware of those screenings.

The distribution and exposure problem thwarted even the pioneering film historian and archivist Dome Sukvong,[7] who wanted to exhibit films outside the commercial circuit. He believed that the student film is one kind of independent film that needed to be encouraged. During the 1980s he had tried to organize the screening of student and amateur films every now and then at the film archive, but he was never able to raise the profile of such films significantly.

In the mid-1990s, the Communications Arts Faculty at Bangkok's Chulalongkorn University invited the director and producer Jira Maligool to teach a film course.[8] He initiated a mini film festival, called "Kangjor" (Unfurl the Screen), to premiere his students' final projects. Both the public and members of the film industry were invited to the screenings. This was the first time that student films received exposure beyond the classroom, and were accessible to members of the public. Previously, student films were only shown in class and had no afterlife.

After the Kangjor festival, Dome Sukvong and I had the idea of initiating student film screenings organized by the film students themselves, since we knew that a number of student films were being made each year yet were rarely seen in public. In 1995, we managed to organize *Jallakam nang naksueksa* (Student Film Mini-festival) with students from different universities. However, it was hard for a given group of

---

[6] Dome Sukvong, *Phrabat somdet phra pok klao kap phapphayon* [King Rama VII and Cinema] (Bangkok: Ton-Or Grammy, 1996).

[7] Dome Sukvong is also the founder of the Thai Film Archive and the Thai Film Foundation. He has recently published a diary of his twenty-five-year struggle to set up the archive and keep it going; see Dome Sukvong, *Poom 25 pee hor phapphayon* [25 years of the Film Archive Diary] (Nakorn Pathom: Film Archive, 2010).

[8] Jira Maligool is the director of *Mekong Full Moon Party* (2002) and *Tin Mine* (2005). He also produces films for his former students, such as Songyos Sukmakanan (*My Girl*, 2003; *The Dorm*, 2006) and Komkrit Treewimon (*My Girl, Dear Dakanda* [2005]).

students to keep the event running continuously, since most of them graduated after four years.

In 1997, Dome Sukvong and I decided to start Thailand's first short-film festival, to be organized under the aegis of the Thai Film Foundation. This is a competitive festival to showcase short films made by students and non-students alike. During its first decade, the Thai Short Film and Video Festival (Tessakan Phapphayon, TSF&V Festival) opened up a new arena in which independent filmmakers could explore, express, and exhibit their creativity. Thailand's short-film scene, which has developed around this festival, both reflects and shapes the definition of the Thai independent film (see May Adadol Ingawanij's contribution to this volume).

NO-BUDGET FILMMAKING

When the TSF&V Festival was starting out, the 16mm era was coming to an end in Thailand. The few 16mm film labs that had been operating in the country closed down in the early 1990s, including those that processed students' film. Back then, the quality of the images produced by video cameras was still not very good, and, besides, the technology was not sufficiently affordable to facilitate its adoption for independent filmmaking. Editing labs for videotape were only available for commercial purposes, so it was costly to make video work.

Given the expense and limited access to equipment, filmmaking was particularly hard for those who did not belong to any film institutions. One such filmmaker was Boonsong Nakpoo, who made *Klang deuk* (After Midnight, 1997), a thirty-seven-minute film about three men who get drunk and then plan to do something wild. It was shot on 16mm, and subsequently projected onto a wall. The projected film was then captured with a video camera for final editing. When I first saw *Klang deuk*, I could tell from the production quality that Boonsong had struggled to finish it, but he did not let the lack of proper equipment stop him.

Without the limitation of funds and lack of access to technology, however, we would not have seen a film like *Sil 4* (The Four Precepts, 1997), by Kullachat Jitkajornwanich and Leurchai Pothisakul. Shot on a small video camera and edited using two video-playback machines, this five-minute film is about a man who sermonizes about the five precepts of Buddhism while drinking alcohol. His metaphor for the five precepts are five lit candles, and when he comes to the last precept, which is Do Not Drink Alcohol, he simply puts out the last candle with his bare hand without mentioning the last precept. The crudity of *Sil 4* brings out its sarcastic message, a slap in the face of the conservatives who moralize about drinking. Given its production quality, this type of film can be described as a product of "no-budget filmmaking." *Sil 4* did not win any prize at the TSF&V Festival, but it was highly praised by Dome Sukvong: "It is so evil; that's why I love it so much."[9]

Kullachat and Leurchai returned to the festival with more ultra-low-budget films in the following years. *Mangkorn kin mee* (Dragon Eats Noodle, 1998) is a mystery about a man who makes instant noodles and discovers strange hair in it. *Swadee kha*[10] (1999) is about a man who brushes his teeth after eating a hamburger, an activity that degenerates into a crazy bloody end. All of their films are extreme in presentation

[9] Dome Sukvong, catalogue published for The Tenth Thai Short Film and Video Festival, August 17–September 3, 2006, no page number.

[10] The title ("This is Crap") is a pun on the Thai greeting *sawasdee kha*.

style, and it is possible to interpret them as making implicit criticisms of capitalism in modern Thai society. More obvious is the fact that these films are characterized by offensive images and vulgar language, and for that reason they are regarded as cult films. A small group of enthusiastic fans recognizes these films' value and has been following the duo for many years.

The advent of digital cameras opened up new opportunities for no-budget filmmaking. Now, with the availability of cheap cameras and editing applications ("suites") on personal computers, whoever dreams of making a film has the chance to do so. One indication of the growing number of people gripped by this dream is the increase in the number of short films submitted to the festival. In the first year, the festival received thirty films; now, more than a decade later, it receives in excess of five hundred submissions each year. Despite the fact that the name of the festival implies "short film," in recent years we have begun to include another programming strand, which we call Digital Forum. The aim is to encourage filmmakers to create independent feature-length digital films, since we believe that soon it will be time for independent films to compete with mainstream films in the same cinema space.

THE FILM SCHOOLS

Since the very first year of the TSF&V Festival, the majority of submissions were student films made by those in film schools. Although formal education in filmmaking started in the 1970s in Thailand, the aim of most of those educational programs was to produce laborers for the film industry, and so the focus was on developing craftsmanship in filmmaking. Yet universities' limited budgets made it impossible to procure the kind of up-to-date equipment that would enable the students to be fully skilled upon graduation. In terms of the intellectual, critical, or theoretical aspects of film education, the situation remains problematic. Each university offers only one or two courses in international film history and criticism, and to this day there does not appear to be any university in Thailand that offers a course on Thai film history. Many film students, therefore, have little knowledge about the history of their nation's cinema. Thus, the limitations of film education in Thailand include inadequate equipment, a lack of historical perspective, and the imbalance between teaching practical skills and encouraging creativity.

Since the focus of film schools is on developing production skills, or meeting the requirements of the school or the instructors, those two factors become the frame that shapes the work of most students. In some cases, the instructors' influence may be so strong that a kind of censorship comes into play. Some schools "pretend" to be film studios: before students can make their films, they have to "sell" their ideas to the instructors. Fortunately, this artificial "wall" imposed by film schools inspires some students simply to scale it. As a result, a number of students have managed to create quality work beyond the level of achievement their schools could ever have imagined for their students. Such limitations in Thailand's film-education programs might, therefore, be regarded as the first obstacle for independent filmmakers. Film schools are the places where future filmmakers may learn to think and act independently and outside institutional expectations.

Usually, however, student films conform to classical narrative structures, followed by some moral or message at the end. Generally, instructors do not encourage documentary and experimental work, but, occasionally, there are those black sheep that stand out from the flock. One of my favorite student films is Suwan

Huangsirisakul's *Baan si chompoo* (Pink House, 2001), which is about a boy who collects soda-bottle caps by the thousands to sell to recyclers. It is an unconventionally naturalistic film that is also confident in its minimalist aesthetics, which leaves a lot of room for the audience to fill in the gaps. *Baan si chompoo* is an unusual student film, as it is the kind of work that film schools frown upon. It was controversial for Suwan's school, and his next film was even more so. This talented filmmaker's forty-minute feature, *Fah-amorn* (2002), about the search for love through sex, went on to win the best student film award at the International Student Film Festival in Kyoto.

For those filmmakers who were born gifted, the film school experience gave them the opportunity to stand out. Chookiat Sakveerakul, also called Madiew, the director of the popular gay teen film *Rak haeng Siam* (Love of Siam, 2007), has been an energetic mover and shaker ever since he was a film student at Chulalongkorn University. He has been making short films (which are usually not very short) since his second year at university. One of them, *Dong rok fah* (2001), is a mystical tale featuring young people in his hometown, the northern city of Chiang Mai. In the film, the characters speak in the northern dialect. His potential as a director was already clearly visible in *Dong rok fah*, and his talent has since been confirmed by successful features such as *13: Game of Death* (2006) and *Love of Siam*. As his graduation project, Chookiat made a feature-length digital film, *Story of Li* (2003), which was given a limited release in a Bangkok cinema.

Those are just some examples that came from the Thai film-school experience. A few filmmakers have managed to strengthen their talents within the film-school framework, while other students developed their talents on their own initiative, sometimes by going against the conventions prescribed by their schools. But where do these filmmakers go after graduation? There are few options for film graduates in Thailand: they can either seek employment at film-production houses, or they must find any job they can and make films in their free time.

Looking for Talent

Over the past decade, some production houses have begun to encourage their staff to make short films to hone their skills. *The Bug* (1997) by Nawajul Boonpaknavik, which won the TSF&V Festival's first Pestonji award, is an example of this. Boonpaknavik worked at Siam Studio, a famous production house in the 1990s, and was able to use the company's equipment and crew. He received a promotion after *The Bug*'s success at the festival, and then developed a feature-film project with the company (although it never got produced).

Phenomena is another production house that evaluates its assistant directors' short films to determine whether those filmmakers are ready to direct commercials. Among the first batch of Phenomena's filmmakers were Pakpoom Wongpoom, Banchong Pisanthanakul, and Songyos Sukmakanan, who have now all directed their own features. The three of them had already started making short films when they were in university. Pakpoom earned some measure of fame prior to joining Phenomena by winning the Best Student Film prize at the 2000 TSF&V Festival with *Luang ta* (The Abbot). Afterward, *Luang ta* traveled to many festivals outside Thailand. It was clear from the beginning that Pakpoom's form and style would be easily embraced by mainstream film companies. For his test project with Phenomena, Pakpoom made *In the Eyes* (2002), which demonstrated his skill at creating suspense with a controversial subject: a young boy's sexual desire. In the same group of short films for the production house, Banchong made *Colour Blind* (2002), a romantic satire about a color-blind mechanic who fixes color televisions. After that, Pakpoom and Banchong worked together on the extremely successful horror feature *The Shutter* (2004). In the same group, Songyos Sukmakanan made *My Elephant* (2002), which went on to win the best short-film prize at the 2002 TSF&V Festival. Thereafter, he worked with his Chulalongkorn University friends to make the retro feature *Fan chan* (My Girl, 2003), followed by his solo success as the director of *Dek hor* (Dorm, 2006). It may be going too far to claim that making short films first was the singular reason for these filmmakers' success, but certainly the practice was a steppingstone for each of them, helping them to gain confidence in making films their own way.

FROM THE COUNTRY TO THE CITY

Since most of the filmmakers live and work in Bangkok, the contrast between urban and rural lives seems to be another central theme for Thai short films. The filmmakers tend to romanticize rural life as one of peacefulness, while the city always represents a hostile force. The life of taxi drivers from upcountry is one of the favorite subjects of Thailand's short filmmakers. Santi Taepanich, the director of the feature documentary *Sua rong hai* (Crying Tiger, 2005), made a short film debut called *Kor tor 2541* (Bangkok 2541, 1998). The film observes the lives of urban residents through the eyes of a taxi driver. A girl works as a prostitute to buy an expensive handbag, and the taxi driver becomes the victim of gang rape by several men. This kind of anti-city theme shows the ugly side of Bangkok, while the countryside holds dreams of a better life.

Nevertheless, there are filmmakers like Boonsong Nakpoo (mentioned earlier) whose educational and professional background is in theater, art, and acting, but who still identifies himself as a farmer by origin. His *Ta kap lan* (Grandpa, 1998) is adapted from Manop Chomchaloa's short story, set in a provincial train station, about a grandfather and grandson. The grandfather has to choose between either filling their hungry stomachs or using the money to buy train tickets to Bangkok. Boonsong won the TSF&V Festival's prize for the best short in 1998. For his next two films, he stuck with the farmer theme: *Chaona klap baan* (Taxi Goes Home, 1999) is about a taxi driver who robs a bank because he needs to go back to his home province. *Mae* (Mother, 2000) portrays an elderly mother in her country hut in Sukhothai province.

A significant filmmaker who makes very beautiful films about rural life is Uruphong Raksasad. After graduating in filmmaking from Thammasat University, and having worked in Bangkok's film industry for four years, he decided to go back to his rural roots. Uruphong once made eight short films in one year, which he later combined into a successful digital feature, *Ruang lao jak mueang neua* (Stories from the North, 2005). This collection portrays the everyday life of the inhabitants of the northern province of Chiang Rai, accompanied by the sense that Uruphong is recording a way of life that will soon disappear. Later on, he made *Khaeng bung fai* (The Rocket, 2007), which observes a cheerful festival where homemade rockets are fired. The film won the best short film prize at the TSF&V Festival in 2007. *Agrarian Utopia* (2009), Uruphong's latest digital feature project, combines narrative storytelling with his documentary style. It portrays the life of a debt-ridden farmer in the midst of current political changes in Thailand. *Agrarian Utopia*'s international success is helping to mark Uruphong as a leading cinematic chronicler of rural life in Thailand.

TOUCHING TABOO, CHALLENGING THE CENSORS

Up until recently, one of the advantages of short and digital films has been that the censors have yet to consider them as part of "cinema." For this reason, neither the censorship board, operating under the previous Film Act (1930), nor other bureaucratic bodies had ever attempted to control these works. This is also the reason why the TSF&V Festival has, up to now, been able to sneak all sorts of films into its programs. However, the situation may change in the near future. The new Film and Video Act, which came into full effect in 2009, is aimed at controlling all kinds of moving images made and screened in Thailand.[11] The challenge the TSF&V Festival faces now is whether it can continue to stand as a censorship-free zone.

One of the characteristics of Thai short films is that they reflect the filmmakers' attempt to transgress barriers. Many films address social taboos or subjects that are difficult to present in the mainstream media. One of the all-time sensitive issues in the Thai media is religion, or, to put it more specifically, Buddhism. There are a few examples of short films that both portray and critique Buddhism. *Chang teuh* (Forget it, 1998), by Namthong Tongyai Na Ayutthaya, poses this question: if a monk finds a prostitute in a near-dead state one early morning, should he rescue her? (Buddhist monks are not meant to touch the female body.) This obvious dilemma had already been written about in short stories, but as a theme in a film it was still controversial. *Manokam* (2004), by Jakrapatr Promsing, also tackles the same issue in a story of a young monk who comes across a drowning girl. He struggles with the conflict posed by his morality versus his religious discipline.

Pakpoom's student film *Luang ta* strikes it harder. It is about a boy who comes to live with his father, who obtains money by stealing some of the cash donated to an old, paralyzed monk. The boy feels that what his father does is not right and tries to return the money to the old monk. However, the boy discovers that the monk is only pretending to be paralyzed, and is therefore no better than the boy's father. Pakpoom was asked by his film school to add a statement that "this film does not intend to insult religion." This is just one example of how nervous institutions such as film schools are about shorts that come across as critical of Buddhism or the conduct of monks.

With the unrest in the far south of Thailand, Muslim identity as well as ethnic Malay identity have gained widespread interest among filmmakers of shorts. Many works still reflect the misconception of Thai society toward Muslims in Thailand. Watching these films, I sometimes have the feeling that they are just reproducing the central government's dominant message about the need for unity. One of the ironic consequences of this message is to widen the gap between Thais of different religions and ethnicities. One exception to this filmmaking trend is Panu Aree, who started off as an experimental/documentary filmmaker focusing on ordinary people's lives. In the documentary *Khaek* (In Between, 2006), the result of Panu Aree's collaboration with the filmmaker Kaweenipol Ketprasit and the energetic film critic Kong Rithdee,

---

[11] The full text of the legislation, "Por ror bor phapphayon lae videtad 2551" [Film and Video Act 2008], available at www.thailandlawyercenter.com/index.php?lay=show&ac=article& Id= 538974653&Ntype=19, last accessed January 21, 2011.

the trio sets out to explore Muslim identity through representing the lives and thoughts of four Muslims in contemporary Bangkok. *Khaek* drew an unexpected reception: a lot of criticism from the Muslim community (apparently for the liberal statement of the film), yet a warm welcome from the non-Muslim audience. Panu, Kaweenipol, and Kong then made their first feature documentary, *The Convert* (2008), about a Buddhist Thai woman who converts to Islam when she marries a Muslim. *The Convert* was given a limited release at Lido Cinema in Bangkok, and it was well received at international film festivals. The trio is continuing their project of exploring the lives and cultures of Muslims in Thailand. Their most recent work is a musical documentary, *Baby Arabia* (2010), about a band that has been playing Muslim–Malay songs for over three decades.

Citizen Juling (2008) is another work concerning the situation in the far south. The context of the documentary is the death of Juling Pongkanmul, a teacher from northern Thailand who moved south to a village in Narathiwat province to teach art. She became a national hero, feted for her idealism, after the abduction and brutal assault that left her comatose for many months. *Citizen Juling* was made as a collaborative effort involving the controversial filmmaker Ing K.,[12] the politician Kraisak Choonhavan, and the famous photographer Manit Sriwanichpoom. The film is structured as a trip following Kraisak Choonhaven to the far south to meet and talk to a wide range of people: students at the school in which Juling used to teach, villagers living in a state of fear, parents of young people killed by anonymous ambushes, and Juling's family and well-meaning officials. To the filmmakers' surprise, *Citizen Juling* actually passed the censorship board and was given a limited release in Bangkok. It has won many national awards.

Apart from religion, sexuality and nudity have always been taboo subjects in Thailand. In a transgressive gesture, many short films portray those sexualities that are made invisible or are reductively represented in the mainstream media. For example, the short film has been used as a platform both to tackle the subject of homosexuality and to explore the identity of the filmmakers. Michael Chawanasai's *Bansai chaiyo: The Adventure of Iron Pussy* (1999) stunned the audience at the TSF&V Festival when it was first shown. The protagonist, Iron Pussy, is a transvestite hero who attempts to save a boy go-go-dancer in Bangkok's sex district, Patpong. The reason why people who saw *Bansai chaiyo* at the festival laughed so much was probably because it brought on the realization that a film like this could be made at all in Thailand. The short was later developed into a super-camp musical digital feature, in a sequel called *The Adventure of Iron Pussy* (2003), directed by Apichatpong Weerasethakul.

Another artist who has challenged these boundaries is the filmmaker with multiple identities first known as Chumpol Thongtab, who then changed his name to Thatthep Thongtab, and finally Thanwarin Sukkhapisit. His first film is called *Waen* (Ring, 2001), featuring a mute transvestite, a prostitute, and a motorcyclist—each connected to the other by the circular shape of the narrative. This low-budget film impressed many viewers, and inspired Thanwarin to give up his teaching job to make more films. His triumph is *Deep Inside* (2001), a melodrama with fine acting. The quality of the performance in his short films has since become his signature (and

---

12 For more information about the filmmaker, see Graiwoot Chulphongsathorn, "Love Letter to *Khon graab maa/My Teacher Eats Biscuits, Criticine,*" www.criticine.com/feature_article.php?id=44&pageid=1277891554.

he usually stars in his own films). In *Queer from Hell* (Kratheuy Narok, 2006), Thanwarin took the step of including some explicit sex scenes, but that does not seem to suit his style. Perhaps because he received a lot of unfavorable comments about that film, he reverted back to his "melodramatic" approach. *In the Name of Sin* is about a gay teacher who tries to conceal his feelings for a student; this film proved very successful at the 2006 festival.

Thunska Pansitivorakul is another filmmaker with a great deal of self-confidence—his films expose his private life. He started out as a film critic before making *Private Life* (2000), which is his first film to be shown in public. Currently, he is one of the most productive filmmakers on the independent scene in Thailand, having made several feature documentaries, including *Voodoo Girls* (Huajai Tong Sab, 2002) and *Happy Berry* (2004), and a number of short films in the past five years or so. He was also the founder of Thaiindie, an independent filmmakers' group, which has been active in screening and promoting their own films, thereby creating a strong group character. Ironically enough, in recent years Thunksa has been given the Ministry of Culture's Silpathorn Award for outstanding mid-career artists—a surprising decision since the ministry is regarded as a conservative organization. However, in 2009, Thunksa's feature *This Area Is Under Quarantine* was banned from screening at the World Film Festival in Bangkok. The film features gay sexuality, though this alone might not necessarily have been an issue with the censors. Thunksa's incorporation of banned footage of soldiers brutally arresting people at Tak Bai district, Narathiwat province—an incident in 2004 that resulted in eighty-five deaths—was probably regarded as a threat to national security by the censorship board.

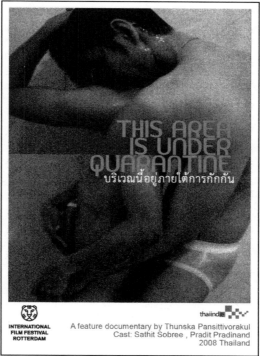

Poster for Thunska Pansitivorakul's, *This Area is Under Quarantine*

It would not be right to discuss independent films in Thailand without referring to Apichatpong Weerasethakul. He is exceptional in terms of both his talent and his opportunities. Through the experience of studying abroad, he understands how to survive as a non-mainstream filmmaker. At the same time, he has always had the strong will to make films his own way. In Thailand, his films challenge both public taste and social righteousness (see Benedict Anderson's article in this volume). As the inspiration for many young filmmakers, Apichatpong encourages them to be bold and to make unconventional films. He has demonstrated that one way to be independent is not to rely on funding from Thai studios, and that it is possible to make Thai films without local funding. Up until recently, his films have not received widespread theatrical distribution in Thailand. Following his reception of the recent Palme d'Or prize from the Cannes International Film Festival for his feature *Lung Boonmee raleuk chat* (Uncle Boonmee Who Can Recall His Past Lives, 2010), a multiplex chain decided to release Apichatpong's film to a small number of screens in Bangkok and several other cities. The success of *Lung Boonmee raleuk chat* may go some way to help other Thai independent films reach a general audience.

Back in 2007, Apichatpong's film *Saeng sattawat* (Syndromes and a Century, 2006) was submitted to the censorship board for consideration prior to the film's release in Thailand. The board gave permission for its release on the condition that several scenes be cut from the film (for details, see Benedict Anderson's article). The incident galvanized the independent film community to start the Free Thai Cinema Movement, a campaign to change the 1930 Film Act. However, the campaign has had only partial success. A classification system has now replaced the old system of censorship, but the new Film and Video Act, which was passed by parliament in 2008 and became fully operative after August 2009, still contains many controlling and undemocratic elements. In the new rating system, films are classified according to seven categories: P (films that should be promoted on the basis of cultural or artistic merit), G (suitable for the general public), 13-plus (not recommended for anyone under age 13), 15-plus, 18-plus, 20-minus, and Ban. The latter is a rating for films that are deemed to threaten Thailand's monarchy, national security, national unity, and public morality, among other categories of harm. The category 20-minus is a restricted one; those under the age of twenty are not allowed to see the film. But the other age-related rates are only recommendations. Since the law's adoption, its application seems inconsistent. Many violent blockbuster films have been given the G rating, while *Jao nok krajok* (Mundane History, 2009), an independent film by Anocha Suwichakornpong, was given 20-minus despite the fact that only one scene might be considered obscene. In short, even with the new law in place, the censorship system remains a challenge to independent filmmakers, and especially when the political situation in the country is totally unsettled.

PEOPLE IN THE DARK

Reaching the audience is always a big issue for independent filmmakers. While the number of short and independent films is growing rapidly, the audience is growing very slowly. Most filmmakers do not watch each other's films, either. This is the real problem of independent cinema: how can filmmakers cultivate an audience? Without the audience, for whom should filmmakers make films? At the same time, ordinary people complain that it is hard to gain access to short films: "Where are they shown? Where can I get a copy? How can I see them?"

There have been many attempts to increase audience access to independent films. Thai Short Film, a group led by the soundman Sirote Tulsuk, tried to help distribute DVDs of short films through his shop at Bangkok's Jatujak weekend market, but the shop did not last long. There have been attempts to distribute short films via the Internet by some broadband and satellite companies, but so far those efforts have not been successful. What is more firmly established is the short-film program on some cable channels and public TV, but the selection criteria for such programs are very stringent (a work cannot be too arty and controversial), which limits the choice of films that those channels show.

Within the online community, a few serious bloggers have been writing about independent films. One of these is Jit Phokaew, who writes in a personal way (in Thai and English) on his webpage, Limitless Cinema (celinejulie.wordpress.com), about the hundreds of short and independent films he sees each year. His writing has persuaded some readers to see the films, contributing to the emergence of a small group of film enthusiasts who engage in online discussions about cinema on the Web. With the popularity of social networking sites such as Facebook, more people are writing and sharing thoughts about short and independent films. This type of activity creates a positive synergy around independent filmmaking, and may, I hope, encourage the growth of a robust film culture.

Image from Anocha Suwichakornpong's *Graceland*

CONSOLIDATING INDIE TERRITORY

During the first half-decade of independent filmmaking, some filmmakers might have made shorts to get a foot (or just a toe!) inside the industry. But later on, when a number of them did get the chance to make their feature films, they came to experience firsthand the difficulty of working in the studio system. Consequently, a number of filmmakers are starting to become fully conscious of the necessity and possibility of making films independently.

In the case of Pimpaka Towira, after making *One Night Husband* (Kheun rai ngao, 2003) with the studio GMM Pictures, she moved towards independent production with *The Truth Be Told* (Khwam jing phood dai, 2007). This is her first documentary about an activist who was sued by Shin Corporation, the company once closely linked to the family of ex-Prime Minister Thaksin Shinawatra. Under her own company, Extra Virgin, Pimpaka now produces feature projects of her own and those of other independent filmmakers, such as Uruphong Raksasad and Jakrawal Nilthamrong. Besides producing films, Pimpaka's company is working on increasing the presentation of independent films in commercial cinemas in Thailand.

In the past five years or so, a small number of independent film companies have been cropping up. Under Pop Pictures, Aditya Assarat, who made a successful short film, *Motorcycle,* in 2000, finished his first feature, *Wonderful Town* (2007), with funding from outside the Thai studio system. A similar case is Anocha Suwichakornpong, who made her debut feature, *Mundane History,* with her own company, Electric Eel Films. Anocha started making feature films after her short *Graceland* (2006) was selected for the Cannes International Film Festival. Both Aditya and Anocha have the same producer, Soros Sukhum, who is an important player on the independent film scene.

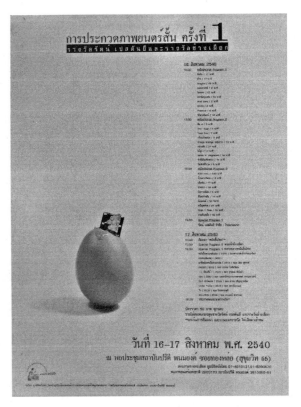

Poster of the first Thai Short Film and Video Festival.
An egg is presented as a symbol of the festival every year.

CONCLUSION: THE PATH OF INDEPENDENCE

At the end of the first decade in which the concept of Thai independent film has been germinating, we are witnessing the slow appearance of its fruit. In 2010, the Thai government, for the first time, announced a fund of two hundred million baht for filmmaking. However, this one-off fund does not, by itself, promise to make filmmaking any less of a struggle in Thailand. Independent filmmakers will still have to struggle for the funds to produce their films, then for their films to be screened; and they will still have to challenge the audience with films of unconventional taste. We are only halfway down the path of independence, and those of us already on it are eagerly awaiting the appearance of more free-spirited filmmakers in the future.

SELECTED FILMOGRAPHY

Baan si chompoo (Pink House, Suwan Huangsirisakul, 2001)
Bansai chaiyo: The Adventure of Iron Pussy (Michael Chawanasai, 1999)
Chang teuh (Forget It, Namthong Tongyai Na Ayutthaya, 1998)
Chaona klap ban (Taxi Goes Home, Boonsong Nakpoo, 1999)
Colour Blind (Banchong Pisanthanakul, 2002)
Deep Inside (Thanwarin Sukkhapisit, 2001)
Dong rok fah (Chookiat Sakveerakul, 2001)
Fah-amorn (Suwan Huangsirisakul, 2002)
Happy Berry (Thunska Pansitivorakul, 2004)
In the Eyes (Pakpoom Wongpoom, 2002)
In the Name of Sin (Thanwarin Sukkhapisit, 2006)
Jao nok krajok (Mundane History, Anocha Suwichakornpong, 2009)
Khaek (*In Between*, Panu Aree, Kaweenipol Ketprasit and Kong Rithdee, 2006)
Khaeng bung fai (The Rocket, Uruphong Raksasad, 2007)
Klang deuk (After Midnight, Boonsong Nakpoo, 1997)
Kor thor 2541 (Bangkok, Santi Taepanich, 1998)
Luang ta (The Abbot, Pakpoom Wongpoom, 2000)
Mae (Mother, Boonsong Nakpoo, 2000)
Mangkorn kin mee (Dragon Eat Noodle, Kullachart Jitkajornwanich and Leurchai Pothisakul, 1998)
Manokam (Jakrapatr Promsing, 2004)
Motorcycle (Aditya Assarat, 2000)
My Elephant (Songyos Sukmakanan, 2002)
Private Life (Thunska Pansitivorakul, 2000)
Queer from Hell (Thanwarin Sukkhapisit, 2006)
Sil 4 (Kullachart Jitkajornwanich and Leurchai Pothisakul, 1997)
Swadee kha (Kullachart Jitkajornwanich and Leurchai Pothisakul, 1999)
Saeng sattawat (Syndromes and a Century, Apichatpong Weerasethakul, 2006)
Ta kap lan (Grandpa, Boonsong Nakpoo, 1998)
The Bug (Nawajul Boonpaknavik, 1997)
The Convert (Panu Aree, Kaweenipol Ketprasit and Kong Rithdee, 2008)
The Struggle of Hara Factory Workers (Jon Ungpakorn, 1976)
The Truth Be Told (Pimpaka Towira, 2007)
Tongpan (The Isan Film Collective, 1977)
Waen (Ring, Thanwarin Sukkhapisit, 2001)
Wonderful Town (Aditya Assarat, 2007)
Voodoo Girls (Thunska Pansitivorakul, 2002)

PIRACY BOOM BOOM

John Torres

It's going to be a strange summer afternoon. I am in my neighborhood, Katipunan, a prime educational, commercial, and residential district, enveloped by the usual buzz of jeepneys (taxis, small cars) and semi-septic smog. Katipunan also happens to be home to the nation's top universities. Today I feel like an undercover agent, a spy, documenting the goings-on in the multi-million-peso, underground business of media piracy. There are no big fish to fry here, only the small ones: door-to-door salespeople selling cheap entertainment to students, teachers, and fellow "entrepreneurs."

I am carefully planning my next move. Let me finish, three more fish balls to chew before he goes. He doesn't carry a knapsack or a bundle of those DVDs he peddles around Katipunan in broad daylight.

I will try not to sound too proper or legal as to scare him away. It helps that I am in faded jeans and a plain shirt; I'm wearing the slightly brushed-up look of tricycle drivers who wait along Fabian de la Rosa Street, in front of my alma mater, Ateneo de Manila University.

This is one of those times when my long, unkempt hair comes in handy. I happen to wear a long, printed garment wrapped around my waist, completing my motif. Give me some DVDs, and I'm ready to go.

But I forget all that, and hurry to get his attention.

He seems good-natured, judging by how he greets me with his arched brows and wide smile. I grab that chance to come up to him. I have an idea.

"Do you know Saddam? Saddam and JR from Commonwealth?"

He wonders.

"Glo-ri," I say.

He smiles, nodding.

"Wait, I'll show you something."

Thank God he knows them. In my debut feature, *Todo Todo Teros* (2006), Saddam and JR are young video pirates whom I met when I was shooting along Commonwealth Avenue. Saddam is the kid in my film who offers bootlegged DVDs to the terrorist's wife. JR is the older one, the one who tells the wife about the curiously reflexive plot points in the DVDs he sells.

I happen to have my laptop, and I have an AVI file of my film. Perfect! I need to look both credible and trustworthy, but not so aloof as to scare him away. This is, indeed, a good way to warm up to him.

• • •

Before anyone accuses me of having nothing at stake in all of this, let me just say that my family has taken a direct hit from piracy. You see, since the 1980s, my father has been in the business of writing, publishing, and selling educational materials that help parents "raise brighter children."

My father pioneered the sale of instructional books and audiocassette tapes in the Philippines. To boost sales he used direct advertising and channeled his vast network of thousands of independent dealers from all over the archipelago as door-to-door salespeople. He offered his dealers up to a 50 percent discount on their wholesale purchases, so half of the retail price went directly to the dealers, who were mainly housewives, part-time traders, sari-sari store owners, and even jeepney drivers.

In less than five years, my father's business grew into a one-man self-help industry that was teaching millions of Filipino children outside the classroom. The enterprise branched out to produce video versions of his book-and-tape titles like "English Grammar Made Easy," "ABC and Numbers," "Reading and Speech Improvement Made Easy," and "Musical Multiplication."

Fast-forward to the present: my father's once-prosperous business is in shambles. We have lost so much: cars, our comfortable house and some luxuries, a few friends, and trust in a stable future. I can say that we took a hit, partly because of piracy.

Why would Filipinos buy a twelve-video set from us at P3,000 (US$65), discounted, when they can get two DVD compilations in Quiapo at P100 (US$2) each?

• • •

I'm here in the street today to find out whether I can use the pirates as my own sales force, to sell DVDs of my films, and take advantage of the pirates' vast network and "outlets" in the streets.

My sales pitch to them is that they are one of us: Filipinos striving to earn a modest living. I admit that I am entering into a compromise. I am appealing to our being Filipino, so we should support Filipino movies by pirating only foreign films. It is my plea to the pirates to spare Filipino independent films by focusing their efforts on selling Hollywood and other foreign-studio blockbuster hits.

"Piratahin mo na ang iba, huwag lang ang ating mga pelikula" (pirate everything except local films) is a sentiment echoed by other filmmakers and DVD buyers. From what I can observe, fellow artists who buy pirated videos of foreign films feel that they are absolved because they don't buy pirated Filipino DVDs. There is also a romantic notion of bringing down foreign capitalists who are making tons of money out of us.

Then, there is that culture of sharing among us that makes it impossible to completely eliminate media piracy (which I explain in more detail later on).

• • •

From what I can gather, my fellow independent filmmakers are open to the idea of selling through the pirates. This is especially true of those filmmakers who own their films, however, they are afraid to take the lead.

I am less fearful than the others because, for one, I funded my film, *Todo Todo Teros,* entirely from my own pocket. Another reason is that I didn't spend a lot in making it: I didn't spend anything on lighting, crew, actors, production design, editing, or musical score. Everything was done with the help of friends and the talents that they offered, for free, to make the film. I spent a hundred dollars for the raw film stock, and that was pretty much it.

Of course, it's not as simple as it sounds. Working full time on this movie for almost a year, I had to give up other projects that came my way. I turned down offers to direct corporate videos and design multimedia projects, as well as passing on television ads and writing jobs. Meanwhile, I still had to pay my condominium rent and electric and credit-card bills.

Because I was turning down paying jobs, I had to find other ways to get money while I was making the film. Good thing I had saved up, and a few relatives pledged just enough support to get me through it all. Nowadays, I get by with the help of the Hubert Bals Fund of the International Film Festival Rotterdam and the National Commission for Culture and the Arts. By winning an award at the Vancouver film festival, I also received a cash bonus, which I wisely invested on a laptop computer and other mobile editing hardware.[1]

Still, it's several months later, and I'm running on fumes, relying on the generosity of others. I cannot keep asking for money and expect to get it forever. I have to find a more stable and regular revenue stream.

I am an independent filmmaker working outside the studio system. In the Philippines, that means I have to do almost everything myself, from production to distribution, including: buying blank DVDs and burning them, designing the covers, printing and photocopying labels, delivering the DVDs to retail outlets, and actually shelving the DVDs in those store fronts.

The independent filmmaker pours her or his soul into a project, and then faces the practical challenge of how to make money from the film. In my case, *Todo Todo Teros* is both "too experimental" and too "low res" for the movie-going public. Filipinos perceive *Todo Todo Teros* the way they perceive documentaries, which is to say *"hindi totoong pelikula"* (not a real film) because there are no celebrities, no special effects, and no gloss. Even my mother echoed those sentiments when she asked me to "make a real film next time." I perfectly understood what she meant when she said that.

Fellow filmmakers know that working with pirates will cause quite a stir among other filmmakers, who are protective of their own interests, which is not a bad thing, because everyone wants to recoup what he or she has invested.

We all have bills to pay, tacked on our refrigerator door or piled on our desks, I understand that. To pay mine, I want to see whether cooperating with street vendors—pirates—can somehow open the door to a mutually rewarding venture. So,

---

[1] In 2006, *Todo Todo Teros* won the Dragons and Tigers Award for Young Cinema at the Vancouver International Film Festival. The award honors the most creative and innovative feature by a new director from the Asia–Pacific region.

that is why I'm selling my DVDs and not just giving them away. We filmmakers have to earn a substantial amount from this somehow to make it worth our while. There has to be a way we can legally transact and do business, just like any tax-paying entrepreneur, armed with all the necessary permits.

• • •

It was surreal. I was screening my movie amid the heat and smog of Katipunan, playing it on a Macbook, and waiting for the pirate's reaction. He was watching attentively and appeared amused, and I took that as a good thing. I looked forward to the scene of Saddam and JR, where they convince the terrorist's wife to give them the copy of the home movie left by her husband, one that exposes his affair in Berlin with Olga, a Russian spy.

My pirate, named Al, was oblivious to what was happening around him.

Will he distribute my film? (photograph by author)

A patrol car came and parked in front of us.

When you see a pirate and the police, you think of a raid or at least an inspection of the pirate's DVD cases. But in the Philippines, bootlegs are sold in plain view of pedestrians and even in the malls, in stalls with highly visible signs offering the latest video game titles, software installers, cracks, hacks, and ripped movies.

My pirate looked up, directed his attention to the police, and went to speak with them. They all seemed on good terms, so I figured it was just plain old extortion. *Kotong*, as we call it here.

Sure enough, the car moved on, and Al went on with his business. This time with a smile.

"What did they say?"

"Oh nothing, they're friends," he said in Filipino.

Friendship in this case has a lot to do with "grease money," of course. In order for Al and his Katipunan team to go about peddling DVDs, they have to keep the cops happy.

"They get DVDs from us. Sometimes cash, but mostly DVDs. We carry around a hundred titles a day each, and sometimes they get all of them, the stuff I have to sell for the day."

Movies are sold for P60 to P90 each (about US$1.50), and they range from Hollywood hits and art-house films to experimental and independent cult flicks. Of course, porn is available, too, especially now that the "university scandals" are hot. These are mobile phone clips supposedly taken by lovers of unsuspecting *kolehiyalas* (college girls) having sex. In truth, the university-scandal DVDs are collections of five- to thirty-minute clips taken by various pornographers, using amateur actors and plain old exhibitionists.

I learned that pirates buy the DVDs at a wholesale price of P35 each. Al didn't disclose his main source, but I guess it is common knowledge that Quiapo is the center of all trade.

I proceeded to reveal to Al my package, my offer of mutual trade cooperation.

• • •

I told him my plan.

"If I give you a movie that I own, can you sell it in the streets?"

"Yes, that's easy." He didn't even bat an eyelash. He didn't mince words at all. "Give me a DVD copy that I can show them."

Who's them? I thought. But I didn't think I should ask him that.

"Okay, so how do I do it?"

"Give me a DVD so they can see if it's any good. There are many of them, my *kababayan* [town mates]."

"So you will be the one to approach them about this?"

"Yes, I will go to Quiapo in a few days to meet the bosses and talk to them."

Of course, I knew going into this that I needed someone from within the pirates' circle to act as liaison and guarantor. It would be a gamble on my part to entrust the DVD—my first film!—to Al, but I also knew I had to take a certain leap if I wanted this arrangement to materialize. So I told him the significance of this transaction.

"If we do this right, Al, a lot more filmmakers may follow our path. I have many other colleagues who, I believe, are interested in showing their own films to more people. If we show them that we can work together and make some money from this deal on a regular basis, others will follow our lead, and we can at least turn the tide in favor of independent, guerrilla filmmakers

There was a sense of urgency in his eyes. I think I made sense, and I felt that I was also convincing the Doubting Thomas in me.

"So," I asked, "when do I see you again?"

"Oh, you'll see me here every day, selling my stuff."

At that moment he seemed cool, and I thought maybe he didn't trust *me*.

"Hey, I know him," I said, and pointed to Al's friend Boy, a cigarette vendor and parking attendant at KFC on the corner of Katipunan and Fabian dela Rosa Street. "He can attest to my credibility. He knows me and where to find me."

Then I asked, "Do I need to worry about printing the covers and the packaging? I am open to giving you just the master copy or I can provide the DVD cases and the covers as a finished product. I don't care if I make only P5 [about a dime] per DVD as long as it gets seen by more Filipinos. You can sell them for whatever price you want, of course. Tell the bosses, and let me know."

"Okay, but don't think about those things first. Give me the DVD and let's see what happens," he said, nicely.

Well, what happens is that one DVD master can give birth to an unlimited number of DVDs being sold in the street without my knowing about it, I thought.

I was getting too far ahead of myself.

• • •

At the Conference on Media Piracy and Intellectual Property in Southeast Asia, held in Quezon City in late 2006, Tilman Baumgärtel, a visiting professor at the University of the Philippines, made a good point: in digital piracy, there can really be no dwindling of resources. There is no depletion in the simple act of downloading or copying-and-pasting. A digital file can be duplicated an unlimited number of times, unlike a *pan de sal,* which is consumed by a limited number of people and then it is all gone.

Piracy is truly a fascinating process, and Baumgärtel described it as globalization's underbelly involving American and Canadian businessmen, the Chinese triad, Muslim vendors from Quiapo, enterprising individuals from Malaysia, and so on and so forth. Piracy, he stated, is the most advanced and aggressive development of illegal capitalism. I agree.

And these are also the same pirates who have exposed us to the experimental-film and art-house genre (as Baumgärtel points out in his article in this book). Even the classics, the Criterion Collection DVDs, cult movies, old black-and-white silent films of Eisenstein and Lang. A Cassavetes box set, as well as fifty years of Academy Awards winners—all of them are available to us here.

The pirates have taken good film education to the streets. I truly believe that if I never saw any films by Kieslowski or Bergman, and had just been exposed to Hollywood cinema, Regal Films productions, and a plethora of soft porn, cheesy massacre movies by aging action stars, and teeny-bopper hits, I would have acquired a different range of tastes, aesthetics, and sensibilities, and I would have made a different movie than *Todo Todo Teros.*

Without art-house and avante-garde films to see, I could be rich by now, and I would have never had to use art as my defense.

Because as long as you make your films according to the whims of your producer, and rely on the proven formula of sex, violence, and star power; as long as you fashion yourself to be agreeable and a star-maker, you'll be fine. Once so established, you can go into TV and advertising, where a director makes more in a few days than what an independent filmmaker hopes to make in a year.

• • •

Roughly ten million people in the Philippines, or about 10 percent of the population, have access to the Internet. Half have Internet service at home, be it via cable, DSL, or dial-up. Yes, technology has a lot to do with the boom of piracy, and many Filipinos are loving that technology because it finally brings them access to places they want to visit. I think it is a big equalizer between the rich and the poor, and here, regardless of your financial standing, you can easily click where you go and see or hear or know where you are headed.

Piracy definitely didn't start at the turn of the millennium, when Napster and Kazaa were the craze. Not even in the 1980s, when bootleg slow rock and glam rock audiotapes in white plastic cassettes were being reproduced in the Middle East and sold everywhere.

In his talk, Baumgärtel claimed that Filipino piracy goes back to the American period, when a certain Kapitan Moy advanced the Philippine shoe industry in 1887 by way of reverse engineering: taking apart good shoe designs from Europe to see how those were made. Kapitan Moy copied the process and shared what he knew with everyone, so that others could benefit from his discoveries.

I am not at all surprised. Filipinos are good at copying, to their credit or discredit. Our show bands play cover songs of foreign artists, and you can find them in Japan, Singapore, and even aboard ships cruising the Caribbean. Filipinos can convincingly mimic Americans, from personal features to fashion to accent. And some of our performance artists make good Elvis or Tina Turner impersonators.

Filipinos are not hesitant to share. We see the act of sharing DVDs or DVD players as a mark of status. It is in our culture, especially in the provinces, to slaughter our last cow when relatives from the city visit just so we can have a big lunch feast. It is automatic for us to offer our best room to friends, not minding about sleeping on the sofa so that our guests are as comfortable as possible. It is understandable to borrow your uncle's video player and rent a good movie so that your friends can feel at home.

As much as we are hospitable, we admittedly like to show off things we only borrow, sharing things we like our friends to see. We like to show that we can afford to give them *lechon* (roasted pig), an air-conditioned room, and all the latest Hollywood hits that they want to see.

We are all entertainers this way.

• • •

I was sick for a few days after my first meeting with Al, so I wasn't able to meet him right away and give him the DVD. All that time I was afraid he would think that I balked at his offer, that I was not serious, after all. Once I recovered, I spent a week in Katipunan trying, in vain, to chance upon him. I asked Boy to pass a message to Al so we could meet at a specified time. I even gave Boy a DVD, along with a small piece of paper for Al to sign, for him to acknowledge that he got the DVD.

Days passed, and although Boy saw Al a few times, he never took the DVD. I thought maybe it was because of that little piece of paper, my request for a signed "receipt." It was just scribbled lines and words written on scratch paper, something informal but could be binding just the same, and a lowly pirate is unlikely to look for such trouble. For me, I imagined that it was some protection against future claims, I guess. And I understood why he wouldn't sign the paper.

• • •

I talked to a friend, Enuh Iglesias, who is a lawyer and an instructor in the Department of Sociology at the University of the Philippines about my radical, pirate-dependent plan for distribution. She was kind enough to offer some nice points and insights as to how or why piracy thrives in our culture.

Enuh noted that the prices of DVDs and VCDs went down at the start of the new millennium. The reason why we have a thriving black market is because we Filipinos are practical, getting the most value for our money. We are used to haggling with vendors, and it gives us satisfaction to get goods at bargain prices. This is because we do not agree on the monetary value of a product set by the market. She says that it is in our culture to get the best deals.

For Filipinos, it is true that an especially good deal conveys non-monetary value to that item or service. The bargain itself becomes a small victory, an achievement, a chance to brag to friends and loved ones that we got the best deal. Thus, obtaining a well-known, desirable movie (DVD) at a great price is a real achievement.

Besides, there's not much difference, quality-wise, between legitimate and bootlegged DVDs and VCDs. The buying public doesn't really care much about the extras, special features, and glossy packaging of box sets and limited editions. They can't tell if the film is ripped from online sources and recompressed to fit a single layer DVD-R. Heck, even great films are compressed even further to make space for other films to be compiled on a single DVD, such as, say, the Akira Kurosawa collection, or recent Hollywood action movies. Overall, there's no pretension or even a slight hint of misrepresentation that what you are getting is the original. Pirated films look the part: there are no movie labels on the surface to cover "Sonee" brand DVD-R logos bought from CD-R King, and they are most often merely packaged in transparent plastic sleeves with hastily printed inserts, complete with the wrong celebrity pictures and captions, as well as amusing misspellings of movie titles.

Pirates' customers know what they are getting for their money, and they don't complain if the DVD occasionally skips after only a few viewings. Besides, a viewer needs to see a film only once *na malaman ang kwento* (to know the plot), as some would say. And even if the DVD freezes midway, regular customers can always count on their *suki* merchant to either replace the bad copy or give a full refund. Yes, pirates generally ensure quick and efficient customer service, without the hassle of corporate retail red tape. At worst, buying another copy is still cheaper than buying one original.

Bootleg goods and used goods from other countries are shipped to the Philippines and sold in *ukay ukay* or *wagwagan* (secondhand) shops. We know that what we're getting are the outworn, branded clothes of the Hong Kong rich, shiny boots from German soldiers, and surplus SUVs used up by the Japanese, but we still buy such things to taste those luxuries we cannot afford to have brand new.

Again, it is the satisfaction of finding a bargain under other people's trash. Consider the Philippine jeepney, the commuters' transport. These vehicles are merely recycled and overly decorated American military jeeps left over from the war. Taste our food. Some dishes are mainly leftover poultry, pork, and beef cuts made tasty: barbecued chicken feet, pig's ears, cow liver and tripe, and a lot more.

Enuh said that we Filipinos like to share the things that we have "in our bedroom and our backyard." One person's belongings are enjoyed by the whole community. DVDs are lent, borrowed, and sometimes not retrieved or returned. We do not ask our friends and relatives for payment to "rent" our DVDs. It is our experience of poverty that makes us willing to make life comfortable for our neighbors whenever we can. In this way, we have learned to adapt to the scarcity of wealth by using and reusing, and sharing and borrowing, what we have until things wear out.

Enuh then made an interesting point about compromise: watching DVDs is a luxury available to those who have the time to rest and relax. It is still admittedly a low purchase priority, so buyers will compromise regarding the DVD's video and audio quality. Thus, we buyers—already familiar with imperfection—have gotten used to watching films that are taken from video cameras in cinemas, looking over other people's shoulders and listening to them laugh or cry or shout during the movie's climactic moments.

We like to share. And we point to the importance of *pakikisama*, which generally means to go along with the collective decision of the group you are in. Thus, when the overly zealous housewife brags that she either downloaded or bought a pirated DVD of the latest season of *Sex and the City*, her *amigas* not only ask about what has been happening to Samantha, they ask whether they can they borrow the DVD to watch for themselves. The housewife is *nakikisama* when she agrees. In reality, she has no choice but to lend it out, if she wants to be called kind and generous: *pakikisama*.[2]

In this way, our concept of property—what is really ours—is truly changing.

• • •

It is 2008, and more than a year has passed. I saw Al a couple of times in the same vicinity. The first few times, he said he was still talking to his boss about the proposal I made, so I waited and waited. I didn't see him until a few months afterward, when he finally said his boss was wary of such an arrangement. By this time, Al didn't sound as optimistic, or, at the very least, as excited about *Todo Todo Teros* as he had seemed at first. He implied, in not so many words, that "they" weren't interested in the film anymore.

• • •

Days ago, I saw my father browsing through e-books about digital encryption and DVD protection. Earlier in the year, our hopes had risen, seeing that sales of his tutorials were improving. But then we saw that more and more of my father's educational materials were being sold in the streets at dirt-cheap prices. Now, the business can hardly sustain itself. My father is still putting his hope on beating piracy by studying the latest technology to prevent the copying of his stuff.

But we know that this is an exercise in futility; it only takes one DVD master to proliferate into a million copies.

---

[2] On the other hand, *pakikisama* sometimes carries the negative implication of succumbing to peer pressure, going along with the drinking sprees of your friends to fit in, for example. You are *nakikisama* when you drink with them and buy more bottles of beer for your friends.

It is an exercise in futility, knowing that other businesses are now seeing pirates as a non-conventional marketing ally. This time, money is being poured into producing pirated DVDs, for example, to make use of the back of the DVD covers as marketing leaflets and advertising space. This is true in the case of one particular liquor brand.

It is an exercise in futility, knowing that police raids can stop the sale of these wares just for a day. It is an exercise in futility when we see stalls upon stalls of pirated items doing a brisk business in commercial malls and in front of police precincts.

I think of viruses and anti-virus software makers existing and coexisting forever. It is a cycle of stop and go. I think of the game of cops and robbers, and real-life crime going on forever. It is a cycle of surrendering and escaping. It is the same when I think of the struggle between filmmakers and video pirates being fought on the same digital playground. Film producers may use the newest digital encryption tool, but there is always time and money on the side of the pirates to enable them to maneuver, eventually, around the most sophisticated security tools.

I should tell my father to stop and not bother anymore—to surrender and move on. Things change, and battles are sometimes lost; oftentimes, we simply cannot keep up. But I have to let him be and let him fight the war that he needs to wage. It inspires me. It inspires me to look for other ways to embrace or to counter the pirates' challenges, to think out of the box, to use technology to my advantage. My opinion of piracy is slowly changing, but I think I am headed in the same general direction as what I described here at the beginning. There is a way we can make it work. But I think we just need to be swayed more by technology, and by time.

AKU, PEREMPUAN, DAN PEREMPUAN ITU: ME, WOMAN, AND THAT WOMAN

Chris Chong Chan Fui

Location: A restaurant somewhere in Jakarta, Indonesia, June 2007
An interview with John Badalu, director of Q! Film Festival

For those whose sexualities are a bit off the beaten track, representations of themselves and their experiences in the cinema might be hard to come by. Within the region of Southeast Asia, the terms represented by the acronym LGBTIQ et al. (Lesbian, Gay, Bisexual, Transsexual, Intersex, and Queer, et al.) tend to be blurred, which allows their representation in the public media to be more fluid and ambiguous. It's hard to peg down where the region stands when it comes to filmic representations of sexuality, given the disparity that exists between such liberal environments as ultra-sexual Bangkok compared to the ultra-desexualized Kuala Lumpur.

While there are over fifteen film festivals in Southeast Asia, only two concentrate their programming on sexual identities. Other festivals have made the attempt but tend to lose their stamina over time. Some do one-off screenings, but it takes a lot of gumption and fortitude on the part of the organizers to keep such an event rolling year after year. Despite the censorship of bureaucracies and the opposition of staunch religious zealots, Q! Film Festival (Q!FF) in Indonesia is one such festival that plows through the odds to showcase works that challenge all Indonesian audiences and not simply the homo-typical ones.

I first met John Badalu, founder of Q!FF, in Kuala Lumpur during the Third Annual New Southeast Asian Cinemas Conference, in December 2006, at which I was moderating a discussion on the ins and outs of queer filmmaking and the exhibition of such films in the region. A few months later, we were able to meet up once again, but this time in Jakarta, where we had a chance to talk about how a festival on alternative sexualities could thrive for over five years in the world's largest Muslim country, Indonesia.

Q!FF 2007 festival poster, courtesy of the festival

PART 1: Q!FF COMES OUT

Chris Chong Chan Fui (CCCF): Let's start from the very beginning. When did Q!FF start and how did it come about?

John Badalu (JB): Q!FF started in 2002, but the idea came to me a year before that in Jakarta. I had a freelance job as a journalist and would go to premieres of films to write film reviews. There I met a few people who were also journalists and interested in films. We started to chat, usually at lunch, about the films that we just saw. I mentioned the idea of Q!FF, and they were interested. They said, "Yah, let's do it together." There were a few of us, all journalists. There were seven of us in the beginning.

I had worked for the Jakarta International Film Festival (JIFFest) in 2000, so had experience in organizing film festivals as the operations manager. I thought I could do it and knew more or less how to set up a festival.

We didn't have any budget, so I started sending out emails to directors saying we would like to do this festival—we didn't have any budget, but we would like to show your film. Some of them agreed. At the same time, most of us had collections of queer films, so we said, "What the heck, we'll just screen them, and we won't get the permission at the beginning." We tried to get permission for every film, and of course there were a few directors who didn't reply. We thought this was a small event, anyway, very limited, so we took the risk and screened them without permission, including international works. I think the ones we couldn't get permission for were *Farewell My Concubine* (Chen Kaige, 1993) and *Priscilla Queen of the Desert* (Stephan Elliot, 1994). With the others, we got the permission to screen using DVD [digital video disc] or VHS [video home system, video cassette format] whatever we had.

CCCF: Finding queer works is one challenge, but what about finding a place to screen them?

JB: I knew a few venues because I had been working in culture/arts for quite a while. I was still working for the Goethe Institute, so they let us use their theater for free. We got Ruang Rupa, which is also a community-based artists' initiative, and we got Theatre Utan Kayu, another alternative art space, which had done something like this two years before with their monthly screenings. At that time, I was thinking, "There is an audience for this kind of film, so why not do it, not only in one venue and only for one weekend, but try to do it as a festival?"

Most of the organizers of this festival are queer, but they are not out yet. They are also sensitive about their involvement with the festival. In the first year, for instance, they decided to put only one name on the poster. I am the only one listed there—my name and the name of our group, the Q Community.

CCCF: How did you feel about being the only one labeled as part of the festival?

JB: I have been out for a long time and everybody knows that. I think that the first thing they will remember about John Badalu is: "Oh yah, John Badalu, he's gay." I don't really care about that. It makes it a lot easier for me because I don't have to explain myself, so I don't have to pretend.

CCCF: How did the fall of Suharto [president of Indonesia, 1967–98, d. 2008] affect the rise of Q!FF?

JB: It [Indonesian society] was still highly conservative here at that point. After 1998 and the fall of Suharto, everybody started to speak out. They had the freedom to say what they wanted to say. That meant I could also say what I wanted to say. But at the same time, it was still very difficult because the media was still writing negatively about queers. So it was time to start something more positive. As organizers of Q!FF, we were all journalists who wrote for different forms of media. That was our strategy: to write something positive about queer life and at the same time to promote the first Q!FF.

CCCF: Did the government try to interrupt the event?

JB: We actually didn't have much communication with the Indonesian government. We considered this event as something underground. We just did it. We didn't ask for permission, we got foreign embassies and foreign cultural centers to support us. They participated in the festival by helping us obtain films.

CCCF: I heard there were some complications outside the cinema during your first year.

JB: There was a small demonstration by an Islamic group, Front Pembela Islam [FPI, Islamic Defenders' Front], at one of our more progressive venues, Ruang Rupa. They came and blocked the entrance so the audience couldn't go in, but they were not violent. They were just there saying, "You have to stop this festival." The venue organizers explained to FPI that this was just a film festival, that it was not anything political. They even invited the FPI to watch the films. None of them wanted to go in. They didn't say anything, they just left.

There was a journalist from an Islamic magazine, *Sabili,* who came to the festival and watched the films. He said, "I will try to write the article nicely because I like the festival. I like the films, and I think it's important to let all these Islamic people know." When the magazine article came out, he said that this festival was a sin, horrendous, don't go there! All bad things. There were also further negative comments from leaders of the Islamic communities. But then, I don't care—good publicity, bad publicity, they're all okay.

CCCF: Were you scared about being the target of a backlash?

JB: I didn't have any fear. When I was doing the festival, I didn't even think about the risks involved. I took it really easily. Then all these things happened, and I thought they were really harsh. I really had to think what would happen if I got killed. We had an emergency meeting with the organizers during the festival. We talked about the *Sabili* magazine article and that my name was now made public. If something happened to me in the next few days: "What are you going to do? Where will you be? Will you be there or will you disappear as well?! What would you like to do?"

The Q Community organizers were scared, but they still wanted the festival to go on, so I gave them a list of things to do: "If I die one of these days, these are the things you have to do." [Laughing] It's like a melodrama: "I'm doing this festival, and this is what has happened so far. Whatever happens to me, this is what you all have to do."

CCCF: What kind of audience came that first year?

JB: The audience was mostly not gay and lesbian. It was surprising, from my point of view, that those who were gay and lesbian were too scared to come. I got more film people to come, and more arts people, all who were not gay or lesbian. But in a way I find that it's good, because it makes me think that we are not exclusive. Non-queers are interested in those subjects, even though they are not queer. So that's even better for me, in a way, to broaden the audience, which I had never thought about before. In the beginning, I just thought about inviting friends and those who were gay-friendly to come to the festival. But actually it was the general public that came to see the films, people I had never met before.

There was also a lesbian group that wanted to help. When the festival was about to start, they said that not all of them were really out and that they didn't want their names made public. They only wanted to volunteer, which was okay by me. But on the day of the festival, they never showed up. I asked why, and they said, "If we show up, people will say that the audience at the festival is gay and lesbian, and we don't want to be known as gay and lesbian." Then they asked if their group could borrow the films and have a private screening at someone's house. I said, "No! The aim of the festival is that you come to the festival. We don't want people to hide inside and enjoy themselves. You have to come out." This festival is for the public. It's not exclusively for gay and lesbians.

PART 2: Q POLITICS

CCCF: Is Q!FF too queer?

JB: We used the letter Q instead of "gay and lesbian" because we didn't want to make it too far "out there." We didn't want people to think it was too provocative. We tried to make the risk a little bit smaller, not in your face. There is one art gallery that also has a screening room. One of the managers there is queer, but she is also very closeted. When we were organizing the first festival, we decided to send her a proposal, and her reaction was totally shocking. "Gay and lesbian film festival? I don't want those kinds of films here! You can forget about this place, I'm not going to give it to you!" After hearing that, I didn't want to push anymore. Let others decide for themselves at their own pace.

At the time of the first festival, we didn't have a political agenda. We just wanted to have some fun, show some different films—that's it. We never thought further than that at the time.

CCCF: But now? Has Q!FF taken a more political point of view?

JB: In our second year [2003], we had a public discussion on homosexuality and religion. We invited three speakers. One is an editor-in-chief for a lifestyle magazine, openly gay and openly Christian, another is a leader of a modern Islamic group, and the third is from the Human Rights Commission for women. The three of them talked about how homosexuality is seen by their respective religions. It was a very interesting discussion, attended by three hundred people—I had expected fifty. It was astonishing that all these people showed up. Women with *jilbab* [Islamic headscarves] came, along with religious people, and some outspoken queers—all in one room, talking.

Of course, there are people who say you can't mix it up. If you are religious, you cannot be gay. But in general, most of the people at the discussion were more tolerant about people and other religions, instead of looking through [the frame of] their own religion all the time. Some [members] of the audience came up to the public forum and said, "My name is this, and I'm gay. I have a big confusion in my life because I'm religious, and I'm gay, too. Both sides are not going well together, so what should I do?" There are a lot of cases like that, which came out of the forum in 2003. We never expected it.

With this festival, since we had already received some threats from Islamic groups—some people already thought it was dangerous—then, [we thought], why not go political, completely? So for the upcoming year [2007], I chose films that are political, like *Fight Back, Fight Aids: Fifteen Years of Act Up* [James Wentzy, 2003], which is about the US political movement Act Up, and I also included documentaries on adoption among gay couples. We're trying to bring out all these political issues that now face the queer community. We are now doing discussions every year, and they are becoming more and more political.

I am now considered one of the gay leaders in Indonesia by the Human Rights Commission. They now include [the commission recognizes] queers as a minority whose rights need to be protected, and they put my name in there as a representative without telling me. People just claim you there. I know that when they crosscheck with me, I will agree and be supportive of the commission. We will now have the Human Rights Commission's protection for queer people. This means you can ask for legal assistance, or any assistance, from the commission. Some of the members of the commission came to the festival, and it made them realize they had never thought about the queer community. Some of them were inspired by the festival. Things are gradually changing. I personally have become political, and I want to make the festival more political as well.

CCCF: How much more political are you talking about?

JB: I personally will go all the way. With a few other friends who share the same vision, we are looking outside of the festival to be part of the gay political movement. I believe you have to act more outside of the festival.

CC: Do you think cinema has a role in defining what queer is?

JB: That's more Western—to categorize people in boxes. It's difficult not to, identity is important. People like to be clear about what they stand for, but I don't think people have to do that all the time. Here, it's more like picking up on all the Western ideas: "We're gay, we have to do gay things." It's up to each individual, of course. Film is freely interpreted. Some people relate to it, some people say they don't relate, but at least it opens their eyes. Now I'm not even sure about my sexuality any more.

CC: Q!FF started in Jakarta, but it has expanded in recent years. Where else has it gone?

JB: I started to go to other cities in 2004. The second year of the festival [2003] was a breakthrough. It became very big—Indonesia's second largest [film] festival. Other film communities in other cities heard about us and were keen to explore the possibility of doing this festival in their cities. We got an invitation from Purwokerto, and we were keen to bring it to this small, conservative Islamic area. The people who invited us wanted to have the festival and guaranteed that it would be okay. So we offered them free films and helped with the organization of the festival there.

We showed at Purwokerto, Yogyakarta, and Surabaya in 2006. There were also other groups that wanted to be involved. My line is that I'm not interested if it's just a bunch of your friends wanting to have a private screening.

CCCF: Q!FF has moved politically, but what about socially? How has it affected the general queer community?

JB: Q!FF is becoming one of the alternative ways of meeting up. Nowadays, we all just chat online to meet people. Only the rich ones go to Heaven [a dance club in Jakarta], and they go in groups, they're not close to other groups. People are quite shy, and you usually go home alone. The most realistic way to meet people is through the Internet. At OhLaLa [a franchise café with locations in various middle-class shopping areas], you don't go to a table of strangers to introduce yourself, whereas the Q!FF parties are a kind of specific event with people who like films and like to party. They're becoming a meeting place in a way. That's why people are quite anxious about the events and want the festival to happen every three months. There are a lot of male prostitutes who would come if we opened it to the public, so we have to be selective with the guests.

Q!FF 2005 festival poster, courtesy of the festival

PART 3: GLOBAL AND LOCAL ALLIANCES

CCCF: Did you find it hard to build up an international network when you first started Q!IFF?

JB: In our second year, we had some international guests: filmmaker Paul Lee from Canada, Tom Abell from Peccadillo Pictures in the UK, and Japanese filmmakers Imaizumi Koichi and Iwasa Hiroki. Koichi and Hiroki were a real surprise. Apparently, they had heard about the first year of the festival, so they sent me an email asking if they could submit [their film]. I saw their film, it was a very low-budget DV [digital video] film, and I liked it. I thought it would be fun to show an underground Japanese film, so I said yes. Then they said, "We would like to come." Oh! We're not ready for this! [Laughs] We don't have any budget. But they said, "Doesn't matter, we will come." Oh wow, this is big! I tried to provide accommodations, but told them it wouldn't be fancy. They said it didn't matter, and they just came. It was the same thing with Tom Abell. I met him in Rotterdam in 2003 when we were sharing the same table in a cafeteria. I was selected as a juror for the Berlin International Film Festival [in 2003, and later in 2006], so I decided to go to Rotterdam before Berlin. I was just talking about my festival, and Tom overheard the conversation. He said that it was great, he didn't know there was a festival like that in Indonesia. He also said if I needed some films to let him know. Then Tom said he wanted to come. Oh dear! [Laughs] How can I manage this? We got Paul Lee from Canada through Tintin Wulia, a renowned video artist from Bali. In his case he already had plans to come to Indonesia. So, altogether, we had four international guests for our second year.

CCCF: Has your involvement with Berlin's Teddy Jury affected Q!FF?

JB: I was invited into the Teddy Jury [the queer film competition of the Berlin International Film Festival], which meant I got to see all these queer films screened in competition. So I approached the filmmakers one by one and asked them to screen at Q!FF. I got the DVDs directly from the filmmakers. There is a sense of solidarity, they think, "I would like to show my film at your festival because I know it must be difficult to show this kind of work. I would like to support festivals like yours by showing my film."

We are now officially part of the Teddy On Tour program. Teddy has its own jury and gives out awards for best feature. [The name] "Teddy On Tour" means some of its films will tour to other countries. Now I have more access to films shown in Berlin, and I can ask for screening rights for free. If you screen your film in Berlin, you also have to agree to show it for free in Indonesia as well.

CCCF: What about the domestic picture? Have you tried co-presentations with other festivals?

JB: Our problem is that we mostly show on DVD format. If we want to work with JIFFest [Jakarta International Film Festival], for instance, we would have to use 35mm prints. Maybe I can organize a queer program at JIFFest, but people pay to watch films at that festival, which means that the censorship board will be involved. Queer works will not pass the Indonesian censorship board; any queer content will be banned. That's why we have Q!FF—because we don't screen films at cinemas [public theaters], we don't go through censorship. We screen them free of charge only at cultural centers, which are non-commercial and attract a limited audience.

CCCF: Speaking of censorship, Masyarakat Filem Indonesia [MFI, Film Society of Indonesia] was formed to rally everyone in the Indonesian film industry to present a stronger, more unified voice. How will the formation of MFI affect Q!FF, especially the issue of censoring queer content?

JB: MFI tries to talk about all elements of the film industry: film education, film schools, film communities, festivals, copyright, government policies on censorship, subsidies, quotas, and the need for some kind of protection from Hollywood. It's [the society's manifesto is] a recommendation to the government, and is huge for everyone involved in film. We want to change the classification board into a proper classification board—not [with] censorship! We want a new kind of board, "This film is [rated] twenty-one and above and you can see the full version without cuts." At the moment they just simply cut.

I personally don't see a lot of significant changes with this manifesto in terms of Q!FF itself. We will still join the MFI and be involved. It will be better if we take advantage of it now, but we will still continue either way.

CCCF: What about Q!FF's long-term goals, especially in the light of the inception of MFI?

JB: Maybe in the end Q!FF can be accepted as an official film festival and doesn't have to be underground in Indonesia. Maybe in the future we can go to the censors and talk to them. Maybe we can change the mind of the audience. It will take time to change the perception and lack of tolerance of the audience over certain issues, and I don't know how long that will take. So far they are quite open, but we have so far also been very careful with the audience.

PART 4: QUEER FILMS AND INDONESIAN CINEMA

CCCF: How do you define queer works?

JB: There's no clear definition. There may be only one queer character [apiece] in films that are selected to queer festivals around the world, but a lot of festivals would still consider that queer work. We do it the same way at Q!FF. Basically, we're looking for good films, it doesn't matter if queer is the main topic or not. Even if it's just a side issue, it's okay. If it's good, we show it.

CCCF: Has there been a Q!FF profile on Indonesian queer directors?

JB: There isn't such a thing! If there are gay Indonesian directors, then they haven't produced so many films, and they're not really out. They may be out to me, but not publicly.

CCCF: But there have been filmmakers, whether queer or not, who wanted to show their films at Q!FF. How did they find you?

JB: When I worked at JIFFest, I met a lot of filmmakers, so they were familiar with my name. Suddenly I started my own festival, and all the filmmakers knew about this. Some filmmakers, even the small underground indie ones, were inspired to make films for Q!FF. For example, Ucu Augustina wanted to make a documentary on the Miss Waria Indonesia transsexual beauty pageant, just because there was Q!FF. She just had this idea and realized that it couldn't really go anywhere other than Q!FF.

Then there was the filmmaker Aria Kusumadewa, who had made a forty-five-minute film for TV a few years back. The TV station didn't like the film, so they never showed it. It's about a woman who gradually evolves to become a man, called *Aku, Perempuan dan Lelaki Itu* [Me, a Woman, and that Man, Aria Kusumadewa, 1996]. The film is interesting because the character is played by a famous actress, Nurul Arifin. I showed it at the second year of the festival, four years after it was made for TV. That was the first time ever that the film was publicly shown. Kusumadewa came with his crew as well as the actress. He was almost crying. His film was finally screened, even if it was at a small festival. He was happy, and I was very happy.

CCCF: Maybe we can take a small step back in time. Do you remember what the first queer film in Indonesian cinema is?

JB: *Istana Kecantikan* [Palace of Beauty, 1989] by Wahyu Sihombing! It's based on a true story, where a gay man gets married to a woman who's pregnant. He makes a deal to get married to the woman so people don't think he's gay. They open a beauty salon and live together. This man then starts to see another man, and the wife gets jealous. In the end, the salon owner murders his boyfriend. During the end credits of the film, you get a moral message saying, "Don't be gay, this is what happens."

CCCF: Have you shown it at Q!FF?

JB: No, I don't like the message at the end. The film is well-known and has a famous actor playing the effeminate character. It became a hit because of the gay issue and the fact that the actor is playing a gay character.

From the late 1980s to the late 1990s, not many films were produced. For almost twelve years, Indonesian films were not being made. There were a few reasons for this: people turned to TV, the financial crisis, and the birth of Cinema 21, a commercial cinema franchise. At that point, Cinema 21 made a deal to show Hollywood films and did not show any Indonesian films.

After *Istana Kecantikan*, the next [Indonesian] film, I think, that dealt with queer issues was *Kuldesak* [Cul de Sac], Riri Riza, Mira Lesmana, Nan T. Achnas, Rizal Mantovani, 1999]. *Kuldesak* consists of four stories, one of which is about a gay couple. It's the first feature film that shows the positive side of a queer couple. It doesn't show that being queer is wrong. The couple is just like any other couple, with their faults and their joys.

Then you've got *Arisan!* [The Gathering!, Nia Dinata, 2003] and *Berbagai Suami* [Love for Share, Nia Dinata, 2006). But none of these films are really queer or full-blown queer films.

CCCF: That aside, which film, in your view, made the greatest impact on queer representations on screen?

JB: I think *Arisan!* is the most important. When the film was about to be released, I asked the director if I could show it at Q!FF. The gay character in it caught everyone by surprise. *Tempo,* the Jakarta news magazine, and the BBC wrote about it. *Arisan* was a big box-office hit—seen as the first ever gay film in Indonesia, with the first ever gay kissing scene. People never thought it was possible to make this kind of film. People had a pessimistic side: "Oh, we won't get to see this sort of film at all." It was a breath of fresh air—a film with all new faces, all unknown actors at that time.

CCCF: Another thing you're doing is presenting films that are blurring the line of what is considered queer work, like *Terima Kasih Dan Selamat Malam Ibu* [Thank You and Goodnight, Mother, Ivan Handoyo, 2006].

JB: That's a very interesting case. Last year I programmed a selection on homoeroticism, looking at male bonding, female bonding, whatever—if it's sensual, I put it in. I included *Gie* [2005], a biopic about an Indonesian activist. It's not a gay film, but the Gie character has a very special friend during childhood. Even Riri Riza, the director, had the assumption that Gie was gay because his love life with women was always a miserable story.

In the case of the surfers in the documentary *Terima Kasih Dan Selamat Malam Ibu,* it's their sensuality. They touch each other and laugh together; the images are strong. I told Ivan we wanted to include his film in the homoeroticism program, and he was okay with it. Then we decided to have a discussion on homoeroticism in Indonesian films. I asked Riri to be a speaker, and he agreed, as he wanted to know what people thought, whereas Ivan wanted to know what he should say. I don't think he knows what homoeroticism means, though. During the discussion, he was the one who said, "I don't understand why my film is in the festival. I think it will kill the film because it will limit it to gay and lesbian audiences only." Riri was really mad, saying that it will broaden your audience by letting people interpret for themselves. Ivan tried to cancel the screening at the last minute, but I said it was already in the printed program. Maybe he was just uncomfortable showing it at Q!FF and having it considered a gay film. But outside Indonesia, then that's okay, no one in Indonesia will hear about it.

Not a lot of people know the definition of homoeroticism. I read in one media [publication], "They put a lot of Indonesian films in Q!FF. But I don't know why it is queer. They [Q!FF] said that this year's theme is homoeroticism, but I don't see why these films are queer." I, as a programmer, must be able to see things from different sides. For me, it's more important to show my point of view. It's also a learning process for others to see my point of view. The program's simply a different perspective on homoeroticism. Some people just see a given film as political rather than a queer film. Some people think, "What is Q!FF? What is that? I don't care, I'm going to see *Gie.*" They don't see Q!FF as a festival. Some of the audience at Kineforum, a theater supportive of the kind of alternative films shown in Q!FF, simply walk in and don't see it as part of a festival. For them, it's just a free screening. Most people don't know what the term "queer" means. Maybe if you say a gay and lesbian film that would be different.

My goal for the first ten years of Q!FF has been to raise awareness. We still have a long way to go to build up the audience, and I don't want to push it. It's better to let people know little by little, through word of mouth, from whatever they've seen. At the moment, it's not that bad, they know the name of the festival, but they don't know what it's about. I want them to see the festival as an exhibitor of films that are an alternative to Hollywood [movies]. When they come to see alternative films, then they can ask further questions about what "queer" means. The first goal is to show that there are alternative films, then after they can ask—what's "queer." If they want to know more, they can read the catalogue. Coming to see the film and then reading that there is an alternative viewpoint is important.

CCCF: How has your audience changed from the first year till now?

JB: The number increases every year, it never goes down. The first year we had 750 people, then 1,500 in the second year, and after that three thousand. Now it's around six thousand. There are more and more people coming to the festival, and more queer people. Friends bring friends, the non-queer people are becoming more tolerant and they're bringing friends. It's a communal experience at Q!FF. You don't attend a film alone.

What we do is bring commercial films to attract people, but then when they look at the rest of the catalogue, they think, "Oh, there are other films as well." Because the tickets are free, it's easier for them to see five or six films. If they have to pay, then they can only go to one or two films. Our main concern is how to find the money to run the festival. This is only an organization, not a foundation, so it's more complicated to apply for funding.

CCCF: Where do you see Q!FF going?

JB: I would like to run it properly. I want everyone to have a salary, a proper job. I would like to include more high-quality films, and to show more of them in proper cinemas. I don't want the festival to grow very big, though, I would like it to be a medium-sized festival. Even right now, people already have to choose too much. We will continue to have discussions, queer karaoke parties, et cetera. I wish we could get more funding to bring in a greater number of directors. We did a workshop on filmmaking, but that didn't work very well. Our audiences are more filmgoers than people who want to make film. We do discussions on all aspects linked to political movements, but I still want to maintain film discussions.

John Badalu is currently traveling the world, from Bangkok to Los Angeles, searching furiously for the latest filmic pickings on alternative sexualities.

SELECTED FILMOGRAPHY

Aku, Perempuan dan Lelaki Itu (Me, a Woman, and that Man, Aria Kusumadewa, 1996)
Arisan! (The Gathering!, Nia Dinata, 2003)
Berbagai Suami (Love for Share, Nia Dinata, 2006)

Gie (Riri Riza, 2005)

Istana Kecantikan (Palace of Beauty, Wahyu Sihombing, 1989)

Kuldesak (Cul de Sac, Riri Riza, Mira Lesmana, Nan T. Achnas, Rizal Mantovani, 1999)

Terima Kasih Dan Selamat Malam, Ibu (Thank You and Goodnight, Mother, Ivan Handoyo, 2006)

PART II

<u>REFLECTION</u>

CIRCUMVENTING CHANNELS: INDIE FILMMAKING IN POST-SOCIALIST VIETNAM AND BEYOND

Mariam B. Lam

I have been concerned about what independent filmmaking means, or signifies, in Vietnam ever since I had a brief conversation about the lack of a clear definition with the late Filipino critic Alexis Tioseco in 2006. While we were chatting, it seemed so clear in my mind that there is, indeed, a form of independent cinema in Vietnam, but it soon became even clearer to me that I needed more time to pinpoint how and where film practices that qualify as "independent" might be identified in Vietnam's context, as well as to articulate this mediated form of independence to foreign film critics and audiences. The definition of "indie" film that I attempt to develop here entails the complicated involvement of the state, and does so to a much greater extent than do the "indie" phenomena traced in the other chapters of this collection. Because the Vietnamese state and state funding are involved in the production of all Vietnamese films, both mainstream and indie, the concept of "indie" is different in the Vietnamese context relative to other cultures. These compromising factors constitute the more mediated form of independence that this chapter traces.

Diasporic Vietnamese director and screenwriter Stephane Gauger defines "independent film" as "a work displaying a unique voice and singular vision."[1] Gauger's concise definition represents the generally accepted historical understanding of independent cinema as a cinema that is less driven by the domestic and international commercial film markets, compared with the more conventional (e.g., mass appeal, formulaic genre) products of the industry, and that exists outside or in a tangential relationship to the major Hollywood studios and production houses. In addition to this *différence* in its commercial standards, independent cinema is usually understood to involve accessible and replicable production methods, and

---

[1] Interview with Stephane Gauger in Palm Springs, CA, February 1, 2008. For more on the dominant history of independent filmmaking, see Emanuel Levy, *Cinema of Outsiders: The Rise of American Independent Film* (New York, NY: New York University Press, 1999); Greg Merritt, *Celluloid Mavericks: The History of American Independent Film* (New York, NY: Thunder's Mouth Press, 2000).

to be endowed culturally and historically with its unique range of aesthetic styles common to those less expensive methods. When asked about the added difficulties of making "indie films" in the Vietnamese context, where censorship is enforced, another diasporic filmmaker, Tony Bùi, stated that red tape is really an ongoing "test of patience" and persistence. "Honestly," he explained, "it isn't any different from [conditions imposed by] the studios because you have to draft, draft, draft. There's a higher order, a hierarchy, you have to get through ... but once you knew the rhythm, once you learned how to play that game, I kind of liked my censorship guys. You learn how to do the dance."[2]

From the late 1980s to the mid-1990s, Vietnamese films exhibited internationally consisted primarily of state-funded productions made under heavy regulations and approved by a censorship review board. During this period, socialist realist films and literature dominated the cultural climate of a nation undergoing rehabilitation, which was only beginning to reintroduce itself to a global audience. However, the general perception was that these in-country films were not as popular domestically as the imported or pirated Hollywood blockbusters, Asian dramas, and martial arts flicks, or the more upbeat domestic variety shows.

Similarly, during this early revival period, diasporic Vietnamese audiences—many of whom were politically conscious war refugees forced to flee Vietnam and resettle abroad—also tired of what they called "propagandistic" filmmaking practices and greeted the screenings of Vietnamese films internationally with protests and jeers. They interpreted the limited selection of films produced and permitted to tour, as well as most of the content of these films, as direct evidence of the state's stifling control over its people's cultural citizenship and freedom of expression.

From the mid-1990s to the present time, however, we have witnessed occasional, drastic sea changes in the directions of Vietnamese film production, education, distribution, and circulation. These more recent historical shifts and cultural phenomena are the backdrop of this chapter. They provide the context for my proposal that Vietnamese independent cinema does exist to a smaller extent than is true of other Southeast Asian countries, yet it deserves close attention because it is much more intricately tied up with foreign and diasporic capital, and with global cultural activism than our traditional notions of "alternative" media would generally accommodate. Vietnamese indie cinema is rooted in the fraught terrain of a booming post-socialist ASEAN nation-state that has only recently become engaged with the World Trade Organization. It also comes with a young and hungry postwar generation of upwardly mobile transnational cultural consumers and producers who want to participate fully in the creation of a new Vietnamese film wave.[3]

This new circuit of Vietnamese independent filmmakers, producers, exhibitors, distributors, and activists is the primary focus of the chapter. Before turning to the indie film community, it is crucial first to consider briefly Vietnam's recent cultural history, as the embedded cultural–political tensions and socioeconomic contradictions create the context within which this new community of filmmakers

---

[2] Filmmakers' roundtable discussion at the Viet Art Center in Garden Grove, CA, November 11, 2007.

[3] Richard Chang, "A New Film Wave," *The Orange County Register*, July 13, 2007, www. ocregister.com/ocregister/entertainment/homepage/article_1766832.php, accessed April 21, 2011.

practices and grows. Fascinatingly, it is the collective downplaying (if not outright omission) of recent Vietnamese political and cultural history that has, to some extent, established the conditions of possibility for these transnational collaborative projects to develop. Because no domestically produced film intended to circulate within Vietnam is free from vetting by the state, and because the state's national film industry can no longer afford to monopolize the creation and production of all films in Vietnam (as the state itself has been privatizing the industry over the past fifteen years), independent film and media in Vietnam are both beholden to the constraints of national political history, as well as free from national commercial sectors. Considering this political and economic cultural context necessarily leads to a very complex treatment and understanding of "indie film" analysis.

CIRCUMNAVIGATING VIETNAMESE FILM HISTORY[4]

Many postwar Vietnamese and Western critics, such as Ngô Phương Lan or Panivong Norindr,[5] appear to be comfortable with, or at least resigned to subscribe to, four periods of film historiography that came to be defined after the "civil war" years, which ended in 1975. These consist of: 1) an early period aligned with French colonialism through 1954 and the signing of the Geneva Agreements; 2) the "civil war" years (1954–75);[6] 3) a reunification period joining North and South Vietnam; and 4) the contemporary period, dating from the 1986 policy innovations of the Sixth Party Congress of the Vietnamese Communist Party, which initiated the *Đổi Mới* economic reforms. Indeed, Wikipedia fans may find this same version of filmic history presented online.

The dominant history recounts that Vietnamese filmmaking began in the 1920s, in Hanoi, of course, with the Hương Ký Film Company. This company is credited with the production of documentaries on the funeral of Emperor Khải Định and the enthronement of Bảo Đại, in addition to some silent feature films. Between 1937 and 1940, at least five more films were made by the Asia Film Group and the Vietnam Film Group. The films produced throughout the rest of this early period are often described as a hodgepodge of victorious battle films and documentaries celebrating the First Indochina War against the French, produced by the government's Ministry of Information and Propaganda from 1945 until 1954.

Postcolonial French scholarship paints a different picture, however, as it documents the fact that the first cinema houses in Vietnam were established before World War I. European films were shown in French-owned movie theaters, while imports from Hong Kong and China were shown in theaters run by the Chinese. While this account of early screenings in Vietnam is difficult to trace, the total number of movie theaters in Vietnam in 1939 was recorded to be sixty-three. Roy

---

[4] For my fuller discussion of the complexities of Vietnamese film history, please see Mariam B. Lam, "Viet Nam's Growing Pains: Cultural Education and Transnational Politics," in *Vietnam and "Vietnam" Since 1975: Transnational Legacies of the Second Indochina War*, ed. Scott Laderman and Edwin Martini (Durham, NC: Duke University Press, forthcoming).

[5] Panivong Norindr, "Vietnam: Chronicles of Old and New," in *Contemporary Asian Cinema: Popular Culture in a Global Frame*, ed. Anne Tereska Ciecko (Gordonsville, VA: Berg Press, 2006), pp. 45–57.

[6] This Cold War fiasco is, of course, called many things by different players, from the "Vietnam War" or "Second Indochina War" to the "American War" or the "War of Liberation."

Armes explains the international make-up of the early cinema production staff and describes how early film activity was ended after the French surrendered to the Japanese in 1940, and how Vietnamese filmmaking was reborn as part of a national guerrilla cinema during the subsequent struggle against the French following the end of World War II. He parallels this complex nationalist history to that told by Vietnamese critics who date the birth of an "authentic" national cinema from the signing of a Decree on Founding the National Agency of Cinema and Photography in March 1953 by Hồ Chí Minh.[7] In Armes's version of Vietnamese cultural history, even at Vietnam's most anti-colonial nationalist moment there was clear evidence of collaborative international film practices and activities.

Michel de Certeau has envisioned history as:

> ... *a text* organising units of meaning and subjecting them to transformations whose rules can be determined ... if historiography can have recourse to semiotic procedures in order to renew its practices, it likewise offers itself to these procedures as an object of study, inasmuch as it makes up a story or a discourse of its own.[8]

This adulterated history of global filmic miscegenation offers an alternative origin myth for the current trends in collaborative transnational independent Vietnam cinema.

In a departure from mainstream historiography, I date the contemporary cinematic period from circa 1994, when the United States' nearly twenty-year economic embargo against Vietnam was lifted. Prior to this date, only a handful of documentaries created by diasporic filmmakers were licensed to be shot in Vietnam; these included Vietnamese American Tiana Thị Thanh Nga's film, *From Hollywood to Hanoi* (1993), and films by the mainstream French auteurs Régis Wargnier (*Indochine*, 1992) and Jean-Jacques Annaud (*The Lover*, 1992). Even French-Vietnamese director Trần Anh Hùng's first feature film, *Scent of Green Papaya* (1993), was shot for the most part on a sound stage in France. Though these early transnational works set the stage for what would become more ambitious cinematic "indie" projects, they were not in themselves independent films. These filmmakers relied on traditional funding channels for their projects, and they sought distribution in their own national contexts. These films did, however, highlight the advantages of Vietnam as a potential site for a new wave of film production, advantages such as its surplus talent, potential as profitable industry, and natural resources. These foreigners and diasporics made use of existing cinematic resources and spurred a Vietnamese domestic need to address Vietnam's own film culture in response to international inquiry. We even begin to see film scholarship being produced during this period.[9]

---

[7] Roy Armes, *Third World Film Making and the West* (Berkeley, CA: University of California Press, 1987), pp. 146–47.

[8] Michel De Certeau, *The Writing of History*, trans. Tom Conley (New York, NY: Columbia University Press, 1988), p. 41.

[9] See, for example, the collections *Diễn viên điện ảnh Việt Nam/Vietnamese Film Actors and Actresses*, eds. Hoàng Thanh and Phạm Hải Vân (Hanoi: Nhà Xuất Bản Văn Hóa Thông Tin, 1994); and *Đạo diễn phim truyện Việt Nam/Feature Film Directors of Vietnam*, ed. Trần Luận Kim and Lê Dinh Phương (Ho Chi Minh City: Trung Tâm Nghiên Cứu Va Lưu Trữ Điện Ảnh, 1998).

Overseas director Trần Anh Hùng filmed his second feature, *Cyclo*, in 1995, one year after the American embargo was lifted. In *Cyclo*, he juxtaposed the constant bombardment of rapid commercial industrialization on the streets of Saigon with the malaise of its fledgling flock of young city dwellers, looking for love in all the wrong gangster–poet places. Edward Soja needs to look no further than Ho Chi Minh City for evidence of his notion of the postmetropolis.[10] In *Cyclo*, Trần's critique of the economic conditions governing social and interpersonal relationships displays a politicized departure from his quietly colonial and subtly historical film, *Scent of Green Papaya*. *Cyclo*, however, was not shown on Vietnamese screens, though the state contends that the director never applied for permission to screen in Vietnam, suggesting this was because he knew that permission would be difficult to acquire from the censorship bureau. Even today, sixteen years later, and despite the *đổi mới* renovation policy, there remains a censorship bureau in Vietnam with the authority to inspect scripts pre- and post-production and to send its staff on site to oversee scenes and shots. Vietnam has only seen twenty-five censorship-free years in its entire history, which occurred during its modernist period in the mid-1920s through the 1940s. Often, Vietnamese film directors and critics themselves must serve as members of the censorship board.

Vietnam proved to be popular with foreigners searching for cinematographic novelty, at the same time that it beckoned its expatriate auteurs to return home. Tony Bùi's Sundance Film Festival success, *Three Seasons* (1999)—the first Vietnamese production by a diasporic filmmmaker shot entirely in Vietnam—captured the hearts and minds of an international audience ready to embrace the rebirth of Vietnam and its culture. While *Three Seasons* starred Hollywood celebrities like Harvey Keitel, Patrick Swayze, and Forest Whittaker, the Bùi brothers' films, *Three Seasons* and *Green Dragon* (Timothy Linh Bùi, 2001), were independently produced and seemed to suggest a schizophrenic, dislocated development for "Vietnamese Cinema," as well as the bipolar anxieties of Vietnamese and diasporic Vietnamese cultural identity. Bolstered by the influx of expatriate talents, domestic Vietnamese directors also synergistically strove to produce less dogmatic and more emotionally complex narratives, such as Nguyễn Thanh Vân's *Đời cát* (Sand Life, 2000), Đặng Nhật Minh's *Mùa ổi* (Guava Season, 2001), and Phạm Nhuệ Giang's *Deserted Valley* (*Thung Lũng Hoang Vắng*, 2002). In the last decade, this transnational filmmaking community and its international audiences also began to inquire after the status of women in the Vietnamese film industry. Though both domestic and diasporic Vietnamese film communities are predominately populated by male screenwriters, directors, producers, and distributors, female directors are starting to receive overdue attention. Phạm Nhuệ Giang and Việt Linh now have their own feminist fans and critics, for example.[11]

---

[10] Edward W. Soja, *Postmetropolis: Critical Studies of Cities and Regions* (Malden, MA: Blackwell Press, 2000).

[11] Phạm Nhuệ Giang's films include The *Coolie Child* (1992), *Escape* (1995), and *The Deserted Valley* (2002). Việt Linh has directed *The Birds Were Singing in the Quiet Place* (1986), *The Trial Needs a Presiding Judge* (1987), *The Traveling Circus* (1989), *The Devil's Mark* (1992), and *Collective Flat* (1999). Chương- Đài Võ, a 2010 doctoral graduate of the University of California, San Diego, herself a Vietnamese American, has written on Phạm Nhuệ Giang, while British cultural critic Carrie Tarr is currently writing on the works of Việt Linh.

CONTEMPORARY "INDIE" CIRCUITS

Not until very recently have efforts to modernize cinema in Vietnam taken off and moved beyond complete state control. Contemporary diasporic and Vietnamese filmmakers have gained wider audiences with films such as *Mùa len trâu* (Buffalo Boy, 2004) and *Bar Girls* (2003). Nghiêm-Minh Nguyễn-Võ's *Buffalo Boy* was shot primarily in Vietnam, with Vietnamese, French, Belgian, and Singaporean cooperation. Due in part to its predominantly external funding sources and internationally collaborative network, and in part to its very minimal political historical content, Nguyễn-Võ's film exemplified a new transnational species of Vietnamese independent cinema.

Although Minh Nguyễn-Võ is an overseas Vietnamese currently residing in California, *Buffalo Boy* was Vietnam's official submission to the 2006 Academy Awards. The film was selected only after it had won numerous awards at festivals throughout Europe and the United States. Considering the lagtime in the film's formal distribution and international circulation, the ultimate selection of a diasporic director's contribution to Vietnamese cinema by the Vietnamese state further displays the benefits of "claiming Vietnameseness" both for diasporic filmmakers and, now, finally, for Vietnam as well. Indeed, the powerful imaginary, symbolic, and interpretive functions of differently situated publics and counterpublics and their receptions as viewers,[12] and their ambiguous involvement in the shaping of our modern life and our unfolding of cultural traditions, reveal themselves in Vietnam's continuously changing attitudes towards its *việt kiều* (the common politically and historically loaded shorthand term for returning overseas expatriates). These attitudes have historically vacillated between disregard for those who supported the losing side in the civil war and subsequently fled the country, to appreciation for the billions of dollars in remittances and NGO development that helped to rebuild the postwar nation-state, to disgust for the apparent *nouveau riche* expatriate tourists who flaunt their feigned wealth on visits home, and ambivalence towards friends and family members who share the same but conflicted national history.

Similarly, the orientalist attitudes of many Western audiences, critics, and industry practitioners also pose dilemmas for these filmmakers. The film poster for *Buffalo Boy*'s French release—with its exotic display of the beauty of poverty at sunset—might be contrasted with Nguyễn-Võ's own graphic design for his film (see below). Nguyễn-Võ translates the French: "Water is normally a symbol of purification and life; here it is associated with decaying and death. At the same time, fish and rice, two essential sources of food, come from this water. Water becomes a mixed metaphor for life and death, opposite but inseparable."

Compare Nguyễn-Võ's design, below, to the jacket cover of the DVD released in the United States (also second image below). In his interview with me, the director expressed his hope that his image "conveys the metaphorical layers of the film effectively." At the same time, he worried that, all too often, the "artwork" designed to promote foreign films portrays overly "exotic and commercial" perspectives and "a Western gaze." One might read the cover of *Buffalo Boy*'s US DVD release as a prime example of the commercialization of foreign films. In this case, Nguyễn-Võ's own graphic design—stripped of its accompanying text—is only one of many eroticized images of the peasant pastoral.

---

[12] Michael Warner, *Publics and Counterpublics* (New York, NY: Zone Books, 2005).

"L'eau est normalement un symbole de la purification et de la vie, elle est ici associee
a la pourriture et a la mort. En meme temps, le poisson et le riz, duex sources de nourriture
essentielles, viennent de cette eau. L'eau devient une metaphore mixte pour la vie
et la mort, opposees mais inseparable." Nguyen-Vo Nghiem-Minh

Gardien de buffles

UN FILM DE
NGUYÊN-VO NGHIÊM-MINH

Nghiêm-Minh Nguyễn-Võ's own design for the inside of French-released *Buffalo Boy*
DVD jackets

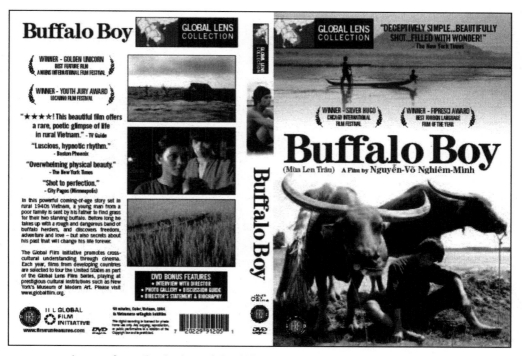

Image from the jacket of the US release of the *Buffalo Boy* DVD

Conversely, Lê Hoàng's privately funded *Gái nhảy* (Bar Girls) is set among the Vietnamese dance clubs, with depictions of both the eager attractive women and the vibrant dance club scene that is geared toward Westerners, expatriate Vietnamese tourists, and an "urbanized" Vietnamese male clientele. While this box-office hit first garnered attention from native auteurs and Western critics as a low-brow film, the work manages to highlight the global capitalist underbelly of sex tourism, rampant AIDS/HIV infection, drug addiction, media and police corruption, and out-of-synch NGOs. Here it is important to note that the Vietnamese nationalist film critics' dismissal of the film as "low culture" and of poor quality was not actually a response to weaknesses in the film that resulted from a lack of funds, or a limited production budget, for *Bar Girls* was produced with private funds totaling more than the money available to underwrite average state-produced films, and it readily employed modern technology.[13] The criticisms aimed against this work betrayed a desire, on the part of its nationalist critics, to link Vietnamese cinema essentially, and exclusively, with either familiar socialist genres or a globally resonant, elite art-house aesthetic. Despite the statist criticisms of *Bar Girls*, representatives of the ministry of culture predicted, or anticipated, that there would be more state funding for such films with which "the youth" seem to identify, and as diasporic communities come to import and mass produce in Little Saigons across the globe. *Bar Girls* belonged to a newer breed of film animal, however, and it had a provocative relationship to global cultural consumption that the state needed to tap into economically even though its censors and critics were compelled to distance Vietnam socially and culturally—or morally—from the film's content. At a 2008 UCLA (University of California, Los Angeles) film panel discussion including both leading Vietnamese film critic and state cinema department representative Ngô Phương Lan and director Phạm Nhuệ Giang, funding offered by the state was said to have dwindled. Whereas there was enough funding in the 1990s to produce and complete twenty or more full-length feature films per year, within the past decade the state has only been providing partial funding for a handful of feature films.

Once *Bar Girls* broke the one million-US-dollar mark in revenues, making it the highest grossing film in Vietnam's history, the national and foreign press began to interview the director, Lê Hoàng, about his reasons for making such a film. In several interviews, Lê blamed the relatively small film audiences in Vietnam and the slow progress of Vietnamese cinema on the overly serious, dull content of Vietnamese motion pictures: "State-owned film companies receive billions of *đồng* from the state fund every year, but the money is still not enough. We can't fully develop the film industry without producing hit movies." In response to inquiries about why he had forsaken his own more serious, earlier cinematic style for such "low quality" new material, Lê added: "I want to change my own direction to create films that lure audiences, particularly young people."[14] His determination to continue pushing the national film industry towards a different register of filmmaking than that mandated by the state is evident in the comment that "the important thing is to change our approach towards producing movies. They should be based on interesting plots and

---

[13] In Vietnam, private funding does not necessarily equate with "independent" production or substance, in the sense that all films are still beholden to state regulations and restricted by state inspection of both material content and funding sources.

[14] "Filmmakers Clash after Bar Girls Triumphs at Box Office," *VietNam News*, March 18, 2003.

good acting"[15] —suggesting perhaps that these qualities had not been given a high priority in the past.

Armes reminds us that for the Third World and some developing countries,

> ... film is an imported form of communication ... Unlike the later systems of radio and television broadcasting, the cinema has not been a tool or direct expression of the state: as a "free enterprise" system, its inception and development are closely tied to the profit motive as it is expressed in and through Western capitalism.[16]

What I am arguing here is that we cannot disentangle state expression and enterprise from the projection of potential global profits motivating Vietnam's transnational independent film circuits. The state's discourse on the future of its film industry helps to motivate Vietnam's transnational independent film circuits at the same time that the state's desire to claim some of the profits that could potentially be reaped from internationally successful Vietnamese films has begun to affect the state's own rhetoric and activities.

Today in Vietnam, foreign markets, diasporic film directors, and touring Vietnamese motion pictures are diverse factors that serve to speed up commercial production and distribution processes. To take advantage of superior technology and to save costs with assistance from various foreign film industries, Vietnamese post-production is often handled in Thailand, Singapore, Hong Kong, or France. Until relatively recently, all Vietnamese film production companies, institutes, and archives were funded by the state. Now the socialist state must compete with the substantial resources of a globalized Hollywood-like film industry[17] and its diasporic communities. So, it has begun to once again warmly receive *việt kiều* who are now aesthetic co-creators with Vietnamese nationals, state-owned production houses, and foreign film industries, or the new ticket and reigning talent for this contest.

In the last decade or so, foreign investors—usually overseas Vietnamese relatives of native filmmakers or supportive Western filmmakers—have ghost-produced and financed Vietnamese films designed to be commercially successful. There has been a further shift in production funding away from complete reliance on government commissions toward individual or private financing, as well as a tendency to initiate joint productions involving both the state and the private sector. Aaron Toronto, an American director, for one example of completely private individual financing, plans to build a film studio to fund young Vietnamese filmmakers in the production of independent films. Toronto has already shot music videos for local artists screened on Vietnam Television and has promoted Vietnamese director Lê Thanh Sơn's short film *Who am I?* at various film festivals.[18]

---

[15] Ibid.

[16] Armes, *Third World Film Making and the West*, p. 35.

[17] See, for example, Richard Maltby and Melvyn Stokes, eds., *Hollywood Abroad: Audiences and Cultural Exchange* (London: British Film Institute, 2005); and Toby Miller, Nitin Govil, John McMurria, Richard Maxwell, and Ting Wang, eds., *Global Hollywood 2* (London: British Film Institute, 2005).

[18] Quynh Nhu, "U.S. Director Encourages More Vietnamese Indie Films," trans. Le Phuong Anh, *Thanh Niên News*, May 12, 2005.

The director of the Ministry of Culture and Information's Cinematography Department, Nguyễn Phúc Thanh, believes that the film industry talents are Vietnamese screenwriters, directors, and cinematographers, rather than well-known actors who drive top-down film projects, as had often been the case: "From now on, private producers can choose the stories and scripts they want. We aim to provide better conditions for young filmmakers to produce quality movies to satisfy young fans."[19] In the past, the national Cinema Department might appoint a director to a project after it was already deemed worthy of funding and producing. Around the time *Bar Girls* went into production, the Socialist Republic began changing its approach to the future of national film-funding practices. The new direction encouraged more proposals, initiated from the bottom-up, that had access to other funding sources. A report indicates: "At the end of 2002, the ministry unveiled a new policy that abolished the pre-filming censorship of scripts and permits the establishment of private film studios." The aim was to encourage "competition, initiative, and investment to revitalize Vietnam's film industry."[20] However, the other stages of vetting carried out by the Cinematography Department's Censorship Bureau have remained in place. The Enterprise Law reform policy came into being in this context. (It apparently took effect in 2001, but was not enforced until February 2003.) The policy outlines very specific requirements and conditions for filmmakers:

(1) The owners or directors of film studios must be Vietnamese citizens who have their own office buildings and behavioral capability according to law;

(2) The owners and directors of Vietnamese film studios must have no criminal record related to the illegal distribution of banned cultural products;

(3) They must have graduated from a cinematographic college or university, or, alternatively, they must have been operating in the cinema industry for at least five years; and

(4) If the owners or directors of the studios are not qualified according to these criteria, they must employ film directors with cinematographic university diplomas.[21]

Of course, debates continue over the question of Vietnamese thematic content and de facto state censorship. *Bar Girls'* director Lê Hoàng states frankly, "Filmmakers usually choose scripts treating traditional subjects—war memories and socialism building—because it is the safest way to win state approval and funding."[22] But Nguyễn Văn Nam, director of the Việt Nam Film Company, expresses the following concerns: "To solve our problems, we need to look at longer term solutions. We need to pay attention to serious movies to attract audiences rather than

---

[19] Tran Dinh Thanh Lam, "Vietnam's Gritty Reality on Film," Inter Press Service, April 24, 2003. Available on *World Press Review*: http://worldpress.org/Asia/1118.cfm#down.

[20] Ibid.

[21] This announcement was found on the Vietnam Embassy English information website in the United States on February 19, 2003. It originated from the Vietnam News Agency (Government Permits Private Sector to Produce Films).

[22] Tran Dinh Thanh Lam, "Vietnam's Gritty Reality on Film."

blindly following the temporary tastes of the audience."[23] Elsewhere, Nguyễn indirectly snubs Lê: "For me, movies are art. Making films is not a game or a business."[24] Though Lê is sought out by private film companies, his contemporaries and colleagues (many of whom are funded by the state) remain critical of his more recent works, which depart from his previously renowned "serious" dramas addressing war and morality, such as *Lương tâm bé bỏng* (Pure Conscience) and *Lưỡi dao* (The Knife Edge). Lê laments, "In their view, I have betrayed the country's traditional movie-making rules by taking on commercial projects." He also adds: "The young generation, especially those living in big cities, prefer to look to the future instead of the past. They enjoy stories they can relate to, dealing with love and work conflicts. Through films, they want to see a reflection of themselves and learn realistic lessons."[25] Lê Hoàng's case is therefore an excellent Vietnamese example of how an "indie" filmmaker's decision to change direction and take on a global commercial project simultaneously enables him or her to become more independent of the state *and* representative of the national film industry's future.

Like the tourists who have flocked to Vietnam in recent years, expatriate filmmakers have fallen for Ho Chi Minh City's affordable and entertaining sights and sounds. Diasporic Vietnamese filmmakers lease or purchase (using the legal names of their relatives who are legal Vietnamese residents) single-family homes that are then converted into sound studios and digital editing rooms, allowing them to employ local technical labor and homegrown talent. Ringo Lê, born Lê Quang Vinh, a UCLA Film and Television graduate, recently directed his first feature, *Chuyện tình Sài Gòn* (Saigon Love Story, 2006), whose estimated production cost was just over US$400,000. (In comparison, the cost of producing *Bar Girls* was only US$78,000.) Lê intended to make a film with "Hollywood flair' and take it on tour to international film festivals.[26] After shooting the film, he declared: "I have gained profound impressions of Vietnam during my visits here. *Saigon Love Story* will feature a new outlook on Vietnam as a rising country where today's young generation is trying to achieve its noble goals."[27]

Jumping on the production bandwagon, the first Vietnamese talent agency sprang up in 2003. The company, Việt Ảnh (literally translated as "Vietnamese Image"), is run by Bá Vũ, whose previous job included casting Vietnamese actors for the adaptation of *The Quiet American*, the first Hollywood movie shot in Vietnam. Việt Ảnh helps domestic film producers find young talent, as well as handling outsourcing for foreign productions. As a one-stop shop, his firm also specializes in building backdrops and scouting out locations.

The current trajectory for those who aspire to be up-and-coming Vietnamese "talents" often follows the Hollywood crossover model, so that actors and actresses who achieve success are often "double threats" and even "triple threats," such as Kim Khánh (*Heaven's Net*), a model, singer, and actress. Ngô Thanh Vân, aka

---

[23] Ibid.

[24] "Evolving Film Industry Faces New Challenges," *VietNam News*, October 13, 2005.

[25] Tran Dinh Thanh Lam, "Vietnam's Gritty Reality on Film."

[26] Mariam Beevi Lam, "Cultural Tourism and Phantasmatic Vietnam," in *Charlie Don't Surf: Four Vietnamese-American Artists*, ed. Việt Lê (Vancouver: Centre A, Vancouver International Centre for Contemporary Asian Art, April 2005), pp. 28–40.

[27] Trâm Anh and Lê Phương Anh, "Overseas Vietnamese Flock to Vietnam to Make Movies," trans. T. H., *Thanh Niên News*, November 19, 2004.

Veronica Ngo, began her career studying hotel management in Norway, returning after only a few years to work as a model in Vietnam. She gained celebrity as a pop/dance musician for transnational media companies and now can add actress credits to her credentials after playing roles in Ringo Lê's *Saigon Love Story*, Charlie Nguyễn's *The Rebel* (2007), and Johnny Trí Nguyễn's *Clash* (2010)—all movies by Vietnamese American directors.

Director Charlie Nguyễn in brown (top) and in white (bottom left) t-shirts on the set of *The Rebel* with his international crew[28]

While Asian American and other Vietnamese diasporic actors and actresses can barely afford the costly services of agents and other public relations personnel who typically represent professionals in the United States and in other mainstream Western film contexts, affordable talent agencies have sprung up throughout Vietnam. Producers and directors in Vietnam have also begun to import and publicize diasporic talents, such as action star and *Spiderman* stuntman Johnny Minh Trí Nguyễn, the actor Dustin Nguyễn (*21 Jumpstreet*, *V.I.P*, *Little Fish*, and Lưu Hùynh's *The Legend is Alive/Huyền Thoại Bất Tử*, 2009), and French Vietnamese reality television personality Marjolaine Buì. Just as the overseas Buì brothers employed their uncle Don Dương, the local veteran actor, in their films, so too do brothers Charlie and Johnny Nguyễn cast their uncle Nguyễn Chánh Tín, a local veteran actor and producer, in their projects. This close circuit—an extended global family of sorts—provides the basis for mutual support and cooperation between native

---

[28] Images courtesy of Charlie Nguyễn and The Weinstein Company (distributor for English territories), First Independent (theatrical), and Lightning Entertainment (foreign market).

Vietnamese and diasporic practitioners and begins to rebuild a foundation of trust among Vietnamese cultural producers, trust of the kind that has not been seen in decades past. These diasporic Vietnamese directors are not "independent" in the sense assumed in traditional Western film studies, which define "indie" films, in part, as those critical of global capitalism and its cinematic aesthetic manifestations. Often, however, their critical lenses do zoom in on the Vietnamese state's conflicted relationship to the economically expanding film industry itself. Neither do the methods adopted by these filmmakers fit the expectations that define "independent" film-funding practices as those free from any Hollywood-affiliated or corporate sponsorship. Nevertheless, the international institutions, foreign cultural foundations, and the diasporic investments from which these networked filmmakers cobble together new projects, as well as new film production and independent distribution companies, represent a new form of transnational independent film practice. Together, this network of practitioners attracts and crafts new audiences in both Vietnam and the various populations of expatriates. They must negotiate literal and cultural translations for diverse subtitling and distribution venues, and they must conform to, while pressing for changes in, the state's film studio practices and the state's cinema department's policies.

DIRECTIONS IN DO-IT-YOURSELF (DIY) VIETNAMESE CINEMA

The new wave of Vietnamese films is a bottom-up creative venture made up of contributions from both homegrown and diasporic filmmakers. It has picked up momentum, and attracted the state's interest in its wake. While it is certainly correct to note that both independent film practices in Vietnam, and the state's response to such practices, reveal "a series of ad hoc responses to a highly fluid situation where opportunities are taken as they arise and an appeal to an audience is paramount,"[29] I would argue that this global, semi-independent network is most important for its valuable and highly proactive (rather than reactive) role in pushing further what could otherwise become a nationally hegemonic enterprise.[30] DIY production companies have begun to garner huge commercial successes in recent years. Lưu Huỳnh's *Áo lụa Hà Đông* (The White Silk Dress, 2006) is a lovingly told narrative coproduced by the Anh Việt Company, Phước Sang Entertainment, and the Vietnam Feature Film Studio—only the latter is a state-run entity. Đòan Minh Phượng's and Đòan Thành Nghĩa's *Hạt mưa rơi bao lâu* (Bride of Silence, 2005) is a German and Vietnamese coproduction involving Thuy Trieu Films, Moonfish Films, and James Gerrand.

---

[29] I thank one of my anonymous reviewers for this insightful observation.

[30] I use the term "semi-independent" because in Vietnam producers and directors cannot gain access to production funding free from regulation by the state film enterprise. Even if nearly all of a feature's funding derives from the private sector or foreign investment, the production must retain assistance and participation from the state's Cinema Department, resulting in some form of "coproduction" carried out in partnership with the state, a partnership that might involve partial "funding" from the Vietnam Feature Film Studio facilities or censorship production assistance or other sorts of engagement. This is a deeply complex political and economic relationship that might help to explain how film-funding sources—as well as the crediting for a specific project like *The White Silk Dress*—are cited in Vietnam in general.

Vietnamese International Film Festival 2007, featuring Lưu Hùynh's *The White Silk Dress*[31]

Other individual producers, directors, and investors have grouped together to start up small film companies. The production team of Charlie Nguyễn and Jimmy Phạm established the comparatively small Nón Lá Films before moving on to establish Cinema Pictures. Literally translated as Rice Hat Films, Nón Lá and Cinema Pictures together coproduced films such as Charlie Nguyễn's *Hùng Vương the Eighteenth* (1994) and *Chances Are* (2001). The latter was made through a collaboration with Vân Sơn Entertainment, a leading diasporic music, comedy, and variety production house that has employed many of Vietnam's budding filmmakers. By the time Charlie Nguyễn was ready to make *Dòng máu anh hùng* (The Rebel), his brother-in-law, Jimmy Nghiêm Phạm, had cofounded Chánh Phương Pictures in Vietnam in cooperation with his wife and Charlie Nguyễn's sister, Tawny Thanh Trúc Nguyễn. Lâm Nguyễn and Trúc Hồ, head of Asia Entertainment and Saigon Broadcasting Television Network, coproduced Hàm Trần's *Vượt Sóng* (Journey from the Fall, 2007) with other private, individual investors. Hàm Trần edited Vietnamese American director Victor Vũ's *First Morning* (2003), and Charlie Nguyễn's *The Rebel*, while Gauger acted and directed lighting in *The Rebel*. Timothy Bùi, Hàm Tràn, and Jimmy Nghiêm Phạm together served as executive directors for Gauger's *Cú và chim se sẻ* (Owl and the Sparrow, 2007). The latter stars *Journey from the Fall* actress Cát Ly alongside local Vietnamese actors. Gauger decided to cast Cát Ly based, in part, on her performance in Trần's film, and he first met his male lead, domestic actor Lê Thế Lữ (also the lead in *Buffalo Boy*), while watching casting auditions for *The Rebel*. These contemporary indie filmmakers all work with local, individual actors and crew members, as well as state-funded or operated networks. Likewise, an actor like Johnny Minh Trí Nguyễn would work in Vietnamese American (*First Morning, The Rebel*), French Vietnamese (*Saigon Eclipse*), and "native" Vietnamese films (*Hồn*

---

[31] Image courtesy of VAALA (Vietnamese American Arts and Letters Association) Curator and VIFF 2007 Co-Director Ýsa Lê, and Director Lưu Hùynh.

Trương Ba da hàng thịt, Souls on Swings, 2006).[32] Indeed, respected mainstream domestic filmmakers, such as Nguyễn Vinh Sơn (*Đất Phương Nam,* Song of the South, 1998), are also learning more about the process of digital video production from Gauger and others in order to find and develop alternative indie channels.

Stephane Gauger and his Vietnamese film crew on the set of *Owl and the Sparrow*[33]

To the extent that these works are neither fully state controlled and funded, nor Hollywood produced and marketed, they represent a newly negotiated form of "global indie networks." Although the global and the local are brought together in these circulations, and international audiences continue to conflate Vietnamese and expatriate filmmakers, increasingly these films are not about the nation as a unified entity—a condition that perhaps conflicts with the desires of the national Vietnamese audience. The state must also ride the new transnational Vietnamese film wave, which means it must work with overseas filmmakers and diasporic communities nurtured on a certain level of aesthetic liberty and cultural freedom. In her contribution to the volume *Global Networks, Linked Cities*, Saskia Sassen elucidates the role of increasingly crucial regions and cities in international economic processes.[34] This kind of linkage extends now to California's Westminster and Garden Grove, the

---

[32] I have not included Vietnamese American director Victor Vũ's large body of work here as he has shot more centrally in the United States. However, he is part of this same network, as evidenced by his casting of actors Long Nguyễn (*Journey from the Fall*) and Johnny Nguyễn in his 2003 film, *First Morning.*

[33] Photo courtesy of Stephane Gauger.

[34] Saskia Sassen, ed., in her introduction to *Global Networks, Linked Cities* (New York, NY: Routledge, 2002).

hotbeds of diasporic media production, and Ho Chi Minh City, Vietnam, which offers a wealth of natural and urban resources. Writer Andrew Lâm has analyzed the ways in which a successful transnational indie martial arts flick like *The Rebel* has the potential to "reconcile feuding Viets," referring to the long-standing history of anti-communist protests by diasporic Vietnamese communities and the consequent alienation of expatriates from the Vietnamese.[35]

Those responsible for these indie collective ventures have been savvy in placing their work at Asian and Southeast Asian film festivals, as well as at choice European, Canadian, and American film festivals. In addition, allies of Vietnamese indie cinema have started their own festivals. One such success story was the founding of the Vietnamese International Film Festival (VIFF) in 2003 by the community-based, not-for-profit organization VAALA (Vietnamese American Arts and Letters Association) in Westminster, California. Founding coproducer Ýsa D. Lê has led VIFF in its evolution as an enriching and complex festival that screens both Vietnamese and diasporic films from around the world; she accomplished this by organizing the festival within Orange County, California, home of the largest Little Saigon outside of Vietnam. She maintains frequent contact with a global range of filmmakers, introducing them to one another and offering a portal for Vietnamese film news. In essence, she is putting some indirect pressure on Vietnam to build its own institutional infrastructure for promotion of the film industry by exerting effort and achieving results that overshadow and contrast with the state's own minimal output.

Despite the successes achieved through this new wave of Vietnamese collaborations, problems do still exist for indie filmmakers. Active efforts to cooperate with international companies and individuals might evolve into increasing dependence on foreign and diasporic collaborators without the accompanying construction of a homegrown cinema infrastructure, no matter how limited. The biggest concern, however, is probably domestic: political censorship in Vietnam still threatens to restrict creative content. For example, director Hàm Trần could not shoot his award-winning *Journey from the Fall* in Vietnam for the simple reason that it depicts the postwar re-education camps of political prisoners, another history the current administration prefers to render invisible. After an unsuccessful attempt to acquire permission through proper formal channels from the Vietnamese Cinema Department, Hàm Trần was forced to make his film in Thailand, a decision that translates into an economic and professional loss of opportunities for actors, artists, and film crews in Vietnam. If Malaysian filmmaker Amir Muhammad and Singaporean director Martyn See could joke at the 2006 Annual Association for Southeast Asian Cinemas conference about the fact that they had managed to produce and screen politically critical films by releasing them in a sister country in order to bypass strict censorship laws at home, perhaps "the Vietnamese diaspora" and "the Vietnamese homeland" can serve similar functions for one another.

---

[35] Andrew Lâm, "Martial Arts Film Reconciles Feuding Viets," *New American Media*, August 6, 2007, http://news.newamericamedia.org/news/view_article.html?article_id=65fc83306d13dfbe0c0204ee394a3397, last accessed April 21, 2011.

Official poster of Hàm Trần's diasporic indie favorite, *Vượt sóng* (Journey from the Fall) highlights its impressive film festival distinctions[36]

Other industry concerns include shared difficulties with distribution and circulation that trouble filmmakers on both the Vietnamese and diasporic sides of the Pacific. The reasons why many "indie" films are given only a limited release in Vietnam may have to do with state control over piracy and diasporic control of revenue, but this does not explain the confinement of film archives, the limited materials available through libraries, and the restricted access to film scholarship in-country. Film criticism is rarely sold in bookstores, and once the first print run of such a book has been sold out, the few available copies tend to be scattered through a handful of national libraries and accessible through no other outlet. Domestic film

---

[36] Permission to reprint poster courtesy of Hàm Trần and Imaginasian.

criticism, education, and scholarship must also catch up with international academic audiences.

For Vietnamese filmmakers, the effort to reel in a reliable American or European distributor is just as taxing as the initial pitch to secure production funds. Hàm Trần's film had difficulties penetrating the so-called "respectable" independent theater chains Laemmle and Landmark, even though these are known in the United States as art-house friendly promoters of foreign films. (Some people have criticized these companies for being biased in favor of European foreign films rather than those from the global South.) *The Rebel* was picked up for distribution by the Weinstein Company, but still had to do much of its own "ethnic" promotion and help facilitate domestic and international circulation.[37]

The possibilities for indie filmmaking in Vietnam and among Vietnamese diasporic communities are inextricably linked. It is extremely difficult to salvage and follow the lineage of this form of independent transnational cinematic collaboration from Vietnam film historical records alone because of the limited amounts of prewar scholarship available and accessible to postwar critics and researchers; any serious attempt to follow this thread is both a multidisciplinary feat and political gesture. On November 1, 2007, the Cinema Department of Vietnam was moved from under the authority of the Ministry of Culture and Information to the National Administration of Tourism, Leisure, and Sports. What will this mean for the amounts of funding domestic filmmakers can hope to receive? What will this mean for the kinds of content produced by foreign film companies that will be encouraged to invest heavily in Vietnam's natural and developing commercial resources? Given its current directions, how Vietnamese and diasporic indie filmmaking develop in the next few years will have far-reaching implications not only for the film culture of Vietnam, but for future revisions of Vietnamese cultural history itself. Critics and audiences can continue to encourage the state's loosening of arts regulations and restrictions, at the same time that they challenge Vietnamese and diasporic filmmakers to craft inventive, novel stories about Vietnamese life, love, and loss. The political and historical scope of this kind of transnational cultural citizenship is something critics in Vietnam are not currently comfortable discussing overtly, but one that they certainly have on their minds. For better and for worse, this global film activism can only help to bolster and enliven the state's film industry, and thereby increase its cultural tourism revenue as well.

SELECTED FILMOGRAPHY

Gái nhảy (Bar Girls, by Lê Hoàng, 2003)
Hạt mưa rơi bao lâu (Bride of Silence, by Đòan Minh Phượng's and Đòan Thành Nghĩa, 2005)
Mùa len trâu (Buffalo Boy, by Nghiêm-Minh Nguyễn-Võ, 2004)
Chances Are (Charlie Nguyễn, 2001)

---

[37] I extend my gratitude to Ýsa Lê, Hàm Trần, Minh Nguyễn-Võ, Charlie Nguyễn, and Stephane Gauger for sharing their works and experiences to assist me in my larger research project. I also want to note that what may appear to be an imbalance in the number of images from Vietnam relative to those from the diaspora results from the difficulties of acquiring reproduction permissions rather than a desire on my part to privilege a particular filmmaker over others.

Clash (Lê Thanh Sơn, 2010)
Collective Flat (Việt Linh, 1999)
Cyclo (Trần Anh Hùng, 1995)
Deserted Valley (*Thung Lũng Hoang Vắng*, by Phạm Nhuệ Giang, 2002)
Escape (Phạm Nhuệ Giang, 1995)
First Morning (Victor Vũ, 2003)
Green Dragon (Timothy Linh Bùi, 2001)
Mùa ổi (Guava Season, by Đặng Nhật Minh, 2001)
Hùng Vương the Eighteenth (Charlie Nguyễn, 1994)
Vượt sóng (Journey from the Fall, by Hàm Trần, 2007)
Cú và chim se sẻ (Owl and the Sparrow, by Stephen Gauger, 2007)
Passage of Life (Lưu Hùynh, 1999)
Đời cát (Sand Life, by Nguyễn Thanh Vân, 2000)
Saì Gòn Nhật Thực (Saigon Eclipse, by Othello Khanh, 2007)
Chuyện tình Saì Gòn (Saigon Love Story, by Ringo Lê, 2006)
Scent of Green Papaya (Trần Anh Hùng, 1993)
The Birds Were Singing in the Quiet Place (Việt Linh, 1986)
The Coolie Child (Phạm Nhuệ Giang, 1992)
The Devil's Mark (Việt Linh, 1992)
The Deserted Valley (Phạm Nhuệ Giang, 2002)
The Legend is Alive (*Huyền Thoại Bất Tử*, by Lưu Hùynh, 2009)
The Rebel (Charlie Nguyễn, 2007)
The Traveling Circus (Việt Linh, 1989)
The Trial Needs a Presiding Judge (Việt Linh, 1987)
The White Silk Dress (*Áo luạ Hà Đong*, by Lưu Hùynh, 2006)
Three Seasons (Tony Bùi, 1999)

Auteur-ing Malaysia: Yasmin Ahmad and Dreamed Communities

Benjamin McKay[1]

On March 8, 2008, the citizens of Malaysia went to the polls in their twelfth general elections of the postcolonial period. Those same citizens surprised themselves and the political pundits by shaking up the established political order and opening the possibility that a time might soon come when a new political order could take over the corridors of power in this most diversely complex of Southeast Asian nations. The ruling coalition, Barisan Nasional (National Front), was returned to power, but with a much-reduced majority, and, more tellingly, they lost control of five of the key states of the federation to the emerging coalition of opposition parties, the *Pakatan Rakyat* (People's Alliance). The certainties of the political order that was created in the wake of the racial riots of 1969 had been thoroughly contested by an electorate that chose, in part, to consider an alternative political, social, economic, and cultural vision for Malaysia. Many commentators detected in the electorate a heartfelt shift away from a belief in the race-based politics that has been the norm in Malaysia since its independence. Is a politics of inclusion now possible?

One of the consistent themes of Malaysian political discourse is the vexed question of what might constitute the inherent features of Malaysian identity. Who can lay claim to a sense of belonging that transcends the merely bureaucratic imprimatur of citizenship? How do you reconcile the emotional and cultural legacies of ethnic Malay-centricity, bound up as it is in a range of contested notions of Malay identity, modes of custom, and the powerful claims of Islam, with the competing aims and ideals of an inclusive polity that embraces its ethnic diversity and seeks to

---

[1] *Editor's note:* After Yasmin Ahmad passed away in 2009, Benjamin McKay intended to make some minor revisions to this draft. But his turn came too soon, and just a year later Benjamin, too, was gone. Thus, this version of his essay, complete in itself and representative of the warmth and clarity of his intellectual voice, should be read in conjunction with the beautiful love letter that Benjamin contributed to the Southeast Asian cinema online journal *Criticine* in remembrance of Yasmin, available at www.criticine.com/feature_article.php?id=44&pageid=1262670272, accessed on June 8, 2011.

create by 2020 a *Bangsa Malaysia* (Malaysian "race")?[2] Indeed, can the development of a truly national and cohesive Malaysian identity produce cultural products that actually reflect such an emerging supra-identity?

There is a rather spurious assumption that modern postcolonial Malay(si)a was born out of an elite-driven negotiation between Malay aristocrats and their British colonial overlords, and that the birth of Malaysia was largely undisturbed by the bloodier and more ideologically driven national awakenings that characterize so many of Malaysia's immediate neighbors. Such an assumption merely grants triumph to those who were triumphant, ignoring, as it, does the very bloody contestation of the so-called Communist Emergency and the competing visions of how a postcolonial Malay(si)a might have taken shape. Maintaining the postcolonial status quo has also not been without its challenges, but the effort to maintain harmony alongside fast-paced development has largely been achievable, to date, through a sometimes uneasy alliance between an ethnically Malay dominated hegemonic elite and a coalition of political groups that claim to represent the diverse numbers of "other" ethnic groups that make up the Malaysian mosaic.

Malaysia seems, on the surface, to conform to Benedict Anderson's notions of an "imagined community,"[3] but, as I will examine further, there is a gulf between surface reality and actual practice. Given the very plural nature of Malaysian society, with its multiethnic, religiously diverse peoples speaking a variety of languages, who all find themselves economically situated on different sides of the very palpable barriers of class, it is also possible to see contemporary Malaysia as akin to what Gayatri Spivak describes as an essentially "artificial construct."[4] It is, naturally, not difficult to connect the somewhat vague certainties of the imaginary with artificiality, and some of the assertions and assumptions that this chapter makes are not always necessarily speaking to Malaysia alone—but there are historic and cultural legacies of the Malaysian imaginary that can and do shape a peculiarly localized brand of artificiality.

This chapter explores the interface between the imaginary and artificiality of Malaysian identity as seen through a critical examination of three films by the independent Malaysian filmmaker Yasmin Ahmad. Those films are *Sepet* (Slit-eyes, 2005), *Gubra* (Anxiety, 2006) and *Mukhsin* (2007). I argue here that her vision of Malaysian plurality and the liberal humanist tone and tenor of her films help to define those characteristics of her work that mark Yasmin Ahmad as a serious contender for the title of "indie auteur." That her filmic work also shapes an imaginary (*her* imaginary) of contemporary Malaysia leads me to ponder whether or not a truly imagined community actually exists in Malaysia. The critical examination to follow argues that, rather than seeking a fully-fledged imagined community, we might better argue for the possibilities of a "dreamed community."

---

[2] Former Malaysian Prime Minister Tun Dr. Mahathir Mohammad developed a policy known as *Wawasan 2020* (Vision 2020), which sought to achieve fully developed nation status for Malaysia by the year 2020. As part of the grand scheme of such development, it was envisaged that a key component in the process (one of nine such components) would be the emergence of a truly Malaysian identity that would supersede the narrow confines of ethnic plurality. Dr. Mahathir articulated a Malaysian "race" as *Bangsa Malaysia*.

[3] Benedict Anderson, *Imagined Communities: Reflections on the Origin and Spread of Nationalism* (London: Verso, 2006).

[4] Gayatri Spivak, *The Post-Colonial Critic* (New York, NY: Routledge, 1990), p. 39.

If my use of the term "auteur" appears at times to have multiple meanings, then that is deliberate. I argue that Yasmin, in her films, is authoring a dreamed image of Malaysia that speaks to a variety of contested realities. I also argue that, as a director, she employs a recognizable cinematic style in rendering such authorship; and that, in terms of cinematography, editing, *mise en scène*, narrative structure, pace, and the use of music and sound, Yasmin has created a unique visual and aural presence on the screen that speaks to more traditional theories of cinematic authorship. What will largely inform the assessment that follows is the manner in which the three films discussed here collectively become emblematic of a palpable body of work that speaks as much to style and form as it does to theme and content.

If the historical legacy of Malay-language cinema is considered alongside much of the output of the contemporary Malaysian mainstream cinema, then a mono-ethnic Malaysia, largely defined and inhabited by ethnic Malays, would seem to predominate. In his own particular contribution to defining the concepts of national cinema, Anthony Smith has utilized the term "ethnoscape" to evoke a sense of "ethnic atmosphere,"[5] where "the territory mirrors the ethnic community by the communal events and processes whose relics and monuments dot its landscape, so that the land comes to belong to a people in the same way as the people belong to a particular land."[6] Cinematically, is it possible for non-Malay Malaysians to enter their own ethnoscape, and can such an ethnoscape be shared? In Yasmin Ahmad's *Gubra,* Alan, a Chinese Malaysian character, says to Orked, a young Malay woman, "Sometimes I wonder if you guys realize just how hard it is for the rest of us to live here. It's like being in love with someone who doesn't love you back."

Since the early years of the new millennium, a burgeoning indie film movement in Malaysia has challenged such mono-ethnicity, and a particularly dynamic and collegial community of young filmmakers has brought very personal visions of life in a cosmopolitan Malaysia to the screen. Filmmakers as varied in approach and style as Amir Muhammad, James Lee, Bernard Chauly, Ho Yuhang, Deepak Kumaran Menon, Tan Chui Mui, Woo Min Jing, and Azharr Rudin have challenged the established imaginary and sought, instead, to infuse their works with a diversity as marked as the very diversity of the country in which they shoot their films. Yasmin Ahmad has been a key player in rejuvenating Malaysian cinema.

In 2007, Yasmin Ahmad released *Mukhsin,* the third film in a trilogy that details several stages in the life of Orked, the young Malay woman mentioned earlier. Considered a champion of the spirit of independent filmmaking, Yasmin Ahmad brought her trilogy well and truly into the mainstream. This chapter assesses the manner in which this filmmaker confronted the contested terrain of Malaysian national identity and the conflicting claims for inclusion within that terrain. Her work has generated, at times, some heated controversy within Malaysia, as she has deliberately challenged certain shibboleths of Malay identity—both in terms of *adat* (Malay customs) and Islam—but, as the following assessment reveals, her challenges and critiques are also, at times, paradoxically shaped and reshaped in her work by the hegemonic claims and demands of mainstream political, social, and religious discourses. Her work tends to illuminate the precarious and confused process of

---

[5] Anthony Smith, "Images of the Nation: Cinema, Art, and National Identity," in *Cinema and Nation,* ed. M. Hjort and S. Mackenzie (London and New York, NY: Routledge, 2000), p. 51.

[6] Ibid., pp. 54–55.

attempting to make something real and tangible from that which may, ultimately, be only dreamed.

POSITIONING YASMIN

Regarding *Sepet*, Yasmin Ahmad has said that all she wanted to make was a simple little love story.[7] If one considers only the surface of this work, one might agree with her, for *Sepet* largely conforms to many of our genre-bound expectations of a romantic love story, but the politics of "race" in Malaysia makes an interracial love story a matter far more complex than the simplicities of romance. Indeed, there is ample evidence in the media coverage and online debates that took place after the release of the film to suggest that there were great divisions in Malaysian society about the representation on screen of a Malay girl (Orked) in love with a Chinese Malaysian boy (Jason). The manner in which the unfolding narrative of their love for one another explores a range of identity issues peculiar to Malaysia, including those that pertain to notions of perceived purity and to cultural hybridity, proved problematic.

With the release of the sequel *Gubra,* a television forum took place on a program called *Fenomena Seni* (Arts Phenomena), which aired on April 23, 2006, on the national broadcasting station RTM1. The episode was titled "*Sepet* dan *Gubra* Pencemar Budayar" (*Sepet* and *Gubra*: Cultural Corruptors). Three speakers attempted to debate the issues raised by the two films, with two of the participants virulently opposed to a range of on-screen images, including a husband cooking in his wife's kitchen (*Gubra*), an Islamic religious official (*bilal*) patting a stray dog (again, *Gubra*), and the appropriateness of the representation of the relationship between Orked and Jason in *Sepet*. One of the closing comments from a forum participant, herself a film producer, summed up the tone of the evening: "Malaysia belongs to the Malays. That's why it was called Tanah Melayu before."[8]

Prior to the success (and, some might add, notoriety) of *Sepet*, Yasmin already commanded a relatively high profile in Malaysia. After beginning her career as a copywriter with the advertising firm Ogilvy & Mather, she eventually rose to the position of creative director at Leo Burnett in Kuala Lumpur. Among her many high-profile clients was the national petroleum company, Petronas, for which she created long-running ad campaigns. Those advertisements are much talked about amongst television viewers in Malaysia. Often coinciding with national holiday celebrations, Petronas ads are noticeable for their "selling" of nation and national identity, rather than anything as prosaic as petroleum. In these ads, which are innovatively shot, aesthetically commanding, and often warmly sentimental, Yasmin developed a visual and narrative command of the advertising medium. Her first feature (originally made for television) was *Rabun* (My Failing Eyesight, 2003), a highly personal film that allegorically equated failing eyesight with an inability to see the true worth of those around us. It was a noticeable debut, no less for the fact that it centered upon a very loving relationship between an aging married couple, said to be in part based upon Yasmin's own parents.

---

[7] This was revealed in conversation with the author and is a statement articulated by Yasmin Ahmad in numerous interviews and public forums since the release of the film.

[8] *Tanah Melayu* is literally "Land of the Malays." For more on that forum, see Jacqueline Ann Surin, "One Reality to Rule Us All," *The Sun,* Kuala Lumpur, May 4, 2006, available at www.sun2surf.com/article.cfm?id=14019 (last accessed on May 1, 2011).

Yasmin has been a staunch supporter of her fellow indie filmmakers, even though she herself finds the term "indie" problematic. In conversation, she decries the term "indie," arguing that it no longer serves as a reliable label, but now suggests that "indie films" constitute an exclusive genre in and of themselves. Her works do challenge any rigid definition of "independent"; *Mukhsin*, the third film in her trilogy, was released locally by a mainstream Malaysian production house, and therefore may have compromised notions of what "independent filmmaking" means. Yet I will ascribe the label "indie" to her overall body of work based on her strong authorial voice, independent spirit, and stance. Others have also recognized that her work is at odds with the content and sensibilities of mainstream commercial Malaysian cinema, and I will discuss the fact that her oeuvre complements the overall output of indie films in Malaysia. Her work has been successful on the international festival circuit, winning numerous awards, and has been the subject of several retrospectives internationally.

Sepet

Set in the city of Ipoh, in the Malaysian state of Perak, *Sepet* is largely concerned with the relationship between Orked, a Malay high-school student, and Jason, a Chinese Malaysian who makes a living selling pirated VCDs (video compact disc). The two youngsters meet at a market while Orked is out with a friend. The attraction between the two protagonists is apparent from the outset, and the narrative follows them as they commence dating. Orked has a supportive and loving family that allows her the freedom to pursue her relationship with Jason. He, on the other hand, comes from a troubled home and remains secretive at first about his relationship with Orked. He has a close and loving bond with his Peranakan mother, but his father is a violent and abusive figure.[9]

Jason's loving relationship with Orked is soon complicated by Jason's peripheral involvement with local gangsters. He and his group of friends are often at the mercy of these gangsters and pay them protection money. He finds himself coerced into having an affair with Maggie, the sister of a gangster, and she becomes pregnant. Her brother has been apprehended by the police and faces a jail sentence. Under those circumstances, Jason agrees to try and stand by Maggie and their unborn child. Orked ends the relationship after Jason confesses his situation to her in a letter.

Orked is awarded a scholarship to further her studies abroad. While driving to the airport, Orked realizes that she still harbors great affection for Jason. Her mother gives Orked an as-yet-unread letter from Jason, and suggests that she should read it. Upon doing so, Orked attempts to call Jason, who is also en route to the airport in an attempt to say farewell to her. The narrative is difficult to translate to the written page at this juncture, as we are soon aware that Jason has had an accident on his motorcycle and appears to be dead, but in a parallel shot we see Orked talking to Jason and offering him a loving farewell. The film ends on this ambiguous note.

This ambiguity led to much conjecture upon the release of the film. Many people surmised that it was a deliberate ploy on the filmmaker's part to impart a surrealistic air to the finale of the film, but such a ploy would be at odds with the rest of *Sepet*

---

[9] "Peranakan" is a term for the hybrid culture that developed as a result of the intermarriage of Chinese migrant men with local Malay woman. The distinctive culture is largely found in Malacca, Penang, and Singapore.

stylistically and would have compromised the narrative integrity of the film up to that point in the storyline. Others accused the director of lacking the courage to fulfill the promise of the interracial love affair and of deciding, therefore, to remove Jason from the equation. Again, I believe that reading to be too simplistic. A more nuanced and politically grounded examination of the film itself is needed to account for the ambiguous ending.

The film opens with a swathe of images and juxtaposed dialogues that affirm that what we are about to encounter in *Sepet* is a celebration of the Malaysian capacity to transgress otherwise rigidly defined cultural boundaries and recognize the "other" that dwells within. The opening slide is in Arabic, and soon afterwards we hear a male voice (Jason's) reciting poetry in Mandarin. The translated poem, we soon learn, is by Tagore, and is being read to Jason's mother. The mother speaks to her son in Malay, and he replies to her in Cantonese. She wears a traditional *baju kebaya* (a fitted blouse worn over a sarong), and he looks like he might be off to a karaoke bar. We then segue to a scene of a Malay girl (Orked), dressed in her *telekung* (prayer clothes), reciting the Koran. When she removes her prayer veil, we see in her wardrobe pictures of the Taiwanese-Japanese film star Takeshi Kaneshiro. Her mother calls out for her in Malay, to which she replies in English.

Both linguistic fluidity and cultural hybridity are features of Malaysian life, but the opening scenes described above are staged to reinforce a perception of multiculturalism rather than truly reflecting the linguistic and cultural mélange of contemporary Malaysian practice. These scenes are more thematically driven than grounded in performed realism. Given the manner in which the narrative later unfolds, these establishing scenes tend to reflect optimistic possibilities rather than grounded practice.

Among the many criticisms raised by conservative Malaysian commentators in response to this film was a recurring objection to the liberal and open manner in which Orked and her family conducted their relationship. If they meant to point out that such a familial environment was not truly reflective of family practice in broader Malay society, then perhaps the criticism has some merit, but I would argue that this film never attempts to document mainstream normative cultural practices but instead celebrates a particularized example of an exception to normative mainstream behavior. As Alfian Sa'at commented in his review of *Sepet*, "One function of art is of course to reflect reality as we know it. But another much-neglected function is to propose other realities, to portray exceptions, because these lead us to imagining possibilities."[10] In imagining possibilities, Yasmin the auteur is fashioning a dreamed Malaysia cloaked in a liberal openness that evokes one of the many competing visions of what a concrete and palpably imagined Malaysian community might mean.

What the detractors of *Sepet* and Yasmin's later films have failed largely to notice is the manner in which the liberal humanist vision of the director is paradoxically reshaped, and subversively nuanced, by the very forces of cultural hegemony with which they claim she is in conflict. How else can we understand the ambiguity of the ending of *Sepet*? How else do we explain the conclusion of the trilogy in the nostalgic resuscitation of an older Malay film genre with the romance in the idyllic *kampung* in

---

[10] Alfian Sa'at, "Eyes Wide Shut," *Kakiseni*, February 21, 2005, previously available at www.kakiseni.com printpage.php?page=articlebody&id=629 (accessed on January 15, 2009).

Mukhsin?[11] How else can we account for the failure of liberal possibilities to translate into fully fledged liberal certainties?

By analyzing the essentially transgressive nature of the representation of women in *Sepet*, and the manner in which such representations may "contravene some of the teachings of *adat* and Islam, rendering [Orked as] potentially a 'threat' to communal purity and integrity," Melissa Wong contends "that the film encourages a reassessment of the liminal space that is the Malaysian community as either liberating and promising, or fraught with unspoken bigotry and division."[12] Wong believes that the ambiguity of the ending of *Sepet* reinforces the latter sense of bigotry, even though the film to that point largely worked at the level of celebrating what was liberating and promising. Wong claims that this anomaly, in fact, reflects the same ambivalent and ambiguous lack of substance in the definitions and possibilities inherent in the Malaysian government's rhetoric about the creation of an inclusive Malaysian "race."

I would further argue, therefore, that *Sepet*, like *Gubra* and *Mukhsin*, is an exploration of a possibility that is ultimately thwarted by the filmmaker's incapacity to resolve matters of purity and hybridity in any other realm but that which is dreamed. I therefore see the ambiguity of the ending of *Sepet* as neither surreal (except where we accept the surreal nature of dreams themselves) nor as a failure on the part of the director to allow the love affair to reach its interracially concrete fulfillment. Instead, the voice of Jason on the phone, even after we have witnessed him lying in a pool of his own blood, is, in fact, an element in a dream sequence, and my reading of this scene is supported by the intertextual references to the love affair between Jason and Orked that occur in their own dreamlike fashion in key sequences in the two subsequent films of this trilogy. To imagine a Malaysia that could reconcile purity and hybridity lies at the heart of the vague and contested rhetoric of *Bangsa Malaysia,* and if such rhetoric sits uncomfortably between competing hegemonies—of nation and "race"—then is not the "ambiguous" ending of *Sepet,* even after all the possibilities of liberal humanism that preceded it, paradoxically a nod to a confused but nonetheless real status quo?

Gubra

In *Gubra,* we again meet up with Orked, who, having returned to her native Ipoh after years studying in the United Kingdom, is now married to a man named Ariff. We again see how she relates to her warm, loving, liberal, and decidedly eccentric family. *Gubra* has more narrative complexity than *Sepet*, weaving in and out of a number of seemingly unrelated stories that all build to a rumination on the redemptive power of love.

Orked's story follows her through the disintegration of her marriage to a weak and pathetic Malay womanizer while at the same time it explores her burgeoning

---

[11] The *kampung* is described by historian Jim Baker as an integrated and self-sustaining social unit whose values and customs "still help define what it means to be a Malay." James Baker, *Crossroads: A Popular History of Malaysia and Singapore* (Singapore: Marshall Cavendish, 2008), p. 26. Often translated into English as "village," the *kampung* is the geographical, social, economic, and cultural entity that developed Malay *adat* and continues to be seen as a repository of Malay traditional values, justice, and customs.

[12] Melissa Wong, "The Paradoxes of *Sepet*: Hybridity, Women, and the 'Bangsa Malaysia' Dilemma" (MA thesis, Monash University Malaysia, 2006), pp. 3–4.

friendship with Alan, the brother of the deceased Jason. Concurrently, we explore the relationships among a *bilal*, his wife, and their neighbors, two female sex workers.[13] Interspersed throughout the film are vignettes that further explore the thematic issues of love and cross-cultural connectivity—in scenes that again revisit the family dynamics of both Orked's and Jason's parents, siblings, and the reappearance of Orked's family's maid.

In a review of the film that I wrote for the online arts journal *Kakiseni,* I observed that:

> [in] Yasmin Ahmad's Malaysia, it appears possible for a Chinese Malaysian man to give a Malay woman a ride in his truck and discuss his unrequited love for his country and then for her to show great empathy and understanding in return. It is also possible for us to believe that a *bilal* and his wife can and do extend true love, support, and commitment to their sex-worker neighbors and that those neighbors are more complex than our usual sex-worker stereotypes.[14]

The fact that these elements of the film, among others, ignited considerable controversy and debate in Malaysia perhaps only reinforces the gulf that exists between the dreamed Malaysia, so awkwardly articulated in political rhetoric, and the much more rigidly divided communities of Malaysia that exist in practice.

In giving shape thematically to her authored Malaysia, Yasmin Ahmad also concurrently reinforces, through her cinema practice, many of the traits that give her work auteur credibility. Through her characteristically long takes, nicely framed and shot scenes that fuse character and place, and her interestingly paced segues and vignettes, Yasmin Ahmad demonstrates her strong visual capacity to bridge cinematic form and content. In creating her complex ethnoscape, she blends polyglot musical, cultural, and religious references, and weaves these with a deft flair for capturing both space and place. I wrote in that same *Kakiseni* review:

> [o]ne of the inherent strengths of *Gubra*—and this makes it a better film in fact than *Sepet*—is its attempt to explore the Malaysian emotional landscape by deftly pitching that examination at the borders between the private and public spaces of Malaysian life—between what occurs on the domestic front and in the shared spaces of a city like Ipoh.[15]

On screen, Yasmin blurs the boundaries of space and place, of the domestic and the public spheres, and this method may also have contributed to some of the conservative backlash her work has often incited. The *bilal* and his wife are seen flirtatiously playing around in their kitchen—this may indeed happen, but detractors are uncomfortable with its representation on screen. Technically and stylistically, these terrains are often nicely juxtaposed by the contrasts of night and day, of light and dark, and the visually powerful and emotionally resonant contrasts between bright light and shadows. Like *Sepet*, this film is perhaps at its most awkward when

---

[13] A *bilal* looks after the *surau*, or house of prayer, and recites the call to Muslim prayer.

[14] Benjamin McKay, "Imaginary Homeland Gubra: Does a Tolerant Malaysia Only Exist in Yasmin Ahmad's Movies?," *Kakiseni*, April 14, 2006, previously available at www.kakiseni.com/print/articles/reviews/MDg1MA.html (accessed on January 15, 2009).

[15] Ibid.

the themes of multiculturalism are verbally articulated and more powerful when they are visually conveyed.

It is in this film that we see Orked finally addressing her depth of feeling and grief resulting from having lost Jason. This is most simply reflected in her friendship with his brother, Alan, and in the scene where Alan presents her with a box of photos, letters, books, and other memorabilia from Jason's and Orked's relationship that he had found among Jason's possessions. Included in this box is the damaged cell phone that lay at the heart of *Sepet*'s ambiguous conclusion. Earlier, Alan had told Orked how strange it was that Jason's cell phone had been found ringing at his accident scene by passers-by. While looking at this box of memorabilia and while holding the damaged phone, Orked weeps, and if the audience of the earlier film had had any doubts about whether a conversation had indeed taken place between the two lovers at that ambiguous moment of closure in *Sepet*, it appears to be laid to rest here.

The link to the dream element that I mentioned earlier involving the ending of *Sepet* comes, indeed, at the end of *Gubra*, after the final credits have rolled. In perhaps a cheeky nod and wink to her audience, Yasmin closes the film with a dream sequence that has Orked in bed asleep. She is awakened by a phone call. From across the bed there emerges a hand and a slight sweep shot reveals that Orked is in bed with Jason. He asks her who called, and she replies that it was her mother, of course. They snuggle together and return to sleep. It would appear that Yasmin is implying that true eternal love can and will survive in the heart, even if it, in fact, remained unconsummated. That theme is again revisited in *Mukhsin*. Love lasts eternally in our cross-cultural dream sequences, but becomes again more problematic in the grounded realities of contemporary multicultural Malaysia.

If *Sepet* explored the dynamic cultural diversity that makes Malaysia what it is and the manner in which two young lovers attempt to traverse the boundaries inherent in that diversity, then *Gubra* explores the spiritual complexities of Malaysian life and the collective capacity for redemption that can be found in both love and in the spiritual domain. The film ends with multiple segues that link—visually and thematically—devotees at a family altar, in a church, and in Muslim prayer. Linking the search for solace and redemption in their seemingly seamless closing rituals, the film concludes with a dark screen emblazoned with the words of a Sufi poet, "The Lamps Are Different, But The Light Is The Same." Here the filmmaker touches upon a sense of universality that lies at the heart of the very contested Malaysian contemporary discourse on interfaith connections, and these obvious references to interfaith and universality were additional causes of controversy in the reception of this film in Malaysia.[16] Her depiction in this film of a loving, caring, and forgiving Islam proved to be most unpopular with religious hardliners.

With the film *Mukhsin*, Yasmin Ahmad ties up her trilogy on cross-cultural connectivity, universality, and the manner in which love can be harbored forever in our dreams, if not in practice. Given the current political and social climate in Malaysia, it is perhaps not too surprising to see the director return to youthful simplicity by way of resuscitating an old Malay film genre that is centered in the certainties of the *kampung*. This chapter now concludes with an assessment of

---

[16] Recent attempts in Malaysia to conduct interfaith dialogues have met with public protests and condemnation from many quarters, including from the prime minister, who claimed that such forums only ignite passionate debate on "sensitive" issues that should not be discussed.

Mukhsin, arguably the best of the three films, if not also the most politically problematic.

Mukhsin

Mukhsin is essentially a prequel to the earlier *Sepet* and *Gubra,* which transports us back to a time when Orked was just ten years of age and living in the idyllic world of a rural *kampung.* It is also the film that most succinctly brings the independent ethos that Yasmin Ahmad explored in her earlier films into the mainstream commercial Malaysian cinema. In this film, we again meet her eccentric parents and the loving maid, and we see, too, in the development of the young Orked, many of the feisty and independent traits she displayed in those earlier films that looked at her adolescence and adulthood.

In many ways this narrative mirrors that of the earlier film *Sepet*. Into Orked's life comes a young boy, Mukhsin, aged twelve. Like Jason, he comes from a troubled family background. He enters this film as a visitor who has come to stay with his aunt during the school vacation. With him is his perpetually angry and self-destructive elder brother. Mukhsin meets Orked, and the film tells of their innocent friendship and of the pangs of early adolescent love. On many levels, this is the simple little love story that Yasmin Ahmad claims she was making with *Sepet*, and the narrative is rendered all the more simple here because no cross-cultural complications have been added to the mix.

Where this film is interesting politically is the manner in which the issues that the director wishes to tackle are given fresh aesthetic and stylistic terrain through Yasmin's resuscitation of the old Malay film genre that looks specifically at *kampung* life—its idyllic setting becoming a site for the contestation of values that is shaped on screen through a heady but balanced mix of melodrama, romance, music, and comedy. The distinctly Malay *kampung* genre had its heyday in the golden era of commercial Malay cinema in the 1950s and 1960s. Many of those films used the locale to explore the battle between traditional values and encroaching modernity. Rather than revisiting those issues, Yasmin Ahmad in *Mukhsin* chooses instead to explore the battle between her own values and those of her detractors. In this sense, this is a highly personal film. The values that her two previous films explored, and the debates that those values ignited among many in the public sphere, are transplanted into fresh milieux where they may be brought to some sense of cinematic closure. Revisiting the *kampung* genre was an inspired, if albeit unintentional, move on the filmmaker's part.[17]

The film opens with a musical number during which the family, friends, and the family maid all gather around to sing and play music. The song that they sing is "Hujan" (Rain) and the performance is again not unlike the impromptu musical numbers found in old Malay movies. Yasmin has an interesting way of playing with diegetic sound, and the musical scores of her work are important. This song

---

[17] I mentioned the resuscitation of the *kampung* genre in my (online) review of *Mukhsin* in *Kakiseni,* where I elaborated further on the manner in which, stylistically, Yasmin Ahmad had given new life and purpose to an old genre (Benjamin McKay, "The Golden Age," *Kakiseni,* March 30, 2007, previously available at www.kakiseni.com/printpage.php?page=articlebody &id=1076, last accessed January 15, 2009). The filmmaker contacted me personally to say that resurrecting a genre was unintentional, but that she found my observations interesting, especially in light of my broader critique of the film.

introduces us in languid manner to the principal characters of the film, as well as to the visual styles the director employs.

Like a number of the Malay film directors of the 1950s and 1960s, Yasmin Ahmad and her cinematographer Low Keong have clearly been influenced by the great Japanese filmmakers. Some scenes are Ozu-like in terms of framing, composition, angle, and pace. There are few close-ups in the film; instead, an array of long and medium still shots capture both the frenetic pace of some scenes and the gentler, laid-back *kampung* ambiance of others. Windows and doorframes are utilized to frame actions, and this again makes for an interesting exploration of private and public spheres. Gossip is never far away in the *kampung*, often taking place on front steps and in doorways—where private domains seep into public spaces. Yasmin addresses her critics and detractors by exuberantly capturing the warmth, love, and humor of Orked's liberal family contrasted with the pious and sanctimonious hypocrisies of those unhappier souls who live near to them.

Midway through the film, there is a scene that I believe captures much of what is recognizably the essence of Yasmin's auteur ingredients, both in terms of form and content. It is night, and Orked and her family are at home with their maid and a family friend. Orked had previously had a falling out with Mukhsin and is being comforted by her parents. They put a record on the record player, and slowly they begin to dance to a song by Nina Simone. Outside in the dark of night stands Mukhsin, longingly looking in on this scene of family warmth and love—the window of the house framing him as an outsider and observer. Suddenly, the song changes diegesis as well as volume and becomes a part of the soundscape of the village as we segue to the wider world outside the previously intimate scene where we observed our characters dancing together to the recording.

When first reviewing this film, I found it to be both exuberant and intelligent and I still stand behind that assertion.[18] This is a good film, and in rereading my observations I still find much there that I agree with. It has, however, been through a reading of the three films together and in reassessing them through a small, but still necessary, window of hindsight that I find that many of the paradoxes I discerned in the politics of *Sepet* are fulfilled finally for me in *Mukhsin*. I will elaborate on this point further by way of concluding this chapter, but, for now, let me just explore how *Mukhsin* actually works.

To begin, there is the fact that the idyllic halcyon days of late childhood, early adolescence, work well with the resurrected genre format itself. For what is that genre but a reminder for contemporary audiences of the halcyon days of the nation's own early postcolonial existence? Yasmin cleverly mutes the nostalgia here, but the references and images are there for all to interpret. Those heady younger times were, of course, complex, and contested visions of the future nation were not without a degree of sometimes bloody political volatility, but there was culturally a sense of immense possibilities, and no genre in earlier Malay cinema explored those possibilities better or more consistently than the *kampung* genre. Like early postcolonial Malay(si)a, the young Orked and her immediate world have the potential to revel in the fluidity and diversity of what youth (or a young nation) might offer. Traditional values (and they are espoused often in Yasmin Ahmad's oeuvre without necessarily compromising her essentially liberal humanist position)

---

[18] Ibid.

are not necessarily at odds with a nuanced diversity that might lead, perhaps, to a fully realized and modern adulthood (both for Orked and her country).

There are, however, problems with this reading, not the least of which is: why are we returning to a halcyon past? Is it that the film is, itself, a recounted reflection of a past incident? Orked in *Gubra*, the last of the trilogy in terms of the character's development, is left alone at the end with nothing else but the dream of what might have been—the promise of cross-cultural connectivity that lay at the heart of her adolescent love for Jason, a love that was so painfully dissolved in the ambiguously "dreamed" ending of that affair in *Sepet*. The trilogy's overriding theme of the capacity of love to endure in the hearts of the lovers years after the love affair has ended is brought home to viewers most strikingly in *Mukhsin*. Again, Orked and Mukhsin are pulled apart by misunderstanding, and even though, at the end of the film, Orked attempts to find Mukhsin, she is too late, and both are left with nothing but the memories of their time together.

While *Mukhsin* is set in a decidedly more homogenous ethnoscape of a largely Malay *kampung,* the theme of multiculturalism is maintained—we learn, for instance, that Orked is being educated at a Chinese language school—a fact that clarifies certain elements in the earlier films and explains the character's linguistic fluidity and capacity. The intertextual referencing of the dreamlike eternity of Orked and Jason's partnership again is present here. Mukhsin and Orked are out in the fields flying kites when they are met by a young couple with a baby. Those familiar with the two earlier films will recognize this couple as Orked and Jason, who appear to have traversed time and space, and even death, to appear to the younger Orked in her youth. Can this be read as surreal? Or can we read this, again, as an allegorical representation of the manner in which culturally transcended love in the Malaysian context is sustained in the dream, rather than in practice? Love, consummated or not, transcends, through the dream, the barriers of a much more rigidly confused present reality.

Mukhsin closes with a musical number that reminds us that we have been on a storyteller's journey in these three films. An elderly couple sits behind a piano in the grounds of a house in the *kampung.* These are not actors; in fact, Yamin Ahmad has recruited her own parents to act in this last scene. As the classic Malay song they perform gains momentum, they are joined by the director and her film crew. As a closing scene to the film, and to the trilogy as a whole, this small celebration reminds us that we have collectively been witnessing a fiction, even while the scene remains in harmony with the older film genre that brings this trilogy to a close. It also brings us firmly back to the present.

DREAMING MALAYSIA

The general elections that took place in March of 2008 have shown that it is possible a future politics could evolve in Malaysia that might transcend rigid race-based politics. The election raised many issues that directly confronted Malay supremacy, and many voters appeared to have questioned the economic and cultural policies that have maintained that supremacy. The post-election environment has, however, reinforced the deep divisions that exist in Malaysian society, not merely between ethnic groups, but within those groups as well. In Malaysian politics, the murky divisions of ethnicity are always further complicated by the very real complexities of class. How close is Malaysia to fulfilling its 2020 goal of creating a

Malaysian "race"—a people who think outside of plural boundaries and see each other as partners in a truly imagined community? Can the competing claims of cultural purity and cultural hybridity be reconciled?

The Malaysian imagined community, as it stands now, is very much akin to Spivak's notion of an "artificial construct."[19] It is there in rhetoric, and it is performed in national rituals, and the policies designed to further the creation of *Bangsa Malaysia* have been awkwardly articulated, but the possibilities for full inclusion and the development of a concrete national imaginary conflict with hegemonic claims for Malay ethnic purity and supremacy. On the poster for Yasmin Ahmad's *Sepet* the tag line reads: "One Chinese boy—One Malay girl—One unforgettable love story." The promise of that first film in the trilogy was left unfulfilled, even though it haunts the trilogy in a series of dreamed sequences that speak to a notion of everlasting love and the possibilities of shared ethnoscape.

For all of the inherent celebration of cultural diversity and hybridity apparent in these three films, the authored nation on screen remains a fundamentally problematic place. In discussing the ending of *Sepet,* Wong suggests "that the film finally resorts to an ambiguous ending because the narrative cannot, in the final analysis, overcome the entrenched ideologies regarding race in this country, but does not wish as well to close off the possibility of a new form of identity for which Malaysians should strive."[20] For all of Yasmin Ahmad's liberal sentiments on inclusion and her celebration of diversity and hybridity, the films are ultimately framed by the schizophrenic demands of two seemingly irreconcilable strands in the contemporary Malaysian discourse on identity. The ambiguous ending of *Sepet* and the dreamed sequences of the two later films hint at possibilities that are, to date, still seemingly only attainable through dream. Perhaps this observation is further reinforced when we consider that the closing film of the trilogy cloaks its optimism by taking us to an idyllically rendered present that is fashioned through the resuscitation of a genre from a purportedly gentler and less contested past.

The authored nation here is a problematic one that straddles the lines connecting the imaginary with the limitations of artificiality. The attempt to reconcile the dream with the contemporary reality in these three films has, however, been a valiant one. In the process, a filmmaker has emerged in Malaysia who has taken the ethos of the independent cinema movement, with its desire to celebrate diversity, firmly into the mainstream culture of the country. In that journey, an auteur of recognizable talent has emerged. It now remains to be seen whether it is possible for the dreamed community that she has captured on her screen to transform itself in the long term in Malaysia, paving the way for the development, perhaps, of an inclusive, fully fledged imagined community.

SELECTED FILMOGRAPHY

All films are by Yasmin Ahmad:
Gubra (Anxiety, 2006)
Mukhsin (2007)
Rabun (My Failing Eyesight, 2003)
Sepet (Slit-eyes, 2005)

---

[19] Spivak, *The Post-Colonial Critic,* p. 39.

[20] Wong, "The Paradoxes of *Sepet*: Hybridity, Women, and the 'Bangsa Malaysia' Dilemma," p. 50.

SMOKING, EATING, AND DESIRE: A STUDY OF ALIENATION IN THE FILMS OF JAMES LEE

Gaik Cheng Khoo

"What's the point of living when there's no true love?"
"It is easier to kill than to love."[1]

This essay is a follow-up of my initial reflection on the development of James Lee since 2002 as a serious auteur.[2] Together with Amir Muhammad, Lee spearheaded the current wave of independent filmmaking in Malaysia that began in the year 2000. He was part of the Malaysian Independent Filmmakers (MIF), an informal, core group that also included the late Yasmin Ahmad and members Ho Yuhang, Tan Chui Mui, Deepak Kumaran Menon, and Woo Ming Jin. MIF "members" collaborate with one another on their films, thereby influencing each other's works. However, each filmmaker has also developed a quite distinct style, perhaps none more so than James Lee, whose films are the most avant-garde and experimental among those directed by MIF members. Lee works closely with the same actors from one film to the next, and shares similar minimalist aesthetics with some of them. The definitive hallmark traits of his *mise en scène* lie in his firm directorial control and in his theater background: the urban, minimalist landscape of a James Lee film is usually depopulated, and the actors' muted acting and deliberate slowness to react almost suggest a sense of calculated inaction and non-emotion. Among his actors, Lee counts as friends and collaborators Butoh and modern dancers and choreographers Lee Swee Keong and Amy Len.

In this chapter, I trace the signature elements of Lee's filmmaking through a significant body of work that includes experimental as well as more naturalist acting styles and forms. I will sum up themes and ideas, sounds and sights, from his DVD (digital video disc) short film collection, as well as from his features made before

---

[1] From James Lee's film *Ah Beng Returns*.

[2] Gaik Cheng Khoo, "Contesting Diasporic Subjectivity: James Lee, Malaysian Independent Filmmaker," *Asian Cinema* 15,1 (Spring/Summer 2004): 169–86. For the current essay, I thank the editors and the anonymous referees for their valuable feedback.

2006, by focusing on his cinematic representations of eating and smoking in order to talk about love and desire. His trilogy of features focusing on unfaithfulness or faithlessness (*Before We Fall In Love Again,* 2006; *Things We Do When We Fall In Love,* 2007; and *Waiting for Love,* 2007), demonstrates a continuity of themes and style. The difficulty with writing about Lee's work is keeping up with this prolific filmmaker. Since the initial writing of this essay in 2006, Lee has made several mainstream Malay-language horror films: the slasher movie, *Histeria* (2008), horror comedies *Sini Ada Hantu* (Here Got Ghost!, 2010) and *Tolong! Awek Aku Pontianak!* (Help! My Girlfriend Is a Vampire!, 2011), and a more serious horror Chinese-language family drama involving cannibalism, *Clay Pot Curry Killers,* scheduled to be released in 2011, which twice already has not received the censorship board's approval. The commercial projects help fund his independent films, such as the indie gangster film *Call if You Need Me* (2009). Lee is also trying his hand at action films; he has just wrapped up his martial arts film *The Collector* (in production) and is commencing production of *Petaling Street Warrior,* a period-set kung fu comedy. This essay will only discuss the body of work up to 2006.

Contrary to the views of some critics, I argue that Lee is less interested in capturing the racial alienation of the Chinese minority in Malaysia.[3] Instead, an analysis of his body of work (at least up to 2006) shows a preoccupation with more universal themes confronting the modern subject living in an urban, global, capitalist society. Lee's typical minimalist landscape, on view in all of his films except *Snipers* (2001), is usually denuded of particulars, forcing the viewer to engage at the level of the psychological interior, though with little help since he does not usually portray outward emotion or use close-up shots. This "universalism" allows room for me to read "alienation" in his cinematic representations of smoking, eating, and desire/love through a combination of Lacanian psychoanalysis and Marxist philosophy. Through representations of smoking and eating, Lee's films hint at the fundamental alienation of the psychoanalytical subjects who can never be satisfied or achieve complete happiness so long as they are workers alienated from the products of their labor through capitalism.

James Lee's DVShorts is a collection that combines some of his earlier and later, more mature, short films (2000–05). In this six-year span, the prolific filmmaker also made five feature films, and a short film called *Waiting for Them* as part of *Visits: Hungry Ghost Anthology* (2004). The DVD Shorts' subtitle, *120 Minutes of Separation, Reunion, Betrayal & Love,* supposedly captures the general themes of Lee's work as an auteur. Yet this description seems somewhat inadequate and inaccurate. Rather than experiencing separation, too many characters seem to be in the process of saying goodbye; awkward meetings or brief linguistic exchanges replace the joyous excitement of reunion; and all meetings are mostly conducted with deadpan expressions, bored detachment, little movement, and muted acting, sometimes punctuated with stage business (attributed to Lee's background training in theater) like smoking or eating/drinking. Moreover, long takes, the absence of intimate close-up shots, and the depopulated modernist settings (which resemble still photographs

---

[3] Critics tend to attribute the general sense of alienation in the works of Chinese Malaysian independent filmmakers, such as Ho Yuhang and James Lee, to racial marginalization, but I believe this explanation may be somewhat reductive as it does not take into account emotional, interpersonal alienation provoked by modern urban conditions. See, for example, Baradan Kuppusamy, "Saying it with 'Indie' Films," *Asia Media Forum,* March 1, 2006, http://v2.theasiamediaforum.org/saying-it-with-indie-films/(last accessed on May 28, 2011).

in which Lee's characters seemingly wander or pose), all serve to alienate viewers, while at the same time representing the characters' physical and spiritual isolation. Certainly demonstrations of betrayal and love appear in his gangster films; but his consistent decision to restrain any sign of emotion (the exceptions being his more collaborative, improvisatory films, e.g., *Emu Kwan's Tragic Breakfast,* 2002) probably suggests a less dramatic sense of invested emotion and energy—disappointment and rejection in love, outcomes that seem inevitable given the sense of bleak irony that underlies Lee's work. Love is elusive, callous, painful, and, if it exists at all, impermanent. Many of Lee's works begin with the ending of love relationships or show the difficult process of navigating such relationships.

In a James Lee film, love is more often a philosophical subject to be discussed in an abstract manner, rather than a euphoric feeling emoted overtly. For example, *Ah Beng Returns* (2001) has a gangster moll who expounds on love; and May, in her callous rejection letter to her boyfriend, conveys succinctly the film's title, *Sometimes Love is Beautiful* (2005), by referring to her new love. Lee remarks that he is "interested in small stories that are filled with big emotions and complex characters, but as a filmmaker, [does not] always choose to present those emotions and feelings in a very direct manner."[4] Here, Lee is referring to *Before We Fall In Love Again*, which revolves around two men who love the same woman. Love triangles or triadic relationships thread through Lee's work: A might love B who loves C; or men pimp women to other men or men exchange women. Lee's films speak to the complexities of desire in a modern capitalist setting, suggesting that monogamous love relationships are somehow unfulfilling or insufficient in satisfying desires. This may be due to the choices available, one's idealism, or the inability of characters to confront their own wrongdoings in failed relationships and to acknowledge their weaknesses while pursuing that thing (the *objet petit a* in Lacanian terms, or the cause of desire) in another. In Lacanian psychoanalysis, the *objet petit a* is:

> … an expression of the lack inherent in human beings, whose incompleteness and early helplessness produce a quest for fulfillment beyond the satisfaction of biological needs. The *objet petit a* is a fantasy that functions as the cause of desire; as such, it determines whether desire will be expressed within the limits of the pleasure principle or "beyond," in pursuit of an unlimited *jouissance,* an impossible and even deadly enjoyment.[5]

Many critics and reviewers have noted the theme of urban alienation in James Lee's work. Notably, they point to the distanciated style à la Tsai Ming Liang, with long takes, few cuts, a focus on the banal, class alienation,[6] and, in *The Beautiful Washing Machine,* a focus on the "interpersonal alienation brought on by the modern consumer society."[7] But perhaps, rather than interpersonal alienation alone, Lee's

---

[4] El Topo, "Director's Statement," September 16, 2006, www.dahuangpictures.com/blogs/bwfla.php/2006/09/16/director_s_statement (last accessed June 1, 2011).

[5] Lewis A. Kirshner, "Rethinking Desire: The *objet petit a* in Lacanian Theory," *Journal of the American Psychoanalytic Association* 53,1 (2003): 83.

[6] Khoo, "Contesting Diasporic Subjectivity."

[7] Robert Williamson, "Affection and Disaffection: Ideas, Themes, and Styles in Current Malaysian Independent Cinema," *Firecracker Magazine* 8 (July 2005), previously available at www.firecracker-magazine.com/ but no longer accessible online.

films hint of the fundamental alienation of the Lacanian subject, where private desire, hinged to a shared social reality, might be constrained by a symbolic boundary that is defined by rules, customs, and narrative models, and as such cannot be transgressed. These limits are central to the recognition of the absolute separateness, or otherness, of the love object. Hence, "the lover must accept that his or her passionate fantasies are inventions that even when apparently reciprocated do not erase the gap between one's private feelings and the reality of the other."[8]

Yet, more critically, the fundamental alienation within each individual means that we can never achieve *jouissance* (the sense of wholeness that the child had with its mother) once we become subjects of the Language of the Father (patriarchal society); we are always looking to return to that earlier state of completeness. Being a (socialized) subject leaves "a permanent ache of desire," which is realized in our fantasies of sexual, romantic, narcissistic, and materialistic fulfillment. "Desire thus becomes 'libidinized' and diverted to existing symbolic objects,"[9] such as the woman/ghost of the washing machine in *The Beautiful Washing Machine* or cigarettes. Even more importantly, love relationships are further distracted by a consumerist, individualist, and status-conscious ideology in a James Lee film.

I approach love/desire obliquely in this article by focusing on Lee's representation of banal, everyday rituals, like eating and smoking. The banality of everyday reality has become the shared vocabulary of Malaysian independent filmmakers. In Lee's minimalist *mise en scène,* each prop and piece of stage business assumes symbolic proportions. These mundane "necessary habits" (necessary only in the world of a James Lee film) potentially suggest a human desire for nourishment, pleasure, fulfillment, and sociality, yet perversely lead to more interpersonal alienation. Brotherhood, family ties, friendship, and heterosexual love are constantly tested and found wanting. In these early films,[10] Lee's bleak vision seems to negate that most "Malaysian" of traits: the love of food and the sense of commensality and sociality derived through food-giving and food-taking. While these traits are common to other cultures that celebrate food—Singaporean films also celebrate food/eating as a form of national pastime—the act of eating in Lee's films predominantly negates these traits, as his films do not show happy people sharing food together. Food (or at least the types of food a character is eating) is not central in his films; rather, Lee's films focus on the mundane habit of "eating" that characterizes everyday life, whereby eating is as routine and ordinary as smoking, copulating, shopping, watching television, and doing domestic chores.

To discover what eating and smoking tell us about love/desire and sex in Lee's work, I explore the manner whereby these acts are represented. Whether one smokes and eats alone or with others explains a lot about desire and interpersonal communication. Moreover, such an analysis helps us chart the subtle nuances and changes in Lee's body of work and the issues explored. I will begin with a discussion of smoking first before focusing on eating and the relationship of each with sex/love.

---

[8] Kirshner, "Rethinking Desire," p. 87.

[9] Ibid.

[10] Lee's later gangster film, *Call If You Need Me* (2009), has scenes of the gangsters and their girlfriends cooking and eating together to suggest how tight-knit they are, if only to make the eventual betrayal and fracturing of relations between the two men even more poignant.

SMOKING

Fellow independent filmmaker Bernard Chauly points out that the uncomfortable silences, protracted gazes, and long, slow bouts of cigarette smoking are consistent in Lee's films.[11] As stage business and visual composition, smoking fulfils aesthetic and narrative functions. It both kills time[12] and is productive of time.[13] This resonates for the bored and lazy unemployed Berg (*Room to Let*), the useless husband in *A Moment of Love* (2005), gangsters who patiently await their next assignment (*Ah Beng Returns, Bernafas Dalam Lumpur,* 2005) and the office worker Teoh (*The Beautiful Washing Machine*). Cigarettes are also used as "a universal token of exchange [that is] linked to their insertion in a gift-giving economy."[14] In *The Beautiful Washing Machine*, Mr. Wong's son Ah Dee bonds with his father by secretly bringing him packs of cigarettes that, due to his health, he is not allowed to smoke. After Mr. Wong's heart attack and hospitalization, Ah Dee visits him in the ward and again brings two packs of cigarettes, which he leaves at his father's bedside. By doing so he ignores completely the potentially harmful effects of this gift, only hoping to convey a sense of home and comfort and to communicate his love. When Ah Dee meets the silent woman who is living in his father's house for the first time, he introduces himself and offers her a cigarette as an ice-breaker (she declines).

Teoh offers the silent woman a cigarette in *The Beautiful Washing Machine*

Cigarette smoking signifies patriarchy, and binds the main male characters in *The Beautiful Washing Machine*. Like Ah Dee, Teoh tries to seduce the silent woman by

---

[11] Bernard Chauly, "In Conversation with James Lee," *SEA-Images*, 2004, http://film.culture 360.org/magazine/interviews/in-conversation-with-james-lee/(last accessed on June 1, 2011).

[12] Richard Klein, *Cigarettes Are Sublime* (Durham, NC: Duke University Press, 1993), p. 21.

[13] Helen Keane, "Time and the Female Smoker," in *Women Making Time: Contemporary Feminist Critique and Cultural Analysis*, ed. Elizabeth McMahon and Brigitta Olubas (Crawley: University of Western Australia Press, 2006), p. 111.

[14] Klein, *Cigarettes Are Sublime*, p. 137.

offering her a cigarette, and then blows smoke in her face when she coughs as a reaction to her first taste. Teoh's actions and reactions make him seem more inhuman than the silent woman (she might, at the most extreme, be an extraterrestrial alien from the spaceship sighting that was heard announced on the radio). This scene is sexualized as Teoh gestures for the woman to sit on the counter, and then parts her knees before running his fingers up her thigh. However, instead of sleeping with her after this smoking scene, he pimps her to another man. Later in the film, the scene where Mr. Wong, Ah Dee, and Yap (the daughter's boyfriend) all meet for a quiet, complicit smoke in the garden after Sunday lunch suggests their phallic power over the silent woman: Mr. Wong asserts his phallic power through patronage and paternalism, his son through sexual harassment, and Yap through rape.

The phallic power signified by the cigarette is one that is asserted without self-reflexivity for Teoh and Mr. Wong. We are told that Teoh's girlfriend has left him recently and taken the washing machine with her. Teoh's exploitation of the silent, nameless woman, who appears magically next to the second washing machine he bought, conveniently solves the hassles that resulted from the loss of his girlfriend. She cooks and cleans for him while he sexually objectifies her, buying her a sundress and high heels and taking photos of her mopping the floor in the dress and heels. Yet enslaving her, while smoking or eating instant noodles, allows him to avoid dealing with the reasons for the demise of his relationship with his girlfriend; his behavior also suggests probable causes for his girlfriend's departure. Similarly, middle-aged widower Mr. Wong's lonely existence is filled only with cooking when his children periodically visit him, and with gay video pornography, which he watches from behind a Japanese *manga* mask. This tedium is disrupted by the mysterious appearance of the silent woman in his car one night. He focuses all his efforts on her, so much so that when she disappears he is crushed and resorts to buying six hundred ringgit's worth of beer at the supermarket.[15] Nothing—not the silent woman, smoking, cooking, or pornography—succeeds in making him alter his life or deal with "the psychological dead end in which [he and Teoh] have found themselves."[16]

Perhaps the act of smoking occurs most often and noticeably in *Room to Let*. The house tenants take turns telling the newcomer, Berg, about the story of a former tenant, an artist, who ran away from marriage to his cousin. In a scene of social camaraderie, Berg and a fellow housemate (a writer) smoke and drink together, and Berg asks, "How does one express lost love?" The writer suggests lending Berg some of his scripts to practice expressing lost love. However, it is clear that Berg, quite depressed, already does this through solitary acts such as smoking, watching video pornography, and eating instant noodles. If, as Klein writes, smoking provides "an occasion for reverie and a tool of concentration,"[17] then Berg indulges in his contemplation of the past through chain-smoking, unable even to leave the house to go job-hunting. From another perspective, he is a smoker who "adopts an aesthetic standpoint, outside the realm of utility or ethics, that kills the time of work or

---

[15] RM600 is approximately US$200.

[16] Nenad Dukic, "Destructive Alienations," Bangkok International Film Festival 2005, FIPRESCI Festival Report, www.fipresci.org/festivals/archive/2005/bangkok/bangkok_dukic.htm (last accessed on June 1, 2011).

[17] Klein, *Cigarettes Are Sublime*, p. 21.

responsibility in order to bear witness to the time [...] of pure passing."[18] Smoking, drinking, and eating in the house with Berg are all activities the men carry out while discussing relationships. Berg, caught in a perpetual state of ennui while recovering from a failed relationship, rejects the expressed love of the male friend who takes him in. Rather than respond to the generosity of this friend, Berg wants to leave the house with a woman he has discovered bound up in one of the rooms. There is a suggestion that she may be the same overweight woman who came to rent a room from the landlord sometime earlier and who might then have been held captive and starved. Berg finally leaves with her, though his depression does not allow him much emotional expression except when he finally breaks into tears in front of the bathroom mirror.

While smoking provides a meditative quality to James Lee's characters, meditation is possible without smoking. Nevertheless, smoking carries other meanings and reveals the personality traits of those who smoke. For example, in *Sometimes Love is Beautiful*, the laundry girl, May (played by indie filmmaker Tan Chui Mui), tries smoking a cigarette after having sex with her lover. Unlike the clichéd scenario of a couple smoking in bed after sex, where sharing a cigarette in bed signifies mutual sexual gratification or fulfilled pleasure, in this film she smokes alone next to a sleeping lover. This act betrays the "narcissistic self-sufficiency" of the modern, sexually liberated woman.[19] Her post-coital smoking is performed almost out of curiosity, perhaps for the first time. Taking a cigarette from his pack, she sniffs it before attempting to light it; at first she fails, but then lights it. She does not choke upon inhaling, and so continues reading her book, looking contemplative and philosophical as she smokes and reads. As Klein tells it, "Love, like cigarettes, is for killing time, aborting the duration of whatever tediously endures."[20] Thus, smoking becomes merely another new experience to be tested by May as she moves from one boyfriend to another; her constants are her love for reading and her reliance on her best friend, Bike Girl. Smoking does for May what it does for Berg in *Room to Let*, "creat[ing] time outside of ordinary duration, like other technologies and practices valued for their temporal otherness [such as] reading novels, sex [and] listening to music."[21]

I have suggested an expansive repertoire of meanings for smoking characters that highlights their obsessive-compulsive and self-interested natures. Their nicotine addiction is a reflection of their inability to manage their lives, as well as a sign of unfulfillment, if not an act of resistance. Smoking provides a quick fix and short-term pleasure in place of unfulfilled, long-term desires. It short-circuits and distracts from the pursuit of other desires that are more difficult to achieve. Chain-smokers, insofar as they endlessly repeat their cigarette consumption, are unable to break from this cyclical habit, their alienation not unlike that experienced by the factory worker under the conditions of modern capitalist industrial production that Marx discusses:

> [T]he worker is related to the *product of his labor* as to an *alien* object. For on this premise it is clear that the more the worker exhausts himself, the more powerful the alien world of objects which he creates over and against himself becomes, the

---

[18] Ibid., p. 119.

[19] Ibid., p. 130.

[20] Ibid., p. 118.

[21] Keane, "Time and the Female Smoker," p. 111.

poorer he and his inner world become, and less there is that belongs to him as his own. [...] The worker puts his life into the object; but now it no longer belongs to him, it belongs to the object. The greater this activity, therefore, the greater the worker's lack of objects. What the product of his work is, he is not. The greater this product, therefore, the less is he himself. The *externalisation* of the worker into his product does not only mean that his work becomes an object, an *external* existence, but that it exists *outside him* independently, as something alien to him, as confronting him as an autonomous power. It means that the life which he has given to the object confronts him as hostile and alien.[22]

The smoker invests so much effort in smoking as an expression of his desires, that the cigarette comes to hold an inordinate power over him, denuding his sense of self but also simultaneously driving his desires. However, it never quite suffices or fulfills him. In the logic of this argument, the cigarette symbolizes the capitalist ideology that enchains characters in a James Lee film.

EATING

Food anthropologists regard eating as a way of placing oneself in relation to others;[23] it "make[s] concrete one of the specific modes of relation between a person and the world, thus forming one of the fundamental [social] landmarks in space-time."[24] Yet in James Lee's films, most characters either eat or drink alone or they eat merely to survive—munching slowly and automatically, with no sign of pleasure. Indeed, eating to survive is what the central character, Berg, does in *Room to Let*. His daily food intake consists of instant noodles, a commodity snack that has become a universal signifier of solitary eating and eating for survival. In keeping with Lee's critique of urban consumption and the multiple ways this condition alienates humans from one another, whether in the form of technology or mindless shopping and advertisements (as in *The Beautiful Washing Machine*), the instant noodle becomes another symbol of mass industrial production that isolates and individuates. Rather than interact with the cook or vendor who prepares one's noodles, the instant noodle is an industrialized convenience food, made so easy that those who have no cooking skills can whip up a tasty noodle in three minutes themselves, using the pre-packed spices provided. Moreover, instant noodles come in single-serving packets, thus assuming individuated consumption. At one point, Berg cooks instant noodles for a woman who has been held hostage in the shared house; but in that case, he only watches her eat. In Lee's ultimate critique of patriarchal capitalism and alienation, *The Beautiful Washing Machine*, the silent woman first appears squatting beside Teoh's washing machine eating a bowl of instant noodles. Analogous to the noodles, she provides the men with instant domestic, sexual, and affective labor.

---

[22] Karl Marx, *The Portable Karl Marx*, ed. Eugene Kamenka (New York, NY: Penguin Books, 1983), p. 134.

[23] Jack Goody, *Cooking, Cuisine, and Class* (Cambridge: Cambridge University Press, 1982).

[24] Michel de Certeau, Luce Giard, and Pierre Mayol, *The Practice of Everyday Life, Volume 2: Living and Cooking* (Minneapolis, MN: University of Minnesota Press, 1998), p. 183.

Instant male gratification as Teoh eats instant noodles while eyeing the silent, sexily dressed woman doing his laundry in *The Beautiful Washing Machine*

James Lee acknowledged in an interview with Bernard Chauly that during meals his characters sometimes "just look down and don't talk," and that this behavior may not necessarily be an "Asian" trait but merely a reflection of his personal experience.[25] While Lee explains his own silences during dinner with his in-laws as normal and presumably not uncomfortable ("they eat, I don't talk, occasionally we smile"), the meaning of the meals Lee's film characters have together can be interpreted differently by viewers depending on the films and individual scenes.

Meal times are social opportunities for interpersonal communication; yet, in a James Lee movie, meals are usually fraught with unspoken tension. For instance, in Lee's films, couples may sit at the dinner table but only one person will be eating. In *Bernafas Dalam Lumpur*, Lina's husband, who has just come out of prison, eats dinner with some relish while she sits and watches him, smiling. While he eats, he asks her whether she "saw" (slept with) anyone while he was in prison. In *A Moment of Love*, the characters played by Bok Lai and Amy are supposed to be having dinner, but only he is eating. She is too upset with him for forgetting to pay the water bill yet again. This scene is merely one of many that captures the power struggle and unhappiness of the couple who cannot eat together. At the same time, the representation of matrimonial tension hearkens back to an earlier film, *Ah Beng Returns*, featuring the same actors eating at a long table without looking at each other (and talking about their impending divorce). If part of the intention behind producing the meal is to produce home, family, and unity, the inability of two people to savor food together may suggest the tenuousness of family and marital relations. As a common saying goes, the family that eats together stays together. In *Bernafas Dalam Lumpur*, Lina's husband is murdered the day following their tense meal; and Amy, in *A Moment of Love*, magically disappears into a full water tank shortly after the unhappy meal noted above.

---

[25] Chauly, "In Conversation with James Lee."

Couples who do eat and talk together in Lee's films end up quarrelling and separating, as we see in *Emu Kwan's Tragic Breakfast*, which features Emu's three different lovers, and in *A Moment of Love*. In extreme cases, they divorce (Bok Lai's character and his wife in *Ah Beng Returns*). In the case of Emu Kwan, the improvised conversations with her lovers over breakfast tell us much about her and her pursuit of love ("someone I can love and who loves me back"). It also shows that—although the breakfast food, her clothing, and posture are the same at each breakfast—Emu's personality is different depending on the personality of her current partner. The contrasting relationships, broken into three screens, expose her contradictory principles and desires. Food comes after sex, and it is through the breakfast conversation that she connects with her one-night stands at an emotional, social, and rational level, rather than through physical or sexual intimacy. Each of these encounters reveals her to be judgmental, playful, and vulnerable in turn as she negotiates the emotional complexities of ephemeral relationships as a supposedly sexually liberated, slightly bohemian modern single woman living in cosmopolitan Kuala Lumpur.

In *The Beautiful Washing Machine*, food, cigarettes, and sex are strongly interconnected. Mr. Wong's relationship to cooking and food proves him to be a man capable of nurturing and supporting others. Food is perhaps the only thing he is allowed to enjoy openly: his daughter approves neither of his smoking nor his "girlfriend." Mr. Wong, who is happy when cooking in the kitchen, possesses a certain transformative power over raw chicken and vegetables. A lonely widower living by himself, whose two grown children periodically come to visit, he seems only too glad to cook for them. The family's Sunday lunch is a crucial scene for establishing relations among characters around the table: Ah Dee and his sister exchange knowing glances when they see their father scooping food into the silent woman's bowl (his "girlfriend"). Mr. Wong's nurturing gesture suggests he cares for her, but rather than becoming sexual, this relationship remains a paternalistic one. His dominance in the kitchen, his power over food, is the only power he commands in the house, for he is nowhere as successful as the other men in sexually exploiting the silent woman. Instead, Mr. Wong becomes a passive witness to Ah Dee's seduction of the woman in the kitchen,[26] and later to the rape scene in the woman's room.

Mr. Wong is not the only character who loves cooking and eating, but displays passivity in matters of love. In these early films, those among Lee's characters who love food are pathetic creatures to be pitied for their inability to control their bodies and consumption. This is true of the bike girl in *Sometimes Love is Beautiful*. She is secretly in love with the laundry girl, May, her childhood friend. Overweight and loyal, Bike Girl is treated callously and taken advantage of by May.[27] We see Bike

---

[26] In this scene, Ah Dee is standing very close to the woman, who is washing dishes in the sink. He demonstrates to her how to wash the plates: "You're scratching the plate. You must do it like this, in a circular motion. Front, back, and around the edges. OK? You try it." He takes her hand deliberately and puts it over the plate: "Round and round the edges," he says, as if getting her to masturbate him slowly. "And on the back, too." She looks visibly disturbed and embarrassed, as if she knows that this is somehow wrong.

[27] Bike Girl functions as May's ride/driver by taking May to and from her sexual trysts. Bike Girl also acts as love-messenger when May tires of her present boyfriend and asks her to convey a letter to him. When May returns after a sexual liaison with her new lover, Bike Girl tells her that her boyfriend called May's mobile phone. May, wanting to avoid a confrontation, asks her friend, "Can you tell him for me?" Bike Girl does not answer, but it is implied that she

Girl buying food and juice for the two of them, but we only see her sipping the drink, and talking about having a stomachache the previous night. May, always shown reading a book, says to Bike Girl, "I told you not to eat so much," and asks whether she has been to see a doctor. Bike Girl responds that she is just waiting for the pain to go away. Her passivity in this instance mirrors the way she has accepted her role in her relationship with May. Thus, she is doomed to sublimate her unrequited love for May into overindulgence in food.

In an earlier Lee film, *Ah Beng Returns*, the female passivity and masochism of "the woman in love" is manifested through food and eating. The wife of gangster Ah Wai reminisces to Ah Wai's friend (another gangster) about her husband's food habits. "Ah Wai loves to eat and drink red wine," she begins. "For breakfast, he'll have a bowl of bird nest soup. Lunch, a plate of roast goose rice and herbal chicken soup, and for dessert a bowl of red bean soup. For teatime, he'll have a cup of coffee and egg tart. He usually doesn't take rice for dinner, but beef noodles. He likes the beef to be medium rare with some blood. And some red bean soup. Then for supper, noodle soup with dumplings. Ah Wai still loves me." This account of Ah Wai tells us that his meticulous relationship with food is more intense than his relationship with his wife (whom he is cheating on), a woman who knows his daily ritual by heart but who is obviously in denial about the nature of their relationship.

Again, this Lee couple (Ah Wai and his wife) sits at a table, but only one is eating. Ah Wai is clearly enjoying his *yong tau foo* (a soybean curd dish), while his wife is smoking. He stops and asks her, "Aren't you hungry? Skipping breakfast and smoking is bad for your health. Come, I'll feed you." She turns away as if not interested. In the next shot, using his chopsticks, he pokes food at her firmly closed mouth; the food just falls. She is expressionless. He keeps at it, trying out *kway teow* (noodles), dumplings, even a stuffed chili, to no avail. After the chili, he puts down his chopsticks and says, "You must be full by now. Have a drink." She stands up robotically and bends at the waist to lay her head sideways on the table. He pours first a glass of beer over her, then, standing up, empties the whole bottle over her head. Such a bizarre scene of domestic abuse, initiated through the rhetoric of a lecture from a loved one, is a strong statement about power and gender. The gangsters, oppressed by and unable to escape from a hierarchical paternalistic system that is dominated by a tyrant, in turn oppress others. Allowing for experimental stylistics, the couple's negotiation of food is completely one-sided. Ah Wai continues to try to force feed his wife even as she rejects his food (and him), and he seems oblivious to her passive but stubborn rejection when he utters "you must be full by now." Yet, she is also complicit in staying in the relationship and perpetuating the abuse when she lays her head on the table and lets him pour beer over her.

Ironically, Lee's earliest feature was more optimistic about the redemptive quality of food and food negotiations than his subsequent films. In *Snipers*, a lone gunman fails to carry out his assassination of the red-bean-soup seller's gangster boyfriend after she kindly gives the assassin free bowls of soup. Instead, he saves her and her boyfriend by killing the two gangsters who come looking for her boyfriend.

---

will tell him. The subsequent long, inactive take, as the two women sit on the bike looking stiff and uneasy with the motor running, sharpens the dynamics between the two characters, as if the filmmaker wants us to contemplate the awkwardness of this moment that tests their friendship.

CONCLUSION

Lee's major theme concerns the difficulty of knowing the other in love (or what Kirshner calls "the otherness of the object, the beloved person's absolute separateness").[28] In such relationships, a certain alienation prevails when love is inadequate and unfulfilling, and the other, through actions and behavior, seems incomprehensible. In such a world, it may perhaps be "easier to kill than to love," to quote a character from *Ah Beng Returns*, easier to experience sexual intimacy vicariously through chain smoking, scopophilia (e.g., Teoh, in *The Beautiful Washing Machine*, when he buys the mute woman a halter-top dress and high heels and photographs her vacuuming the house wearing that outfit), or pornography, which, much like the consumption of material goods, offers only fleeting, empty satisfaction.

Overall, James Lee's work captures characters in search of something or someone to give them that which they themselves lack. Nevertheless, they are lost in a perpetual cycle, caught up in the repetitive banality of everyday urban life that is mediated through ideologies of work, consumption, and sociality. In this regard, as a commodity, the washing machine best symbolizes this cycle of non-self-knowledge, repetition, and the modern domestic trap for its characters, while smoking and eating become acts of consumption representative of personal and interpersonal alienation.

Lee's trilogy about faithfulness and unfaithfulness further expands on the Lacanian pursuit of love in and through the elusive object of desire. In *Before We Fall in Love Again*, Ling Yue, despite her presumably happy marriage, resumes her love affair with her married former colleague, Tong. The film suggests through her lovers' contemplative flashbacks that the elusive object of desire may be wholeness with oneself, as the two men keep confronting their egos either in Ling Yue or in each other through the film's mirroring devices. The second installment of the trilogy, *Things We Do When We Fall in Love*, focuses on a masochistic relationship in which two lovers, played by Amy Len and Loh Bok Lai, continue to love and hurt each other with their bouts of jealousy, possessiveness, or adultery, and yet stay together. Here, subtle aesthetic changes, together with the portrayal of Bok Lai's character's struggle to quit smoking, may signal the possibility of a new language for the filmmaker.

Though treated quite differently by the different artists, the theme of love seems to be popular with Lee's indie film compatriots—Tan Chui Mui, with *Love Conquers All* (2006), and Yasmin Ahmad, whose Orked films may be said to revolve around love: familial (*Rabun*, 2003), romantic (*Sepet*, 2004), adolescent or first love (*Mukhsin*, 2006), and spiritual love (*Gubra*, 2006).[29] Nevertheless, Yasmin's films do not lend themselves easily to a psychoanalytic Marxist reading of alienation in capitalism since her worldview of social relations is more optimistic than Lee's. Furthermore, rather than critiquing the larger structures of inequality in an abstract and deterritorialized fashion, Yasmin illustrates the humanist possibility of ordinary individual Malaysians resisting racialisation and dogmatic interpretations of

---

[28] Kirshner, "Rethinking Desire," p. 87.

[29] See Gaik Cheng Khoo, "Irreconcilable Differences? The Politics of Love vs. Wahhabist Exclusivism," paper presented at the Seventh International Malaysian Studies Conference, Universiti Sains Malaysia, Penang, Malaysia, March 16–18, 2010; and Benjamin McKay's chapter in this volume.

religion. While such elements in Yasmin Ahmad's films may invite the critic to frame her work in the context of a "national cinema," Yasmin and other indie Malaysian filmmakers were/are also quick to use the language of common humanity when discussing their works. Indeed, indie Malaysian filmmakers' works are infused with a cosmopolitan sensibility.[30] Such simultaneous contemporary global and local influences must necessarily open up their works to theoretical frameworks (including psychoanalytical readings) that go beyond discussions of national cinema that continue to buttress Jameson's notion of Third World texts as narcissistic national allegory.[31] This openness to diverse theories would substantially enrich discussions of Southeast Asian films, particularly since many parts of Southeast Asia are undergoing processes that follow from intense neo-liberal capitalism, giving rise to possible disillusionment, and repeating the universal condition of alienation under historical capitalism. Still, the universal does not have to preclude the particular, and vice versa. Lee's first two features, *Snipers* and *Ah Beng Returns,* which consciously attempted to capture a more diverse Malaysian society in the *Reformasi*[32] spirit, contain the seeds of more universal ideas about individual alienation that he explores in his later "made for festival" films.

Nevertheless, it is difficult to state categorically whether the content of his "festival films" is self-consciously departicularized for a broader international niche market. While Lee stopped making films that reflected Malaysia's multiethnic and multilingual diversity when he realized that there was a limited local audience for his early multiethnic and multilingual features,[33] this avoidance was not permanent. In the Chinese-language *Call if You Need Me* (2009), there is a Cantonese-speaking Tamil gangster and a Malay policeman. Lee also made the political short film *Gerhana* (2009) for 15Malaysia, a short film project that dealt with socio-political issues in Malaysia.[34] *Gerhana* (Eclipse) sees Lee returning to the aesthetics that made him famous: minimalist settings, almost expressionless acting, and dialogue that can alienate viewers. Yet *Gerhana* is Lee's most contextually based and, in that sense, most political film. It features an interethnic, upper-class couple having a secret tryst in a hotel. As we watch this couple, the high-powered Malay man eats at a table by himself, while his non-Muslim mistress watches a television news program from the bed. That the couple is filmed as if they are in separate rooms is again suggestive of modern alienation. Viewers unfamiliar with Malaysian politics and current events will not grasp the numerous references made by the newscasters on the television. Viewers might interpret the film as a critique of the capitalist bourgeois lifestyle, common anywhere in the world. Here, in the couple's hotel room, the rich do not quite know what to do with their lives—they are beautiful and powerful, but isolated from the real world of events, where people are poor, hungry, and exploited (as

---

[30] Gaik Cheng Khoo, "Just Do-It-(Yourself): Independent Filmmaking in Malaysia," *Inter-Asia Cultural Studies* 8,2 (2007): 227–47.

[31] Fredric Jameson, "Third-World Literature in the Era of Multinational Capitalism," *Social Text* 15 (1986): 65–88.

[32] This refers to a movement in Malaysia that was initiated by former deputy Prime Minister Anwar Ibrahim.

[33] The Malaysian film market is divided according to language, and James Lee found that even the Chinese–Malaysian audiences were not ready for a multi-dialect film like *Ah Beng Returns*. Consequently, his later films are mostly in Mandarin and/or Cantonese.

[34] The films can be viewed at: http://15malaysia.com/. The comments for *Gerhana* are also interesting to read.

overheard on the television news reports). This couple cannot make the link between their wealth and the means of production (i.e., the workers' desperate lives). The wealthy live in a bubble that seems sterile, unruffled. The TV news broadcast is represented merely as a flickering blue screen, though we can hear its political content. The woman makes an effort to engage in a dialogue about the news stories, but her words and voice are emotionless, and she seems hypnotized, as if in a dream or bubble. Her partner asks her not to worry and to go to sleep; he takes a picture of her lying on the bed fully dressed, just as the news report warns women that they should not allow their male lovers to take intimate photos of them for fear that such photos could be posted on the Internet. The familiar tropes of solitary eating and scopophilia hint at interpersonal alienation, and in this film, each character's inability to connect directly to the object of desire persists.[35]

For Malaysians, this couple allegorically represents the gendered relationship of the state with the *rakyat* (citizens). The messages emanating from the television seem hyperbolic and lend a humorous and surreal air to the serious point about how citizens (the woman) are fed nonsense by the media, which is completely one-sided. When the camera in the closing shot shows us the television screen, we see that the woman has been watching an empty blue screen. This indicates that no matter which station one watches, private or state-run, the news is controlled by the state, as represented by the voices of the female newscaster and male authorities being interviewed. The reason Lee does not keep the television news as background sound when the couple is talking is because he wants to show that the man who speaks to his mistress with such paternalistic authority in the hotel room is akin to the voice of the government. Both speak on the same "channel." Even the gender relationship on television parallels the gender of the couple: the newscaster who asks questions and reports the news is female, while the politician is male.

All this is to say that a film like *Gerhana* illustrates several levels of alienation: a more universal class alienation as understood by its international audiences, and political alienation, or apathy, as interpreted by its local audiences. Does the "eclipse" in the title refer to the temporary nature of the chaos that ensued when the ruling Barisan Nasional (National Alliance) attempted to wrestle power back from the opposition, sparking a constitutional crisis in the state of Perak, as mentioned in the film? Or, in a far more pessimistic view of Malaysian society, does it mean that the gains made by the opposition in the 2008 general elections were ephemeral? These are questions worth pondering. Suffice it to say that Lee's auteur vision provides a dark contrast to Yasmin Ahmad's "dreamed communities."[36]

---

[35] Rather than lying down beside her in the bed, he goes off to the bathroom after taking the photos.

[36] See Benjamin McKay's essay in this volume.

SELECTED FILMOGRAPHY

Films cited below are all directed by James Lee:
Ah Beng Returns (2001)
The Beautiful Washing Machine (2004)
Before We Fall In Love Again (2006)
Call if You Need Me (2009)
Clay Pot Curry Killers (2011)
Gerhana (Eclipse, 2009)
Histeria (Hysteria, 2008)
James Lee's DVShorts: 120 Minutes of Separation, Reunion, Betrayal & Love (2000–05), which contains:
    Sunflowers (2000)
    Emu Kwan's Tragic Breakfast (2002)
    Goodbye (2003)
    Teatime with John (2003)
    Goodbye to Love (2004)
    A Moment of Love (2005)
    Bernafas Dalam Lumpur (2005)
    Sometimes Love is Beautiful (2005)
Petaling Street Warrior (in production)
Room to Let (2002)
Sini Ada Hantu (Here Got Ghost!, 2010)
Snipers (2001)
Things We Do When We Fall in Love (2007)
Tolong! Awek Aku Pontianak! (Help! My Girlfriend Is a Vampire!, 2011)
Waiting for Them in *Visits: Hungry Ghost Anthology* (2004)
Wall (2006)

INDEPENDENCE AND INDIGENOUS FILM: THE FRAMING OF TIMOR-LESTE[1]

Angie Bexley

In 2005, a striking film titled *Rock 'n' Roll with Jakarta* (SAMEP, 2005) was made in Timor-Leste.[2] Produced by the Sahe Media Popular Film Unit (SAMEP) of the Sahe Institute for Liberation, it examines the failed efforts to seek justice for the Timorese people and to achieve retribution relating to crimes against humanity committed by Indonesia during its occupation of Timor-Leste (1975–99). *Rock 'n' Roll with Jakarta*, which focuses on the Commission for Truth and Friendship, is a window into how the younger generation—known collectively as the *Geração Foun* in Tetum (the Timorese lingua franca)—mediates issues concerning Timor-Leste's independent identity as they struggle to assert themselves as legitimate citizens of the new nation while engaging with a transnational movement striving for democracy in Indonesia. The film deals with postcolonial social memories and negotiates the narratives of the "resistance struggle," "truth," and "justice," and the experience of "Indonesia."

This article discusses one attempt to produce a Timorese film during a period when independent film in Timor-Leste could be considered fundamentally "indigenous." Accordingly, a definition of indigenous film production must be understood in the light of socio-political, historical, and postcolonial contexts. Timor-Leste gained independence after four hundred years of colonialism and oppression, and the Timorese people are now taking hold of the camera, producing scripts and directing films that highlight issues of importance to them.

The cultural producers from the *Geração Foun* are an important group within Timorese society. *Rock 'n' Roll with Jakarta* focuses on the issue of justice by accusing the political elite of Timor-Leste of failing to make forceful demands for the much

---

[1] This chapter is based on a conference paper presented at the Third Annual New Southeast Asian Cinemas Conference, Theory and Practice: Southeast Asian Cinemas and Filmmaking, Kuala Lumpur, December 14–17, 2006. I thank May Adadol Ingawanij and Benjamin McKay for their thoughtful comments.

[2] I use "Timor-Leste" in this paper to refer to the Democratic Republic of Timor-Leste, a name that, here, encompasses the country during both its periods of independence and occupation. Under Indonesian occupation, the region was referred to as *Timor Timur* (East Timor).

needed international and UN support to bring Indonesian perpetrators to justice. Through this film, these cultural producers have articulated the concerns of their generation and continue to do so through the cultural practices of dance, music, and filmmaking. Youth culture in Timor-Leste continues to pervade discourses concerning the direction of the nation, and this culture plays an important role in maintaining the continuity of memory and identity in an era of independence.

LOCATING TIMOR-LESTE

Timor-Leste, once described as a pebble in the shoe of Indonesia by Indonesia's ex-Foreign Minister Ali Alatas, made a significant contribution to the Indonesian New Order regime's history of human rights.[3] Under occupation, Timor-Leste continued to make itself known as a province that aspired to independence, despite Indonesia's assurances to it and the rest of the world that the annexation of Timor-Leste was a *fait accompli*. It was formally incorporated as Indonesia's twenty-seventh province on July 17, 1976, with the Bill of Integration, which was passed by a manipulated People's Assembly of Timor-Leste, made up of a handful of pro-Indonesian supporters. The passage of the bill halted the decolonization process that had already been set into motion by the Portuguese in 1974.[4] Over the course of the next twenty-four years, Timor-Leste suffered the loss of an estimated one-third of its population—nearly 200,000 people—from causes related to the Indonesian invasion and occupation.

Indonesian President Suharto resigned from office in May 1998, after thirty-two years of authoritarian rule, and the end of his New Order regime provided the necessary conditions for a popular consultation to be held in Timor-Leste. Despite widespread voter intimidation by militia groups backed by Indonesian security forces, almost all eligible voters cast ballots, and nearly 80 percent chose independence.[5] Announced on September 3, 1999, the result sparked a widely predicted rampage by Indonesia's militia groups, violence that claimed over one thousand lives in a brutal scorched-earth campaign and razed over 90 percent of the country's infrastructure.

Since Timor's independence, officially declared in 2002, the United Nations has acted as a sovereign body administering the country, and there have been two changes of government. As a site of post-conflict connection and disconnection, the presence of international agencies and the focus on economic development has had a considerable impact on defining difference and marginality among the citizens of Timor-Leste.

The violent history of Timor-Leste remains incredibly important to the Timorese people and their sense of identity. During the initial years of Timor's independence, the politics of belonging dominated personal, collective, and national concerns. Interpretations of historical narratives and memories of violence were contested as

---

[3] Suharto became president of Indonesia and successor to the disgraced Sukarno, with overt support from the United States and its allies, following a failed coup, on October 1, 1965, and a subsequent bloodbath in which more than 500,000 people were killed under the guise of ridding the nation of communism. Sukarno coined the term "New Order" to characterize his regime as he came to power in 1966.

[4] Portugal colonized Timor-Leste between 1511 and 1974.

[5] Dionisio Babo-Soares and James J. Fox, eds., *Out of the Ashes: Deconstruction and Reconstruction of Timor-Leste* (Canberra: ANU Press, 2003).

Timorese struggled for recognition as legitimate national subjects. A group of young Timorese, in particular, mediated these issues through film.

INDEPENDENCE AND INDEPENDENT FILM

Timor-Leste's independence has provided conditions that made the birth of indigenous film production possible. To date, there is no censorship board in the country. This situation, combined with a substantial injection of international aid money, assisted in the establishment of two independent audio-visual units. The Centro Audio Visual Max Stahl Timor-Leste Film and Sound Archive (CAMS) was established by filmmaker Max Stahl in 2003.[6] This unit has two main functions: to gather and preserve Timor-Leste's history and culture in audio-visual form, and to record music, culture, and events related to the nation-building process in Timor-Leste. The second institution, SAMEP, mentioned above, has a different focus, as it not only records events but also actively directs and produces documentaries.

SAMEP is a part of an NGO—the Sahe Institute of Liberation. The Sahe Institute originated as the Sahe Study Club, formed by Timorese students and Indonesian pro-democracy activists in Jakarta in the mid-1990s to discuss the implications of independence and what the activists' roles would be in a post-independent Timor-Leste. Despite certain disagreements with the older '75 Generation (those who were educated under the previous Portuguese administration and experienced and resisted Indonesia's initial occupation of East Timor), members of the younger generation appreciate that the anticolonial movement of the 1970s, which was conducted and endured by their precedessors, remains relevant for their struggle today. Recognition of this debt prompted members to name the Institute after Vincente Sahe, a Portuguese-educated Timorese intellectual who formed the cultural wing of the anticolonial movement. (He was killed shortly after the Indonesian invasion.) Furthermore, the phrase "Media Popular" in "SAMEP" echoes rhetoric used to describe South American approaches to education, rhetoric employed by Timorese activists involved in transnational engagement with countries such as Brazil.

Transnational engagement of Timorese filmmakers with Indonesia exists on multiple levels of production and distribution. The films are collectively produced, with the tasks of scripting, shooting, and editing shared among those involved. This collective ethos, which provides a framework for cultural production, has its roots in Yogyakarta, Indonesia, where there is a strong history of engaging collaboratively in artistic pursuits. SAMEP's audiences are urban and rural Timorese, and include young and old, as well as an undefined international community of NGO workers and social movement types. *Rock 'n' Roll with Jakarta* was launched at Kinoki, one of the café/cinemas that emerged in the liberated post-*reformasi* era in Yogyakarta.[7] The film was then launched in Timor-Leste, where it toured as part of a traveling cinema (*bioskop keliling*) around the thirteen districts of the country. The Sahe Institute for Liberation received donor funding from the Finnish and Canadian governments for the establishment and maintenance of the Film Unit.

---

[6] Max Stahl is a journalist, cameraman, and producer, and has made many award-winning films. He now lives in Dili and is the director of CAMS.

[7] Budi Irawanto is currently researching independent filmmaking communities in Yogyakarta. The Yogyakarta-based LBK Taring Padi art collective has worked with the Sahe Institute, and two of its members were based in Timor-Leste with the Sahe Institute for four years.

SAMEP is clearly influenced by the documentary exposé styles of John Pilger and Max Stahl, and independent Indonesian filmmakers such as Lexy Rambadeta. The latter was involved in the pro-democracy student movement during the 1990s and filmed many important events, such as the violence directed against Indonesians of Chinese ancestry in May 1998. He also produced footage of the Falintil (Forças Armadas da Libertação Nacional de Timor-Leste, Armed Forces for the National Liberation of East Timor) fighters in the Timor-Leste hinterlands. In 2001, Rambadeta and several Indonesian multimedia artists established Offstream Production House in Jakarta. Offstream produced films imbued with a sense of social justice, often in collaboration with community groups. One of these productions is *Mass Grave* (2001), which "digs up" memories of 1965 from the perspective and experiences of villagers in central Java. These filmmakers in Indonesia and Timor-Leste are united in their concern to find ways to deal with a violent past.

FRAMING TIMOR-LESTE DURING THE NEW ORDER

Before the nation secured its independence in 2002, there were relatively few films made about Timor-Leste. The films produced during the New Order regime can be categorized into two genres. The first is the New Order genre of fiction dramas; the second is made up of documentaries exposing mass human-rights atrocities. Both have influenced the form and content of indigenous Timorese film production, and this is particularly true of the *Geração Foun's Rock 'n' Roll with Jakarta*, with its references to the New Order and it focus on violence.

The New Order's policies regarding the media acted as a mechanism to control social memory, and melodramatic fiction served the purpose of legitimizing Indonesia's occupation of the province. Resistance to the regime was downplayed in New Order films by representing the agents of resistance as "troublemaking mobs" (GPK, *Gerakan Pengacau Keamanan*) and highlighting the military's role in "maintaining stability and order," a phrase that effectively became the New Order's mantra for the next thirty years. Almost all media produced in Indonesia during this time were required to highlight the themes of security and national stability.

Pengkhianatan (Treacherous 30 September Movement, Arifin C. Nur, 1984) was the first film made in support of the official myth outlining General Suharto's rise to power. The film, written by Suharto's favorite military historian and minister for education, Nugroho Notosusanto, was shown in schools and on television annually up until 1998 to invoke the nation's fear of troublemaking mobs and renew people's belief in the military as a force for "maintaining stability." The archetypal film of the New Order, whatever its genre, style, or theme, contained the same basic narrative structure, which moved from order through disorder to a restoration of order.[8]

Langit Kembali Biru (The Sky Returns Blue, Dimas Harring and S. Dias Xiemenes, 1991) illustrates how Indonesia created a particular image of Timor-Leste in the popular imagination during its twenty-four years of occupation. The film stars Sonia Carrascalão, daughter of the pro-autonomy governor of Timor-Leste, Mario Carrascalão. It tells the story of a family feud—between families led by members of rival political parties, Fretilin (Frente Revolucionária do Timor Leste Independente, Revolutionary Front for an Independent East Timor) and The Timorese Democratic

---

[8] Krishna Sen, *Indonesian Cinema: Framing the New Order* (London and New York, NY: Zed Books, 1994).

Union—that splits up two young lovers. The film paints a simplistic, dichotomous picture of the Fretilin soldiers as violent and brutal and the Indonesian soldiers as gentle and kind-hearted.

The film was shot in a number of locations in Timor-Leste and Indonesia. Although it was screened widely throughout Jakarta,[9] it attracted relatively few viewers in Timor-Leste, most of whom were pro-Indonesian Timorese. Many Timorese reflect that *Langit Kembali Biru* was regarded, for the most part, as Indonesian New Order government propaganda and was ridiculed within the emerging clandestine movement at the time.

Langit Kembali Biru was nominated as the year's best film at the 1991 Indonesian Film Festival, and it won a Citra (a film industry award in Indonesia) in the "history" category, as well as receiving nominations for best actress in a leading role, photography, and art direction. The production and promotion of *Langit Kembali Biru* broadcast and amplified Indonesia's justification for the invasion of the tiny island, and helped perpetuate the "maintenance of stability" myth. It was perhaps no coincidence that the film was released two weeks before the Santa Cruz massacre in Timor-Leste, which killed over two hundred Timorese youths.[10]

To counter the state-controlled view of the relationship between Indonesia and Timor-Leste, independent documentaries made by foreigners and produced outside of Indonesia's borders played a vital role in alerting the global community to the violent actions of the Indonesian military, masked under the guise of maintaining stability and order, and the failure of its "development" strategies to win the hearts and minds of the Timorese. The year 1991 put Timor-Leste on the international stage with the release of Max Stahl's smuggled footage of the Santa Cruz Massacre, a documentary titled *In Cold Blood: The Massacre of East Timor*. The footage revealed the systematic encircling of the cemetery before the massacre. The scenes of the Indonesian military opening fire on the Timorese sparked a shocked realization in the audience by portraying the actual nature of Indonesian domination. Another film produced during this period was the informative documentary by John Pilger, *The Death of a Nation: The Timor Conspiracy* (1994). Pilger first went to Timor-Leste in 1993 and was concerned about the complicity of Western governments in the measures taken by Indonesia. These two documentaries typify the ways in which Timor-Leste was presented by filmmakers who opposed the occupation and how its subjects were constructed by foreign film producers.

Since independence, there have been a number of Australian films on Timor-Leste, but none as widely publicized as director Robert Connolly's *Balibo* (2009). This dense film is packaged as a political thriller. It intelligently relates the story of five Australian journalists who became victims of the Indonesian invasion of East Timor in a small border town called Balibo in 1965. The story centers on Roger East, a sixth Australian reporter, who went in search of the five missing journalists at the prompting of young José Ramos-Horta. In the film, we follow a reenactment of East's investigative journey to Balibo and his violent death. His individual story is set against the larger historical backdrop, the critical turning point of Timor-Leste's

---

[9] Ibid., p. 6.

[10] The Santa Cruz massacre galvanized the *Geração Foun* and remains a touchstone for identity formation. The long march through the center of Dili to the cemetery of Santa Cruz, in protest against the killing of a young boy, was the first large public demonstration carried out against the Indonesian occupation that involved such large numbers of young people. Of those who marched, 271 youths were killed by soldiers at the Santa Cruz cemetery in Dili.

colonial history, when Indonesia invaded the tiny region, a former Portuguese colony, with the support of the Australian government. The film was released just weeks before the Australian Federal Police announced they would conduct an investigation into the killings of the six journalists. The probe followed a 2007 coroner's inquest that concluded that the Indonesian military had summarily executed the journalists to cover up the invasion and that they were not caught in crossfire, as the Indonesian government previously claimed.

Balibo won three Australian Film Institute awards and has received broad and extended screenings in Australia since its cinema release in mid-2009. The response in Indonesia has also been enthusiastic. While the film has been banned by the Indonesian film censorship board, the Alliance of Independent Journalists (AJI) has defied the ban by arranging a series of free screenings throughout the country. As many as seven hundred people were reported to have attended the screening of the film in Bandung, West Java. This impressive attendance rate verifies that censorship can sometimes act as a spur to a film's popularity. Indeed, copied versions of the DVD of *Balibo* continue to be widely circulated.

The film was also screened in Timor-Leste on August 30, 2009, ten years after the independence referendum of 1999, on the lawn of the president's palace in Dili. Although the event was not widely publicized, many came to see the English-language film that had been dubbed in Tetum. The actor Anthony Lapaglia, who starred in the film, was also in attendance. However, this celebrity was of little significance to the Timorese viewers, who were more occupied with spotting their relatives or friends on the big screen. Riotous laughter would erupt from the audience every time local artist Osme Gonsalves appeared in the background playing the driver for the journalists. This response seemed to give the film another possible interpretation. While the Westerners sitting next to me were deeply moved by the abhorrent execution scenes, many young Timorese were entertained. They are members of a new generation of youth who came of age after independence and are learning of the pain and trauma of the Indonesian invasion not through direct experience, but through family reports and mediated scenes on screen. They may be a new generation of youth growing up in dramatically different contexts, but many embody the same youthful optimism and hope for peace, justice, and independence that the youthful generation of Ramos-Horta and the slain journalists had once fought to attain.

THE *SUPERMI* GENERATION OF TIMOR-LESTE

The producers of *Rock 'n' Roll with Jakarta* are politically active young Timorese whose common characteristic is that they grew up during the Indonesian occupation between 1975 and 1999. They have a shared past, strongly marked by the resistance struggle, Indonesian schooling (an estimated fifteen thousand attended university in Indonesia during this period), and a fluency in Indonesia's languages and cultures. They also share a concern for Timor-Leste's future. The imagined community of the *Geração Foun* continues to inform the attitudes and outlooks on life of young people, more so than members of the generations that went before them.

The *Geração Foun* was pejoratively dubbed the *Generasi Supermi* (the Supermi Generation) by members of the Portuguese-speaking '75 Generation. *Supermi* is an iconic Indonesian brand of instant noodles, and the label suggests that the youngsters are metaphorically soft like noodles. They lack strength and wisdom;

they have an *instan* attitude toward life, and do not possess strong morals or leadership qualities. This negative marking of the younger generation by the power-holders, which is intensified by the younger generation's links to a discredited Indonesia, questions their legitimacy as subjects of national belonging. An important distinction needs to be made between "official" citizenship, which signifies a formal recognition of one's national status by the state, and practical national belonging, which refers to a person's everyday sense that he or she has been accepted by the dominant community and so belongs to the nation. This process is determined by a cumulative logic, whereby citizens mobilize certain practices that translate to national belonging.[11] Through the creation of *Rock 'n' Roll with Jakarta*, young Timorese could give meaning to the Indonesian past through their cultural gaze, and thereby asserted their legitimacy as citizens of national belonging.

Questions regarding the best ways to deal with the painful memories of Indonesian occupation color many Timorese postcolonial concerns, and in this sense constitute an inherent part of the Timorese quest for an independent identity. The approach of the governing elites, who belong to the Portuguese-speaking '75 Generation, was to search into a past prior to the Indonesian invasion to forge an independent identity based on a history distinct from the horrific experience with Indonesia. The result was to construct Portugal as the legitimate and authentic root of the Timorese national imaginary. President Xanana Gusmão, in his Independence Day speech, said the Timorese should pay their respects to Portugal for giving rise to their nation. Many groups in society, particularly the youth, found this recommendation to be irreconcilable with their own point of view, as the younger generation did not share any experience of Portugal.

Young Timorese focus on cultural practice such as poetry, performance, music, text, and film in order to assert their patriotic subjectivity in postcolonial Timor. This cultural practice combines approaches from the 1970s anticolonial movement (of which the Portuguese-speaking elites were a part) and highlights suffering at the hands of Indonesian forces. At the same time, the youths' cultural practice is informed by a transnational engagement with progressive Indonesian cultures and cosmopolitan discourses of justice and democracy. Indonesia represents, at once, both cultures of resistance and cultures of violence (and, most importantly for young Timorese, suffering). Indonesia forms a central component of Timorese youths' subjectivities, and therefore cannot be forgotten.

FRAMING THE *GERAÇÃO FOUN*

Rock 'n' Roll with Jakarta focuses on the issue of justice by pointing the finger at the political elite of Timor-Leste for failing to make forceful demands for much needed international and UN support to bring Indonesian perpetrators to justice. The film is a rejection of President Xanana Gusmão's assertion that independence and peace are the rewards for the Timorese independence struggle. *Rock 'n' Roll with Jakarta* contests the notion of "truth" and "friendship," and argues relentlessly that friendship must be based on a sound understanding and implementation of justice. It portrays the Truth and Friendship Commission (TFC) as an act of surrender, carried out with impunity. Gusmão wishes to move beyond the devastating tragedy and

---

[11] Ashley Carruthers, "The Accumulation of National Belonging in Transnational Fields: Ways of Being at Home in Vietnam," *Identities: Global Studies in Culture and Power* 9 (2002): 423–44.

accelerate both healing and reconciliation, and the TFC is based on this logic. However, in the opinions of the younger generation, the ongoing debate on justice and reconciliation in Timor-Leste has deeper implications, and principles informed by a wish to maintain "friendships" and act pragmatically are not workable, given the situation.

Rock 'n' Roll with Jakarta actively engages with issues of national concern. One can argue that, at this point in Timor's short history, there is no issue more important than recent history, shaped by Indonesia's dominance. The film actively engages issues of identity politics on a personal and collective level. For the youths of Timor-Leste, to disregard the importance of the brutal Indonesian past is an inconceivable act, which contributes to national amnesia and erodes democratic legitimacy in Timor-Leste. Furthermore, to disregard the importance of the Indonesian past, while promoting Portugal as the authentic root of the Timorese imaginary, has made many who were born after the Portuguese colonial era feel that their histories and contributions to the nation have been ignored.

Shot with digital cameras, the fifty-eight-minute *Rock 'n' Roll with Jakarta* portrays interviews with Timorese and Indonesian political actors, along with intellectuals and survivors of New Order violence in Indonesia and Timor-Leste. The opening scenes introduce the main antagonists—Xanana Gusmão (Timor-Leste's prime minister) and Jose Ramos Horta (president), along with Indonesian allies Susilo Bambang Yudhoyono, Ali Alatas, former military chief General Wiranto, and the infamous militia leader, Euricco Gutteres—engaged in a slow-motion dance together, accompanied and mocked by the soundtrack, which features Elvis Presley crooning *Don't be Cruel*.

The film then introduces the protagonists: members of the *Geração Foun,* their reactions captured in footage shot throughout the 1990s. Activist students are shown on podiums with megaphones and at the forefront of demonstrations, campaigning for Timor-Leste's right to independence. Here, the young activists are represented as contemporary youth warriors (*klosan funu nain* in Tetum) as they go into "battle" with the Indonesian forces on the streets of Jakarta, on Jalan Thamrin outside the United Nations office and the Indonesian parliament's building.

The young Timorese in these scenes sing about Maubere, which represents the essence of what it means to be Timorese. Maubere is a negative term, denoting dirty and poor peasants, that was commonly used by the Portuguese to describe the Timorese during colonial times. There are, in fact, two indigenous, derogatory terms in Tetum for "poor peasant," defined by gender: Maubere (masculine) and Buibere (feminine). Ramos Horta picked up on and used the term "Maubere" during the early years of the resistance movement in the 1970s to signify Timorese pride by appropriating a formerly dismissive word. Young Timorese in this film clip sing the powerful "Maubere," a national independence song. The chanting of the lyrics, "Our insides are Maubere. We are Maubere," while they dance the *tebe-tebe* (a traditional welcoming dance), is a personal and bodily reaffirmation of their authentic, traditional, and therefore legitimate Timorese identity, and a reference that surpasses in power the associations with Portugal that the '75 Generation have attempted to legitimize as the genuine Timorese past.

In Timor-Leste, the land of the Maubere, both the nation and its history are contested concepts, and the politics of the Timor-Leste postcolonial state is the politics of remembering and forgetting. Hersri Setiawan, an Indonesian poet and human rights activist, claims that recalling the past is a matter of justice and a necessary process for both countries. In *Rock 'n' Roll with Jakarta*, he says:

> The act of collecting and expressing victims' voices is actually an act of reclaiming historical memory. And if you, or I do that, as a private practice ... [it] will become that of collective memory. And, if these memories of a dark past become collective memories, I think this will become a powerful tool against the alliances and false promises made by the political elite of both my country, Indonesia, and yours of Timor-Leste. [Author's translation]

Young Timorese find it imperative both to remember and to continue working with Indonesia in areas such as cultural production, but they want justice in the form of an international tribunal. Meanwhile, Xanana Gusmão is in favor of seeking regional diplomatic and economic stability to appease Indonesia. It is in this light that the film about Xanana, *A Hero's Journey* (Grace Phan, 2006), was allowed to screen at the 2007 Jakarta International Film Festival, whereas the film *Passabe* (James Leong and Lynn Lee, 2005), about Timorese village perspectives on justice, was banned at both the 2005 and 2006 festivals. The decision to ban this film illustrates the continuing self-censorship operating in Indonesia. "Maintaining stability" remains a priority for the Timorese and Indonesian government, but it comes with a cost, for it represses discussions of a potentially flammable past. However, the co-director of *Passabe*, James Leong, has suggested that the film's viewing could also have a cathartic effect on Indonesian audiences by developing an understanding of what happened in Timor-Leste during the occupation.

FRAMING TIMOR-LESTE

Rock 'n' Roll with Jakarta can be seen as an attempt by members of the *Geração Foun* to assert their subjectivity as legitimate Timorese citizens—those who "own" the Indonesian past by contesting the narratives of Timor's past offered by the elite. The film deals with the memory of Indonesia, and with practical issues of justice and reconciliation, through examining the implications for the establishment of the Commission for Truth and Friendship. (Its better-known name is the Indonesian acronym TFC, humorously referred to as the Timor Fried Chicken by Indonesian and Timorese activists alike.) The TFC was formed in March 2005 by the presidents of Indonesia and Timor-Leste. This was an unsuccessful effort to dissuade then United Nations (UN) Secretary-General Kofi Annan from appointing a Commission of Experts (CoE) to make recommendations for the establishment of an international tribunal to ensure justice for those whose human rights were violated in Timor-Leste in 1999. Members of the younger generation involved in civil-society organizations, as well as representatives of the Catholic church, supported both the conclusion of the UN-sponsored Commission for Truth, Reception, and Reconciliation in Timor-Leste (CAVR) and the CoE, which relates justice to the establishment of an international tribunal.

The final two-thousand-page report published by CAVR, entitled *Chega!* (Enough!), is the most comprehensive historical record to date of this painful period.[12] It is based on 7,669 statements from survivors and victims' families. It reports that large-scale military attacks in the regions, and later in Indonesian detention camps and resettlement areas, where food and medical care were grossly insufficient, were common practice. Responsibility for this carnage, in addition to widespread torture, starvation, and rape used as a weapon of war, rests largely with the Indonesian military, according to the report.[13]

Rock 'n' Roll with Jakarta was a reaction to the failed justice mechanisms that were implemented in Timor-Leste. Citing extensive evidence, the CAVR report clearly documents that the highest echelons of the Indonesian army knew that a scorched-earth campaign was being planned for Timor-Leste. However, the report's recommendations for implementing justice at the level of an international tribunal have not been acted upon.

The first of the justice-seeking measures was the establishment of the Ad Hoc Human Rights Court on Timor-Leste in Jakarta, followed by the Special Panels for Serious Crimes in Dili. These two institutions were widely acknowledged to have failed in fulfilling their mandates. The Judicial System Monitoring Programme (JSMP) observed that the processes of the Ad Hoc Tribunal were "highly irregular and critically flawed ... [T]he Special Panels have been under-resourced and starved of international political support and cooperation."[14] These efforts were followed by the appointment of the CoE, which also agreed with the recommendations of the CAVR that formal justice is fundamental to the healing of the nation.

Through interviews with survivors and their families, *Rock 'n' Roll with Jakarta* supports the evidence in the CoE report, which states: " ... 52 percent of the population responded that justice must be sought even if it slows down reconciliation with Indonesia."[15] The report concludes that it "may provide the last opportunity for the Security Council [to establish an international tribunal] to ensure that accountability is secured for those responsible for grave human rights violations and human suffering on a massive scale and delivery of justice for the people of Timor-Leste."[16] However, as the film *Rock 'n' Roll* illustrates, the United Nations failed to keep its promise of prosecuting perpetrators and did not provide sufficient funding or political backing for judicial mechanisms to be implemented.

The complexity of Timor-Leste's independence colors the form and content of the birth of Timorese indigenous independent film production. The themes and

---

[12] Commission for Truth, Reception, and Reconciliation in Timor-Leste (CAVR), "*Chega!* Final Report of the Commission for Truth, Reception, and Reconciliation in Timor-Leste," at www.etan.org/news/2006/cavr.htm, last accessed March 16, 2011.

[13] The CAVR report determined that a small proportion of the toll was due to internecine violence among the four main East Timorese parties, including Fretilin, and reprisals against those who collaborated with the Indonesian military.

[14] Judicial System Monitoring Programme (JSMP), "Justice for Victims Still Elusive. Press Release," May 26, 2005, www.jsmp.minihub.org/Press%20Release/2005/May/050524%20 End%20SPSC.pdf, viewed June 13, 2011; and "Prosecution of Serious Violations of Human Rights in Timor-Leste in 1999: JSMP's Submission to the United Nation's Commission of Experts," http://www.jsmp.minihub.org/Reports/jsmpreports/JSMP's%20Summission% 20to%20CoE.pdf

[15] Commission of Experts, "Report to the Secretary-General of the Commission of Experts to Review the Prosecution of Serious Violations of Human Rights in Timor-Leste [the then East Timor] in 1999," May 26, 2005, p. 90.

[16] Ibid., p. 125.

preoccupations of the films noted here, exemplified through the case study of *Rock 'n' Roll with Jakarta*, are concerned with contested memories that occupy different generations of citizens and the unique relationship between youth culture and collective memory. The continuity of memories of the Indonesian occupation, the violence and the role of the young people in the independence movement, are vital to the continuity of the identity of the *Geração Foun* and their place within independent Timor-Leste. The conducive conditions of independence have made Timorese indigenous filmmaking possible, and the production of *Rock 'n' Roll with Jakarta* attests to its firm beginnings.

SELECTED FILMOGRAPHY

A Hero's Journey (Grace Phan, 2006)
Balibo (Robert Connolly, 2009)
Death of a Nation: The Timor Conspiracy (John Pilger, 1993)
In Cold Blood: the Massacre of Timor-Leste (Max Stahl, 1991)
Langit Kembali Biru (The Sky Returns Blue, Dimas Harring and S. Dias Xiemenes, 1991)
Mass Grave (Lexy Rambadeta, 2001)
Passabe (James Leong and Lynn Lee, 2005)
Pengkhianatan (Treacherous 30 September Movement, Arifin C. Nur, 1984)
Punitive Damage (Annie Goldson, 1999)
Rock 'n' Roll with Jakarta (Sahe Media Popular, The Sahe Institute for Liberation, 2005)
The Diplomat (Tom Zubrycki, 2000)

THE STRANGE STORY OF A STRANGE BEAST: RECEPTIONS IN THAILAND OF APICHATPONG WEERASETHAKUL'S *SAT PRALAAT*[1]

Benedict R. O'G. Anderson

In 2005, at the end of a talk for perhaps one hundred professors and students at Thammasat University in Bangkok, I took the opportunity to ask those in the audience who had heard of Apichatpong Weerasethakul and his astonishing film *Sat pralaat*[2] (2004) to raise their hands. I was quite surprised when only about fifteen hands went up. When I made the same request for those who had actually seen the film, only about eight or nine people identified themselves. How was this possible? After all, Apichatpong had won the Special Jury Prize at the 2004 Cannes International Film Festival, which is generally regarded as the single most important international film festival in the world. Nor was this triumph a one-time fluke. Two years earlier, he had won another important prize at Cannes for his *Sut Saneha* (2002).[3] One would have thought that a Bangkok public eager to claim Tiger Woods as a "world-class Thai," even though he speaks no Thai, would have been enormously proud of, and excited by, Apichatpong's impressive success. But no. The question is: why not?

If one watches the very intelligent, biting, and funny mockumentary of "Alongkot," entitled *Room kat sat pralaat* (Ganging Up on *Sat pralaat*, 2004), the

---

[1] A shorter version of this essay first appeared, in Thai, in *Sinlapawatthanatham* magazine, July 2006, pp. 140–53. I wrote the expanded version specifically for this collection under the editorial guidance of May Ingawanij. At Apichatpong's request, and in a gesture of friendship to him, May and I granted permission for "The Strange Story of a Strange Beast" to be published also in the Austrian Film Museum's book about him.

[2] The English language version of the title is the rather exotic *Tropical Malady*. The Thai title, which means literally "Strange Beast," refers to the shape-shifting were-tiger of folklore and legend. Curiously enough, in the first gay magazines of the early 1980s, one can find the term occasionally used as gayspeak for a penis, or for a male homosexual. When I asked Apichatpong whether he knew of this usage, he said he'd never heard of it, and it must have died out when he was still very young.

[3] *Sut saneha* means something like "total happiness." But the English title given it was *Blissfully Yours*.

beginnings of an explanation emerge.[4] The mockumentary repeatedly (and wrongly) tells watchers that *Sat pralaat* played in only three Thai cinemas (all in Bangkok), and for only one week in each.[5] Why so? A series of short interviews follows with various types of Bangkokian minor celebrities and "talking heads," who say that the film is "great," "extremely interesting," and reaches a "global level above that of other Thai films." (They are responding to the Cannes prize rather than to the film itself.) But their descriptions of it as "surreal," and "*abstrak maak*" (extremely abstract) indicate both that they do not understand the film at all, and also that they are sure that it would be pointless to circulate the film in provincial cinemas. It would be way over the *cheuy* (hick, unsophisticated) heads of the *khon baan nork* (up-country people).

The mockumentary then proceeds to wonderful extended interviews with four genuine *chao baan* (villagers, rubes), three boys, one girl, after they have been brought to Bangkok to see *Sat pralaat* at a special screening put on by the Alliance Française. After the show, the unseen interviewer tells the four that many Bangkok intellectuals find the film "*yaak*" (difficult) and "*lyk lap*" (mysterious), and asks them whether they share that reaction. The *chao baan* all say that the film is great, that there is nothing especially *yaak* or *lyk lap* about it, and that they would like to see it shown at cinemas back home. They say they understand it perfectly. We shall discuss some details of their reactions later on.

Before turning to the question of why both Cannes and the *chao baan* really liked the film, while many Bangkokians did not, it is worth reporting on a brief, amateurish research trip that I recently took with Mukhom Wongthes and May Ingawanij. We decided to spend two days interviewing personnel working at video stores in Chonburi, Samut Sakhon, Samut Songkhram, Ratburi, Suphanburi, and Ayutthaya, in a rough half circle around Bangkok, all about an hour's drive away. These businesses come in two types: stores that are in the rental outlets, mostly in downtown areas, and stores, always located in malls, that sell legal and pirated DVDs at quite low prices. What did we discover? First, that all the people interviewed, except in one small store in Suphanburi, knew about *Sat pralaat*, and a good number had the DVD of this film on their shelves. How did they know about it? Not from newspapers or magazines, but from references on TV and, most interestingly, from customers' requests. When we asked what kind of customers were interested in *Sat pralaat*, the most common answer was "oh, all kinds, mostly families." Others said, "young people who already have jobs"—i.e., in their twenties and early thirties, as opposed to teenagers. But still others said they also had requests from teens. How did the film do with the public? "Not bad," "average," "in steady demand" … in other words, not outstandingly successful, but not a flop, either. One store clerk told us the customers were mainly male, but others denied there was any difference between the sexes. One should note that these customers were not *chao baan*, but people living in small provincial towns.

At this point we can profitably turn to the film itself, in order to deepen our inquiry. Except for an enigmatic opening scene—in which a group of young soldiers

---

[4] "Alongkot" is actually Alongkot Maiduang, who writes film criticism under the penname "Kanlaphraphruek." He has published an excellent, searching survey of Apichatpong's films in his collection of film criticism, *Asia 4: si yod phu kamkap haeng asia tawan ok* [Four Top East Asian Directors] (Bangkok: Openbooks, 2005). He has also made a number of short films, which were shown at the Fourth Bangkok Experimental Film Festival in 2005.

[5] Apichatpong has written to me that it was actually shown in only one cinema, the Lido, but for three weeks.

out in the countryside come across a corpse, while the viewers see in the distance the obscure figure of a naked man moving through the high grass on the edge of a jungle—the first half of *Sat pralaat* shows us how a handsome young soldier (Keng) woos an odd-looking youngster (Tong) who works in a local ice-business. The two men never take off any clothes, never kiss each other, let alone have sex, but the film shows us the progress of this *chao baan* courtship in a wide variety of village and small town settings.

"What do you think of the two men courting?" The interviewees in
Room kat sat pralaat

In *Room kat sat pralaat,* the interviewer, pretending to be a middle-class Bangkokian, on several occasions asks the four *chao baan* about this courtship: "Up-country, are there really men who are in love with other men?" The villagers matter-of-factly answer, "Oh yes, it's quite ordinary." All agree that Tong and Keng really love each other, and the shyest of the boys goes so far as to say that the courtship is very "romantic."[6] The girl comments, with a broad smile, that the scene where Keng lies with his head in Tong's lap gave her goose pimples (*khon luk*). The interviewer pretends to be surprised by all this, and asks the girl whether she thinks Keng is maybe a *kratheuy* soldier.[7] She giggles and replies: "Yes, the soldier mostly likely is a

---

[6] He actually uses a Thai-ified form of the word "romantic."

[7] *Kratheuy* is an old Khmer word adopted into the Thai language. It means an effeminate man who likes to dress in women's clothes. It should be noted that the *kratheuy* are a recognized group in traditional Thai society, even if usually stigmatized. The word and the concept of "gay" only entered Thai in the late 1970s. Note that the interviewer deliberately poses his question as an oxymoron—could a macho soldier really be an effeminate?—to see how the villagers will react.

kratheuy." And Tong? "Well ... he's a bit coy ... um ... mostly likely he is the same." It is plain that the mockumentary is trying to show how ordinary a romance between two young men is up-country, while for some Bangkok people it might seem "trendy, aping the West," "shameful," or even "un-Thai." (But it is the interviewer who introduces the word *kratheuy*, and before he does so the *chao baan* just use *chai* [man] or *khon* [person]; the boys never describe Keng and Tong as *kratheuy*.)

The attentive viewer, however, will quickly notice one very striking feature of the first half of *Sat pralaat*—the soundtrack. For the most part, there is no background music at all: instead, we hear the sounds of everyday country life, motorbikes, dogs barking, small machines working, and so on. The mostly banal conversations are also essentially "background," and one does not need to pay careful attention to their content. Foregrounded are faces, expressions, body language, and silent communication with eyes and smiling lips. The elderly woman whom Tong calls *mae* (mum) shows by her expression that she understands the courtship going on, but she says nothing about it, nor does anyone else in the village. A Bangkok viewer who does not pay attention to the strangeness of the soundtrack could easily dismiss the first half as something very *cheuy*, even wondering when the two men will finally undress and fall into each other's arms.

Keng recovers from the beast's attack, in *Sat pralaat*[8]

The real problem for such viewers, however, arises in the astonishing second half of the film, in which almost no human word is spoken. It shows us Keng setting off alone into the jungle to track down a *Sat pralaat*, which has apparently been killing the villagers' cattle. In this half, the soundtrack moves into the foreground, and what we hear, most of the time, are the sounds of the jungle and the sounds that Keng makes as he moves deeper and deeper inside it. Much of this half takes place at night. As Keng tracks the puzzling foot or paw prints before him, human and animal, it seems to dawn on him that they belong to one creature, and this creature is

---

[8] Images included in this chapter are reproduced from the Mangpong DVD of *Sat pralaat*.

a *seua saming,* or were-tiger, but also, perhaps, Tong. Eventually, he is attacked by a "beast" in whom viewers will recognize the strange naked figure from the opening scene. It is Tong, and completely human in shape, except that he has tigerish stripes self-painted on his face, and he growls and snarls without saying a human word. In the hand-to-hand fight that ensues, Tong is the winner. He drags Keng's stunned body to the edge of a steep hill, and shoves it down. No attempt is made to kill (let alone eat) Keng, who is not seriously hurt at all, and the last we see of Tong is the silhouette of him standing at the top of the hill as if to reassure himself that Keng is really all right. In the remaining part of the film, the viewer follows Keng as he resumes his search, experiencing various "magical" events (a dead, half-eaten cow getting up in perfect condition and disappearing into the jungle, a wise monkey giving him advice, and so on). The film ends with Keng on his knees in the mud looking up at a motionless tiger crouched on the high branch of a tree in front of him. We hear his inner voice saying: "Strange beast, take them, my soul, my blood, my flesh, my memory … In every drop of my blood there is our song, a song of happiness … there it is … do you hear it?"

What to make of this second part? When I showed the film to some highly educated, bourgeois Filipino gays in Manila, they quickly decided that it was "another type of the now very popular genre of Asian Horror Film," pioneered in Japan, which has spread to Korea, China, Indonesia, the Philippines, and so forth. This is not the reaction of the young up-country people interviewed by Alongkot. Two of the boys have had personal experience of the jungle, and say it is like that: *sayong* (scary) and *tyn-ten* (tense, exciting), sometimes even "hair-raising." They have never seen a *seua saming,* but are sure that "they existed in the old days." The only thing that puzzles them is the very last scene, which they felt was cut short, unfinished.

The tiger looks at the hunter, in *Sat pralaat*

An even more interesting reaction was that of my bosom friend Ben Abel, an Indonesian Dayak who was raised by his animist grandfather on the fringes of what was then, forty years ago, the immense, largely untouched jungle of Borneo. When I asked whether he found the second half "difficult," he said "Not at all. I understand it perfectly." He had often gone hunting in the jungle, also at night, with his grandfather, his friends, and even alone, and could immediately identify all the animal and bird sounds on the film's soundtrack. "The jungle is where you really have to listen all the time, and keep as quiet as possible yourself. Yes, it can be frightening, but it is like a strange and wonderful world all of its own. You keep wanting to go back. You know you are testing yourself, and learning about yourself, too."

When I asked him about were-tigers, he confirmed what Professor Nidhi Iowsriwongse told me from his childhood days.[9]

The true *seua saming* are always human males. Only men have the spiritual power to change their shapes as they wish. They can appear as tigers, but inside the tiger is a human intelligence and soul. Usually they change shape to escape some danger, mostly from other human beings. There is another kind of *seua saming* which is female, but it is a spirit, not a human being. It can appear as a tiger or as a beautiful woman, but it is always a malevolent spirit.

Drawn image of the were-tiger in *Sat pralaat*. The lines say, "Once upon a time, there was a Khmer shaman whose magical power enabled him to change his body into various beasts."

A very short scene in the second half of *Sat pralaat*—which at first seems inexplicable—shows one of Keng's experienced, older military comrades on night-guard at the fringe of the jungle. Suddenly a beautiful woman appears and asks him to go with her to help her sick mother. But the soldier refuses to leave his post and tells her to go home at once, as the jungle at night is too dangerous for women. As she turns away, the man notices a long tiger tail protruding from under her skirt. She

---

[9] Nidhi is, by general agreement, Siam's greatest historian, as well as a brilliant essayist, columnist, satirist, and principled social activist.

is there, one could say, to show exactly what Tong is not: she is a malevolent spirit, but Tong is human.

In any event, Ben Abel went on, more or less in the following vein:

> You know, if you grow up in or near the jungle, as I did, the distance city people feel between human beings and the animal world is hardly there. You begin to understand the meaning of the different sounds the birds and beasts make hunting, mating, escaping, warning, and so on. Also, people can pass from one world to the other—an uncle who died recently can be recognized in an owl hooting at night. When they sleep, people's spirits leave the body, and bring back messages, sometimes in dreams.

He added that he thought that in the second half of the film, Keng is looking for something, answers to what he doesn't understand about himself, Tong, and many other things. "What is so wonderful about the ending is that Keng's love is so deep that he is willing to give up 'his soul, his body, even his memory,' in other words, a certain idea of human beings as gods, apart from the rest of the natural world. His spirit is in the process of finding Tong's." His final comment to me was: "This is the most wonderful movie I have seen. I can't believe that anyone making a film today could get inside the world in which I grew up, and present it with such perfection. I've never seen anything like it."

In the summer of 2005, I was invited to a scholarly convention in Fortaleza, a remote town on the north coast of Brazil, just in front of the vast, empty, wild interior prairie called the Sertão, which is the source of many Brazilian legends and also films. In the municipal museum, I found something remarkable, an exhibition of tiny hand-sewn booklets of about twenty pages, with rough etchings on the covers. These booklets are sold mainly at bus stops, and to very poor people. They are written in poetry, often beautiful, and usually without a named author. The subjects are typically famous rebellions, massacres, and miracles in the past. But the collection included a section devoted to deeply felt romances between unhappy girls and their goats, and between cowboys and their horses and donkeys. When I asked my educated friends about them, their answer was rather Bangkokian. "Well, you know, on the ranches out there deep in the Sertão, there are no women, so the men either have sex with other men or with their animals. What can you expect?" I replied that this seemed difficult to believe. "What about the poor girl who flees her cruel master in the company of her beloved goat? What about the wife who cuts the throat of her husband's horse out of jealousy? So far as I can tell, the cowboy and his horse are in love, but they don't have sex." "Hmmmm! Hmmmm! I see what you mean." But what did I mean?

If, as it seems to me likely, Apichatpong was trying to make a film, not "about" the world of the *chao baan* of Siam, but rather "from inside" that world, from inside its culture and its consciousness of itself, then one can easily see why Alongkot's four young interviewees found the film both clear and gripping. At the same time, one can see why many of the city people of today's air-conditioned Bangkok find it "difficult," and "mysterious." They are accustomed to films about themselves and their social superiors, with *chao baan* included only for local color or comical side effects. They do not find it at all odd that the poor Isan[10] lad who plays the main role in Prince Chatrichalerm Yukol's otherwise excellent film *Thongpoon khokpo ratsadorn tem khan* (The Citizen, 1977) should be played by a fair-skinned, utterly Bangkokian pretty-boy. They enjoy Tony Jaa's stunning martial arts skill in *Ong Bak* (Prachya Pinkaew, 2003), only adding, as I heard some well-dressed girls say to each other as they came out of the multiplex of the Central Mall in Taling Chan: "What a pity, the hero isn't handsome."[11] They like, up to a point, films using Thai legends, but to be agreeable, these films have to be versions of well-known "legends" and the viewers have to be able to take a certain anthropological distance from them. A good example is the very popular recent version of *Nang naak* (Snake Girl, Nonzee Nimibutr, 1999). It recreates an originally eerie folktale, which everyone knows at least in rough outline, in the Bangkok TV bourgeois manner.[12] The folktale is about a young woman who dies in childbirth while her husband is off at war, and returns as a vengeful widow ghost; the film, however, has the woman so deeply in love with her husband that she returns as a spirit who magically reappears to him as if she were still alive. When the villagers try to get the entranced husband to see the truth, she retaliates violently. So: "It's a love story!" The Snake Girl is not a Strange Beast at all, but a nice woman who can't bear to leave her husband even after death. Here we can detect Apichatpong's cunning. *Sat pralaat* is, in some respects, legendary in character, yet it is not based on any legend with which people are generally familiar. But he makes sure that the film cannot be Bangkokized and banalized by strategically introducing the theme of *chai rak chai* (men love men).[13] Just imagine if *Nang naak* were turned into *Num naak* (Snake Boy)?

But I suspect there is even more to the resolution of the puzzle with which this essay is concerned. This is the difficult problem of "Thainess" (*khwampenthai*). Some years ago, the famous novelist, poet, and critic Sujit Wongthes's pioneering and iconoclastic book *Jek pon lao* (Jek Mixed with Lao) caused a stir by its argument that "Thainess" was not something truly ancient, but was the relatively recent product of the osmosis between longstanding "Jek" and "Lao" cultures.[14] As I have heard it,

---

[10] Isan is the usual name for northeastern Siam, the poorest region of the country. The people's main language is a dialect that is closer to Lao than Central Thai. The area is especially famous for its popular folk-derived music. Isan people are usually looked down on by Bangkokians as dark-skinned, rough, and unsophisticated.

[11] Tony Jaa's debut was a huge commercial success in Siam, and the film went on to become a hit in the international market as well. Tony comes from Isan and is rather dark-skinned. In fact, he is quite good-looking, but the girls' idea of masculine beauty was centered on skin color. Perhaps I should add that Taling Chan is a part of Thonburi on the western ("wrong-side of the tracks") bank of the Chao Phraya River, facing Bangkok proper. Charmingly still full of gardens, orchards, and canals, it retains a somewhat rural atmosphere, and very few foreigners live there. But it is being gentrified, and the Central Mall is a magnet for west bank, upwardly mobile, middle-class people. Not far away is the "hick" Pata Plaza (alas, it closed in 2010), frequented by the lower classes. If one watches a film there, one hears the audience loudly commenting and cheering on the hero—in the Isan dialect.

[12] The translation is not really satisfactory. *Naak* is not an ordinary snake, but a Naga, a fabulous kind of serpent.

[13] Not to be confused with Thai Rak Thai (Thai Love Thai), the name of ex-Prime Minister Thaksin Shinawatra's huge political party.

[14] The title was deliberately provocative. We have seen earlier how the Lao-speaking people of Isan are often looked down on by Bangkokians, who also regard Laos as a "little brother" of Siam. *Jek* is a derogatory word for Chinese, analogous to "chink."

Sujit was quite surprised by some of the grateful letters he received from readers. They were touched and stirred by his positive invocation of *khwampenjek* ("jek-ness"). (This emotional response reminds one of the reaction of gay men and women to the first serious novels with attractive gay and/or lesbian leading characters. "Finally, we are represented respectfully and honestly.") In the 1990s in Thailand, many books followed in the spirit of "coming out of the *jek* closet." There really was a lot to be proud of in the history and culture of Chinese immigrants to Thailand and their descendants. What is less clear is whether these books were carefully read by many who were not in this closet. We have yet to see "*jek*-ness" celebrated in the textbooks of Thailand's primary and secondary schools.

In the nineteenth century, Bangkok was still overwhelmingly a Chinese city, and, even on the eve of World War II, a majority of the capital city's working class consisted of poor Chinese and Vietnamese immigrants—before the huge waves of migrations from Isan got under way. Today, Bangkok's successful middle classes are heavily *luk jin* (children of Chinese, Sino-Thai, a polite substitute for *jek*).[15]

In many countries the successful urban bourgeoisie is culturally removed from the countryside, yet not ethnically so; but in Siam, this removal is twofold, because of the ethnic origins of the bourgeoisie outside the country.

One might think about it this way: the *luk jin* middle classes are, as elsewhere in the world, energetic, ambitious, and social climbing. Hence, they are inclined to assimilate upwards (at least to a certain point) to the culture of the upper classes and the state. London's House of Lords today is full of successful middle-class people who adore getting titles as Baroness This or Baron That. Bangkok has plenty of female *luk jin* who would love to become *khunying* (a lady, noblewoman).[16] It follows—always up to a point only—that such people are attracted to Thailand's "official nationalism"[17]—especially as performed in TV "historical" dramas and ritual celebrations, and through the "River of Kings" advertising machine.[18] They can find themselves reflected in talk shows and television soap operas, but only in their roles as "Thai bourgeois," not *luk jin*. This can't be wholly satisfactory. They are not at all comfortable with popular films like *Tom yam kung* (the name of a popular spicy Thai soup) (Prachya Pinkaew, 2005), a follow-up to *Ong Bak*, which, like *Citizen* before it, features cruel and greedy villains who are patently "*jek*."

Apichatpong's film is, I think, especially "difficult" for today's *luk jin* middle classes not only because they are invisible within it, but also because it presents a form of "Thai culture" with ancient roots that is "below them," as well as alien to

---

[15] The upper class, including the royal family, is also of partly Chinese origins, but this is not widely recognized in the public sphere.

[16] After the coup of 1932, which overthrew the absolutist monarchy, all the titles traditionally granted by the king to favored male officials were abolished in the spirit of egalitarian democracy. Oddly enough, titles for females were preserved; it is said that this anomaly was the result of pressure by the wives of a few of the top coup leaders.

[17] "Official nationalism" emanates from the state rather than from popular movements, and was created in Europe in the second half of the nineteenth century by worried dynastic rulers fearful of just such movements. For a detailed discussion, see my *Imagined Communities: Reflections on the Origin and Spread of Nationalism* (London: Verso, 1991), chap. 6.

[18] This machine, celebrating the palaces, temples, and monuments of the rulers of Bangkok, through which the Chao Phraya River flows, was originally aimed at boosting the tourist industry's *son et lumière* shows, luxury river cruises, and so on. But more recently it has evinced as much a political as a commercial character.

their experience. To be able to dismiss it as "meant for Westerners" is to show one's own patriotic Thai credentials against the implicit threat that the film poses. Self-deception is necessarily involved, since the biggest addicts of Western consumerist culture are precisely the Bangkok bourgeois. This suggestion might bring us back to Thammasat University, which is sometimes, half-jokingly, half-proudly, self-described as the Biggest Teochiu University in the world.[19] If my argument in this article is even partly correct, it might help to explain the surprising student–faculty ignorance of, and indifference to, *Sat pralaat*'s amazing achievement.

Readers will have noticed that at several places above I have emphasized the word "today's." I do so because I suspect that the deep alienation of middle-class Bangkok from "up-country culture" is something relatively new. During the opening credits to *Sat pralaat*, Apichatpong mentions his debt to, and affection for, the popular "jungle novels," collectively called *Long phrai*, written in creative imitation of, *inter alia*, Conan Doyle's *The Lost World*, by "Noi Inthanon" during the early 1950s—before the massive elimination of most of Thailand's ancient forests by legal and illegal loggers.[20] In these novels, *set in the present*, were-tigers are often featured as real, if "strange," beasts, though the hunter-hero Khun Sak is quite rationalist and scientific in his outlook. Noi's readers were mostly young, perhaps also mostly male, townspeople of varied ethnic and class origins, who listened to the radio rather than watching TV, went to noisy, crowded cinemas rather than losing themselves in cyberspace, lived contentedly without air-conditioning like everyone else, and were not locked into a mediocre "globalized" consumer culture.[21] This older kind of urban society (middle class and lower class) still exists, up to a point, in places like Samut Sakhon and Ratburi, but it has largely vanished from the City of Angels.

It remains only to consider the Bangkok "talking heads" who claim to like *Sat pralaat* very much, but who can make neither head nor tail of it. On this question, I owe a great debt to conversations with May Ingawanij, who has been engaged in a big research project on Thai heritage films.[22] I mentioned earlier the importance these "talking heads" attach to the high-prestige awards that the film has reaped. As they are inclined to see the matter, these awards mean that "our country" is producing films at the *sakon* (international, global) level; hence, their approval of the film means that they, too, are *sakon*. The difficulty is that this word has different and sometimes antagonistic connotations. Sometimes it means that nowadays Westerners appreciate some Thai films. But which? The unsettling examples are, for example, *Satri Lek* (Iron Ladies, Yongyoot Thongkongtoon, 2000), *Beautiful Boxer* (Ekachai Uekrongtham, 2003), *Ong Bak*, and a cluster of horror films, since their success overseas seems to mean that foreigners think of "our country" as mainly populated by kickboxers, effeminates, transsexuals, and evil spirits. Sometimes it means that foreigners have helped in the making and distribution of "good Thai films." A case in point is the

---

[19] The great majority of immigrants from coastal Southeast China have been Teochiu-speakers. In fact the sociological profile of Thammasat is not markedly different from that of other prestigious universities in Bangkok, but Thammasat's cheerful self-mockery is unique.

[20] Noi Inthanon is the pen name of the prolific writer and journalist Malai Chuphinit (1906–63). These novels have a real-life element, as Malai himself was an experienced hunter, and, like the hero of his book, who shares a close bond with his trusted Karen guide, counted among his closest friends the Karens who led him into the heart of the Kanchanaburi jungles.

[21] In fact, these jungle novels were serially broadcast, with great success, in the pre-TV age.

[22] May Adadol Ingawanij, "Hyperbolic Heritage: Bourgeois Spectatorship and Contemporary Thai Cinema" (PhD dissertation, London Consortium, University of London, 2007).

role of Hollywood's Francis Ford Coppola in the final editing, as well as the promotion, of his friend Prince Chatrichalerm's huge, nationalist "heritage" film *Suriyothai* (The Legend of Suriyothai, version 2003). Alas, the film was a flop overseas, and even in "our country" it made a lower net profit than the populist, nationalist, and gory *Baang rajan* (Baang Rajan: The Legend of the Village Warriors, Thanit Jitnukul, 2000), which focused not on royalty but on patriotic *chao baan*.

Sat pralaat might seem a good way out of the difficulties, since it is admired by foreign talking heads, film critics, and well-educated aficionados of "world cinema." "Our kind of people," one could say. Unfortunately, of course, they are not really "our kind of people" because they are situated differently. Sophisticated filmgoers in New York and Tokyo, Paris and Berlin, London and Toronto are accustomed by a long, intellectual tradition not to expect to "understand" a film in any fixed, unambiguous way—hence a culture of what is technically called "multiple readings." They can watch Robert Bresson's astonishing, austere *Pickpocket* (1959) as a film about the alienation of modern urban life, or a Catholic meditation on original sin, or a study of repressed homosexuality, or an allegory of French politics in the 1940s, or … without excluding the alternatives. Typically, the intellectual commitment is in the aesthetics of the film, a personal and collective investment that French intellectuals share with their Japanese and Canadian comrades.

This kind of investment is much more difficult for Thai intellectuals, who naturally want a Thai *sakon* film to be both "world-class/global" and also Thai. This means that the investment is primarily nationalist, which by definition is not *sakon*. Since the deeper concern is political, there is bound to be some hostility, open or concealed, towards the opening up of anything "truly Thai" to the fluid operations of "multiple readings." Foreigners, like Cannes juror Quentin Tarantino, can admire *Sat pralaat*'s ambiguities and highly sophisticated narrative technique, and yet still happily say "It is wonderful, and I don't understand it." But this position is not easily available for some Bangkok intellectuals, who find it difficult to say both "It is a great Thai film" and "I don't really understand it." After all, they *ought* to understand it in a straightforward, unambiguous way, just because they are "good Thai." Apichatpong has made their position all the more difficult in that, at least in Siam itself, he has insisted in his interviews that his film is completely Thai and rooted in Thai traditions, *including Thai popular film traditions*.[23] The "talking heads" in Bangkok, even if they are not completely committed to River of Kings official nationalism, still find it hard to see why a very expensive product of that nationalism, such as *Suriyothai*, arouses, at the *sakon* level, no interest. It is merely boring "provincial cinema" for anthropological specialists. It says nothing to anyone who is not Thai. Needless to say, these people do not relish the idea that official patriotism at home is regarded as provinciality on the world stage.

Why should this be so? One plausible line of argument is that there is some failure to distinguish between the tourist industry and world cinema. The Thai industry has been spectacularly successful in getting short-term holidaymakers to rush-enjoy the Grand Palace, the spectacular Phra Kaew temple, the ancient ruins of Sukhothai, Phanom Rung, and Ayutthaya, the beach resorts of Patthaya, Phuket, and Samui Island, as well as Thai food, Thai friendliness, and the polymorphous Thai sex

---

[23] Until quite recently, educated Thai rarely watched commercial Thai films, which they regarded as low-class, unsophisticated, and meant for the "up-country" market. Their tastes ran rather to the products of Hollywood and Hong Kong.

industry. But this enjoyment is superficial, as befits holidaymakers, who, while they are in Siam, form a captive market. On the other hand, this local enjoyment by backpackers, retired people, vacationing Japanese businessmen, and others has nothing whatever to do with the satisfactions of global cinephilia. This discrepancy puzzles some educated Bangkokians, who find it difficult to understand why the droves of tourists who are happy to buy tickets—in Bangkok—to see the Grand Palace have no wish at all to see *Suriyothai* in Berlin or Rotterdam, where these same viewers do not regard themselves as tourists.

Probably this is why Bangkok "talking heads," in their double position as spokespeople for "Thainess" and as members of *sakon* culture, tend to find themselves trapped. Since *sakon* culture admires Apichatpong, they wish to admire him too. But they cannot take any pleasure in the idea that they "do not understand him." The way out of the dilemma is to insist that *Sat pralaat* is "difficult," and "mysterious." We can thus see why it is highly "abstract" and/or "surreal," and therefore completely unsuitable for circulation in the rural and small-town interior of the country.

One can hardly doubt that Apichatpong enjoys all this. This is why his title is so perfectly multivalent. Who, in today's Siam, are the "strange beasts?" Awkward question, no doubt about it.

POSTSCRIPT: RECEPTIONS ELSEWHERE

Events in Siam since the coup d'état of September 2006 have made it plain that discussing the reception of *Sat pralaat* among different strata and regions of Thai society is no longer sufficient, if, indeed, it ever was. Political conflicts have to be taken into account. Early in 2007, Apichatpong's latest big film, *Saeng sattawat* (Light of a/the Century, but given the English title *Syndromes and a Century*), which had been shown very successfully at various *sakon* film festivals, came up for review by the state board of censors (a mix of police, bureaucrats, and intellectuals-of-a-sort), which decided that it could only be released in Siam if four brief scenes were eliminated. In two of these scenes, Buddhist monks are depicted in ways that the censor-viewers could not tolerate—in the first, one sees a young monk strumming on a guitar, while in the second two monks of different ages are pictured in a public park playing with a battery-powered toy UFO. The other two scenes take place in a hospital.[24] First one sees a tired, middle-aged lady doctor at the end of a grueling day pulling a bottle of liquor from its hiding place in a prosthetic leg and sharing a drink with a couple of younger colleagues. Later, one sees a young doctor passionately kissing his girlfriend, while the camera drifts briefly down to the man's middle, where one hand is clutching an erection concealed inside his trousers.

The censors are film-viewers of a special type. They are not interested in either quality or commercial success. While they usually share the Bangkok middle class's disdain for "up-country people," they also, as an arm of the state, share the bureaucracy's traditional paternalism. Thus, they feel entitled to decide what is good for the "infantile" masses of the people to see on the screen—above all, when the

---

[24] The film, which I have not yet seen, is said to be an indirect tribute to Apichatpong's parents, both doctors, who worked in a hospital in Khon Kaen, the "capital" of Isan, while he was growing up. However, I was able to view the banned scenes at an open meeting in May 2007, designed to rally filmmakers and film-lovers against the whole arbitrary system of censorship.

films are Thai rather than foreign. (For them there can be nothing less agreeable than Apichatpong's films, which are deeply sympathetic to "up-country people" and keep the state almost invisible.) They are not required to justify their decisions publicly. It is enough to say that scenes to be deleted are "offensive" to their nannyish notions of "Thai" propriety. In fact, Thai newspapers are full of scandals about monks' sexual misdeeds, financial manipulations, drug-abuse, and so on. But normally the names of these monks are mentioned, i.e., as individuals, and their activities are accessible only through print. What Apichatpong had done, however, was to show in visual motion some unnamed (so to speak, "any") monks enjoying themselves in a way that would interest no scandal-hungry newspaper. Even if in real life one can easily observe monks having fun, the official nationalist–Buddhist position is that monks must be dedicated, wise, austere, and always serious people. So Apichatpong's gentle satire could be regarded as lèse-Buddhism. The Thai are a liquor-loving people, and it would be very surprising if some doctors, at the end of the working day, do not have a drink or two in their hospitals, and take a little time out to kiss their girl- or boyfriends in a private nook. But the state tries to sustain the prestige of Thai hospitals and the public's trust in Thai doctors by cultivating a public image of authority, austerity, wisdom, and seriousness.[25] So to speak, secular monks.

This was not the first time that Apichatpong had run into censorship, as we shall see, but it was the first occasion where this censorship came from the state. Doubtless to the board's surprise, Apichatpong refused to cut anything, and withdrew his request for permission to circulate the film in his own country.[26] This was also the first time any Thai filmmaker had not caved in, or attempted to bargain with, the censors.

One cannot be sure, but it is possible that the board might have acted differently prior to the September coup. It did not, after all, either censor or ban *Sat pralaat*. To be sure, it has long had double standards, such that foreign, especially Hollywood, films often circulate uncensored, despite their gory violence and fairly graphic sex, while Thai films have been much more strictly policed. But since the coup, censorship of the media has become much more intense, elaborate, and arbitrary. Furthermore, the coup leaders, facing their enemy Thaksin's populist nationalism, have felt it necessary to enforce (and reinforce) the traditional official nationalism, with its three icons, Monarchy, Buddhism, and Nation—a recipe for pharisaism, euphemism, and conformity. It is also possible, if not likely, that Apichatpong might earlier have acted differently, at least less brusquely; but maybe in 2007 he saw his own troubles as like those of many others whose freedom of expression was being repressed by the coup-makers and the state apparatus.

One could thus speak of an increased politicization. Though *Sut saneha* is ostensibly apolitical, the central male character is a poor, illegal migrant from Burma,

---

[25] Apichatpong informs me that the censors invited the Medical Council of Thailand and the Council of Buddhist Monks to a special private showing. These organizations are controlled by elderly conservatives, and are by no means representative. Apichatpong slyly wonders whether the Council of Buddhist Monks representatives had ever watched those popular local horror movies that feature monks running amok.

[26] In an unguarded moment, one of the censors, a scaly Thammasat University teacher who doubles as a henchman to "Sia Jiang" (see below), allowed himself to be interviewed on tape. His remarks showed that he had it in for Apichatpong, whom he said was "too big for his boots," "pretending to be a big international star," "running down religion," and "focusing on faggots."

who is warned by the two Thai women who protect and love him that he must pretend to be dumb so that his speech does not give him away. Such Burmese workers, fleeing poverty and interminable repression in their own country, have often been the victims of ruthless Thai employers, police, military men, and gangsters, and subject to social hostility. Without explicitly saying so, the film is on the side of the Burmese boy and his Thai friends. *Sat pralaat* is also seemingly apolitical, but this was the first Thai film that focused seriously and powerfully on the love between two men, and so broke with a long-standing official–national taboo.[27]

Hence, after rejecting the demands of the censors, Apichatpong, along with colleagues, friends, admirers, and activists, began, in May 2007, to organize a serious protest against the whole system of arbitrary censorship, demanding at the very least the establishment of a rational, clear, and even-handed rating-system for Thai (and foreign) films. (See Chalida Uabumrungjit's essay for the outcome of this campaign.)

Yet in some ways state censorship may be less insidious than that practiced by another, less visible, set of "viewers" who mostly generally share the censors' indifference to quality, but are deeply interested in commercial success. These are the Bangkok entrepreneurs who control, more or less successfully, financial backing for new films, own the cinemas and multiplexes of the country, and regulate the production and, especially, distribution of VCDs and DVDs. They are also people rich enough to have formidable connections within the state apparatus. Essentially we are speaking of a sometimes rivalrous cartel of three "family" commercial empires owned by ... *luk jin!* This essay is not the place to go into much detail, since our focus is on Apichatpong and *Sat pralaat*. Suffice it to say that the "big enchilada" is the vain "Sia [Boss] Jiang," aka Jiang Sae Tae, aka Somsak Techaratanaprasert, who controls Sahamongkol Film International, a company that handles the production of local films and the import of popular foreign films. He also indirectly controls the SF chain of cinemas and multiplexes, which has wide influence through its power to decide what films will or will not be shown. It seems that early on Apichatpong approached "Boss Jiang" to get funds for his films. He must have been partly successful, since the Thai DVD and VCD of *Sut saneha* were produced by a distributor contracted to Sahamongkol. Apichatpong reports that the contract included a clause that any cuts required his consent, but, in fact, he was never consulted and the film was mangled. Busy preparing *Sat pralaat*, and feeling helpless, he let the mangled version go through. The authentic DVD, produced in Paris, has not been widely circulated in Siam. The final scene of the film never had a chance to be censored by the state, as private enterprise had already decisively intervened and deleted it.[28] Not surprisingly, Apichatpong and "Boss Jiang" fell out. This is why the only Thai filmmaker to have won a top prize (actually two!) at Cannes has never been included in the lavishly funded official delegations from Bangkok to the

---

[27] It is a matter of public representation. At least two of Siam's post-World War II prime ministers have been widely known to prefer their own sex to the opposite, but the media never showed photographs of them with their lovers or referred directly to their sexual tastes.

[28] The Burmese man and the two women have escaped, for a time, into the jungle, where they happily bathe in a little stream, chat, and doze off. The man falls into a deep, exhausted slumber. The younger woman, his lover, watches him with a contented smile on her face, fishes his penis out of his shorts, and caresses it without waking him up.

festival.[29] It is also probably the reason why *Sat pralaat* was never shown up-country, and shown only for three weeks, at one cinema, in Bangkok.

This fate of *Sat pralaat* cannot easily be explained by citing the actions of Sahamongkol alone, but only by considering, as well, his collusion with another component of the film cartel. This is the Major Cineplex Group, controlled by Vicha Poolvoralaks and his kinsmen, which owns the largest chain of multiplexes (perhaps 70 percent of all multiplexes in Thailand). Major is mainly a very powerful exhibition and distribution empire.

The last member of the cartel is GTH, a film production company created by a merger (compelled by the industry's financial problems) of the production houses Tai Entertainment and Hub Ho Hin into the integrated entertainment empire GMM Grammy, headed by "Ah Koo" Paiboon Damrongchaitham. GTH differs from the other members of the cartel in that its leader, Ah Koo, acting on good advice, has championed a number of talented young Thai directors who are using sophisticated technical methods, but primarily doing edgy mainstream films (for example, *Dek hor* [The Dorm, 2006] and *Beautiful Boxer*). Many of these films are quite good, as well as popular, yet they are nothing like Apichatpong's creations. It is interesting, however, that Ah Koo provided 25 percent of the budget for *Sat pralaat*—at the last minute—allowing it to be finished just in time for Cannes.[30] But GTH does not have the distributional power of Sahamongkol and Major, and so does not seem to have functioned as Apichatpong's censor.

In the end, the cartel probably matters more than the state board of censors because it operates out of the limelight and is rooted in huge, entrenched financial interests. Apichatpong's genius and reputation have enabled him to bypass the cartel at one level, by providing him with financial backers overseas, mainly in Western Europe. But these backers can only help him make the films, not distribute them to his countrymen.

SELECTED FILMOGRAPHY

Room kat sat pralaat (Ganging Up on *Sat pralaat*, "Alongkot," 2004)
Saeng sattawat (Syndromes and a Century, Apichatpong Weerasethakul, 2006)
Sat pralaat (Tropical Malady, Apichatpong Weerasethakul, 2004)
Sut saneha (Blissfully Yours, Apichatpong Weerasethakul, 2002)

---

[29] Since the time of writing this essay, Apichatpong has won the topmost prize at Cannes, the Palme d'Or, for *Uncle Boonmee Who Can Recall his Past Lives*.

[30] As usually happens when three large businesses merge, the leaders of GMM, Tai Entertainment, and Hub Ho Hin share seats on the new executive board and have brought some of their staff with them into the conglomerate's structure. Opposition to the daring of Ah Koo led him to create an autonomous company called Tifa to outflank this opposition. Alas, Tifa has recently been closed down.

THE THAI SHORT FILM AND VIDEO FESTIVAL AND THE QUESTION OF INDEPENDENCE

May Adadol Ingawanij

The eleventh Thai Short Film and Video Festival kicked off with a curious montage. Held in a downtown multiplex, the opening night began with the usual adverts for mobile phones, soft drinks, cars, and beauty products. Since this 2007 edition of the festival happened to take place in the month of August—the same month in which an unelected Thai government was rushing through a referendum to legitimize the new constitution, drafted after the 2006 coup deposing the controversial elected leader Thaksin Shinawatra[1]—a different type of advert followed, extolling the importance of participating in this upcoming exercise of "democratic" rights. The advertisement for the referendum addressed as citizens of a democratic polity a people who, at that point, were being bombarded with propaganda messages seeking to secure their consent to a new constitution that was meant to introduce a new style of governance allegedly capable of staving off the "twin tyrannies" of crony capitalism and representative democracy. Rounding out this promotional package was the playing of the royal anthem, a "tradition" inaugurated some time during the late 1970s, when it became customary to initiate film screenings in commercial cinemas by having the audience stand to attention for the anthem.

---

[1] See articles by Kevin Hewison and Ukrist Pathmanand for their analyses of the coup as the result of an intra-elite struggle. In their view, the coup was a bid to eliminate the authoritarian, yet popular, crony capitalist rule of Thaksin, carried out by the alliance between the (factionalized) military, the bureaucracy, and royalist elites worried about the question of monarchical succession. Another important factor in endowing the coup with the appearance of "popular" legitimacy was the blessing of the "street protest" group People's Alliance for Democracy and its middle-class Bangkokian supporters, who called for royal intervention to topple Thaksin and then embraced the tanks. See Ukrist Pathmanand, "A Different *Coup d'État?*," *Journal of Contemporary Asia* 38,1 (February 2008): 124–42; and Kevin Hewison, "A Book, the King, and the 2006 Coup," *Journal of Contemporary Asia* 38,1 (February 2008): 190–211. For an analysis of the political inclination of this psychologically threatened middle class, accounting for the depth of their aversion to the rural and urban poor, regarded as Thaksin's mass support base, see Pasuk Phongpaichit and Chris Baker, "Thailand: Fighting over Democracy," *Economic and Political Weekly* (December 13, 2008), pp. 18–21.

Since it took place four months after the contemptible censorship of Apichatpong Weerasethakul's *Saeng sattawat* (Syndromes and a Century, 2006), the 2007 Festival was also a crucial moment for representatives of independent cinema in Siam to vocalize their stance against the further erosion of their freedom of creative practice.[2] The next item up on the screen, after the music video featuring the royal anthem, took a tentative turn in this direction, for it was a short film consisting of sound bites from high-profile figures associated with independent cinema or media activism, most of whom made gentle noises in hazy support of freedom. The expression of dissent acquired an allegorical tone with the festival trailer, a silent black-and-white film by Anocha Suwichakornpong. In it, a young woman accepts a birth-control pill thrust at her by an invisible hand. The caption specifies the date of this action, October 2006, or the month following the coup. The action is repeated again, then disrupted in the symbolically suggestive month of December, when she brushes the hand away. The last caption indicates that the scene showing the birth of her "child"—a reel of film—occurs in the same month as the Thai Short Film and Video Festival. Immediately following Anocha's trailer, the opening film commenced: Apichatpong's *The Anthem* (2006), which is both homage to the pleasurable ritual of collective cinemagoing and a conceptual parody of the state-enforced ritual of standing to attention.

In this multiplex space, the festival's symbolic staking of a claim to the democratic right of expression—including what might be interpreted, in Anocha and Apichatpong's contributions, as gestures challenging the interpellation of Siamese as captive royalist subjects—followed, unmarked, from the royal anthem and the promotion of the referendum, both emblems of royalist democracy in whose name conservative forces had attempted to close down political and cultural spheres of dissent.[3] Witnessing this succession of moving images during the opening minutes of the festival was a rueful experience, like watching multiple empty cans dangling in bathetic proximity from the same string off the rear bumper of a wedding car.

---

[2] May Adadol Ingawanij, "Disreputable Behaviour: The Hidden Politics of the Thai Film Act," *Vertigo* 3,8 (Winter/Spring 2008): 30–31.

[3] My use of the term "royalist democracy" here follows Thongchai Winichakul's mobilization of the term in his analysis of the discourse concerning democracy in modern Thai political history. According to his argument, since the fall of royal absolutism in 1932, the signifier "democracy" has been articulated based on the notion that the monarch is the stabilizing force of democratization (acting selflessly in the people's interest against authoritarianism) and the primary agent of its development. In short, the monarch is "above politics" because he has the ultimate moral authority to oversee the parliamentary political realm yet does not habitually intervene in its day-to-day operation. With this moral authority, the monarch can override elected politicians in the name of safeguarding democracy in those instances when politicians are seen to be acting in a "corrupt," "authoritarian," or "self-interested" fashion. Thongchai Winichakul, "Toppling Democracy," *Journal of Contemporary Asia* 38,1 (February 2008): 11–37. In his speculation concerning the near- to medium-term prospects of Thai politics, Thitinan Pongsudhirak has extended the definition of "royalist democracy" to highlight the following features: it is a parliamentary political body "based on the 2007 Constitution, which puts first the interests of the monarchy, the military, and the bureaucracy (the last currently being spearheaded by the judicial branch). This path points toward a bureaucracy-driven body politic adapted to the demands of economic globalization. Elections are held, and the prime minister must be an elected MP, but the appointed half of the Senate is filled with bureaucrats and military surrogates." Thitinan Pongsudhirak, "Thailand Since the Coup," *Journal of Democracy* 19,4 (October 2008): 151.

What are the conditions that would permit and nurture independent cinematic practice in this terrain? What counts for independence in a place where signifiers float remarkably freely, while citizens face the iron force of such laws as Lese Majesty, the Internal Security Act, the Emergency Decree, and the Computer Crimes Act? What does it mean to make, screen, and watch moving images independently in Siam at this moment, this post-coup *now* in the twilight of the reign of the current king? As an accompaniment to the chapter by the festival's director, Chalida Uabumrungjit, my article analyses the festival's championing of the value of creative independence through its first decade of existence, as its agenda was guided, on the whole, by a liberal form of patriotism and a romantic embrace of artisanal production. The key questions pursued are: what types of practice and discourse has the festival instituted in the name of independent cinema? What, among its range of innovative projects and exhibition activities, has been appropriated by other agencies—and in whose interests? Which aspects of radicalizing practice remain underdeveloped, waiting to be adopted by others, whether in alliance with or separately from the organizers of the festival?

NGO OF AN ALIEN FORM

The Thai Short Film and Video Festival was first held in August 1997, coinciding with the onset of the Asian economic crisis. At the time, the idea of an annual festival exhibiting mostly feature films was still an unfamiliar concept in Siam, and the prospect of an event featuring short films even stranger. In its first few years of existence, the festival found itself having to clarify to people that *nang san* (short films) are not filmed versions of short stories. The organizers' funding application to the state's culture-promotion office was turned down based on the logic that short-film competitions were not appropriate vehicles for the promotion of Thai culture.[4] In contrast, there are now at least two major annual pop culture/lifestyle events in Bangkok with their own short-film awards. Competitive calls for participation in short-filmmaking projects or short-film contests are announced on what seems like a monthly basis. These are just a few of the indications of the newly legitimated status of the short film in Siam, and the Thai Short Film and Video Festival has played a crucial part in these developments.

The festival is an annual competitive event held in August or September, usually lasting around two weeks. It is organized by the Thai Film Foundation (TFF), a non-governmental and nonprofit institution established in 1994 by a small group of film cultural activists dedicated to promoting Siamese cinema as part of a "national cultural and intellectual heritage," as the TFF states on its website. The wide range of activities undertaken by the TFF in this spirit have included providing informal film educational programs; carrying out film historical research; supporting non-industrial filmmaking; organizing exhibitions; and archiving films. According to staff members' estimates, attendance at the 2007 edition of the festival numbered a few thousand, at most. The modest scale of actual attendance is outweighed by the festival's towering reputation in the Bangkok-concentrated pop/youth cultural scene, however, and the affection it has won from programmers and curators of

---

[4] Chalida Uabumrungjit, "Kueng todsawat kap karn sang watthanatham nang san [The Half-Decade Mark: Constructing a Short Film Culture]," Catalogue of The Fifth Thai Short Film and Video Festival, August 11–18, 2001, p. 3.

international, Asia-oriented festivals and art institutions. Surprisingly, given its emphasis on noncommercial moving images, the festival also receives a relatively large volume of coverage from the national media, though mostly of the inconsequential kind (see below).

Opening Night at the 2008 festival. Courtesy of the Thai Film Foundation

As Chalida describes in her chapter, the desire to give due recognition to independent-spirited filmmaking motivated the original organizers to establish the festival. The short film—as a vehicle of creativity and personal expression—figures here as a metonym for the persistence of artistic or critical sensibilities, for a refusal to bend to the various pressures of conformism. Dome Sukvong, the film historian and archivist, once defined short films as "films that aren't concerned with the market and aren't afraid of the censors.[5] For him, short films are "art, culture, and protest."[6] Dome's definition has been mentioned several times, over the years, in the festival's catalogues, standing as its quiet motto. The festival's mission is to honor and highlight independent-minded endeavors in Siam. In doing so, it aims to undermine the common preconceptions that *nang* (film) refers only to feature films, or that Thai filmmakers are generally directors of generic flicks made on a budget allocated by studios, and that all "good" films are feature films characterized by high production values and pretentiously moral/didactic content.

The TFF's other equally pertinent, if less perceptible, hope in organizing the festival has been, from the start, to increase viewing literacy among potential

---

[5] Ibid., p. 3.

[6] Pimpaka Towira, "Dome Sukvong phu ri ruem tessakarn nang san [Dome Sukvong the Pioneer of the Short Film Festival]," in *Short Film*, ed. Chalida Uabumrungjit and Wimolrat Aroonrojsuriya (Bangkok: Openbooks, 2006), p. 19.

members of an audience and to encourage a broadminded approach to viewing moving images—one that does not respond with knee-jerk hostility when faced with "alien" forms and the uncertainty that characterizes the experience of encountering them. The organizers' commitment, in this regard, was and is to pave the way for a democratic culture of viewing and criticism, one shaped by aesthetic receptiveness to difference and active critical engagement. However, rather than claiming that this aspiration constituted a concrete goal with accompanying strategies, it is probably more fitting to describe this commitment as a will to activism shared by the organizers of the festival (and of the TFF more generally). Through this film-festival project, the TFF, a "cultural NGO," aspires to lay down the roots of an unalienated and democratic culture of cinema in Siam.

Translated into practice, this original commitment has guided the festival to focus on highlighting the dynamism of "alien" forms of moving image, and on recognizing their local creators. Such focus is evident in two aspects of the foundation's activities: the programming style and the wide-ranging categories of awards. The most prestigious of the awards are the Rattana Pestonji prize for non-student shorts and the Chang Pheuak prize for student-directed shorts. In the inaugural year of the festival, the only prizes given were for short films, but by its third year, awards for other categories of moving images quickly multiplied. There are now documentary and animation awards, indicating the organizers' wish to redress the flawed hierarchy of filmic evaluation in Siam, which has tended to dismiss as "unaccomplished" all moving images outside the category of expensively made, spectacular, generic features. The proliferation of awards categories also reveals an orientation toward youth, and the festival now gives out special prizes for school-age entries (more on its commitment to youth are mentioned below).

It is worth noting that each of the key prizes is christened after Siamese pioneers of independent cinema. The Rattana Pestonji award, for instance, is named after the late Parsi–Siamese filmmaker, who was awarded a prize for his amateur short film in a 1938 contest in Glasgow. In the 1950s and 1960s, Rattana continued to make 35mm sound-on-film features when the "industrial" standard in Siam, at that time, had become the 16mm quickie: films that were shot as silents on 16mm celluloid strips, and subsequently projected accompanied by voice performances, either delivered live at each cinema screening or played via tape machines. Rattana's decision to maintain his self-imposed technological standard has been retrospectively attributed to his possession of the sensibility of an independent-spirited filmmaker. In recent years, an emerging consciousness of what Chalida in her chapter calls the "need to be independent" among marginalized filmmakers and activists has necessitated the search for local roots. And it is mainly in relation to Rattana—a lonely, elite figure in the film world during his lifetime and still not widely known in Siam today—that a myth of Thai artistic origins is being articulated.

In terms of the festival's programming, three features are worth mentioning. As Chalida makes clear in her discussion, this is a festival that has been quietly screening works whose content transgresses those moral and political prohibitions governing TV and commercial screens in Thailand. Secondly, the TFF makes a point of showing all the entries that have been submitted to the many competitions organized as part of each festival (all submissions are shown during its "marathon" pre-launch). In this way, the majority of participants who do not make the shortlists are at least acknowledged for their effort, and can have a sense of what it is like to have their works screened in public. More importantly, since all of the submissions are screened in their entirety—warts and all, so to speak—those dedicated viewers who attend the pre-launch can have a stab at "curating": making up a personal shortlist of works that, to them, are aesthetically valuable or thematically interesting, even if the festival's organizers think otherwise. Theoretically at least, the pre-launch marathon screenings signal the possibility of placing viewers and programmers on an equal footing, asking each, in turn, to exercise his or her judgment over the same raw materials.

Thirdly, the thematic and repertory programs, included each year alongside the competitive aspects of the festival, provide the TFF with a rare context for communicating the search for origins just mentioned. Quite consistently, the organizers have curated programs that signal their intention to disinter the internal or national origins of independent cinema. In its first year, the festival reminded viewers of the existence of forgotten, or simply never-seen, precedents. It recalled Thai cinema's historic precedents by screening Rattana's *Rong raem narok* (Hell Hotel, 1957) and *Phra jao chang pheuk* (The King of the White Elephant, Sunh Vasudhara, 1941), the English-language feature commissioned by the statesman Pridi Banomyong (then finance minister) in an attempt to communicate a global message calling for peace during the Second World War. The organizers have featured, as Siamese "ancestors," those films that were inspired by leftist activism alongside the early products of royal amateurs. The best example of this programming style is the aptly titled 2004 program: Twenty Years of Solitude. This melancholic celebration of the twentieth anniversary of the Thai Film Archive screened, for the first time in many years, the groundbreaking documentary *The Struggle of Hara Factory Workers* (Jon Ungpakorn, 1975). In this documentary, the female workers in a bluejeans factory directly address the camera, elucidating their rationale for organizing a strike and factory sit-in during the early 1970s, and describing their experience of taking over the organization of production despite being intimidated by the factory's owner and state forces. The same anniversary program also included the little-known documentary made for British television, *Green Menace: The Untold Story of Golf* (1993), made by the rebellious filmmaker Ing K. Both of these documentaries were simply juxtaposed to *The Magic Ring* (1929), the thirty-minute film made by Rama VII, the last absolutist king of Siam, who was a keen lover of cinema. According to the TFF's preferred linguistic framing, these are all examples of "independent-spirited" filmmakers—pioneers who blazed the trail at a time when, conceptually, the notions of independent and experimental filmmaking were outside the vocabulary of Siamese cinema.

The TFF's other interest in opening up access to film and video-making has, more recently, taken the festival in the direction of youth-oriented training projects whose outcomes are screened at the festival itself. It would probably be fair to say that the TFF has felt able to be more explicit in articulating its self-defined role when engaged in such projects. The foundation seems to be most comfortable regarding its staff and associates as informal educators of young people, and, correspondingly, it tends to go along with the kind of framing that articulates the festival as a space that nurtures the creativity of youth. As is evident from the catalogue's cover design, the symbol mobilized to communicate this mission represents the festival as a tottering egg, and shows the organizers themselves as "the eggs' incubator."[7] By playing on

---

[7] Wimolrat Aroonrojsuriya, "Rang roi khong prawattisart [Inscribing Historical Traces]," in *Short Film*, ed. Chalida Uabumrungjit and Wimolrat Aroonrojsuriya, no page number.

the phrase *tang khai* (literally, "setting the egg upright")—the Thai idiom for the shaky first steps that must be taken in order to begin anything—this hopeful, modest symbol speaks of a certain kind of investment in the future. It signals a belief that progress can be made through incremental steps, as well as a faith that the "egg" can find its equilibrium without cracking any shells in the process; this is not a symbol that advocates provoking a break with or iconoclastic negation of the existing order.

2001 catalogue cover page. Published by the Thai Short Film and Video Festival

So far, the projects initiated by the TFF in this spirit have tended to take the form of filmmaking camps, whereby amateurs or complete beginners, mostly in their late teens and early twenties, spend a short amount of time and carry out intensive study with the foundation's staff and invited guests. During that period, the participants are taught the basics of shooting and editing (and, in some cases, given a preliminary class in the history of relevant topics), before coming up with a short film idea that each team then has to see through to completion in the remaining days of the session. The organizers consider the outcomes of these experiments, which are inevitably uneven, to be less important than the process of involving amateurs and novices in producing moving images and the experience of creative self-expression. The best example of this kind of workshop is the 2004 October Youth Short Film program: a project undertaken in collaboration with the US-based academic Sudarat

Musikawong, whereby three teams of young adults were invited to create their own works in response to the theme of remembering Siam's October events.[8]

FUNDING IN A BUREAUCRATIC NETWORK

Funding to cover the festival's current annual budget of between 500,000 and 600,000 baht (approximately US$18,000), excluding the labor cost of the small team of staff members, comes from a combination of sponsorships and income generated from the TFF's other activities during the year. That is to say, the foundation partly self-finances the festival by using the staff on its payroll as assistants and covering a proportion of the direct costs. To keep the expenses down, the TFF also relies on in-kind donations from domestic and international cultural agencies, which can help out by securing screening locations for free or having other agencies fund the travel of the various international guests. On top of that, the TFF needs external annual sponsorships to cover about half the total of the direct cost. Sponsorships come from four sources: bureaucratic bodies, corporations, individuals, and foreign cultural institutes. The Thai government's bureaucratic agencies provide the biggest sums, considerably more than the modest donations from the other sources. A mention, then, must be made of the festival's complicated relationship with its key sponsor: the arts and tourism promotion wing of the slumbering Thai bureaucracy.

From this vantage point, the festival's status is perhaps best described as provisionally dependent, or the festival itself described as a marginal event entangled within the network of personal contacts, obligations, and convoluted budgetary arrangements that structures the economy of state-sponsored film festivals. Historically, the modern Thai state has defined cultural promotion and preservation in terms of producing nationalist propaganda and clamping down on counter-cultures. This is the dominant tradition in which the cultural organs of the bureaucracy still languish. Since the globalization of the economy, these government offices have recently added "selling Thai Culture" to their mission. The state now budgets considerable funds for reproducing propaganda and commodifying Thainess, but "investment in culture," under any other definition, is largely a matter of paying lip service to the rhetoric. Accordingly, the construction of a progressive infrastructure of financial support for noncommercial film production, exhibition, or archiving has never been given high priority. Yet at the same time, state organs or enterprises with close links to the bureaucracy (and, in some cases, the palace) would lavishly sponsor films and film events that sell themselves in the language of promoting heritage—especially of the type associated with the commemoration of royal greatness—or tourism. Any organization's ability to secure substantial sponsorship from the bureaucracy or state enterprises is also directly related to the personal contacts and stature of its representatives. Two examples testify to this development: Prince Chatrichalerm Yukol, who was once regarded as the leading light of social realist filmmaking of the 1970s and 1980s, and who now makes expensive, redundant biopics of pre-modern royal figures; and the corruption-tainted, tourism-authority-funded Bangkok International Film Festival (BKKIFF).[9]

---

[8] These were the mass uprising against the military dictatorship in 1973 and the brutal massacre of so-called communists in 1976.

[9] The scandal surfaced with the US Federal Bureau of Investigation's probe into corruption involving US citizens abroad. In early 2010, the film producer Gerald Green and his wife, Patricia Green, were given jail terms for bribing a senior TAT official in exchange for the

This structure of state funding places the festival in something of a dilemma regarding the sources and implications of public sponsorship. For most of the 2000s, one of its biggest sponsors has been the Tourism Authority of Thailand (TAT), the bureaucratic organ with the largest direct budget designated to fund film-promotion events. This sponsorship was granted in a rather strange fashion: as payment for work undertaken by the staff of the TFF during the national festival—the BKKIFF—that once had the pretension to claim it would rival Pusan. Until the eventual scaling down of BKKIFF in 2007, partly due to the reduction of its budget by the junta-appointed government, the TFF's organizers were recruited via a combination of financial incentives and personal pressure to organize the day-to-day running of BKKIFF, and to program a substantial part of that festival. Directorship, however, remained in the hands of the American producers, who were subsequently sentenced to prison in the United States for bribing a Thai official in exchange for the BKKIFF contract. The implicit expectation of the TAT seems to have been that, since the foundation was run by a group of "young" activists committed to supporting Siamese films and obliged to raise money for its own flagship festival, the TFF could always be called upon (by invoking the patriotic goodwill, docile cooperability, and financial needs of its members) to assist in the organization of "the nation's festival"—on whatever disadvantageous terms. After BKKIFF's organizational structure was changed following the corruption scandal, however, the relationship altered, and the TFF was no longer employed to work on the event. As a result, after 2007 TAT "sponsorship" funds for the Thai Short Film and Video Festival dried up.

More recently, another bureaucratic agency has emerged to provide about a fifth of the festival's budget: the Office of Contemporary Art and Culture (OCAC), an arts-promotion institution set up in 2002 under the umbrella of the Ministry of Culture. This institution's relatively straightforward manner of funding—it requires only an acknowledgement in the festival's catalogue—is granted on a year-by-year basis in response to the TFF's application. Whether financial assistance from this source will be affected under the new Film Act, enforced by the very same culture ministry, is worth flagging here as a point of speculation, though I may risk seeming overly suspicious. The difficulty is that centralized bureaucratic institutions with the "cultural" remit and pockets deep enough to sponsor the festival have made no long-term commitment to its continuation. Furthermore, any unspoken condition accompanying the OCAC's financial assistance—such as the expectation that the TFF "won't go too far" in its programming decisions—has, up to now, never been tested. Nevertheless, given this current climate of political repression, there is a possibility that the cultural authorities may decide to scrutinize the Thai Short Film and Video Festival more closely using the new film legislation to clamp down on any perceived waywardness of programming and filmic representation.

Regarding other potential sources of funding, the TFF appears to have made the decision that it would not actively seek out substantial corporate sponsorship. This is, of course, in keeping with the self-proclaimed stance of the festival as an event that supports the artisanal or DIY (do-it-yourself) production ethos. The relatively

---

contract to run BKKIFF. Also in that same year, US prosecutors indicted Juthamas Siriwan, former governor of the TAT, and her daughter Jittisopa, on charges of accepting bribes from the Greens to run BKKIFF. See "Juthamas Charged over Film Fest Scandal," *Bangkok Post*, January 21, 2010, www.bangkokpost.com/news/local/166063/juthamas-charged-in-film-fest-scandal, accessed June 3, 2011; "Couple Jailed for Bangkok Film Festival Bribery," *BBC News*, August 13, 2010, www.bbc.co.uk/news/entertainment-arts-10963317, accessed June 3, 2011.

marginal role of corporate sponsorship sets the foundation apart from other friendly competitors: pop cultural short-film events that appropriate the language of DIY production to enhance the fashionable veneer of the sponsoring brand. Unlike its sister event—the Bangkok Experimental Film Festival—the Thai Short Film and Video Festival has not placed much emphasis on seeking sources of direct sponsorship from abroad. And unlike the South Korean model, which demonstrates how a nation's provincial film festivals can be supported and increased in number, localist ambitions that would organize and nurture provincial and regional festivals outside the metropolis have yet to emerge in Thailand. Given the resurgence of regionalist sentiments over the past three decades or so, it is not inconceivable that, at some point, a shrewd alliance might be made: between entrepreneurial regional or provincial funders and organizers of progressive arts or film festivals who are prepared to seek new audiences beyond Bangkok. If this were to come about, it would provide an extremely interesting alternative to the current pattern of drawing sponsorship from unsympathetic, centralized authorities obsessed with enhancing the country's global status, yet inept in their pursuit of that goal.

SPACES: PHYSICAL, MEDIATED, GLOBALIZED

Before settling in its current downtown location in 2008 (in the newly opened Bangkok Art and Culture Center), the festival had a rather nomadic feel. Unlike Singapore's The Substation,[10] the TFF has not been endowed with a well-located flagship venue at which to hold its full calendar of film events. Its office—a nondescript suburban shop building situated in a neighboring province of Bangkok—was bought with private money. As a result of these limited accommodations, over the years the festival has been shifting its location regularly across Bangkok. The Goethe Institute, multiplex screens, and the Fourteenth October Memorial Institute (a civic space built to commemorate the 1973 anti-dictatorship uprising) have all housed the main programs of the Thai Short Film and Video Festival at some point.

Despite its tenuous physical presence, the festival has come to be featured in the national media primarily for its considerable range of awards. In a mainstream culture that tends to elide the question of the value of an artwork with the hype of the awards ceremonies (of which there are many in Siam), the decision of the TFF to award prizes from the start has been a quite useful, if ambivalent, tool in raising the profile of the short film. The initial decision to offer awards was partly taken in earnest and intended to honor independent endeavors and to encourage the growth of an independent sensibility. But the decision was also a half-ironic gesture towards attracting media attention; as the organizers put it, "the equivalent of a prize draw."[11] In its early years, the awards ceremony made the festival more readily comprehensible by contextualizing the strange and unfamiliar images featured during the event with a familiar framework for endowing cultural value. Since then, as the short film has become strongly associated with fashionableness and the indie

---

[10] See Jan Uhde and Yvonne Ng Uhde, "The Substation and the Emergence of an Alternative Cinema Culture in Singapore," in this volume.

[11] From an interview I conducted with Chalida and Wimolrat on September 13, 2006. On the questionable value of the prizes, see also Pimpaka, "Dome Sukvong phu ri ruem tessakarn nang san [Dome Sukvong the Pioneer of the Short Film Festival]," pp. 12–31.

youth lifestyle in Thailand,[12] the prizes and award ceremonies have remained the primary frame of reference for journalistic coverage of the festival. The media reports are mostly in the style of nightly entertainment news on TV; when other, more sympathetic media channels provide coverage, they tend simply to reproduce the festival's modest PR releases. Substantial reviews of the works screened at the festival are few and far between.[13] Thai-language film critiques and decent interviews used to appear in the pages of the festival's catalogues, though the small TFF team seems to have become too stretched by the expansion of the program offerings to continue producing this more ambitious conception of the festival's self-documentation. Currently, most serious Thai-language film criticism—a minority pursuit that frames itself as an alternative to the insular, smugly pedestrian tone of the majority of film journalism broadcast and published in Thailand—has tended to be restricted to blogs on single-authored websites maintained by individual cinephiles.[14]

Within the transnational space of global independent cinema, the festival is known among programmers and curators who keep a sharp eye on new trends and talents in the Asia-Pacific. For some professionals on the film-festival circuit, this is Siam's showcase festival. The festival has established close ties, for instance, with the prestigious Clermont-Ferrand Short Film Festival in France. In this globalized space, where discourses of world/independent cinema are shaped by the more established film festivals, partly through the cycle of discovery of promising filmmakers and artists, the Thai Short Film and Video Festival has been playing a significant role as a discovery site for international programmers and curators. This was not what the TFF had in mind when it first established the festival, but in many ways its unanticipated role, in this respect, has been, ironically enough, one of its biggest achievements. It is worth noting in this context that in 2000, prior to the global discovery and recognition of Apichatpong Weerasethakul, it was this festival that programmed a small "retrospective" of his videos. The Thai Short Film and Video Festival staff then recommended Apichatpong to the Singapore International Film Festival, which then recommended him on to the Pusan International Film Festival, setting off the initial momentum of the discovery of Apichatpong in Asia.[15] It would not do, of course, to exaggerate the role of the Thai Short Film and Video Festival in nurturing the global reputation of an artist who hardly needs superfluous promotion. Yet, it is indicative of the structure of discovery of global

---

[12] Akiba Takayuki, "The Emergence and Development of Thai Contemporary Arts and Artists: A Case Study of Thai Independent Cinema" (MA thesis, Chulalongkorn University, 2007), chap. 3.

[13] For the occasional exception, see Kong Rithdee, "Strong Homegrown Selection," *Bangkok Post*, September 1, 2006, R5. In this review of the 2006 Thai Short Film and Video Festival's prizewinning shorts, the *Bangkok Post*'s film critic discusses the problem of representing Muslim identities with sufficient complexity.

[14] I refer readers to the blog by the film critic Wiwat Lertwiwatwongsa (Filmsick), http://filmsick.exteen.com/. The lineage of the film education of this cinephile, a pharmacist by day, can be traced to the excellent independent Thai-language publication series *Filmvirus*. For more detail on Sontaya Subyen, the visionary who founded the *Filmvirus* publication and screening space in the 1990s, see my entry in the special Love Letters issue of the Southeast Asian cinema web journal *Criticine*, www.criticine.com/feature_article.php?id=44, accessed June 7, 2011.

[15] In 2011, the Pusan International Film Festival's name was changed to Busan International Film Festival.

independent/world cinema that small, but credible, and locally rooted events such as this festival make the "first contact." They are valued on this basis by the professionals of globally or regionally prestigious festivals—those who have the real power to provide exposure to filmmakers.

The mediated and transnational profile of the short-film festival is addressed here to provide some degree of contrast with the modest scale of attendance at the event itself. A constant source of disappointment for the organizers is that the festival has not been that successful in attracting a larger and more varied constituency of local viewers.[16] Aside from its obvious success with schoolchildren at the special group screenings, attendants of the main programs have mostly been young people whose works have been submitted in the competition, who bring along their families and friends, supplemented by Bangkok's small group of dedicated cinephiles. Why the audience base remains restricted is an important question that cannot be adequately tackled by this article, but, nonetheless, it is probably worth mentioning the following contradiction between the festival's pedagogical aim and its structure. The structure of the event itself—it occurs only once a year—is less likely to be effective in broadening viewers' filmic exposure and improving the quality of film discussions in comparison with the historical model of the cinematheque, or the present day possibility of constructing online a virtual film-education museum, or a virtual cinematheque. (The historical model of the cinematheque is, broadly speaking, defined by a year-round calendar of screenings organized in a specific site containing library or other research facilities.) The film festival, especially if it is accompanied by an awards event, is geared far more toward discovering upcoming practitioners or providing a feel-good platform for social causes (such as the "human rights" festival, the "identity politics" festival) than toward the kind of educational work with viewers on which the TFF would ideally like to focus.

Whatever the reasons for the unsatisfactory size of the festival's audiences, one of the biggest ironies of the festival is that it has, through its mediated presence, become an institution that seemingly certifies the "strength" and liveliness of short filmmaking in contemporary Siam. Yet in private, the organizers say they feel they have not been able to make much of an inroad in encouraging a more varied crowd of the capital city's residents to engage with unfamiliar forms of moving images, or in generating in-depth criticisms about them.

APPROPRIATION OF THE SHORT FILM

Although, in the beginning, the organizers of the Thai Short Film and Video Festival were often called on to explain the fact that a short film is not a filmic adaptation of the short story, activities pioneered by the festival have come to be widely appropriated. Commercial brands, social campaign groups, and bureaucratic agencies are now clamoring to put on short film competitions and filmmaking workshops, mobilizing what, at first glance, appears to be a rhetoric about "nurturing youth creativity" borrowed directly from the TFF. This phenomenon is a

---

[16] This summary is based on personal conversations I have had with TFF staff on several occasions. See also Dome's comments about the lack of audience participation in Pimpaka, "Dome Sukvong phu ri ruem tessakarn nang san [Dome Sukvong the Pioneer of the Short Film Festival]," pp. 12–31.

testament to the success that the TFF has had in legitimizing the short film by associating the form with artisanal production and independent-spirited creativity. At the same time, it is also an indication of the eclipsing of the TFF's effort to place the short film within a non-conformist symbolic terrain, for the TFF's discourse and strategies are being appropriated by agencies motivated by interests quite unrelated to the foundation's mission of defending cinema as both cultural heritage and resistant aesthetic/intellectual experience.

The mobilization of the indie image by cultural entrepreneurs and big brands is a story already extensively told, usually with reference to America's independent cinema of the 1990s. In Siam's case, two essays, one authored by Sudarat Musikawong, the other by Akiba, provide insightful parallel studies that demonstrate the centrality of the rhetoric invoking youthful verve and independent cinema in efforts to promote a particular brand or production house.[17] Rather than go over the same ground, I refer readers to their work, which provide an appropriate context with which to understand phenomena such as the buzzy, annual short-film competition in Bangkok organized by FAT, the popular youth-oriented radio station.

What appears to be more unusual in the global or regional context, and therefore worth addressing here, is the trend whereby bureaucratic organs and NGOs, or single-issue campaign groups, are eagerly funding short-film competitions and workshops on specific themes and topics. These events are usually framed by rhetoric that speaks of raising social awareness and nurturing youth engagement. Such projects, which have taken place in recent years, include the Film for Peace competitive workshop funded by the National Reconciliation Commission, a short-lived group set up in the wake of the 2004 Tak Bai massacre in the far south of the country; a competitive workshop and awards for short films about Alzheimher's disease, organized by an awareness-raising and support group in conjunction with a pharmaceutical company; and an international NGO's 2006 commission, *Withi Moken*, which commissioned four short films about the Moken, or sea gypsies, off the Southwestern coast of Siam. Concerning such projects, a special mention must be made of OCAC's somewhat ironical "independent" film scheme. In 2007, emerging independent filmmakers and amateurs were selected, alongside filmmakers who had been awarded OCAC's Silpathorn arts prize, to make nine shorts commemorating King Bhumibol's eightieth birthday. The theme of this prestigious commission was His Majesty's "tireless diligence, moral excellence, and graceful conduct toward his subjects," and participants were encouraged to "freely [!] choose their own topics."[18]

Subsidized filmmaking schemes of this nature create certain opportunities for artists despite their obvious limitations. For better or for worse, such projects remain the only available sources of domestic, public funding for upcoming filmmakers in Siam—those who have yet to achieve a notable profile or win prizes of the kind that will attract the interest of domestic and/or foreign industrial or cultural funders for their projects. Sivaroj Kongsakul is a good example of a filmmaker who, around

---

[17] Sudarat Musikawong, "Working Practices in Thai Independent Film Production and Distribution," *Inter-Asia Cultural Studies* 8,2 (June 2007): 248–61; and Akiba, "The Emergence and Development of Thai Contemporary Arts and Artists: A Case Study of Thai Independent Cinema," chaps. 3 and 7.

[18] This is my translation of the statement in the Thai language. Office of Contemporary Art and Culture, "Catalogue of *Phapphayon chalerm phra kiat 'dae phra phu song tham'* [The Short Film Project in Commemoration of the Celebration on the Auspicious Occasion of His Majesty the King's Eightieth Birthday Anniversary]," Bangkok, 2007, no page number.

2006, was at the stage of his career where he had few alternatives except to try and take advantage of funding opportunities linked to issue-based films. After he had worked with fellow independent filmmakers in a variety of roles—including as one of the cinematographers for Apichatpong's DV *Worldly Desires* (2005) and as an assistant director for Anocha's *Graceland* (2006)—two of the shorts that Sivaroj then directed, *Meun kheei* (Always, 2006) and *Siang ngiab* (Silencio, 2007), were sponsored by the Alzeimher-awareness and royal-commemoration film projects, respectively. Whether the filmmaker was actually compelled by personal sympathy for the subject matter in each case may not be as relevant as the fact that his reputation has benefited from the publicity earned by the high-quality work he contributed to these projects. *Meun kheei*, the gently observed story of an old couple living with the disease, won the Vichimatra prize (the organizers' choice) at the Thai Short Film and Video Festival in 2007. *Siang ngiab*, a fascinatingly muted take on the theme of honoring HM, was selected for Rotterdam in 2008 and won a special prize at Clermont-Ferrand shortly afterwards.

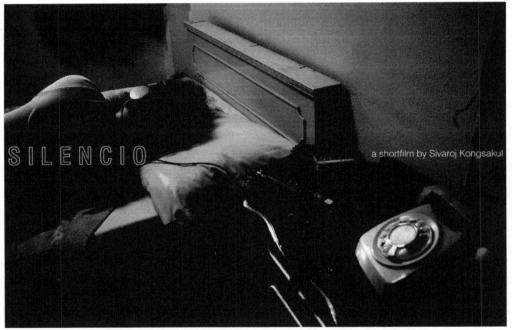

Silencio. Poster image courtesy of Sivaroj Kongsakul

The best that can be said about these filmmaking schemes is that they happen to plug a funding gap for emerging filmmakers who need to build up their portfolios. One can predict that such a pattern of funding will not persist long into the future. Right now, filmmaking workshops and commissions are following the hype associated with the short film: that impression, magnified by the mainstream media, that the short film is the Good Object with which to celebrate youth culture (according to the commercial rhetoric) and/or immerse our youth in worthwhile activities (according to the didactic rhetoric). Once the hype begins to wear off, professionals assigned the task of increasing the profile of their organizations or causes through worthy write-ups will most likely shift their attention to producing budget proposals for other kinds of project.

The majority of schemes of this kind tend not to budget for disseminating the films they have recognized or make much of an effort to reach audiences with the short films that have resulted from myriad workshops and commissions; they are not concerned with determining what contexts of discussion, or textual traces, should follow the PR event celebrating the films' premiere. It is doubtful that previous filmmaking workshops, though numerous, have seriously addressed topics about which ignorance or stereotyping are rife, such as the Moken people or Malay-Muslim existence, or created counter-images to challenge the dominant modes of representation.[19] Lastly, given that hagiographic projects exploiting the spectacular qualities and myth-making propensity of mechanical and digital media are now firmly part of the aesthetic field of royalist propaganda in this twilight period, the proliferation of short-filmmaking projects commemorating HM since OCAC's 2007 initiative raises crucial questions about value. How can non-conformist cinematic discourse and practice survive the move, via projects of this nature, to appropriate the very same rhetoric of independence, creativity, and the "democratization" of participation in moving-image production, only to create demonstratively royalist surfaces? Do practitioners of independent cinema in Siam regard such appropriation as an encroachment to be resisted?

LOOKING AHEAD: THE MOMENT OF COUNTER CRITICISM, PERHAPS

At the inception of the Thai Short Film and Video Festival, its celebration of small-scale production was analogous to domestic critiques of neo-liberal capitalist globalization. The TFF's foundational position of embracing artisanal and amateur production as an alternative to the monopolistic practices of the Thai film industry resonated easily with the key critical positions against consumerism and crony capitalism. In the immediate aftermath of the Asian economic crisis, this anti-consumerism, anti-crony capitalism position was a broad-based one shared by political conservatives (those who laid the blame for Siam's instability on electoralism), cultural conservatives (those who feared the loss of Thainess due to globalization), and critics of a Left-radical persuasion. At the present conjuncture, however, those who would propose that independent cinema is a significant critical force face a new challenge, for any gesture of embracing artisanal production, by

---

[19] As was discussed during a seminar involving the Japanese documentary maker Sato Makoto at the Tenth Thai Short Film and Video Festival, the Film for Peace shorts have been criticized for naively simplifying the problem of violence in the far south, and in some cases reproducing the state's moralizing rhetoric. In my interview with Taryart Datsathean, one of the makers of *Moken, pa?* (Moken, Right?, Taryart Datsathean, Phisan Sangjan, and Nattawit Khaosri, 2006), a team selected for the *Withi Moken* workshop, Taryart indicated that the schedule and funding arranged for the filmmakers only went as far as two short trips to the Moken community featured in the film. The "fieldwork" trip lasted a matter of days, and the following week shooting had to begin. The structure of the project did not accommodate the need for the filmmakers and documentary subjects to develop a relationship. Despite the restriction, however, *Moken, pa?* is unusually egalitarian in the affectionate, teasing way with which it records the interactions between the Moken islanders and the amateur ethnographer—a witty *kathoey* (transgender male) who "crosses borders" with his unpredictable line of questioning while playing the insular Bangkokian. Email interview with Taryart Datsathean on February 27, 2008.

itself, conforms rather comfortably to the dominant affirmative discourse of royalist democracy. This is because the Thai neo-right's resurgence is propelled by a commonsensical, and powerful, rhetoric of anti-globalization: the royal-endorsed rhetoric of "returning to self-sufficiency" is here the signifier mobilized to legitimize the 2006 coup and subsequent attempts to undermine the electoral franchise.[20] In this context, "self-sufficiency" means little in concrete terms, yet its mythic associations with royal wisdom and national heritage (the link to a pastoral past) constitute a powerful discursive tool. With its rhetorical stance against emblematic domestic figures of crony capitalism and neo-liberal economic globalization, and appeal to cultural nationalism, the discourse of economic self-sufficiency legitimizes the hostility of the urban middle- and upper-middle-class elites toward elected politicians and the masses, which are both together branded as materialistic agents of capitalism threatening to destroy national values.

To assert the critical/non-conformist value of independent cinema in this climate requires a broader framework of discussion, one that encompasses topics beyond the scale of production. Questions concerning the politics of signification, the place of the author as producer, in Walter Benjamin's sense of the term,[21] the ethics of representing reality/evoking historical reality, and, not least, the ontology of the image addressed within historically determinate circumstances, now emerge poised to become topics in a far greater discussion—and in a critical language sufficiently robust.[22] If the first decade of the Thai Short Film and Video Festival's existence was the moment of hesitant youthfulness, now may be the moment of counter-criticism. To end on a note of optimism as I write this sentence in the chill of the country's April–May 2010 massacre: With the period of production and circulation of a body of politically radical and aesthetically avant-garde "third world" films, once known as third cinema, now studied as "history" in English-language film studies courses, and the term "Asian cinema" reduced to a bland denomination for the new global blockbuster or the arthouse turkey, the cultural political conditions here in Siam are at least becoming ripe to give birth to something that could make a truly global contribution: a radical cinema movement. These conditions are: the greater accessibility of technology; a growing group of talented and politically frustrated filmmakers (and their teams) unable or unwilling to occupy the gravitational center of the monopolistic film industry; and a crisis of political-cultural legitimacy of a magnitude engendering a massive effort of denial, especially on that most delicate question of what to do with—in Thongchai Winichakul's apt coinage—our "Elder(s)."[23]

---

[20] See the editorial, "*Khwa thai* [The Thai Neo-Right]," *Fah Diew Kan* 6,2 (April–May 2008): no page number.

[21] In his lecture "The Author as Producer," presented in 1934, Benjamin writes: "Rather than asking, 'What is the attitude of a work *to* the relations of production of its time?' I would like to ask, 'What is its position *in* them?'" Walter Benjamin, "The Author as Producer," in *Walter Benjamin: Selected Writings, Volume 2, Part 2, 1931–1934*, ed. Michael W. Jennings, Howard Eiland, and Gary Smith (Cambridge, MA: The Belknap Press of Harvard University Press, 1999), p. 770.

[22] On this point, see also David Teh, Benedict Anderson, Apichatpong Weerasethakul, and May Adadol Ingawanij, "Conversations," in the catalogue of *The More Things Change: The Fifth Bangkok Experimental Film Festival*, March 25–30, 2008, pp. 24–43.

[23] Thongchai, "Toppling Democracy," p. 29.

SELECTED FILMOGRAPHY

Graceland (Anocha Suwichakornpong, 2006)
Green Menace: The Untold Story of Golf (Ing K., 1993)
Moken, pa? (Moken, Right? Taryart Datsathean, Phisan Sangjan, and Nattawit Khaosri, 2006)
Meun kheei (Always, by Sivaroj Kongsakul, 2006)
Rong raem narok (Hell Hotel, by Rattana Pestonji, 1957)
Siang ngiab (Silencio, Sivaroj Kongsakul, 2007)
Saeng sattawat (Syndromes and a Century, Apichatpong Weerasethakul, 2006)
The Anthem (Apichatpong Weerasethakul, 2006)
The Struggle of Hara Factory Workers (Jon Ungphakorn, 1975)
Worldly Desires (Apichatpong Weerasethakul, 2005)

PART III

<u>ADVOCACY</u>

LIKE THE BODY AND THE SOUL: INDEPENDENCE AND AESTHETICS IN CONTEMPORARY PHILIPPINE CINEMA

Alexis A. Tioseco

A very practical undertaking must occur before one is able to discuss, in detail, the aesthetics of independent films in the Philippines. Quite simply, we must first define what we mean when we use the term "independent" in this context, and why a discussion of aesthetics in relation to notions of "independence" will be of particular importance to our overall understanding and appreciation of these films.

It is important to know that, when one speaks of independence in relation to cinema, its definition or significance varies greatly from country to country. There have been heated arguments in the Philippines in recent years about what the term "independent" actually means in relation to our cinema. The debate is very contemporary, as in the past it was much easier to define independent cinema in opposition to commercial mainstream cinema in the Philippines. At that time, one could simply look at the tools being used (16mm, Super 16mm, 8mm, Super 8mm film, and Video, or Digital Video [DV], versus 35mm film); the length of films (short versus feature; the decision to opt for short was usually due to the cost of purchasing and developing film stock); the form (independent was grounded in an alternative aesthetic relative to mainstream); and the distribution (limited versus wide release). Within this framework, there were, of course, a few aberrations—films funded by grants, individuals, or small production companies; short films shot on 35mm or features shot on 16mm—but these were clearly and easily identifiable as such. The situation today, however, is markedly different.

In today's Philippine cinema, the lines that demarcate independent from mainstream are becoming increasingly blurred. The term "independent" was once like a battle cry, but now it is a whimper, a marketing tool, a hip reference to be spouted by those ignorant of its original, and perhaps more easily definable, meaning. With the Philippines's commercial film industry set on a steady decline,[1] and the technology used to produce cinema now much cheaper (in DV form), boundaries have become confused. Studios have begun creating smaller sub-labels

---

[1] While roughly 150 commercial films were produced in the Philippines in 1998, the figure dipped to around fifty in 2004 and has been leveling off at that annual average since.

(such as Digital Viva), which co-opt young filmmakers into producing cheap films, often of the exploitation variety. Festivals have sprouted (Cinemalaya, Cinema One), which aren't exactly "independent" festivals in the commonly understood sense, but rather showcases for films produced by companies (Dream Satellite, ABS–CBN) from scripts that had won a "contest" leading to a "grant." Films are being produced by small companies that wave the banner of "independence." Financially independent in some cases, backed by corporations in others, the films produced by these companies do not necessarily offer alternatives in content or form to the mainstream output, and they benefit from theatrical distribution in more than just a handful of local cinemas.

This is where our problem lies: the tools used for both independent and commercial cinema have become similar (ranging from DV to HDV [high-definition video] to HD [high-definition]); because of these lower production costs, making full-length features on a relatively small budget has become an option for the studios (costs may start as low as 90,000 pesos, or US$2,000); and distribution channels are opening up.[2] Given this transformation, what we have is ultimately the makings of a micro-industry. Where is the significance of independent cinema, as we once knew it? When and how does independent cinema matter? When the infrastructure, tools, and even the filmmakers themselves have been co-opted by this new form of mainstream cinema, what have we left to fall back on, to define and demarcate "independence" by?

Perhaps the answer lies quite simply with form and content. Two examples are worth investigating in this spirit of enquiry.

A RIVER RUNS THROUGH IT: REFLECTIONS ON A SHOT IN LAV DIAZ'S *HEREMIAS*[3]

We walk a narrow dirt path lined randomly with fragmented rocks, working our way down to a clearing that runs parallel to a long river, a river that serves as a divide between the ground I walk on and the grassy terrain on the side opposite. The landscape on this side rises up dramatically: shoddy, low-cost housing is being prepared on the main plain some twenty feet higher. The director Lav Diaz steps gingerly into the water, sporting a worn black t-shirt, which appears to have weathered many battles, and black jeans torn at the knees. He crosses to the midpoint in the narrow river with members of his crew, whose pants are rolled up just below their knees, water reaching their ankles.

The soundman, Bob Macabenta, tests the levels of the DAT (digital audio tape) recording device, which has been borrowed from the cinematographer Neil Daza. There are loud noises coming from the construction site in the main plain above us, and it dominates the audio. Rolly, the stout production manager, and Celso, the diligent AD (assistant director) and line producer, ask the workers to halt briefly for the duration of the shot. They oblige, intrigued by what is going on, and watch intently the proceedings from their bird's-eye position above.

Bob sends Lav a thumbs-up sign, signaling that the sound is clear. Lav takes one more peek through the eyehole of the camera, a glance at the LCD (liquid crystal

---

[2] SM Cinemas, the country's largest chain, has installed digital projectors in ten cinemas by the end of 2007.

[3] A different version of this essay was published in the debut issue of *Kino!,* a Slovenia-based cinema journal.

display) detailing the frame, then a final look at the tranquil river. He folds his arms in front of his chest, and, in his typically crooked stance (he has muscle problems), yells out into the distance, "Action!" The crew looks on, the construction workers are paused, watching. I am observing, too, standing on the dirt road to the side of the river. We wait ...

Since first watching the five-hour long *Batang West Side*, at its world premiere during Cinemanila in 2001, I've been an ardent believer in the cinema of Lav Diaz. *Batang West Side* not only changed the way I viewed cinema and the possibilities of Philippine cinema, but it was *the* film that made cinema matter to me, personally. Its impact was similar to that of *Night and Fog* on the late French critic Serge Daney: a numbing revelation of the power the medium, as mentioned in his essay "The Tracking Shot in Kapo."[4]

Diaz's long takes feel right. I've seen *Batang West Side* (edited by Ron Dale) three times now, and the eleven-hour *Ebolusyon ng Isang Pamilyang Pilipino* (Evolution of a Filipino Family, 2004), which was edited by Diaz himself, four times. The rhythm of each shot in these films seems timed to near perfection. Diaz's shots linger long enough to let thoughts ferment and to let the eyes explore and wander, absorbing in equal measure the crevices of the frame, the ambient sounds of the world captured in it, and the audiences' own personal reflections on the relation of what one is seeing now to what has been shown to them in the film prior to this particular point. The director and editor cuts, in my viewing experience, at the moment when it feels one's attention may soon be diverted.

This, however, is the first time I am on location during the shooting of a Lav Diaz film ...

As minutes pass, the frame remains stagnant, nothing changing, nothing moving, save for the natural ebb and flow of the river. Far in the distance on the dirt road in front of me there is movement. Heremias (played by Ronnie Lazaro) is walking forward towards me at a snail's pace, his cow trailing slightly to his side, guided by a rope he holds loosely. So beaten and worn is this character that he has chosen to leave behind his band of traveling handicraft vendors and venture off on his own. His legs don't walk—they labor. And considering the incredible distances he must traverse—first with his cow, later alone—the toll it takes on the body and the mind must be incredible. We sense that this is his solitude, this is his loneliness, and it is the path he has chosen.

Heremias, feet dragging, head bowed humbly, has finally reached the point of entry into the river. He steps in first, legs weary, and dips his hand into the water as his cow trails him along the slippery path. He walks to the middle of the river, the center of Diaz's frame (which has remained stationary throughout), and places the shirt that has been resting on his shoulder on a rock, dipping his hands into the river to clean them. He turns again to his majestic cow, the soothing sounds of water flowing in the river in the background, and begins to wash it. He gently dabs water from the river onto the cow's body, rubbing water over its torso and legs in an effort

[4] Serge Daney, "The Tracking Shot in *Kapo*," in *Postcards from the Cinema* (Oxford and New York, NY: Berg, 2007), pp. 17–35.

to cleanse the cow from the dirt it must have accumulated over the course of their journey.

> Often when Diaz's characters enter a stagnant frame from a distance, the shot will be held until the character exits the frame; it is a pattern you become accustomed to and begin to expect when watching a Lav Diaz film. For the uninitiated, it can be almost unbearable to endure; for those who have come to expect it, it is therapy.

A shot from a prolonged, quiet scene in *Heremias*

Heremias pauses for a moment and looks out into the distance of the river ...

> The actor Ronnie Lazaro has a magnificent body. This has nothing to do with the splendor of his muscle nor his stature. (His chest looks almost gladiatorial, and he is neither particularly tall nor short.) But it has to do with the relation of his body to the manner in which he carries himself, the way he moves, sits, stands, and pauses. Simply put—it is his way of being. He is representative of the *every-Filipino*: humble yet strong, quiet yet resilient. A "type" that is sturdy and able to endure.
>
> Luc Dardenne, a member of the jury that awarded the Palme d'Or in 2000 to *Anino* (*Shadows*), a short film Ronnie Lazaro starred in, described him as a beautiful, enigmatic image on the screen. I agree with Dardenne, and I believe this enigma, this mystery, is borne out of the contradictions of Lazaro's body (imposing) and his nature (meek). This meekness, however, is not a manifestation of humility without conviction, but rather the opposite: it is a quality marking the demeanor of one who has contemplated the world around

himself, and is choosing if there is a proper time to begin to act and when that should be. The body ensures survival while searching, and the search leads to conviction in moments of action.

He turns back to his cow, placing a hand on its shoulder, and looks diagonally to that which is beyond the scope of our frame (opposite the side he had entered from). His head is barely higher than the back of the animal. The moment passes ... and he returns to washing his companion, darting underneath the animal at one point to better wash its underside

Heremias then rests on a rock near his cow. He seeks a moment to himself, as he rests motionless before his cow, which is as noble as its owner in appearance. Having hardly moved at this point, the cow nudges him slightly with its head, causing Heremias to turn and pat the animal lovingly on the nose. We are now twelve minutes into the shot at this point, and the crew light up with smiles at this sight, as if the cow, reading their minds, was nudging Ronnie to say "get up, let's go!" Knowing Diaz's modus operandi, that "cut" would only enter his on-screen vocabulary once the actor and his animal exited the frame.

Heremias sits undeterred by the prodding, and his cow then lowers its head, resigned to wait, and drinks from the river. After a beat, Heremias walks to the rock where he had placed his shirt, and puts it back on. Again, he takes a moment to sit, head lowered, and lets the water pass between his legs ...

Remember that the workers above us have halted their grind and are watching, quizzically, for in their eyes nothing is actually happening.

I stand silent, alone in my thoughts, still in the same position I was in when the camera began its set-up. I am getting impatient with this spectacle, nervously glancing at the workers, bystanders, and various members of the crew. I am a devout cinephile and a lover of long takes pregnant with meaning, not to mention a believer in the cinema of Lav Diaz; but at this precise moment, I feel I am no better, or more patient, than any other person on the set. We all began the scene with intent concentration, but at this point we've been broken. To me, only Lav, Ronnie, and the cow remain in focus. Or maybe just Lav and Ronnnie ...

Minutes pass, and Heremias stands up, tugging the rope that is tied to his cow, leading the animal out of the river and back to the road in front of me; the road from which they came. They walk slowly, continuing at a pace that is proper to the film. I didn't know this at the time, but, in Diaz's framing, the left side of the shot ends just before the dirt road begins. The view of the path that they walk up is obstructed almost completely by shrubbery. As with many shots in his films, what's important to Diaz is not whether we see the characters; it is that we know they are there.

The crew waits with anticipation, and as Heremias and the cow wander far off into the distance, Diaz yells "cut." The crew applauds, the onlookers wonder why, and the construction workers resume their grind.

When I watched the finished film of *Heremias* for the first time, I noticed this shot. It was one of a small handful of shots that I had the privilege to witness firsthand being filmed on location. In the film, the beginning and ending of the shot are abbreviated—we see Heremias and his cow walking toward us and away from us only briefly. It feels as if I am slipping into the river while watching and listening to this scene, enraptured by the beauty of nature, entranced by the soothing sounds of the water flowing—feeling, understanding what this moment means to Heremias. Diaz's air on set, his resiliency and belief in his art, is the melding of what Ronnie Lazaro's body represents and his meekness seeks. There is humility in Diaz's patience, and a resiliency in his unwavering gaze, the unwavering patience of his camera. It is a patience born from a conviction.

I did not concede to this on the set, but understood when watching the film. Standing on that dirt road, I was anxiously anticipating the word "cut." Sitting in my cinema seat, I wish this shot could go on forever ...

* * *

NIGHT OF THE LIVING DEAD

Notes on Where Raya Martin's Autohystoria *Succeeds and his* Maicling pelicula nañg ysañg Indio Nacional *Doesn't*

Alexis Tioseco (AT): You've told me before that historical accuracy was not your goal, necessarily. You're making a period film, but not a historical film.

Raya Martin (RM): And I'm actually moving away from that, from establishing facts, other than a sense of period, a sense of time.[5]

Raya Martin's *Maicling pelicula nañg ysañg Indio Nacional* is a glorious aesthetic achievement rendered in striking black-and-white 35mm film, for the most part. (The film opens in color, DV, and with sound.) Approximating the aesthetic of the silent period, the film was shot on a budget of roughly 700,000 pesos (up to video finish; 700,000 pesos is about US$15,500). *Autohystoria* was shot in two days on 24P digital video, with a budget of no more than 10,000 pesos (US$225). (The opening shot is on black-and-white video.) The latter, I feel, is the better film.

AT: Correct my phrasing, but you've said that you want to focus on the emotional history of the time, that you want to evoke pathos. Can you tell me about this?

RM: With the history education that I went through—in elementary, high school, in a Catholic private school—it was very much a memorizing of dates and places and events. You would take in characters as one-dimensional. That [José] Rizal was this educated guy, and then you have the other pole, [Andrés] Bonifacio, not knowing anything.[6] It was like the opposition of the heart and the mind. Where is the room for man, for man as maker of history?[7]

---

[5] Alexis Tioseco, "My Own History," *Osian's Cinemaya* 1,3 (2006): 49.

[6] José Rizal's incendiary novels, *Noli Me Tangere* and *El Filibusterismo*, turned him into a symbol of Philippine resistance against colonial rule. He was executed by the Spanish authorities in 1896. André Bonifacio led the revolutionary secret society Katipunan, which initiated an armed uprising against Spain in the same year that Rizal was executed. Bonifacio died in 1897 at the order of his political rival Emilio Aguinaldo.

[7] Tioseco, "My Own History," p. 49.

Martin has always spoken of his interest in history, of making it come alive for present-day viewers, and inextricably, as well, one imagines, for himself. He speaks of his desire for people to *feel* history. In *Indio,* the focus, as Martin describes it, is on man as maker of history.

Indio feels like a reclamation. The most iconic cinematographic images of the Philippines from the years leading to the uprising against Spanish rule in 1896, the historical period in which Martin's film is set, are newsreels from the American Edison Film Company. (The company also shot some reenactments of real events.) From that historical period, moving images shot from a Filipino perspective are nonexistent. However, as Martin's resistance to establishing facts enforces, *Indio* cannot be relied upon to provide, with a historian's conviction, the mood or atmosphere of the time, but rather a sense of this era as conjured by an artist. *Indio* is set in the past, but the subject, material, and focus of its project are undoubtedly all the imagination of its maker. If the focus were measured to determine where, between history and cinema, it rests, the balance would be heavily tipped toward the latter.

A still shot from Raya Martin's *Maicling pelicula nañg ysañg Indio Nacional*

The static images, distinguished by silence, each composition inspired by postcards from the era, are spare yet undeniably beautiful. But these images, which focus on everything from a young bell-ringer to a revolutionary fighter to a theater actor, and with scenes of everyday life spliced in between, manage occasionally to evoke humor, but rarely illicit emotion in themselves. They sing of photographic beauty, but are flat emotionally. Martin has attempted to recreate the mood of the silent-film era by screening *Indio* whenever possible with live music;[8] and experiencing the film with different musical performances only reinforces this notion, as the music dictates one's feeling more than do the images on the screen.[9]

In its creation of images to substitute for historical images that are lacking,[10] the film succeeds brilliantly; in touching emotion and making history come alive for the present viewer, it fails. But it is precisely where *Indio* fails that *Autohystoria* succeeds.

* * *

RM: Once you elevate someone to a historical icon, they lose their right to be human. They [simply] assume their role in history. So previous history making or a perception of history was based on this kind of making a list: one-two-three. I wanted to find articulation in trying to create an atmosphere, feelings, emotions of the time ... [11]

Autohystoria begins with a song played over a black screen—a light, charming tune in which a man plays tribute to his *nipa* (a type of palm with leaves used for thatching) hut—before we are presented a shot in grainy video of a young man leaving an apartment complex. We walk with this young man for over twenty minutes. The traveling shot with the camera situated across the street allows us to watch and listen as he passes karaoke bars and small clubs; the cars zipping past occasionally obstruct our vision; we soak in his environment. He reaches his destination, a small, two-story gated house, enters, comes out, smokes a cigarette, and enters again. Text then appears on the screen—with the shot of the street and house still in the background—announcing approximately this: "Last night I read about Andrés Bonifacio. He was murdered together with Procopio Bonifacio. I wrote about him to my brother. He did not answer." At the end of its first shot, *Autohystoria* declares itself both as personal—through the use of *I, my brother*—and presents the possibility that we are watching a dream—*last night*.

AT: How did you decide on the form of *Autohystoria*?

---

[8] The film does have an original score to use as an accompaniment during those times when a live performance is not possible. It features a piano solo by Martin's fellow filmmaker Khavn De La Cruz.

[9] In addition to watching the film on DVD with the recorded score, I have seen it projected accompanied by live music on the following occasions: a) Philippine premiere in Shangri-La Mall with a renowned Philippine pianist, Rudolf P. Golez, playing selected classical pieces; b) In Podium Mall with Khavn De La Cruz on electric keyboard, with occasional vocal intrusions (moaning); c) At the University of the Philippines with an acoustic quartet; d) At the University of Asia and the Pacific with Khavn De La Cruz on piano solo, with occasional vocal intrusion; and f) At the University of Asia and the Pacific with Khavn De La Cruz, featuring both classical piano and electric keyboard, and another musician on percussions. The dominant emotions elicited in me by these viewings ranged from nostalgia to tenderness, sweet melancholy to the sadness inspired by a requiem.

[10] This is a subject that perhaps deserves further exploration.

[11] Tioseco, "My Own History," p. 49. In the *Cinemaya* interview regarding *Indio*, Martin proceeded to discuss why he focused on the common man. The topic of historical icons discussed in the interview also seems extremely relevant to *Autohystoria*.

RM: When Khavn [De La Cruz, filmmaker] brought up the Bonifacio brothers (he was telling me about a high school play on this [topic] that he had worked on before), automatically I wanted to make a series of long takes about that specific moment when the two brothers were led to the mountains, up until their death. The script consisted of five to seven lines, chapter-like, describing what happens in each shot, basically. When I didn't want to make another costume film, because I didn't have any money for 35mm rolls, naturally it would [have to] be shot on video, and then a costume film wouldn't make any sense … so it became a tie-up with the modern, the two brothers dressing up as me and my brother. Originally I wanted to shoot in the mountain where the execution really happened, then, as all things changed, decided to shoot in the same mountain where I had shot my first feature. It was a tie-up with the modern take on the historical story. With those five to seven lines in my head, I went with a small crew to the location and shot overnight, some shots taken directly from my head, some improvised.[12]

A shot from Raya Martin's *Autohystoria*

The first shot we see after the opening poses a question: it is night and we are given a view, in a static, extreme long shot, of a monument at the center of a roundabout, with cars circling by. We wonder: what is this monument? What are we supposed to be looking at? And what is the monument's relationship to the text that we had just read?

---

[12] "Entretien avec Raya Martin," in *Cinéma du Réel 2008* catalogue, En Asie du Sud-Est section (Bibliothèque publique d'information, 2008), p. 121. Available in French and English at http://www.cinereel.org/IMG/pdf/p98_123_asie_sud_est.pdf, last accessed April 21, 2011.

Knowing that the statue featured in the monument is of Andrés Bonifacio will give you a clue,[13] but it doesn't quite solve the riddle. A few minutes into the shot, you begin to take notice of a sound: the siren of a police car that returns and fades repeatedly. Then we spot the police car driving around in circles again and again. Now we have clues, but we still have no answers, and the shot continues for several more minutes before the cut that finally gives us a clue. An edit thrusts us into two shots taken inside the car. The car holds two passengers. In these shots—given the feeling of claustrophobia, the expressions on the passengers' faces, the restlessness of their bodies, and their petrified silence—we are provided an answer. Inside the car driving in circles are two people who both appear not to want to be there. One of them is the man we saw in the prologue, and the other, a bit older, we imagine to be his brother.[14]

In the next shot, we are transported into a forest, with the camera following the brothers, whose hands are tied, from the car as they are forced by apparent captors to walk forward. What follows is a modern recreation of the Bonifacio brothers' death march: our tragic heroes walking forward gingerly in a dark forest with only a flashlight illuminating their steps.

Argentine cultural critic Beatriz Sarlo has described these scenes beautifully:

> We see them from behind, and we feel how difficult it is to walk in the countryside, at night, in a wooded and irregular terrain, their bodies are twisted by the pain and the fear, harassed by those who had taken them as prisoners, with the certainty that they are advancing towards their deaths. It is almost dawn when the prisoners stop; insects, birds, and the murmur of a river are heard; they look to the camera, they make an effort to stay upright, they tremble from fatigue, they sway. They know the sentence, and they expect the death that soon arrives.[15]

The video then proceeds to its inevitable, stark conclusion, with one brother (Procopio) shot and the other (Andrés) running away (as occurred in real life; Andrés was eventually caught and executed). Then there is a startling cut to three extended shots: a view of a mountain, a picture of serene clouds hovering in the blue sky, and

---

[13] I didn't know this was a statue of Bonifacio the first time I saw the film, though I guessed it may have been so. Knowing or not knowing doesn't hinder one's appreciation of the film.

[14] The story of Jun Lozada provides an interesting footnote to this shot and to the idea of being driven around in circles as a captured political prisoner. A key witness in Senate hearings about the highly controversial NBN-ZTE (National Broadband Network, Zhong Xing Telecommunications Equipment) deal (allegations of corruption had arisen concerning the awarding of a construction contract for a national broadband network to the Chinese corporation ZTE), Lozada claimed he was kidnapped by police at the Manila airport upon his arrival from Hong Kong, then driven around Manila, and that at one point he found himself being driven on a highway, going in the direction of Cavite, a place notorious for an infamous salvage killing that occurred there. Lozada's story was one of the most discussed news headlines of 2008 in the Philippines.

[15] Beatriz Sarlo, "Un cine conceptual," *Punto de Vista* 88 (August 2007): 37. With thanks to Maria Cleofe Marpa for providing a translation of Sarlo's article.

a shot of a flowing waterfall. A jolting cut to three archival Edison newsreels from the era follows,[16] and then deafening silence.

One feels a strange surge of emotion upon observing, in stillness and silence, the Edison clips. (This is heightened, perhaps, by the way the silence contrasts with the raging sound of water in the previous shot.) It is not an emotion one feels when watching these newsreels on their own; it is an emotion brought about by their placement at the end of this trip; and it is in this sensation that the beauty of this film is revealed. This is our history, Martin declares, but it's also a hallucination: sometimes we need to dream, to summon the imagination, in order to feel the past with a renewed intensity.

And herein lies the difference between these films by Martin: *Maicling pelicula nañg ysañg Indio Nacional* presents us with imagination, *Autohystoria* encourages it.[17]

SELECTED FILMOGRAPHY

Anino (Shadows, Raymond Red, 2000)
Autohystoria (Raya Martin, 2007)
Batang West Side (Lav Diaz, 2001)
Ebolusyon ng Isang Pamilyang Pilipino (Evolution of a Filipino Family, Lav Diaz, 2004)
Heremias (Lav Diaz, 2006)
Maicling pelicula nañg ysañg Indio Nacional (Raya Martin, 2005)

---

[16] The clips, in order, are (1) "An Historical Feat," filmed February 5, 1900; (2) "Aguinaldo's Navy," filmed February 18, 1900; (3) "25th Infantry," filmed March 23, 1900.

[17] A short review by blogger Dodo Dayao makes this intriguing, and I believe valid, inference about *Autohystoria*: "Its subtext—that political homicide is in our blood." Dodo Dayao, "Autohystoria/Indio Nacional," September 25, 2007, http://pelikula.blogspot.com/2007/08/autohystoria-indio-nacional.html, last accessed April 21, 2011. Dayao's comment is a reference to the killing of Bonifacio by Aguinaldo, and to the numerous politically motivated murders that have taken place since that event. The murder of Ninoy Aquino, who was killed upon returning to the Philippines in 1983 during Ferdinand Marcos's Martial Law rule, is just one example.

THE PIRACY GENERATION: MEDIA PIRACY AND INDEPENDENT FILM IN SOUTHEAST ASIA

Tilman Baumgärtel

Jo is a Malaysian student who smuggles Malaysian DVDs into England, where he is studying economics. Being a film buff and aspiring director, he saves the money he makes selling those cheap Malaysian DVDs in the hope that someday he will have enough money to attend a film school in New York City. Taking advantage of the fact that pirated DVDs often hit the streets before a movie's cinematic release, Jo has the latest titles before they are shown in UK cinemas. As he is about to graduate, Jo decides to go big with his last shipment. He has promised to smuggle 175 movies into the UK for a buyer, who will pay fifty pounds per DVD. This will cover the tuition for the film school of Jo's dreams, including the necessary means to live in style in New York. Fatefully, the Malaysian police kick off a major operation on the very day Jo is scheduled to pick up his stock of DVDs, and his suppliers are among those caught in the raid. The British film pirates who depend on Jo's wares threaten to "get even" with Jo for not returning with the goods by physically harming one of his friends. To save his friend, Jo must get those promised 175 DVDs in the twenty-four hours before his plane leaves for the UK.

That is the story of *Ciplak* (2006), the exhilarating film debut of Khairil M. Bahar. Despite having been made on a miniscule budget, it is a feature-length movie that both entertains and moves its viewers. *Ciplak* (Malay for "pariah") is a self-conscious piece of independent cinema full of clever ideas and endless cinematic innuendos, references, and puns. Its wry, sarcastic humor is reminiscent of films such as Richard Linklater's early works *Slacker* (1991) and *Dazed and Confused* (1993). It makes good use of very limited resources in a way that resembles Kevin Smith's *Clerks* (1994), and at times manages to turn its material limitations into filmic virtuosity à la Robert Rodriguez's debut film, *El Mariachi* (1993). A potential feel-good and popcorn movie, and at the same time a cineaste's tour de force, *Ciplak* is a film that is smart, enjoyable, and touching in a fashion that one has stopped expecting from Hollywood mainstream movies a long time ago.

This movie is a good starting point to introduce this chapter, because it brings together some of the topics I want to tackle here. Most obviously, it deals with the chapter's main subject matter of media piracy in Southeast Asia. Director Bahar says this about the film:

> In a country such as Malaysia, piracy isn't just common: it's indispensable. Everything from clothes and shoes to CDs and video games are available in bootleg form. Piracy has allowed the underprivileged to afford overpriced sneakers, exposed the ignorant to the wonders of non-top 40 music, and increased the cinema vocabulary of an entire nation through pirated DVDs.[1]

At the same time, *Ciplak* is also a wonderful example from an emergent batch of Southeast Asian independent films. *Ciplak* talks about the way digital media are currently influencing the way films and (pop) culture are created and consumed in Southeast Asia.[2] While *Ciplak* was a critical success in Malaysia, it did not do exceptionally well at the box office. Yet, its subject matter and quirky way of storytelling should appeal to young urban audiences throughout the region—and probably in the rest of the world, too. That young hipsters in Malaysia's neighboring Indonesia, Thailand, Singapore, or the Philippines will most likely never get to see this film shows the deficiencies in the distribution of film (and, presumably, also of music, books, and art) in the region. The phenomenon of piracy responds to these deficiencies.

This chapter examines some of the consequences of piracy for independent film production. In the first part, I look at the phenomenon of piracy and try to outline how piracy works. In the second part, I address some of the effects that piracy has on the makers and consumers of independent films. It does not seem too far-fetched to consider the Southeast Asian filmmakers who have started to make films in the first decade of the twenty-first century the "Piracy Generation." Due to the prevalence of media piracy in the region, these young filmmakers have had access to world cinema in an unprecedented way. While it is still too early to assess the long-term impact of piracy on the contemporary cinema of Southeast Asia, films such as *Ciplak* speak to the fact that the influence of independent and alternative cinema on local cinema is growing. I will end by discussing some of the early signs of changes that may be caused by piracy, while at the same time contrasting those changes with the way earlier generations of filmmakers from the region encountered international cinema. I also emphasize the fact that both piracy and the recent wave of independent films in the region benefit from the same technical advances: the easy and cheap access to digital media tools from cameras to computers to the Internet; peer-to-peer networks; and video-sharing sites, such as iFilms or YouTube.

THE SOCIO-ECONOMICS OF PIRACY

To discuss the mechanisms of piracy is a tricky matter, since hard and fast data on the subject are difficult to obtain. Despite my research into the piracy culture of

---

[1] This quote is from the website of the film that has disappeared from the Internet since this article was written. All other online sources were last accessed on June 20, 2011.

[2] At the same time, *Ciplak* has not been canonized in the same way that films by directors considered to be more art-house oriented (such as Lav Diaz, Apichatpong Weerasethakul, or Amir Muhammad) have been. Also, due to *Ciplak*'s whimsical nature, it most likely will never receive the same type of cineastes' blessings.

the Philippines, which included interviews with some DVD dealers,[3] I still have many unresolved questions regarding piracy in the Philippines, not to mention the rest of Southeast Asia. How do films get to the pirates' markets? Who picks the titles that get distributed? Who compiles the DVD collections of Oscar-winning films produced from 1929 to 1965? How is it that films by the German Marxist directors Jean-Marie Straub and Danièle Huillet—never published on DVD in Germany—are available in a shop full of pirated DVDs, smack in the middle of Bejing's embassy area? Who brought to Thailand the films of Harun Farocki, another German avant-garde filmmaker whose films are not out on DVD in Germany, to sell them at the night market in Patpong red-light district?

In many respects, one has to consider the pirated DVD market as a kind of black box. Research into this field is very difficult, as it is an illegal and therefore very secretive trade. The disc traders themselves know very little about the way the films are obtained and produced, and most of the people who do are not prepared to talk about it. There are numerical estimates concerning the extent of piracy in Southeast Asia, either from local law enforcement agencies or international lobby groups, yet most of those numbers are self-serving, and often the way they have been collected and calculated is unclear, unrealistic, or biased.[4] The mostly American trade groups, such as the Motion Picture Association of America (MPAA), the International Intellectual Property Association (IIPA), or the Business Software Association (BSA), that publish data on international piracy are often financed by US media and software companies and therefore have a vested interest in making their alleged losses seem as dramatic as possible. They try to paint the situation in the darkest colors. Other numbers stem from the police or organizations such as the Optical Media Board (OMB) of the Philippines, which have been assigned the task of fighting piracy. These organizations are often predominantly in the business of making their own work look efficient, or keeping their respective countries off international blacklists (and thus preserving their reputation as a good business location). One way to do that is by keeping loss-from-piracy statistics low. Therefore, I have decided not to include any of these obviously biased statistics into the text.[5] I will

---

[3] Tilman Baumgärtel, "The Culture of Piracy in the Philippines," in *Cinema in/on Asia*, ed. Kim Shin Dong and Joel David (Gwanju: Asian Culture Forum, 2006), pp. 377–401, available online at www.asian-edition.org/piracyinthephilippines.pdf

[4] For example, in some cases the media and software industries' losses that result from piracy are obtained by multiplying the alleged number of pirated DVDs, CDs, and CD-Roms by the typical American retail price. Needless to say, most of the people who buy pirated films, music albums, and software packages would not be able to buy them at the US price, so the "loss" mostly reflects potential sales that never would have occurred.

[5] Writers who subscribe to the notion of piracy as a pernicious international crime include Moisés Naím, *Illicit: How Smugglers, Traffickers, and Copycats are Hijacking the Global Economy* (New York, NY: Doubleday, 2005); and Tim Phillips, *Knock-Off: The Deadly Trade in Counterfeit Goods: The True Story of the World's Fastest Growing Crime Wave* (London: Kogan Page, 2005). For writings on piracy that are not informed by the perspective of the American copyright industry, see J. D. Lascia, *Darknet: Hollywood's War against the Digital Generation* (Hoboken, NJ: John Wiley & Sons, 2005); and Lawrence Lessig, *Free Culture: How Big Media Uses Technology and the Law to Lock Down Culture and Control Creativity* (New York, NY: The Penguin Press, 2004), available online at: http://free-culture.cc. For accounts that take Asian socio-cultural contexts into consideration, see William P. Alford, *To Steal a Book Is an Elegant Offence: Intellectual Property Law in Chinese Civilization* (Stanford, CA: Stanford University Press, 1995); Laikwan Pang, *Cultural Control and Globalization in Asia: Copyright, Piracy, and Cinema* (New York, NY: Routledge, 2006); and Sarai Media Lab, *Contested Commons/Trespassing Publics: A*

not, however, address the ever-popular question of the moral and legal implications of piracy. While piracy is illegal in all Southeast Asian countries, it is also a pervasive fact of life in almost all of them.[6] For the sake of my argument, I will consider this practice to be something that is very much part of quotidian life, without passing any ethical judgment on it.

And what a part of daily life it is. Counterfeit goods are easily obtainable in many street markets throughout most of Southeast Asia, as well as at shopping malls: fake Nike sneakers or DVDs with anything from Hollywood movies to European art-house films, illicit copies of Gucci bags, or copies of the latest albums of Western pop stars. I have found pirated copies of rare Japanese horror movies, such as *Jigoku* (Nobuo Nakagawa, 1960), next to digital gay art-house films from the Philippines, such as *Masahista* (The Masseur, Brillante Mendoza, 2005), and William Burroughs's shorts next to Amir Muhammad's documentary *Lelaki Kommunis Terakhir* (The Last Communist, 2006), which is banned in Malaysia. Manila's neighborhood of Quiapo, *the* centre for pirated DVDs in the Philippines, is jokingly referred to as "the biggest film archive in Asia" due to the massive number of otherwise hard-to-get films available there. Even in the gift shop of the Royal Palace in Phnom Penh, pirated copies of films such as *The Killing Fields* (Roland Joffé, 1984) and the French DVD edition of the Cambodian art-house film *Rice People* (Rithy Panh, 1994) are openly on display next to traditional weavings, postcards, silver trappings, and guide books (which in many cases are pirated reprints of American or European books).

While in Europe and the United States piracy is mostly seen as an online phenomenon that takes place via peer-to-peer networks, the pirate culture in Southeast Asia takes advantage of the fact that most people here do not have access to the Internet and most do not even have a computer of their own. Therefore, the predominant form of piracy in the region is the sale of counterfeit DVDs and VCDs. Most of them are copies of recent Hollywood movies, often for sale on the streets even before they premiere in the theaters. There is also pornography—loads of it, actually—that is illegal in many Asian countries. Then there are art-house and experimental films. Less common, but still available, are movie classics, such as the Shanghai studio Chinese silent films of the 1930s, Godard's *Weekend* (1967), *Gone With the Wind* (Victor Fleming, 1939), and video art by Brian Eno. The majority of these films are not and never were available in regular, legitimate shops, which predominantly carry mainstream movie fare. Consider, for example, Orson Welles's classic *Citizen Kane* (1941). It was never legally available in the Philippines (and presumably in other Southeast Asian countries), and one had to go to great lengths to see this movie. Now it is easy to find it through pirate markets. For a very long time, being a film fan in Southeast Asia meant one either had to limit oneself to viewing whatever was playing in the cinemas or was legally available on video (mostly mainstream US–Hollywood movies and local offerings); pay a fortune to

---

Public Record (Delhi: Sarai Media Lab, 2006), available online at http://www.sarai.net/ publications/occasional/contested-commons-trespassing-publics-a-public-record. The website for the conference, "Asian Edition," that I organized in November 2006, at the University of the Philippines, contains most of the papers delivered there, as well as ample links to other online resources. See www.asian-edition.org.

[6] Even in Singapore, which prides itself on having stamped out piracy, pirated DVDs are still available.

purchase mail-order videos from abroad; or be part of a well-organized circle of friends who swapped and copied the latest movies.

Those days are over for good. Examples of rare films that people have discovered on the pirate markets in Manila include a complete retrospective of the works of Rainer Werner Fassbinder (on three DVDs) and a DVD of *The Cremaster Cycle* films by American video artist Matthew Barney. (The latter was never officially released on DVD; instead, it was only for sale as an art piece for an amount estimated to exceed one million US dollars.) On the other hand, it is not easy to find local films for sale in many Southeast Asian countries. Yet, there have been instances where local films that have been banned or censored, and which therefore cannot be shown in regular cinemas, appear in the pirate markets. I will return to this point later.

In sum, the pirates don't just deliver the latest blockbusters and blue movies. Some pirates are ambitious enough to come up with their own box sets. A staple of pirate markets all over Southeast Asia are collections such as these: all the *Star Wars* films; a complete set of popular Korean soap operas, such as *Jewel of the Palace*; and well-presented selections of films by directors such as William Wyler and Kenji Mizoguchi. Many of these collections reflect a nerdy tendency towards completeness—for example, a set that includes all the films starring Jackie Chan or all the films by Akira Kurosawa. Sometimes the sets are even sold in lovingly handcrafted boxes.

More recently, the pirates have started to create their own film selections. The so-called eight-in-one sets (that squeeze eight feature-length movies on one DVD) often focus on a theme: all the recent horror films involving snakes, such as *Anaconda* (Luis Llosa, 1997) and *Snakes on a Plane* (David R. Ellis, 2006; this film is apparently a favorite in India); overviews of recent Bollywood films; and films on World War II, with weird combinations on one disc, such as *The Pianist* (Roman Polanski, 2002), *Saving Private Ryan* (Steven Spielberg, 1998), *The Downfall* (Oliver Hirschbiegel, 2004), and *Pearl Harbor* (Michael Bay, 2001).

Yet, the package's cover design typically betrays the fact that the people who produce these DVDs are not professional designers or writers. Often, local graphic artists—using pictures obtained from the Internet—design the covers and provide the blurb. The practice of using pictures from the Web can sometimes lead to side-splitting results. Recently, a version of Akira Kurosawa's adaptation of Dostoyevsky's novel *The Idiot* (1951) was sold in Manila with a cover featuring an image from Lars von Trier's independent digital movie *The Idiots* (1998). On the covers of some discs one can find pictures that have nothing to do with the movie in the box, or that have been dramatically enhanced. The covers may show pictures of guns for films that do not have guns, or suggest sexually explicit scenes that are not in the movie. Out of sloppiness, the boxes for many different films present the same credits on the packaging (no effort is made to find the actual credits for each movie). For instance, a widely available, pirated version of *On the Wings of Desire*, by German art-house director Wim Wenders, lists Van Diesel as one of the actors! The covers might also include lists of special features (such as bonus material, subtitles in Spanish, Cantonese, or Arabic) that are not included on the disc. The plot summaries on the back of the box are typically taken from the Internet Movie Database, and are often reproduced in hilarious versions full of typos, poor English, and tortured translations.

The English subtitles of pirated DVDs that come from China usually range from Chinese-flavored to completely outlandish, and sometimes contrast directly with the actual dialogue.[7] A typical DVD cover may include something like this: "The global film is included completely, broadcast the new feeling superstrongly." On the box of another DVD sampler it says: "Unique Color Sensual Desire Cinema." The copyright notice (!) on the same box reads:

> The copyright owner of the video disc in this DVD only permits Your Excellency to run the family to show, owner keeps the copyright all one's life relevantly in the right, not listing exhaustively, "the private family shows the use" not including using, exhibiting in the place such as a club, station, bar, theatre etc, for instance without permission, forbid hiring out, export or distributing, copy issue, alter right, will bear civil and criminal responsibility.[8]

The production quality of these discs varies greatly. The "cam rips" of the late 1990s are on their way out.[9] The majority of even the latest films available through the pirate market are usually from "screeners" (advance copies of movies that are circulated in the film industry) or other digital sources. Often the DVDs contain bonus material and other extras, including trailers for films from the same pirate corporation. Even beer commercials have been spotted on some discs.

The manufacturing quality of these discs ranges from shoddy (as with discs that do not play at all) to excellent. In Thailand, many of the more offbeat films seem to have been reproduced on an ordinary home computer, with the covers reproduced using cheap color copiers or printed out on computer printers, and the artwork coming from websites such as *cdcovers.cc*. The majority of the releases available in Southeast Asia, however, seems to come out of professional disc-pressing plants, complete with titles printed on the discs and packaging-covers produced on a printing press. There have been reports indicating that the same disc-pressing plants that produce regular DVDs during regular business hours also manufacture pirated discs during unauthorized night shifts.

Some customers who patronize pirate markets in Southeast Asia have become aware of quality issues. For example, there are a couple of forums on the Internet where buyers of pirated movies from the Philippines exchange tips on where to find rare films and how to distinguish quality DVDs from bad products. In one forum I looked at called *TheQ*,[10] buyers frequently bragged about their latest discovery. Since *TheQ* has recently disappeared from the Internet, I can only quote from my memory here, but there were a lot of posts along these lines: "Found *Day for Night* by Truffaut in Quiapo in the Muslim Barter Center at Stall No. 16. Ask for Benjie!"

---

[7] Laikwan Pang, "Global Modernity and Movie Piracy," a paper presented at the conference "Contested Commons/Trespassing Publics: A Conference on Inequalities, Conflicts, and Intellectual Property," January 2005, New Delhi.

[8] There is even an online-repository on the Internet that collects especially flawed covers of pirated DVDs, "Crappy Bootleg Covers." See www.flickr.com/groups/crappybootlegs/pool/

[9] "Cam rips" are bootlegged versions of movies that have been filmed in a theater with a digital video camera during a regular, authorized screening of the movie (in other words, a film of the film). The audio quality is typically poor (often one can hear audience members coughing or laughing), and the visuals may include the silhouettes of people headed for the restroom or concession stand.

[10] Q stands for Quiapo, the neighborhood in Manila with the biggest black market.

Other forums provide more general advice on how to distinguish bad DVD copies of a movie from good ones. These expert customers are capable of identifying well-made copies of films from the design of the cover and the occasional manufacturer's name. One poster in the *Pinoy DVD* blog explained crucial differences in manufacturing quality, and pointed out the high quality of the releases from a company that identifies itself with the label Superbit on the cover.[11] In other forums, participants provided detailed technical analyses of different DVD versions of the same film and compared them in terms of picture and sound quality. These tests were obviously conducted with laboratory equipment and software used by professional video studios.

There are notable differences among the "pirate cultures" of various Southeast Asian countries, both in terms of what is produced (to sell) and what is available (to buy) in the respective countries. I have discussed the culture of piracy in the Philippines extensively elsewhere,[12] so would just like to point out here a recent development that I was not able to cover in that earlier essay. The whole piracy landscape in the Philippines has been completely changed with the advent of the eight-in-one sets. DVDs with only one film on them are on their way out and are already unavailable in certain markets. Since eight-in-one collections usually focus on popular Western mainstream fare, this means that art-house and classic films are much harder to find now than they were even one year ago.

A majority of the "quality" pirated art-house films and the increasing number of classic American, European, and Japanese movies come from China. A company from Shenzen called Bo Ying is notably prolific in producing very sophisticated DVD copies—often using as masters the discs from the US-based Criterion Collection, which specializes in top-notch editions of classic films in flawless transfers and with original bonus material. Yet a visit to the website of Bo Ying reveals an "Anti-Piracy Statement"! Emails that I sent to both Bo Ying and the Criterion Collection regarding the copyright situation of pirated DVDs were not answered. Yet it is safe to assume that Bo Ying did not obtain the rights to Criterion Collection films, since the Criterion Collection points out on its website that it only distributes its films in the United States. Yet these Bo Ying titles are easily available in regular stores in Singapore, which prides itself for having extirpated piracy in the last couple of years.

Piracy as "Globalization from Below"

It is unquestionable that media piracy has resulted in unprecedented access to international cinema in Southeast Asia, a region that has a very limited infrastructure for art-house cinemas.[13] Except for a number of film festivals, viewers find few opportunities to watch non-Hollywood movies legally. Regular stores carry

---

[11] From the PinoyDVD forum, June 2002, www.pinoydvd.com

[12] Baumgärtel, "The Culture of Piracy in the Philippines."

[13] While there are a number of art-house cinemas in cities such as Singapore and Bangkok, in Southeast Asia there is nothing that even remotely resembles the art-house scene in most countries in Europe and the larger cities of the United States. In Southeast Asian cinemas, screenings are dominated by Hollywood and local commercial movies; art-house films are screened only occasionally by such cultural institutions as the German Goethe Institute, the Alliance Française, the British Council, the Spanish Instituto Cervantes, a number of universities, and some film festivals (e.g., Cinemanila in Manila or the World Film Festival in Bangkok).

predominantly American mainstream films, and mail-ordering DVDs from abroad is prohibitively expensive. It is therefore safe to say that piracy has added to Southeast Asians' film literacy and even the quality of media education in the region. For evidence of the latter, I only have to look at the rapid transformation that Manila's schools' media studies departments have gone through in the last two or three years. While previously a college's film collection might consist of some shelves full of dusty VHS tapes (sometimes even LaserDiscs!) that often came from the private collections of the professors, more recently the quality of school-based film libraries has improved dramatically. Brand new DVDs are appearing on the shelves of many media studies departments, and professors have started to use top-notch DVD versions of rare and offbeat films in class. Such accessibility not only exposes students to a much wider variety of movies than ever before—including uncommon, contemporary, independent, and cult films—it also allows professors to teach classes that would not have been possible five years ago, due to the lack of films. Needless to say, all of these films come from the pirate market.

Before I look in greater detail at how this new variety of accessible films has influenced the surge of recent independent films from Southeast Asia, I should point out that DVDs of rare and unusual films are not being produced to educate underprivileged students in Southeast Asia. The driving force is market economics. The cornucopia of titles that has become available all over the region is a very peculiar result of the globalization of both markets and cultures that has developed in the last twenty years. The deregulation of many national markets around the world in the wake of the demise of the Soviet Union and its Eastern European satellite countries was one of the prerequisites that paved the way for the kind of globalized media piracy that we see today. In addition, the post-1978 reforms of Deng Xiaoping, which paved the way for private enterprise in the People's Republic of China, and the economic reforms and increased commercial intercourse in formerly socialist countries such as Vietnam and Cambodia, played their role in furnishing large, untapped markets for pan-Asian piracy.

The free movement of capital and data is not only a hallmark of economic globalization, but also of global piracy. The process of economic "liberalization" around the world—in other words, the recent process of privatization and business deregulation internationally—has played its part in facilitating piracy. At the same time—and also in the name of a neo-liberal curbing of the power of the state—many countries have cut back on law enforcement and reduced border patrols, which, obviously, was another advantage for international pirates.

Economic globalization has worked in tandem with technological developments, such as the proliferation of the Internet and comparatively inexpensive access to powerful computers, disc burners, and scanners. While economic liberalization provided the means for distributing and purchasing illicit goods, digital tools supported their production. Moisés Naím points out the importance of new communication and distribution technologies for the pirate business in his book *Illicit*:

> With communication technologies that allow such tasks as warehouse management and shipment tracking to be done remotely, the trader and the goods need never be in the same place at the same time. This flexibility is a

crucial advantage that illicit trade has over governments, and is a defining aspect of the problem.[14]

Other new technologies used by smugglers and pirates include clandestine telecommunication systems and encryption that are often very far ahead of what the respective governments have at their disposal.

In many respects, therefore, piracy is the illicit underbelly of globalization. It is a form or product of globalization from below, in which the participants are not multinational corporations, but illegal enterprises. Flexible, non-hierarchical, speedy, highly efficient, and organized in a way that transgresses national boundaries, these illegal traders are in many respects quite representative of globalized businesses. They gleefully take advantage of newly deregulated foreign exchange transactions, offshore financial havens in obscure venues such as Tuvalu or the Cook Islands, and the benefits of the Internet—the anonymity and convenience of free Web mail accounts and online shops.

The pirate market is paradoxical in the sense that it is the most radically "free" market capitalism, yet at the same time is also a corrective to certain traits of capitalism. On one level, it is a no-holds-barred competition, where the fastest and most ruthless entrepreneur is usually the most successful. At the same time, it has exposed and compensated for some of the inadequacies of the legitimate marketplace. The pirates were flexible and perceptive enough to detect a potential market that nobody had noticed before. They discovered that there was an audience for art-house and avant-garde films in Southeast Asia, and were quick to exploit it.

In most of Southeast Asia, one of the main benefits of piracy so far has been that it makes available films that would otherwise be difficult to see. In more autocratic countries, pirates have had a much more important and libertarian function: as a distribution channel, they have been providing an alternative to the regular cinemas and shops as providers of films that the authorities don't want their citizens to see—in other words, pirates provide a way around censorship. The most extensive examples of circumventing political authority take place in China, where only twenty international films get official permission to be shown per year, yet every American blockbuster—and much more—is available at many street corners on pirated DVDs.

Similarly, among Southeast Asian countries, DVDs can come to provide an important distribution channel for banned films. In the Philippines, as the result of a political intrigue, a television documentary about former president Joseph Estrada was denied a rating by the Optical Media Board and therefore could not be aired. The film was available immediately on the black market. Some of the bestsellers on the pirate market were the so-called *Hello Garci* tapes, illegal recordings that seemed to provide evidence that another former president, Gloria Arroyo, had manipulated the last election to her advantage. To some extent, the pirate market can therefore generate opposition to entrenched institutions and create a public space to counter powerful interests—not out of political or aesthetic considerations, of course, but rather because of opportunism: to cash in on the controversy and the "free marketing" that is usually the result of censorship.

---

[14] Naím, *Illicit: How Smugglers, Traffickers, and Copycats are Hijacking the Global Economy*, p. 19.

"DAMAGED IN A SENSE": DIGITAL PIRACY, DIGITAL INDEPENDENT FILMS

Now we come to the vexed question of how this onslaught of foreign films has influenced Southeast Asian independent filmmaking. Before we consider some statements by the filmmakers themselves, let me briefly reiterate the structural parallels of piracy and the new independent cinema of Southeast Asia—that is, a predominantly digital cinema. Both rely on the recent proliferation of relatively inexpensive digital tools: cameras, the Internet (for both distribution and communication), and fast disc burners that allow for the mass production of DVDs and VCDs. Other important tools-of-the-trade include cheap printers, scanners, and the graphics software that allow for the design and production of covers or promotional materials. The creative, do-it-yourself aspects of digital media, which have been hailed as liberating and revolutionary by many media educators and computer evangelists, also allow for the mass production of illegal media.

Let us look again at *Ciplak* as a typical example of a no-budget indie film. Director Bahar posted this comment on the website for the movie:

> The film was made for less than ten thousand Malaysian ringgit [approximately US$3,000], shot on a single Canon XM2 Mini DV camera, and edited on a home PC. The movie was shot on weekends between October and December 2005. Everybody working on the movie did so free of charge. Given the nonexistence of a budget, we tried to beg, borrow, and steal as much as we could to get the movie made. When I bought the camera, it came with ten free mini DV tapes, which I used to shoot the film (although ten weren't enough), so we saved quite a bit on tapes. I had my old tripod from when I was fifteen, and Ariff had a monopod so that we could be more mobile. Our lighting rig was a borrowed Ikea lamp and a cheap Styrofoam board. Our boom mic was a borrowed stereo directional microphone (which broke down on us). All the sets and locations were obtained without a single penny spent. Most of the locations were houses or apartments where the cast lived. The only thing I really spent money on for this production was food.[15]

While the budget of ten thousand ringgit is extremely low even by local standards, these production methods are not uncommon among many independent filmmakers in Southeast Asia. It is therefore the easy availability and the simplicity of use of digital tools and media that facilitate not only the proliferation of media piracy, but also the production of independent films.

In some ways, the pirate market in Asia today serves a function similar to the French or the German film clubs of the 1950s and 1960s. Both of the European movements screened films that had been blacklisted or simply overlooked during the Second World War, and started their own magazines, initiating the research on and criticism of auteurs whose works are canonical today. In the process, those clubs bred a new generation of filmmakers who were highly conscious of film history and aesthetics. Film movements such as the *Nouvelle Vague* in France or the *Neuer Deutscher Film* in Germany were a direct outcome of this grassroots cinephilia. Today, the pirate market in Southeast Asia seems to have taken on the task of confronting audiences with classical and offbeat, nonmainstream films. That is not to suggest that pirated films have taken on the role of the more institutionalized entities

---

[15] See: www.ciplakmovie.com/

of "film appreciation," but they certainly are in the process of laying the groundwork for a more informed discourse on world cinema and providing material for cinephiles in the region.

The full effects of this proliferation need to be studied in greater detail, yet there are early signs of the impact of increased access to offbeat and art-house films in the region. A number of filmmakers have openly acknowledged their indebtedness to pirated movies in becoming filmmakers. Malaysia's Amir Muhammad reminisces in an interview about the influences of piracy on his generation of independent filmmakers:

> I think we all grew up watching Malaysian cinema to various degrees, but we are also of the generation that was very much exposed to cinema made in other countries. ... (B)ecause we came of age with the pirated VHS in the eighties and the VCD in the nineties, I think our range of influences is wider. If it were not for these pirated things then we would have been stuck with what was brought here, which is extremely limiting. And probably you would have got the sense that to make a movie you had to make a movie like what you see in the cinema. Perhaps you can say that we were damaged, in a sense, as we were exposed to the hype of independent movies, which you can't deny started in America in the early nineties. So we then got the romantic idea of doing it our own way.[16]

Other filmmakers have joined Amir Muhammad in pointing out the influence that pirated DVDs have had on their development. The young Philippine director Raya Martin writes about his first interview at the Festival du Cannes's Cinéfondation: "Here I was, in front of producers and distributors of films I was only familiar with from pirated DVDs, talking about my approach to filmmaking."[17] And fellow Filipino John Torres points out in an interview that "the video pirates have brought ... a lot of good films into our country."[18]

When reading the biographies of other Southeast Asian independent filmmakers, one discovers that it was often the exposure to avant-garde and art-house films from the West that got them interested in making their own films. Kidlat Tahimik, arguably the first independent director in the region, started to work on his debut film, *The Perfumed Nightmare* (1977), after he encountered Werner Herzog and his films in Germany. Raymond Red and other Philippine independent filmmakers who came after Tahimik in the 1980s were among the regulars at the workshops and film screenings that the Goethe Institute of Manila used to organize in the late 1970s and early 1980s. There they encountered films by directors such as Herzog, Harun Farocki, Werner Schroeter, Rosa von Praunheim, and other German directors of the *Neue Deutscher Film* movement.

More recently, internationally renowned Thai directors such as Pen-Ek Ratanaruang and Apichatpong Weerasethakul have described their "filmic eureka"

---

[16] Benjamin McKay, "A Conversation with Amir Muhammad," *Criticine*, October 13, 2005, available at http://criticine.com/interview_print.php?id=18

[17] Raya Martin, "Journal Entry No. 1: Anticipations of Light," *Criticine*, October 5, 2005, http://criticine.com/feature_print.php?id=19

[18] Alexis A. Tioseco, "A Conversation with John Torres," *Criticine*, April 20, 2006, http://criticine.com/interview_print.php?id=22. For a discussion of attempts to use piracy intentionally as a means to distribute independent films, see John Torres's contribution to this volume.

moment during their first encounter with foreign art films. Pen-Ek relates in an interview:

> Since I was in New York, I was always going to see films. And actually, I discovered cinema there, because before that I had no interest in cinema, in film. And even when I was in New York I was watching normal films, all these Hollywood films, and then one day I went to see *8½*, just because of the poster ... [A]t the end of the film, I was completely blown away. I didn't understand shit, I didn't understand at all "what is this?," you know, but ... it was so sexy to me. It was so attractive. That was the first film in my life that actually sort of gave me the idea that—this guy can make films? This is film? Then I started to become interested in Fellini, so I'd see more films by him. And then that lead to Bergman and Godard. And you know, the usual stuff, Truffaut, and Fassbinder. And so I discovered this art cinema that I found really to my taste.[19]

In a similar vein, Apichatpong points to American experimental films by directors such as Stan Brakhage and Jonas Mekas that he watched during his studies in Chicago as one of the reasons why he became a filmmaker: "I went to Chicago and discovered experimental cinema. It was something that made me think, 'Oh, this is what I always wanted to do, but I didn't know how to explain it.'"[20]

While those filmmakers had to travel abroad to get to know foreign avant-garde films, less than ten years after the formative experiences of Pen-Ek and Apichatpong it is possible to find the very same films that made such a lasting impression on them in the pirate markets of Bangkok, Manila, Kuala Lumpur, and Jakarta. Filmmakers such as John Torres are among the first to have been exposed to this flood of films that have become available out of the blue in their home countries. Torres's fast and daring work with hand-held digital cameras and found footage seems to speak of his experience with and exposure to nonmainstream films. The same goes for the trendy and self-conscious filmmaking of Khairil M. Bahar, which is saturated with film history and movie references.

None of this is, of course, meant to suggest that the filmmakers I mentioned are relying on the ideas and approaches of Western directors in their work. Tahimik, Red, Apichatpong, Pen-Ek, Torres, and Khairil M. Bahar have all carved out their respective filmic styles very much in their own way, which, in fact, differ quite substantially from the styles of the films that inspired them to become filmmakers in the first place. Yet, it appears as if these filmmakers' encounters with films outside the mainstream of Hollywood or the film industries of their respective home countries were the impetus that led them to develop their personal styles or even to become filmmakers in the first place. Now that international art-house and avant-garde films have become relatively easy to obtain in the region, those should inspire

---

[19] Alexis A. Tioseco, "A Conversation with Pen-Ek Ratanaruang," *Criticine*, October 18, 2005, www.criticine.com/interview_print.php?id=19

[20] Jonathan Marlow, "Blissfully Ours: A Talk with Apichatpong Weerasethakul," *GreenCine*, February 14, 2005, www.greencine.com/article?action=view&articleID=194

even more young filmmakers. Arguably, we will see the full consequences of this influence on regional filmmaking, which the pirates have brought about, only in the generation of filmmakers that will come after the generation represented by the likes of Amir Muhammad and John Torres. The real "Generation Piracy" might be still poised to emerge.

SELECTED FILMOGRAPHY

Ciplak (Khairil M. Bahar, 2006)
Lelaki Kommunis Terakhir (The Last Communist, Amir Muhammad, 2006)
Masahista (The Masseur, Brillante Mendoza, 2005)
The Perfumed Nightmare (Kidlat Tahimik, 1977)

THE SUBSTATION AND THE EMERGENCE OF AN ALTERNATIVE CINEMA CULTURE IN SINGAPORE

Jan Uhde and Yvonne Ng Uhde

Even in the early years of film's tumultuous history, far-sighted people realized that nurturing an alert and astute audience is an important step in the development of consequential intellectually and artistically significant cinematic forms. The first step in the search for such an audience was the founding of film societies (*ciné-clubs*). Since their emergence in France in the early 1920s, they have served as venues for the exchange of ideas, facilitating the intellectual and social interaction of those sharing the conviction that motion pictures are more than a disposable, ephemeral amusement.[1] More importantly, they provided access to movies neglected or rejected by the established commercial distribution and exhibition systems. In various historical periods and across continents and regions, film societies and other noncommercial screening venues significantly contributed to the formation of discriminating audiences and education of budding filmmakers. One of the most celebrated historical examples of such an influence were the film projections and discussions organized by Henri Langlois at his *Cinémathèque Française*, a key factor in the emergence of the French New Wave cinema after 1959.

In Singapore, the city's first and only film society was formed in 1958, mainly by a group of expatriates. It has been in operation since then, having contributed over the years to the country's film revival and to the maturation of the island's cultural life. Another prominent organization, the Singapore International Film Festival (SIFF), will be mentioned later. The most enduring function of film societies has been to nurture and spread the appreciation of the art of film to wider circles of viewers. They have promoted our understanding of film, led the way to professional criticism and the study of the medium, and, consequently, to its acceptance as an important and influential art form. Film clubs were also the forerunners of other organizations and associations, including informal, communal, and student groups interested in

---

[1] The phrase ciné-club was introduced in 1921 by Louis Delluc, an early French film critic, writer, and filmmaker, who launched the film review journal *Cinéa* in 1921. At present, there are about eleven thousand film societies in France.

film appreciation and in creating a platform for non-mainstream and experimental filmmaking.

Members of Singapore audiences, who, for the last half-century, knew only the bipolar world of mainstream exhibition and the Singapore Film Society, and the related activities of organizations such as the Alliance Française and Goethe Institute, have in recent years witnessed the emergence of alternative venues and activities.[2] This development was stimulated by the revival of film production in the country after 1991, increased government funding in this sector, and the establishment of film and media education in tertiary institutions.

Established and frequented mostly by young film enthusiasts, ventures such as the Sinema Old School, opened in late 2007, are embracing programming experimentation involving critical discussions of films, as well as organizing seminars, workshops, and regional exchanges, and linking movies with art forms such as music and multimedia. A characteristic feature of these types of avant-garde activities is experimentation with new and nascent technologies, including digital video, high-definition cinematography, and computer animation. Participants in such ventures are also exploring nonconventional forms of distribution, such as uploading films on the Web.

Film production in Singapore, as in most countries, reflects two fundamental ideological attitudes and production modes. On one hand, there are movies aimed at mainstream audiences, such as those made by the government-controlled MediaCorp Raintree Pictures, the country's *de facto* film studio. The mainstream producers and filmmakers look to Hollywood and Hong Kong for their stylistic inspiration, preferring genres such as horror, comedy, action, and thriller. This filmmaking strategy was popularized by the star-director Jack Neo and his television-style didactical satirical comedies. Singapore's mainstream cinema industry involves a growing number of international co-productions and multinational investment ventures, as exemplified by *One Last Dance* (2006), by Max Makowski. In general, it shies away from controversial subjects and social or political criticism.

The other side of the production playground is inhabited by a nascent independent cinema—mostly small ventures, many run on shoestring budgets, and all organized outside of Raintree's orbit. Singapore's "independent" films are characterized by reflective and critical subjects, and they typically exhibit more adventurous or experimental styles relative to mainstream movies. This type of filmmaking emerged in the first years of the film revival in Eric Khoo's *Mee Pok Man* (1995) and *12 Storeys* (1997). Since the 1990s, Singapore's independents—and sometimes even mainstream directors—have been examining the aspects of their country hidden under the well-oiled economic machine and ostentatious wealth. This new focus of attention has become one of Singapore's "indie" cinema's key characteristics. Some of the country's best features and shorts relate to the lives of people who have been dismissed as peripheral, such as: social misfits (*15*), the marginalized and forgotten (*Singapore GaGa, Invisible City*), the discarded and the poor (*Perth, Nation Builders*), the disabled (*Be With Me, Cages*), and people with nontraditional sexual orientations (*Solos, Women Who Love Women*).

---

[2] The contribution of the Singapore International Film Festival to the advancement of the country's film audience has been vital and ought not to be ignored. This article, however, focuses on activities and organizations that run year-round.

By choice and necessity, the working medium of new filmmakers has largely been the short-film format. Shorts have, for a long time, offered an economical alternative to feature productions; since the emergence of inexpensive, high-quality digital video technology and Internet-based diffusion, short films have become an even more important factor in contemporary film culture. Specifically in Singapore, the short format offers a convenient outlet for filmmakers who aspire to voice alternative or critical views and to scrutinize sensitive issues that would otherwise be difficult to explore, given the restrictions that hobble the city's tightly controlled professional film and television studios. Inexpensive and inconspicuous digital video cameras help the filmmaker to avoid or ignore the numerous regulations and restrictions for which the country is known. In addition, a short film is more likely than a feature-length film to slip by the official censors: for example, Sun Koh's *Bedroom Dancing* (2006) was rated R21 and passed uncut despite its explicit sex scenes. And should all roads to the viewer be barred for an independent filmmaker, there is the Internet, where a short could easily be made available to virtually anybody who wishes to see it. As Vinita Ramani's chapter discusses, Martyn See's critical documentaries, such as *Singapore Rebel* (2005, banned until 2009) and *Zahari's 17 Years* (2006, banned since 2007), could hardly have been brought to audiences through traditional means of production and distribution, but these films attracted an audience after they were broadcast on the Internet.

THE SUBSTATION

In Singapore, one of the most important establishments for aspiring filmmakers is The Substation. The Substation, the city's only multidisciplinary cultural institution, has devoted a considerable portion of its activities to cinema as part of its general objective. The concept behind The Substation was introduced in the mid-1980s by the esteemed Singapore playwright Kuo Pao Kun (1939–2002), a visionary who saw the possibility of turning an abandoned power substation built in 1926 into an arts center—a powerhouse of creativity. This sort of institution was particularly needed in a highly regulated city that had no comparable space for artistic experimentation and critical exchanges about the arts. With the help of the Ministry of Community Development and the financial support of the Guinness Brewery, the power station was resurrected from its ruinous state and opened as "The Substation–A Home for the Arts" in September 1990. Kuo, The Substation's founder, acted as its artistic director until 1995. The present artistic director (since 2010), Noor Effendy Ibrahim, is a visual artist, theater director, and playwright.

Housed in a building on Armenian Street rented from the National Arts Council (NAC), The Substation is home to local artists in dance, theater, music, literature, the fine arts, and film, as it provides space for rehearsals, installations, workshops, experiments, and performances. Lectures and film series, as well as individual screenings and seminars on film art, are held regularly in the unpretentious, intimate, one-hundred-seat Guinness Theatre. Over a short period of time, The Substation has become synonymous with the country's inspired film activities and a focal point for young film artists. It may be that the old-world charm of the simple three-story building contributed to the site's popularity among the young. Contemporary Singapore is characterized by ultramodern, almost aseptic, anonymous high-rises and shopping centers that lack history, identity, and character—structures one can find almost anywhere in the contemporary world.

Virtually none of the city's old (and even the not-so-old) stand-alone cinemas is in operation today. The power substation, on the other hand, having escaped the wrecker's ball in the 1980s, has preserved for new generations something from the old Singapore that their parents' generation was busy obliterating. Together with the neighboring houses on the centrally located Armenian Street, The Substation building offers cultural continuity and a symbolic link between the old and the new, between the past and the present.

Line drawing of the Substation building

The Substation is a registered charity and an Institute of Public Character (IPC). Its activities are approximately 70 percent self-financed, with the remaining 30 percent coming from external funds and donations. The funds raised by the organization itself come from a variety of sources, including ticket sales, fundraising, donations, corporate sponsorships, course fees, sales of artwork and a variety of other merchandise, and rental of the facility. The majority of its external funding comes from the NAC and the Lee Foundation; these contributions cover both operational costs and The Substation's various programs. The NAC, the Lee Foundation, and the Singapore Film Commission (SFC) provide annual support based on proposals The Substation submits every year. The sizes of their grants have been relatively consistent for the last five years. Other smaller grants are awarded on a project-by-project basis by the Hong Leong Foundation, the SFC, the Arts Fund, and the Ministry of Community Youth and Sport. Depending on the projects seeking support, The Substation may attract grants or sponsorships from foreign institutions such as the Australian High Commission and the American Embassy. This ability to generate income from such a variety of sources is a reflection of The Substation's resourcefulness and reputation among Singapore's artistic community, capabilities that have allowed it to operate for a decade and to develop into an important cultural institution.

Not long after it began operating, The Substation developed into a popular hub for the visual, performing, and literary arts, and for the occasional film-screening run; when films were first shown, the staff used two 16mm projectors donated by the Canadian High Commission in 1991. In October that year, a Canadian Film Festival was held, featuring experimental and animated shorts, including the works of Norman McLaren. Not until March 1997 did film become a regular part of The Substation's programming. That year, the center's artistic co-director, Audrey Wong, launched the Moving Images film program with then-artistic director T. Sasitharan, a program comprising monthly screenings, talks, seminars, and courses to promote film appreciation and encourage aspiring filmmakers in a film industry that was just rising from oblivion. The growth of The Substation's film activities reflected the revival of feature-film production in Singapore, the evolution of short filmmaking, and the rising awareness of film as an art form in the city's cultural and artistic community. One of the crucial impulses was the inclusion of Singapore shorts into the program of the third SIFF in 1990, at a time when Singapore was still without the capacity to produce its own feature films.

The Moving Images film program operates on a year-round basis, complementing the programming of the Singapore Film Society (SFS), Goethe Institute, and Alliance Française. Its programming strategy is primarily oriented towards non-mainstream, short, and local film production, since the organizers aspire to offset the predominance of mainstream feature programming (mostly imported from the United States and Hong Kong) that has traditionally determined what movies appear on the city's screens. One of The Substation's strengths is that its leaders and members embrace experimental works and works-in-progress, a stance that encourages critical discussion and innovation. Its programming strategy concentrates on advancing film appreciation, promoting independent local and regional shorts and feature-film production (Singapore Short Film Festival and the Asian Film Symposium), showcasing first-time filmmakers (First Take), encouraging student short-film production (Young Guns), and the recognition and screening of documentary film (Singapore Indie Doc Fest).

From its inception, the Moving Images program has been broad and bold in its effort to delight, provoke, engage, and educate. For example, among its events in 1997 was a joint venture with SIFF involving a two-day Classic Indonesian Masters Film Workshop, and a double-bill screening of the films *They Call Her Cleopatra Wong* and *Dynamite Johnson*, two movies set in Singapore but not seen since the 1970s. The screening was a fundraising event for the Moving Images program. There was also a five-day Canadian Film Festival featuring films ranging from fiction features, experimental and animated shorts, to award-winning documentaries. Among the pictures shown was the critically acclaimed *Thirty-Two Short Films about Glenn Gould*, a documentary on the Canadian piano virtuoso. This film was brought back by popular demand and screened again at The Substation that same year, when it played once again to full houses.

As part of its Septfest Film Events, another program that ran in 1997 (Septfest is The Substation's annual month-long festival in celebration of its anniversary in September), The Substation organized a four-day long perspective on documentary and experimental filmmaking in Asia, entitled "Beyond the Exit Sign." This event was coordinated by Gina Marchetti and Duncan Holaday, both from the Nanyang Technological University's School of Communication Studies. The seminar was packed with film screenings, talks, and discussions involving Holaday and directors Nick Deocampo from the Philippines, Hasnul J. Saidon from Malaysia, and Evans Chan from Hong Kong.[3] From July 1997 to November 1998, The Substation was also the venue for the now defunct Guerrilla Filmmaking Workshop, then the first of its kind, run by an independent film company, Monster Films, which had just made Phillip Lim's *The Teenage Textbook Movie*.

The Substation in April 2011

SHORT FILM HAVEN

From 2000 onwards, The Substation's focus on film intensified, especially when Wahyuni Hadi (2000–03) took charge of Moving Images. In 2001, twelve film events were organized, and 193 shorts and four features were presented. Among the events organized that year were animation film screenings, an International Youth Video Showcase, the American Short Shorts Film Festival, and Women in Film, a program

---

[3] Duncan Holaday is an American anthropologist and filmmaker whose productions include *Metos Jah Hut* and *Ngaben*. Nick Deocampo is considered the leading theorist of the Philippine independent movement involving filmmakers who produce short films. He has won prizes at international film festivals, and he is well known for a trilogy of documentaries dealing with themes of poverty and prostitution (1983–87). Hasnul J. Saidon is a video artist who uses his own films in installation artworks. He currently heads the Fine Arts Department at Universiti Malaysia Sarawak. Evans Chan is a Hong Kong filmmaker who works in Hong Kong and New York City.

celebrating the short films made by women filmmakers from Singapore and other countries.

What Hadi and her fellow organizers recognized was the significance of the short format as a foundation for feature productions of the future and as a launching pad for new generations of filmmakers. Their acknowledgment of the short film's importance was reflected through the launch in December 2001 of the Singapore Shorts Film Festival (SSFF)—now the Singapore Short Film Festival—the only international short film competition in the city.[4] This festival gave filmmakers from Singapore and abroad the opportunity to present, compare, and discuss their work. The festival includes a competitive section consisting of six films nominated by a panel of judges, out of which three are selected through an audience poll to receive its Voice Awards.

Although the SSFF was originally conceived as a biennial event, the second SSFF was held in November 2002, attracting an impressive 117 entries (up from 80 in the previous year) from Singapore, Argentina, Australia, India, Israel, Romania, Thailand, the United Kingdom, and the United States. It included home-grown entries such as Royston Tan's *15*, Sun Koh's *The Secret Heaven*, and Han Yew Kwang's *The Call Home*. The third SSFF, in early 2006, featured a selection of films from the International Short Film Festival Oberhausen, and in all it received 152 entries from thirty-four countries (including Singapore). From the time of the fourth festival, held in 2008, the SSFF was organized as an annual event.

Wahyuni Hadi's capable successor, Zhang Wenjie (2003–05), shared her view on the importance of the short format. Hadi is currently manager of the Objectifs Centre for Photography and Filmmaking and an initiator of its Travelling Short Film Project, a film outreach program that brings local short films to schools in Singapore. But before she left The Substation to join the center, she had already begun promoting Singaporean films abroad with two trips to the United States in 2001 (to the Sundance Film Festival and the American Cinematheque in Los Angeles), while in 2002 local shorts also participated at the Slamdunk Film Screening, Cannes International Film Festival. Under Zhang's direction, Moving Images played an increasing role in introducing and promoting Singaporean films to the rest of the world, doing so by connecting the filmmakers to and presenting the films at international film festivals. In 2004, Zhang facilitated the Singapore Night Short Film program at the Tenth La Cittadella del Corto International Short Film Festival in Rome, and the Singapore Slings program at the Twenty-Seventh Asian American International Film Festival in New York City. In addition to established annual events, such as Young Guns and Women in Film, several new programs were also introduced in 2004: First Take seeks to provide an outlet for new and first-time filmmakers to present and discuss their work in public and to encourage more people to try their hand at making films. First Take has proven to be very successful among the city's young film community.

Moving Images also launched the biennial Singapore International Documentary Film Festival (later renamed the Singapore Indie Doc Fest), Singapore's first festival dedicated to non-fiction film. Its objective is to encourage documentary filmmaking

---

[4] Not to be confused with the Short Shorts Film Festival, formerly known as the American Short Shorts Film Festival, as it was called when it made its first appearance at The Substation in July 2001. (Since then, the Japanese-born traveling festival presenting award-winning international shorts has been a regular feature of the Moving Images program.)

in Singapore and enable local filmmakers to interact with their counterparts from around world. In addition to six Singapore entries, documentaries from Denmark, India, Israel, Korea, Malaysia, Nepal, and the Netherlands were submitted to and screened at the 2007 festival. In its Focus on Female Directors program, co-presented with Objectifs, the festival featured the American filmmaker Andrea Richards. She discussed her 2005 book *Girl Director: A How-to Guide for the First Time, Flat-broke Film and Video Maker*, highlighting several female film pioneers who were only recently rescued from obscurity, along with the early works of Tamra Davis, Sofia Coppola, and Miranda July.

Cover of the Singapore Short Cuts program, 2006

A most visible and noteworthy program of The Substation today is the Singapore Short Cuts, a selection of some of the best local shorts, organized in partnership with the National Museum Cinémathèque of the National Museum of Singapore (NMS) and co-financed by the SFC. It started in 2004 as a cooperative venture between the Singapore History Museum (now the NMS) and The Substation. This venture has been remarkably successful. In 2006, the Third Singapore Short Cuts screenings moved to the newly opened, multi-functional, 247-seat Gallery Theatre at the NMS; a highlight of this program was a panel discussion on the state of local short filmmaking. Zhang, who was already working at the NMS at the time, was largely responsible for curating the event. (Zhang is now with the NMS as programming manager of its National Museum Cinémathèque, maintaining the ties and cooperation between the museum and The Substation.) Among the twenty-three shorts screened in four sessions during the Third Singapore Short Cuts, there were seldom-seen productions from the 1990s, as well as more recent works, such as Lau Chee Nien's *Old Woman* (2005), a nuanced portrait of an elderly woman who nears the verge of suicide when she discovers an abandoned baby at her doorstep, and *Di* (Little Brother, 2005), by Michael Kam, a deft and delightful depiction of the love-hate relationship between two brothers.

The growing popularity of the Short Cuts can best be illustrated in the words of Zhang, reflecting on the success of its fourth event in 2007: "This year the response was the best so far. All the tickets were taken up within two to three hours of being issued ... I think we have, in a way, achieved the objective of growing the audience for local films!"[5] The Short Cuts 2007 program also included works of Singapore's recently discovered early short filmmaker, Rajendra Gour, borrowed from the collection of the Singapore-based Asian Film Archive (AFA). Singapore Short Cuts remains one of the most successful showcases of short films in the country. The 2010 program featured a selection of recent Singapore shorts as well as a retrospective of local filmmaker K. Rajagopal, a three-time recipient of the Special Jury Award for the Singapore Short Film Category at the Singapore International Film Festival.

The Asian Film Symposium (AFS), introduced in 2001, is an annual highlight of the Moving Images program. Promoting Asian film and regional cultural exchange, it was originally co-presented with the Singapore History Museum. It includes S-Express, a traveling short-film program that now involves filmmakers and their works from Singapore, Malaysia, Thailand, Indonesia, the Philippines, China, and Australia. An innovative Singapore-Malaysia Film Exchange Project was added in 2004, whereby three filmmakers from each country traveled to the other country to shoot a short. The six completed films were shown on the closing night of the symposium. The following year, the AFS screened over fifty shorts and feature films by filmmakers from Singapore and around the region, and included the new program, Forum on Asian Cinema: Social Memory on Film, co-organized with the newly established Asian Film Archive. Thai filmmaker Pen-ek Ratanaruang and Singapore's Khoo were honored with retrospectives of their works.

The sixth AFS, held in September 2006 under the guidance of Zhang's successor, Kristin Saw, acting as the new programmer, invited the respected Malaysian independent director Amir Muhammad to participate. He presented his 2005 movie *The Year of Living Vicariously* and discussed the planned sequel to his new documentary, *The Last Communist* (*Lelaki komunis terakhir*, 2006), which was banned in Malaysia. Another acclaimed Asian guest lecturer at the AFS was Taiwanese documentary filmmaker Wu Yii-Feng. His film, *The Gift of Life*, about the devastating earthquake that struck Taiwan in September 1999, was screened at Cathay's The Picturehouse as the closing feature of the symposium. A new program, Medium, featuring medium-length films just under or above sixty minutes, curated in partnership with the Asian Film Archive, was added to the symposium the same year. This new initiative made available a separate platform for featurettes—medium-length films that did not fit the range for either short-film competitions or the feature-film category. In 2009, the AFS was presented as part of the SSFF, which had by this time become a September event.

---

[5] Zhang Wenjie, in private communication with the authors, September 1, 2007.

Although The Substation has been enormously important as a center of artistic ferment, and in facilitating the emergence of an alternative cinema culture, it would be unjust to ignore SIFF's seminal role in the resurgence and advancement of the country's film production and overall public awareness of the medium. In fact, it was SIFF programmer Philip Cheah who, in 1990, discovered local film talent Khoo, then an independent filmmaker who had been experimenting with Super-8 cameras since his youth. With the inclusion of Khoo's shorts in a new program highlighting independent Asian short-filmmakers, the screening of shorts became an integral component of the festival from 1990 onwards. As the only Singapore-made films at that time were shorts, this visionary initiative opened an international stage for local film artists—an act of fundamental significance for the survival and future revival of Singapore film production. The following year, in 1991, SIFF established the Silver Screen Awards to honor the Best Asian Film and Best Singapore Short. In 1992, the Silver Screen Awards were expanded to include a Best Director Award in both the feature and short film competitions.

SINGAPORE SHORTS: TALL ON SUCCESS

Unjustly obscured in the shadow of feature-film production, some of the most interesting Singaporean films are shorts. As in a number of other countries, the short-film genre acted as the cradle for many successful local filmmakers. Khoo and Royston Tan, today's leading figures of Singapore's independent cinema, launched their careers by making shorts. Not without reason, the noticeable expansion of the country's short-film production coincided with the growth of The Substation's Moving Images program from 2000 onwards; these activities provided both a focal point and motivation for previously fragmented and isolated individual efforts. It was at about the same time that Singapore short-filmmakers began winning festival prizes and awards, both locally and internationally.

One of the earlier overseas successes among local filmmakers was Tan Kai Syng's ten-minute short *All Change!!!*, which won third prize in the Experimental Video Category at the 1999 San Francisco International Film Festival's Golden Gate Awards. At the 2001 Malaysian Video Awards, Royston Tan won the Silver Award in the ASEAN Best Director category for his short film *Sons*; while *Gourmet Baby*, made by former journalist Sandi Tan, premiered at the thirty-ninth New York Film Festival in the same year.

The year 2002 was a stellar one for Singapore's shorts: Tan Pin Pin's *Moving House* was chosen as part of a Discovery Channel project to highlight young filmmaking talent in the Asia-Pacific region. The thirty-minute documentary observes with a critical eye the impact of urbanization on traditional culture through the experience of a Taoist family whose deceased relative must be exhumed to make way for residential development. The film also won a 2002 Student Academy Award (the "Baby Oscar") from the US Academy of Arts and Sciences. Royston Tan presented his award-winning short *15* in Clermont-Ferrand (France); Bertrand Lee's R(A)-rated *La Conquista* won the Silver prize at the thirty-fifth Worldfest–Houston and was invited to the Montreal World Film Festival. Sun Koh won the Silver Hugo Award at the 2002 Chicago IFF and the Best Director prize at the 2002 SIFF for *The Secret Heaven*.

In the following years, the number of Singaporean short-filmmakers successfully participating at festivals around the world grew. For example, Eva Tang screened

While You Sleep at Bilbao (Spain) in 2002 and in Venice (Italy) in 2003; Han Yew Kwang's *The Call Home* was shown in Rotterdam IFF (2003); and Leonard Yip took his *L'envie* to the Kinderfilmfest of the 2003 Berlin IFF. Wee Li Lin's *Holiday* was screened at several festivals, including Los Angeles IFF 2002. These are filmmakers whom Wahyuni Hadi calls the "second generation," the "first generation" being made up of filmmakers such as Khoo and Jack Neo.

Short films have now become an inseparable complement to Singapore's production of feature films. Shorts are more economical to make and much more critical and free in examining problems that bigger producers such as MediaCorp Raintree Pictures sidestep. For example, both Tan's gritty short *15* and Neo's *I Not Stupid 2* reflect on teenage delinquency, but their approaches—philosophically and stylistically—could not be more different. The short-filmmakers in Singapore have used both fiction and documentary to touch on practically every conceivable social issue, from the price of progress to nostalgia, from parental pressure and children's education to old age, from financial woes and job loss to communication and marital problems, and from personal crises to sexual identity and suicide. Personal themes are also expressed in the formal experiments of Victric Tng and Tanya Sng. Khoo's recent *No Day Off* (2006) is a brilliant, socially critical account of the four-year ordeal of an Indonesian maid working in Singapore, which uses an effective technique through which only the maid is visible while other characters remain off-screen. Another reflection of the short's growing status in Singapore has been the establishment of an independent short-film distributor (Objectifs Films)—a much-needed support for those artists seeking to bring Singapore-made shorts to local and international audiences.

THE SUBSTATION AND SINGAPORE'S NON-MAINSTREAM FILM CULTURE

Today, there are a number of venues in Singapore featuring documentaries, shorts, experimental films, and other non-mainstream fare: the National Museum Cinémathèque, the SFS, the Arts House, the privately run Sinema Old School, the Goethe Institute, the Alliance Française, and the universities and polytechnics. Even the repertory halls run by the large feature-oriented exhibitors, such as the Cinema Europa at VivoCity (Golden Village) and The Picturehouse at Dhoby Ghaut (Cathay), have acknowledged the growing interest in non-mainstream films and the significance of the short format by including these works into their screening schedules. Such commercially based arthouses are becoming an important factor in cultivating discriminating viewers recruited from general audiences in Singapore.

Still, The Substation remains the city's foremost location dedicated to promoting the short film and supporting its makers at home and regionally. It not only offers a physical space in which to present these movies to a wider public, but it also acts as a sounding board for creative efforts. The Substation has helped to foster a new kind of viewer—alert, intelligent, open-minded, adventurous, and critical—quite different from what one might call the average audience member for Singapore films. A number of young men and women from the first "Substation generation" have already made their own films—short and also feature-length works—which have been enthusiastically appreciated by viewers at home and earned positive reception overseas.

Perhaps the best way to convey The Substation's impact on Singapore's alternative film culture is through the words of some of those who have been shaped by it:[6]

> The Substation Moving Images film program has helped to give young filmmakers a platform to showcase their talent to the public. In many ways, the Substation gave me a head start as a filmmaker and provided me the opportunity to interact with my audience. With the focus on reaching out to the young, The Substation Moving Images film program plays a vital role in cultivating the next generation of filmmakers.—Royston Tan, filmmaker

> The Substation Moving Images film program is the genuine pulse of independent filmmaking and film appreciation in Singapore.—Sun Koh, filmmaker

> The Moving Images film program at The Substation is invaluable to film education in Singapore. It fills a gap like no other organization for Singapore films. With its strong focus on short films, newer filmmakers learn most from these programs. More importantly, The Substation gives very strong support to the local filmmaking community by giving us a venue to screen our works in a program that is well curated. It is this unfailing support that keeps many of us working away at our craft. There is no other program like it in Singapore, and without it, we are poorer for it.—Tan Pin Pin, filmmaker

> The Moving Images Program is something I look forward to every year as a filmmaker and as an audience member.—Wee Li Lin, filmmaker.

These filmmakers, "children of The Substation," are now among the leading forces of Singapore's independent cinema:

- Royston Tan revised and enlarged his breakthrough short *15* into a feature-length film. He then directed the melancholic aesthetic exercise *4:30* (2006), followed by the popular, commercially inclined *getai* musical *881* (2007)[7] and *12 Lotus* (2008).
- Tan Pin Pin shot two contemplative, stylistically groundbreaking documentaries, the featurette *Singapore GaGa* (2006) and the feature-length *Invisible City* (2007). She released both of them in a nonconventional way, with considerable success.
- Sun Koh registered a daring social commentary with her *Bedroom Dancing*; she is also the producer of the low-budget, Surrealist-inspired omnibus feature *Lucky 7* (2008), involving seven filmmakers.
- Wee Li Lin completed her perceptive first feature, *Gone Shopping,* in 2007.

Although each is working independently now, those filmmakers continue to be a part of The Substation by sharing their experience and expertise with others. The two former programmers of The Substation's Moving Images program, Wahyuni Hadi and Zhang Wenjie, are now continuing their work in influential film-related

---

[6] All of these quotes are from Zhang Wenjie, comp., "Moving Images 2004—Highlights," informational material compiled for The Substation, Singapore.

[7] *Getai* means, literally, "song stage." *Getai* are rambunctious, live stage performances commonly held in Singapore and Malaysia during the Chinese lunar seventh month, also known as the "hungry ghost" month.

institutions, the Objectifs Center and the National Museum Cinémathèque, respectively. Kristin Saw, in charge of The Substation's programming between 2005–08, is now with the Singapore Film Commission. She was succeeded by Low Beng Kheng (2008–10). The present programming manager of Moving Images is Aishah Abu Bakar. They and many others are living testimony of The Substation's role in fostering an alternative film culture in Singapore.[8] In just two decades, The Substation, a modest building with limited facilities and resources, run by a small but passionate staff, has developed into one of the most important centers for Singapore artists, performers, and aspiring filmmakers as a venue for presentations, exhibitions, screenings, and discussions. By making possible a continuous and vibrant exchange of ideas, The Substation provides an essential environment for the growth of film and art in Singapore.

SELECTED FILMOGRAPHY

15 (Royston Tan, 2002)
All Change!!! (Tan Kai Syng, 1999)
The Call Home (Han Yew Kwang, 2003)
La Conquista (Bertrand Lee, 2002)
Di (Little Brother, Michael Kam, 2005)
Dynamite Johnson (Bobby A. Suarez, 1978)
L'envie (Leonard Yip, 2003)
The Gift of Life (Wu Yii-Feng, 2003)
Gourmet Baby (Sandi Tan, 2001)
Holiday (Wee Li Lin, 2002)
I Not Stupid Too (Jack Neo, 2006)
The Last Communist (Amir Muhammad, 2006)

---

[8] Because of their basic relevance to discussions of Singapore cinema, references not cited in the text are recommended here: Timothy P. Barnard, "Film, Literature, and Context in Southeast Asia: P. Ramlee, Malay Cinema and History," in *Southeast Asian Studies: Debates and New Directions*, ed. Cynthia Chou and Vincent Houben (Leiden: International Institute for Asian Studies and Singapore: Institute of Southeast Asian Studies, 2006), pp. 162–79; Philip Cheah, "Film in Singapore from 1972: The Reconstruction of a Film Industry," in *Film in South East Asia, Views from the Region: Essays on Film in Ten South East Asian Countries*, ed. David Hanan (Hanoi: Vietnam SEAPAVAA and Vietnam Film Institute, 2001), pp. 195–210; Ho Tzu Nyen, "The After Image: Traces of Otherness in Recent Singapore Cinema," *Inter Asia Cultural Studies: Southeast Asian Cinema* 8,2 (June 2007): 310–26; Raphaël Millet, *Le cinéma de Singapour: Paradis perdu, doute existentiel, crise identitaire, et mélancolie contemporaine* (Paris: L'Harmattan, 2004); Raphaël Millet, *Singapore Cinema* (Singapore: Editions Didier Millet, 2006); Ben Slater, *Kinda Hot: The Making of Saint Jack in Singapore* (Singapore: Marshall Cavendish, 2006); Kenneth Paul Tan, *Cinema and Television in Singapore: Resistance in One Dimension* (Leiden: Brill, 2008); Jan Uhde and Yvonne Ng Uhde, *Latent Images: Film in Singapore* (Singapore: Ridge Books, National University of Singapore Press, 2009); Jan Uhde and Yvonne Ng Uhde, "Reviving Singapore Cinema: New Perspectives," in *Impressions of the Goh Chok Tong Years*, ed. Bridget Welsh, James Chin, Arun Mahizhnan, and Tan Tarn How (Singapore: National University of Singapore Press, 2009), pp. 491–500; Jan Uhde and Yvonne Ng Uhde, "Singapore: Developments, Challenges, and Projections," in *Contemporary Asian Cinema: Popular Culture in a Global Frame*, ed. Anne Tereska Ciecko (Oxford: Berg, 2006), pp. 71–82; William van der Heide, *Malaysian Cinema, Asian Film: Border Crossings and National Cultures* (Amsterdam: Amsterdam University Press, 2002); Souchou Yao, *Singapore: The State and the Culture of Excess* (London: Routledge, 2007).

Moving House (Tan Pin Pin, 2002)
Nation Builders (Martyn See, 2007)
No Day Off (Eric Khoo, 2006)
Old Woman (Lau Chee Nien, 2005)
Remember Chek Jawa (Eric Lim, 2007)
Singapore Rebel (Martyn See, 2005)
Singapore GaGa (Tan Pin Pin, 2006)
Solos (Kan Lume and Loo Zihan, 2007)
Sons (Royston Tan, 2000)
Speakers Cornered (Martyn See, 2006)
Tanjong Rhu aka *The Casuarina Cove* (Boo Junfeng, 2008)
The Secret Heaven (Sun Koh, 2002)
The Teenage Textbook Movie (Phillip Lim, 1998)
They Call Her Cleopatra Wong (George Richardson, aka Bobby A. Suarez, 1978)
Thirty-Two Short Films about Glenn Gould (François Girard, 1993)
While You Sleep (Eva Tang, 2002)
The Year of Living Vicariously (Amir Muhammad, 2005)
Zahari's 17 Years (Martyn See, 2006)

THE BEGINNINGS OF DIGITAL CINEMA IN SOUTHEAST ASIA

Eloisa May P. Hernandez

This article[1] examines the evolution of digital filmmaking in Southeast Asia, particularly in Malaysia, the Philippines, Singapore, and Thailand.[2] Due to the unprecedented growth of digital cinema in these Southeast Asian countries, emerging modes of production and distribution have begun to take shape, and they are quite different from the more traditional Hollywood-influenced modes that characterize the mainstream cinemas of these countries.

My focus is on the political economy of digital cinema in Southeast Asia. One of the leading figures in the study of the political economy of culture, Vincent Mosco, defines political economy as "the study of the social relations, particularly the power relations, that mutually constitute the production, distribution, and consumption of resources."[3] He encourages a "look at shifting forms of control along the production, distribution, and consumption circuit."[4] This article is, therefore, an attempt to address the core question: how are digital films produced and distributed in Malaysia, the Philippines, Singapore, and Thailand?

Before answering the question, the term "independent," which remains a highly debatable and fluid nomenclature in Southeast Asian cinema, should be discussed. Malaysian scholar Gaik Cheng Khoo writes that "[o]utside of Amir Muhammad's definition of 'indie' as 'a film that is not accepted by the Malaysian Film Festival,'

---

[1] This research was made possible through a grant from the Southeast Asian Studies Regional Exchange Program (SEASREP), funded by the Toyota Foundation and the Japan Foundation Asia Center in 2005.

[2] There are also nascent digital filmmaking communities in Indonesia, Vietnam, and other Southeast Asian countries, but financial and time constraints limit this study to Malaysia, Philippines, Singapore, and Thailand.

[3] Vincent Mosco, *The Political Economy of Communication* (London: Sage Publications, 1996), p. 25.

[4] Ibid.

there is much debate still around the term."[5] Customarily, the term "independent" refers to films produced and distributed without the resources or sponsorship of major film studios. The implication is that creative decisions are the responsibility of the filmmaker, who is free from the pressures of the studios and their commercial interests to realize his/her artistic vision. The focus of the term "independent" is tilted towards, but not limited to, production and distribution. At the same time, there is the common expectation that independent films feature alternative representations, novel narratives, and innovative storytelling, thereby avoiding formulaic plots and conventions. However, *Thaiindie*, a group of Thai independent filmmakers, expresses a sense of unease about the term "indie" on its website:

> We're getting tired with the word "indie," people want to make indie movies because they think they can escape from the rules, but when we all do that, we're following another set of rules anyway. For us, we want to make movies that we really feel strongly about, and in the style that we think is unique, not better or worse, but unique.[6]

Independent filmmakers have largely turned to utilizing the most affordable filmmaking technology of our day: digital technology. Although some major film studios have also used digital technology with the hope of lowering their production costs, independent filmmakers are the more active and impassioned champions of the digital technology. As noted by Paolo Villaluna of the Philippine Independent Filmmakers' Multi-Purpose Cooperative (IFC):

> The new technology undoubtedly took away the monopoly of filmmaking from only those who can afford them. Filmmakers saw this as an affordable opportunity to make films the way they want to, minus producers breathing down their backs, minus the cliché of casting big stars, and minus the pressure of recouping a large return of investment.[7]

Independent filmmakers have used and still use various film formats, but the introduction of digital technology gives independent filmmakers a comparatively inexpensive and more accessible alternative. Villaluna connects the digital technology to its predecessors, "[this technology] mirrors the independence that the previous generation saw in classic tools like the Super 8 and 16 mm."[8] While the importance of other filmmaking media, such as Super 8 and 16 mm film, to the work of independent filmmakers is well recognized, it is the contemporary nature of the digital technology that most merits study in this article.

---

[5] Gaik Cheng Khoo, "Just-do-it-yourself: Malaysian Independent Filmmaking," *Aliran Monthly* 24,9 (2004), at http://web.archive.org/web/20090515113831/http://www.aliran.com/oldsite/monthly/2004b/9k.html, accessed on June 28, 2011.

[6] See: www.thaiindie.com/wizContent.asp?wizConID=202&txtmMenu_ID=62, accessed on June 7, 2011.

[7] Paolo Villaluna, "Bagong Agos: New Currents. New Visions. Emerging Cinema," in *Bagong Agos: The Current Wave of Philippine Digital Cinema* (Manila: Independent Filmmakers Cooperative, 2007), p. 2.

[8] Ibid.

THE INTRODUCTION OF DIGITAL TECHNOLOGY

Several reasons can be cited for the emergence of digital cinema in Southeast Asia. One is the relatively recent establishment and strengthening of information and communications technology (ICT) in the region, such as through state-driven initiatives like the Multimedia Super Corridor in Malaysia, and the Commission on Information and Communications Technology (CITC) in the Philippines. The CITC is in charge of the Philippine Cyberservices Corridor (PCC) and describes it this way: "Stretching 600 miles from Baguio City in Northern Luzon to Zamboanga in Mindanao, the cyberservices corridor currently houses 75,000 call centers and business process outsourcing (BPO) companies, which are being served by a high-bandwidth fiber backbone and digital network."[9] The drive towards ICT development in this country stimulated growth in several industries, such as call centers, Internet gaming, and the recovery of the once robust animation industry. It has also given young digital filmmakers the opportunity to circulate and distribute their works on the Internet.

The Multimedia Super Corridor in Malaysia is a geographically designated area that stretches from Kuala Lumpur City Centre (KLCC) to Kuala Lumpur International Airport (KLIA), and also includes Putrajaya, Cyberjaya, and the wider Klang Valley. The Multimedia Super Corridor encompasses the Multimedia University, where a number of young Malaysian digital filmmakers have been educated. The harnessing of ICT has also spurred the growth of the Malaysian animation industry, which, according to Hassan Muthalib, has meant that "from 1995 to 2005, an unprecedented thirty local animation TV series, three feature animations, and four telemovies were produced for local consumption, surpassing any other ASEAN country. It also resulted in the rise of mostly young digital video filmmakers, beginning in 1999."[10] Khoo adds that indie filmmaking has burgeoned "due to the availability of cheap digital video technology, pirated foreign VCDs, DVDs, and software, not to mention the government's push for IT in its establishment of the Multimedia University and the Multimedia Development Corporation."[11]

The apparent dissatisfaction of young independent filmmakers with the current state of the mainstream film industries in their respective countries is driving them to find alternative ways to make films. Muthalib notes, for instance, that Malaysian mainstream cinema emphasizes pure entertainment: "[d]ishing out clichéd, stereotypical, and un-innovative narratives and characters, many of these films somehow attain box-office success."[12] In the local mainstream film industries, both the quality and the quantity of films produced have suffered. Since the Philippines film industry has been repeatedly described as dead or dying since the 1990s, its decline can be taken as a prime example. While it was once a robust industry that consistently produced around 120 films a year for wide theatrical release, Philippine

---

[9] Commission on Information and Communications Technology, www.cict.gov.ph/index.php?option=com_content&task=view&id=61&Itemid=94, accessed on June 8, 2011.

[10] Hassan Abd. Muthalib, "Malaysian Cinema 2003 through 2005: Beginning of the Crossover," e-mail to the author, May 23, 2006.

[11] Khoo, "Just-do-it-yourself: Malaysian Independent Filmmaking."

[12] Hassan Abd Muthalib, "The Little Cinema of Malaysia: Out with the Old, In with the New," Malaysian Cinema yahoo group, February 17, 2007, http://movies.groups.yahoo.com/group/malaysian-cinema/message/5780, accessed on May 30, 2011.

cinema has experienced a steady decline in film production since 2001. Records from the University of the Philippines Film Institute show that the Philippine film industry produced 103 films in 2001, ninety-four in 2002, eighty in 2003, fifty-five in 2004, fifty in 2005, and forty-nine in 2006. Several factors have been blamed for this decline in film production, such as the rising cost of raw film stock, exorbitant taxes, and the constant influx of Hollywood movies. The substantial cost of making movies using traditional technology commonly compels independent filmmakers to find alternative and cheaper ways to make films. Independent filmmakers who use digital technology find that the cost of production is drastically lower than it would have been if they had used conventional movie cameras and film stock.

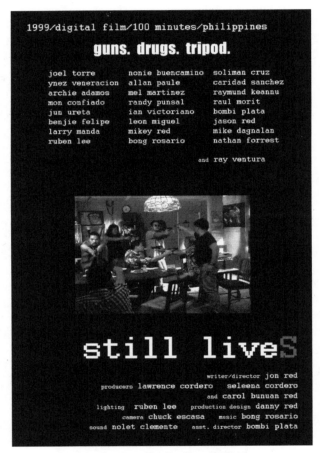

Poster for Jon Red's film, *Still Lives*

The year 1999 remains a landmark year for Filipino independent film, for in 1999 the pioneering filmmaker Jon Red shot the country's first digital full-length film, *Still Lives* (1999). In Malaysian cinema, the year 2000 saw the public screening of Amir Muhammad's *Lips to Lips* (2000), Malaysia's first full-length digital film. Punlop Horharin's *Everything Will Flow* (2000), shown at the Bangkok Film Festival 2000, was the first digital film produced and screened in Thailand.[13] In Singapore, a group of undergraduate students from the National University of Singapore made a digital film called *Stamford* in 1999, while the first Singaporean feature-length digital film was *Stories about Love* (Chee Kong Cheah, James Toh, and Abdul Nizam, 2000), directed by three emerging filmmakers and produced by the internationally acclaimed Singaporean filmmaker Eric Khoo.[14] Since then, numerous independent filmmakers in the Philippines, Malaysia, Singapore, and Thailand have taken up digital as their medium of choice.

MAKING DIGITAL CINEMA

The advent of digital technology has given rise to emerging modes of production that challenge more traditional, mainstream industrial practices. Filmmaking, once limited to a select group of people, is now open to more would-be practitioners due to the drastic reduction in the cost of production. This decrease in cost has allowed filmmakers to make their films without huge budget and studio financing, thereby liberating them from the controls of major studios. In her article, "Art, Entertainment, and Politics," Khoo observes:

> [I]ndies also undergo alternative modes of production, exhibition, and distribution. Digital technology has, to a large degree, democratized filmmaking by making it more affordable. While there are always exceptions, most digital indie films are shot without permits or membership to professional film organizations using digital video, non-actors, and a minimal crew. Made on a shoestring budget on private funds, they can be edited on home computers, then screened in "underground" localities in Kuala Lumpur.[15]

As noted earlier, the cost of production has been drastically decreased as a result of this new technology. Kannan Thiagarajan spent only between 150–200 RM (between $44–58 USD) when he made *Chitappa* (Malaysia, 2005). He did not even own his own personal digital video camera, but borrowed a friend's. Woo Ming Jin spent between RM 600–800 RM ($174–232 USD) to make *Love for Dogs* (Malaysia, 2003). Brillante Mendoza's *Masahista* (The Masseur, the Philippines, 2005) was made on a budget of just one million PHP ($20,000 USD). Even more frugal was John Torres, who did not spend more than the cost of the digital video tapes he needed to shoot *Todo Todo Teros* (the Philippines, 2006), his first full-length film (see his chapter in this volume).

Many digital films are now funded and filmed by the filmmakers themselves—"self-produced." Amir Muhammad produced his own documentaries: *The Year of Living Vicariously* (Malaysia/Indonesia, 2005) and *Lelaki Komunis Terakhir* (The Last Communist, Malaysia, 2006). James Lee, Amir Muhammad's good friend, produced his own first digital film, a Mandarin-language experimental drama called *Sunflowers* (Malaysia, 2000), and he also produced a compilation of his digital shorts entitled

---

[13] Ministry of Culture, Office of Contemporary Art and Culture, *S.i.am Contemp* (Bangkok: OCAC, 2006).

[14] Raphael Millet, *Singapore Cinema* (Singapore: Editions Didier Millet, 2006), p. 86.

[15] Gaik Cheng Khoo, "Art, Entertainment, and Politics," *Criticine*, October 14, 2005, http://criticine.com/feature_article.php?id=20, accessed on May 30, 2011.

James Lee's DV Shorts: 120 Minutes of Separation, Reunion, Betrayal, and Love. Lee's subsequent feature films have all been self-produced, a model that has been repeated by filmmakers across the region. Producing their own films liberates the filmmakers from the pressures imposed by producers who demand commercial viability, which generally requires films to be based on run-of-the-mill stories and to feature highly paid movie stars. Self-production brings control of film production back into the hands of the filmmakers and also enables them to tell the stories about previously invisible sectors of society: gays in Thunska Pansittivorakul's *Happy Berry* (Thailand, 2004) and *Life Show* (Thailand, 2005); lesbians in Connie Macatuno's *Rome and Juliet* (the Philippines, 2006); rural villagers in movies such as Uruphong Raksasad's *Stories from the North* (Thailand, 2006), and Brillante Mendoza's *Manoro* (The Teacher, the Philippines, 2006); and overseas contract workers, in works such as Eric Khoo's *No Day Off* (Singapore, 2006).

Producing their own films gives wider latitude to some independent filmmakers, giving them the means to challenge the usual process of filmmaking. The conventional approach to filmmaking normally starts with writing a script, then looking for producers, auditioning actors, shooting the film, and finally editing and finishing the film through post-production. Instead of starting with a script, John Torres uses unscripted and unstaged footage that he shot months or even years earlier, and with this method he needs no working script. He edits the footage and builds a film from his video library of more than twenty hours of unstaged footage. He does not hire actors or a film crew, but instead works by himself in a process that challenges conventional practices of filmmaking. Thunska also used a similar process for his eleven-minute short film *Sigh* (2001), constructed out of private footage of himself with his ex-boyfriend. It would have been difficult, if not impossible, to experiment with the filmmaking process in this manner using 35mm film, but digital technology has made it possible for independent filmmakers to venture into such challenges.

Filmmakers have also been producing films for their colleagues, most evidently in Malaysia. Through his indie production company, Doghouse 73 Pictures, James Lee has helped produce the digital films of other Malaysian filmmakers, namely Amir Muhammad, Ho Yuhang, David Ngui, and Ng Tian Hann. Amir Muhammad produced Tan Chui Mui's *Love Conquers All* (2006); he was the associate producer of Azharr Rudin's *The Amber Sexalogy* (2006) and James Lee's *Snipers* (2001); and he acted as the executive producer of Woo Ming Jin's *Lampu Merah Mati* (Monday Morning Glory, 2005). Tan Chui Mui produced both of Deepak Kumaran Menon's films, *Chemman Chaalai* (The Gravel Road, 2005) and *Wind Chimes* (2005). Such collegiality is a feature of the Malaysian indie scene and, in addition to Doghouse 73 Pictures, other indie production houses, such as Da Huang Pictures, have emerged. Filmmakers in both Singapore and Thailand have also collaborated in the production of each other's films. Fellow filmmakers have also contributed to the projects of their colleagues by taking on varied roles, for instance as cinematographers, editors, and actors.

Even if digital technology makes it possible for a filmmaker to finish a film as a solo endeavor, the tendency among filmmakers to pursue their craft as lone, independent artists is tempered, often, by an eagerness to collaborate and a strong sense of community among the practitioners. As mentioned previously, the Malaysian film community works with and in each other's films, demonstrating that film is still a collective endeavor. Members of *Thaiindie* have also worked together in distributing their films through their website and to local and international film festivals. Filipino independent digital filmmakers have banded together to form the IFC, and they collectively managed the festival *Bagong Agos* (New Wave): The Current Wave of Philippine Digital Cinema, held at Robinson's Galleria, a major mall in Metro Manila. The IFC also managed to convince the owners of Robinson's Galleria to transform one of its movie screens into a digital theater space, the short-lived but aptly named *IndieSine*. Motivated by idealism or pragmatism or both, in many cases, independent filmmakers form film communities and rely on one another for support.

Several independent film-production companies have begun to surface in Southeast Asia and are providing crucial support for digital filmmakers. An example is ufo Pictures, which produced one of the most commercially successful digital films in the Philippines, *Ang Pagdadalaga ni Maximo Oliveros* (The Blossoming of Maximo Oliveros, Auraeus Solito, 2005). Arkeo Films in Manila produced *Big Time* (Mario Cornejo, 2005) and *Mansyon* (Joel Ruiz, 2005). Red Films, part of Red Communications, was formed in 2004 to produce and distribute films; it focused mainly on the works of digital filmmakers in Malaysia and other Southeast Asian countries. Red Films has produced Bernard Chauly's *Gol and Gincu* (Goalposts and Lipsticks, 2005), Amir Muhammad's *The Last Communist*, and James Lee's *The Beautiful Washing Machine* (2004), among others. These independent film-production companies act as an alternative to the mainstream producers by providing financial and production support while allowing the filmmakers to retain their creative control and freedom.

The formation of Da Huang Pictures was the initiative of Malaysian digital filmmakers Amir Muhammad, James Lee, Tan Chui Mui, and Liew Seng Tat. According to a company profile included in the 2010 "Paris Project Projects Book," "the company's aim is to make Malaysian films according to the director's personal vision rather than having profit as its main motive."[16] Similarly, ufo Pictures is composed of young scriptwriters Michiko Yamamoto, Raymond Lee, Ned Trespeces, Jade Castro, and Emman dela Cruz, all of whom have already had experience working in the mainstream film industry in the Philippines. In the mid-2000s, they agreed to make a movie about a gay boy growing up in the slums of Metro Manila and appointed Yamamoto as the screenwriter. They then asked Auraeus Solito to direct the film for them, a collaboration that resulted in *The Blossoming of Maximo Oliveros*. Raymond Lee said in an interview that the group wanted more creative control over their material:

> We wanted to be involved in projects that start with a story or a character. We knew many of our dream projects would never make it on screen. If we had pitched *Maxi* to the studio, they would have laughed at us. They would have come up with all sorts of reasons why it wouldn't be commercial. We cast unknown actors, which would never fly with the studios, although now, paradoxically, they're famous.[17]

---

[16] See www.pariscinema.org/data/document/pc2010_maquette-projectsbook-net1.pdf, p. 41, accessed on June 7, 2011.

[17] Sonia Kolesnikov-Jessop, "Surprise Success for Philippine Film Shot on Shoestring," *International Herald Tribune*, September 28, 2006, http://www.iht.com/articles/2006/09/28/opinion/fmlede29.php, accessed on March 24, 2011.

Today, even multimedia conglomerates have ventured into producing digital films. For instance, ABS–CBN in the Philippines does so through Cinema One, a popular Filipino movie channel on cable TV. This channel supports digital filmmaking in the country through its Cinema One Originals competition, which encourages the creation of full-length digital films. Several film projects are selected and each given a substantial production grant. Cinema One Originals is a project of Creative Programs Inc., an entertainment subsidiary of ABS–CBN. The main film production unit of ABS–CBN is Star Cinema, which produces films using conventional technology; its participation in digital film production raises questions about the nature of "independence." Are digital films funded by Cinema One grants comparatively less independent than digital films created without such funding? Are these films perhaps semi-independent? If the financing for a project has been obtained from a major film studio, to what extent does the studio control production and creative decisions?

Government institutions in Malaysia, the Philippines, Singapore, and Thailand provide varying degrees of funding to digital filmmakers in their respective countries. Some of these government institutions include the National Film Development Corporation, or Filem Nasional Malaysia (FINAS); the Philippines' National Commission for Culture and the Arts (NCCA); the Cultural Center of the Philippines (CCP); the Singapore Film Commission (SFC); and the Office of Contemporary Art and Culture (OCAC) in Thailand. FINAS, established in 1981, provides production grants to Malaysian digital filmmakers. The CCP is the central organizing institution of the Cinemalaya: Philippine Independent Film Festival, in cooperation with the NCCA and the University of the Philippines Film Institute, and with major funding from private sources. The NCCA also provides production grants to filmmakers, as well as travel grants for those who are attending recognized international film festivals. The SFC was established in 1998, and in 2003 it merged with the Singapore Broadcasting Authority and the Films and Publications Department to form the Media Development Authority.[18] Lacking an established studio system, Singaporean filmmakers have been relying on the SFC for funding. The Film Commission's Short Film Grant has supported the production of more than two hundred films from 1998 to 2005, while the Film Incubator Programme, launched in 2003, provides support for aspiring filmmakers to make their first feature films.[19] In Thailand, the OCAC commissioned fourteen filmmakers to create thirteen short films to commemorate the anniversary of the 2004 tsunami. This was an unprecedented gesture, as no Thai government agency had previously commissioned independent filmmakers in a state-funded project.[20] Although government programs to support digital filmmaking do exist in Malaysia, the Philippines, Singapore, and Thailand, many of those who might take advantage of such support do not view it as adequate. Many filmmakers are probably also wary of the kind of government funding that would come with strings attached, subjecting them to strict auditing rules, finance regulations, and censorship. Since government funds are being used, a grant-giving body such as the NCCA in the Philippines can

---

[18] Millet, *Singapore Cinema*, p. 100.

[19] Ibid.

[20] *Thai Film Directory*, Office of Contemporary Art and Culture, Ministry of Culture (Bangkok: OCAC, 2006).

ask for a detailed breakdown of the expenses claimed by the recipients of the grant, and subject that grant income to taxes. Such funders can also exert some influence over the political content of films that might potentially be interpreted as anti-government, or they could deny grants to film projects that are critical of the state, hence exposing filmmakers to a certain degree of censorship.

An alternative source of funding for digital filmmakers is international foundations. Some filmmakers, like Amir Muhammad, have received grants from sources such as the Asian Public Intellectuals Fellowship of the Nippon Foundation. Amir Muhammad used the grant money to make his films *Tokyo Magic Hour* and *The Year of Living Vicariously* in 2004. Others have received script- and project-development grants and post-production grants from the Hubert Bals Fund of the International Film Festival Rotterdam. Beneficiaries of these grants have included such practitioners as John Torres, Ho Yuhang, Deepak Kumaran Menon, Tan Chui Mui, Lav Diaz, Raya Martin, James Lee, and Anocha Suwichakornpong. The Hubert Bals Fund has also instituted a new grant category for low-cost digital films, with three Southeast Asians as its first recipients: Ho Yuhang, Liew Seng Tat, and Khavn De La Cruz.

DISTRIBUTING DIGITAL CINEMA

Even with the proliferation of digital film production over the past decade, problems in distribution abound. "Distribution" of films generally means getting the films shown to an audience, and the usual distribution route for a film involves a theatrical exhibition—to show the film in commercial theaters to paying audiences. Other options include TV broadcast, cable-network release, and going straight to video.[21] Unfortunately, not all digital films reach commercial theaters. Digital filmmakers usually do not have access to the marketing machinery that major film studios typically use to promote their movies. Hence, digital filmmakers in Malaysia, the Philippines, Thailand, and Singapore rely on film festivals in their respective countries and on international film festivals to obtain much needed exposure. Do-it-yourself distribution strategies, the Internet, and support from local film institutions have also been crucial in the distribution of digital cinema.

As early as 2000, the Philippines already had The First Filipino Full-Length Indie Feature Festival (FFIFF), organized by the Cultural Center of the Philippines. It featured early digital films such as Jon Red's *Still Lives,* JJ Duque's *Journey,* Khavn de la Cruz's *The Twelve,* and *Motel,* by Nonoy Dadivas, Chuck Escasa, and Ed Lejano.[22] The first digital film festival in the Philippines, .MOV, was organized in 2002 by the filmmaker Khavn De La Cruz. As its website proclaims, ".MOV is the Philippines' much-awaited answer to the rousing call of the Digital Revolution."[23] An international array of digital features was shown that year. In 2005, Cebu City played host to .MOV International Digital Film Festival, at which Lav Diaz's ten-hour epic, *Ebolusyon ng Pamilyang Pilipino* (Evolution of a Filipino Family, 2004), won the grand prize in the digital feature film category.

---

[21] Steven Ascher and Edward Pincus, *The Filmmaker's Handbook: A Comprehensive Guide for the Digital Age* (New York, NY: Plume, 1999), p. 556.

[22] Edward Cabagnot, "The Road to Cinemalaya: Some Random Rants on Pinoy Indie Cinema," SEA-Images, 2004, available at http://sea-images.asef.org/ArticlesDetail.asp?ArticleID=140, accessed on June 7, 2011.

[23] See http://indieyo.tripod.com/mov/mov.htm, accessed on May 30, 2011.

In the Philippines, 2005 was a banner year for digital cinema following the establishment of two major film festivals dedicated solely to digital films: Cinemalaya and Cinema One Originals. Cinemalaya gave production grants of 500,000 PHP (roughly $10,000 USD) for the completion of nine full-length digital films, which were subsequently shown at the festival. The most successful entry was Solito's *Ang Pagdadalaga ni Maximo Oliveros* (The Blossoming of Maximo Oliveros). It was subsequently transferred to 35mm film and had a relatively successful commercial run in theaters. Even though most of the Cinemalaya entries do not really enjoy commercial success, Cinemalaya still provides Filipino filmmakers with a venue in which to exhibit their works.

In its first year, Cinema One Originals gave production grants of 600,000 PHP (roughly $12,000 USD) to six film projects. The finished films were screened at the Cinema One Originals Film Festival. In the following year, Cinema One Originals began to present awards in addition to the production grants. *Huling Balyan ng Buhi* (Woven Stories of the Other), directed by Sherad Anthony Sanchez, won the 2006 Grand Prize. The finalists in this contest are assured commercial theater screenings, and their films are aired on the Cinema One cable TV channel. The Cinemanila International Film Festival, the Philippines' longest running film festival, also instituted a digital film competition in 2005 with Digital Lokal: Cinemanila Digital Film Competition.

In Malaysia, the Festival Filem Malaysia (FFM, Malaysian Film Festival), established in 1980, instituted a new award category in 2007—Best Digital Film. Deepak Kumaran Menon's *Chalanggai* (Dancing Bells, 2007) won over Bernard Chauly's *Goodbye Boys* (2007) and Eng Yow's *The Bird House* (Naio Wu, 2007).[24]

Southeast Asian digital filmmakers have been actively participating in the world's premier film festivals, thereby ensuring that their films reach a global audience. The past few years have seen increased participation by Southeast Asian digital filmmakers in international film festivals, such as those staged in Vancouver, Rotterdam, Toronto, Fribourg, Hong Kong, Berlin, Pusan, Jeonju, and Cannes. At these and other international film festivals, many Southeast Asian digital filmmakers have won some of the most prestigious awards.

Film organizations have been crucial in sustaining the development of digital cinema in Southeast Asia. For instance, one of the most important institutions supporting Malaysian digital filmmakers is the Kelab Seni Filem Malaysia (Film Club of Malaysia), which shows Malaysian digital films to the public for free and on a regular basis at HELP University College. The club's regular projects include "Malaysian Shorts" and "Malaysian Docs," usually curated by independent filmmaker Amir Muhammad. The club's founder, Wong Tuck Cheong, also helps digital filmmakers by collecting and submitting their films to organizers of international film festivals. In Singapore, as Jan Uhde and Yvonne Ng Uhde point out in their chapter in this collection, digital filmmakers are fortunate to have their efforts supported by such organizations and institutions as the Asia Film Archive, The Substation, The Arts House, and Objectifs: Centre for Photography and Filmmaking.

Many filmmakers have started selling their own DVDs using do-it-yourself strategies: they make copies of their own films and sell these to friends, fellow

---

[24] See http://www.sinemamalaysia.com.my/ffm.php?mod=archive&p=info&id=27, accessed on May 30, 2011.

filmmakers, and cinephiles at film screenings and festivals, and in bazaars, small shops, and bookstores (such as Kinokuniya bookstores in Malaysia and Singapore). In Kuala Lumpur, Malaysian digital filmmakers sell DVDs through the independent bookshop Silverfish Books, situated in the Bangsar district. Sirote Tulsook, the founder of Thai Short Film (a group of short-film and independent filmmakers), opened a short-film stall for a brief period of time at the popular Jatujak Weekend Market in Bangkok. In Manila in the mid-2000s, a former shoe center was transformed into an art hub called CubaoX that became home for Vintage Pop, Datelines Bookshop, Futureprospects Studio, and Blacksoup Artspace—all outlets where DIY DVDs were sold. Today, one can find DVDs for sale in Manila at several branches of Mag:net Gallery and other alternative spaces.

Since digital filmmakers typically do not have access to the distribution networks and facilities employed by major studios, they use the Internet and other forms of information and communications technology to circulate their works. Currently, the most popular video Internet site is YouTube, which hosts short films, experimental works, and trailers by digital filmmakers such as Chuck Gutierrez, Jim Libiran, Crisaldo Pablo, Khavn De La Cruz, Raya Martin, Thunska Pansittivorakul, Amir Muhammad, Azharr Rudin, Tan Chui Mui, Royston Tan, Eric Khoo, and Apichatpong Weerasethakul. Martyn See's *Singapore Rebel* (2005), banned for a number of years in Singapore after censors judged it to be a "party political" film, can be viewed in full on YouTube, and it has elicited numerous online comments.

The Internet has become an arena in which virtual film communities may be created. Electronic mailing lists related to Southeast Asian cinemas have proliferated, such as those of the University of the Philippines Film Institute, Cinemanila, and the Malaysian Cinema e-groups.[25] Social networking sites such as Facebook and Twitter have also become electronic venues for disseminating information about digital cinema. Digital filmmakers make resourceful use of their personal websites and blogs. Khavn De La Cruz's Facebook page, "This Is Not a Film by Khavn,"[26] contains several manifestos strongly supporting what he calls "filmless films." Tan Pin Pin's "Notes from Serangoon Road" website[27] contains notes related to all her films. Singaporean digital filmmaker Victric Thng's website[28] contains his biography and filmography. Digital films commonly have their own dedicated websites, such as Solito's "Ang Pagdadalaga ni Maximo Oliveros,"[29] Diaz's "Ebolusyon ng Isang Pamilyang Pilipino,"[30] and Ian Gamazon and Neill dela Llana's "Cavite."[31] Amir Muhammad maintains a blog about the making of his two films *Lelaki Komunis Terakhir* (The Last Communist, 2006), and *Apa Khabar Orang Kampung* (Village People

---

[25] See http://movies.groups.yahoo.com/group/upfilminstitute/; movies.groups.yahoo.com/group/Cinemanila/; and movies.groups.yahoo.com/group/malaysian-cinema/, accessed on May 30, 2011.

[26] See www.facebook.com/group.php?gid=40617170941, accessed on June 7, 2011.

[27] See www.tanpinpin.com/wordpress, accessed on May 30, 2011.

[28] See www.victricthng.com, accessed on May 30, 2011.

[29] See www.blossomingofmaximooliveros.com, accessed on August 17, 2007.

[30] See www.ebolusyon.com, accessed on April 13, 2009.

[31] See www.cavitemovie.com/, accessed on May 30, 2011.

Radio Show, 2007).[32] The Da Huang Pictures blog contains entries on *Love Conquers All, Before We Fall in Love Again,* and *Things We Do When We Fall in Love.*[33]

The Internet also provides a space for several publications, which have been crucial in sustaining digital cinema in Southeast Asia. *Criticine: Elevating Discourse on Southeast Asian Cinema*[34]—edited by the late Alexis Tioseco—is an online publication that specializes in Southeast Asian cinema. It is an important source of information and contains incisive and engaging interviews and film reviews, as well as essays by noted film critics such as Noel Vera, Khoo, and Muthalib. More importantly, *Criticine* builds bridges between film critics, historians, and filmmakers in Southeast Asia. Thai digital filmmakers are fortunate to have *Bioscope Magazine,* which is dedicated to filmmaking in Thailand, available to them and other cinephiles, and to have talented film writers such as Kong Rithdee and Anchalee Chaiworaporn contributing to the discussion of contemporary Thai cinema. In Malaysia, the online news zine *Kakiseni* has been a welcome venue for film critics such as the late Benjamin McKay and Australia-based academic Khoo.

Although the aforementioned alternative modes of distribution are crucial in sustaining digital cinema in Southeast Asia, some digital filmmakers in the region have produced films that have been released successfully in commercial theaters. Initiatives such as the now-defunct Robinson's Galeria IndieSine theater, for instance, have commercially screened the works of Filipino independent filmmakers. In Malaysia, Bernard Chauly, Deepak Kumaran Menon, Ng Tian Hann, James Lee, and Tan Chui Mui are among a growing number of local digital filmmakers who were granted commercial releases with the International Screens division of the multiplex chain Golden Screen Cinemas. This trend has emerged and is growing in other Southeast Asian marketplaces as well.

FUTURE PROSPECTS

The accessibility and manageability of the new technology has given rise to many new filmmakers and digital films. Unfortunately, this does not necessarily translate into a growing supply of well-produced films. In her essay, "Malaysian Indies: The Future of Story-telling," Khoo writes: "With the ease of digital filmmaking, everyone suddenly thinks they can do it without understanding how to tell an interesting story, how to do it well (style), and with some honesty and restraint."[35] James Lee, in an interview concerning the state of digital filmmaking in Malaysia, also expresses reservations:

> It's very encouraging, but at the same time, it has reached a very dangerous point where they [filmmakers] have forgotten what filmmaking means because DV is so cheap. This year, we have two or three young guys making features even before making short films. I don't know if they are really talented, but this is the trend. They skip a lot of work process. I think it's become too easy to become a filmmaker. They just graduate and say "I'm a director"; this is how it is

---

[32] See www.lastcommunist.blogspot.com/, accessed on May 30, 2011.

[33] See www.dahuangpictures.com/blogs/, accessed on May 30, 2011.

[34] See www.criticine.com

[35] Gaik Cheng Khoo, "Malaysian Indies: The Future of Story-telling," *Rentakini,* April 12, 2005, http://www.malaysiakini.com/rentakini/35242.

in Malaysia now. The worst point is that the quality drops. Everybody is rushing to [be] an independent, experimental cinema, without much experience.[36]

For digital cinema to prosper, filmmakers must be able to utilize the technology's strengths, work with its limitations, find novel ways to reach their audience, and fully harness digital's potential. Digital technology has encouraged many filmmakers to create fresh, novel, and innovative films, breathing new life into cinemas in Malaysia, the Philippines, Singapore, and Thailand. It has given independent filmmakers another way to create their films and tell stories that may not have been narrated by movies coming out of the mainstream film industries. There has been an increase in films tackling sensitive subject matters, such as homosexuality, interracial relationships, and religion. Previously unseen and unheard stories about members of different ethno-linguistic groups, overseas contract workers, maids, and people from the rural areas are now being told. Unpopular topics, such as urban alienation, the effects of diaspora, abuse of state power, poverty, and hopelessness, are also portrayed in digital films. Malaysian mainstream cinema is dominated by the Malays, yet Deepak Kumaran Menon and Kannan Thiagarajan are examples of Tamil-Malaysian filmmakers who are now actively making digital films. The digital technology has enabled their voices to be heard and their stories to be seen.

The digital mode of making movies raises several questions about the evolving nature of independent cinema in Southeast Asia. As digital technology becomes more closely affiliated with independent filmmaking, it raises the question, "Is indie only digital?"[37] Moreover, given the increasing involvement of multi-national corporations in digital film production, coupled with government support for digital cinema, we are also compelled to ask whether corporate or government support compromises the independence of the films, or whether we must shift our discourse to consider relative degrees of independence. The debates surrounding what constitutes "independent cinema" will continue as the film environment changes and as technology offers new challenges and opportunities, but digital filmmakers will go on finding novel and distinct ways to produce and distribute their works.

SELECTED FILMOGRAPHY

Ang Pagdadalaga ni Maximo Oliveros (The Blossoming of Maximo Oliveros, Auraeus Solito, 2005)
Apa Khabar Orang Kampung (Village People Radio Show, Amir Muhammad, 2007)
Before We Fall in Love Again (James Lee, 2006)
Big Time (Mario Cornejo, 2005)
Cavite (Ian Gamazon and Neill dela Llana, 2005)
Chalanggai (Dancing Bells, Deepak Kumaran Menon, 2007)
Chemman Chaalai (The Gravel Road, Deepak Kumaran Menon, 2005)
Chitappa (Kannan Thiagarajan, 2005)
Ebolusyon ng Pamilyang Pilipino (Evolution of a Filipino Family, Lav Diaz, 2004)
Everything Will Flow (Punlop Horharin, 2000)

---

[36] Jérémy Segay, "Discussion with James Lee on the DV Film Making In Malaysia," *s.e.a images*, undated, http://sea-images.asef.org/ArticlesDetail.asp?ArticleID=115, accessed on March 24, 2011.

[37] Khoo, "Just-do-it-yourself: Malaysian Independent Filmmaking."

Gol and Gincu (Goalposts & Lipsticks, Bernard Chauly, 2005)
Goodbye Boys, (Bernard Chauly, 2007)
Happy Berry (Thunska Pansittivorakul, 2004)
Huling Balyan ng Buhi (Woven Stories of the Other, Sherad Anthony Sanchez, 2006)
Lampu Merah Mati (Monday Morning Glory, Woo Ming Jin, 2005)
Lelaki Komunis Terakhir (The Last Communist, Amir Muhammad, 2006)
Life Show (Thunska Pansittivorakul, 2005)
Lips to Lips (Amir Muhammad, 2000)
Love Conquers All (Tan Chui Mui, 2006)
Love for Dogs (Woo Ming Jin, 2003)
Masyon (Joel Ruiz, 2005)
Manoro (The Teacher, Brillante Mendoza, 2006)
Masahista (The Massuer, Brillante Mendoza, 2005)
No Day Off (Eric Khoo, 2006)
Rome and Juliet (Connie Macatuno, 2006)
Said Zahari's 17 Years (Martyn See, 2007)
Sigh (Thunska Pansittivorakul, 2001)
Singapore Rebels (Martyn See, 2005)
Snipers (James Lee, 2001)
Still Lives (John Red, 1999)
Stories about Love (Chee Kong Cheah, James Toh, and Abdul Nizam, 2000)
Stories from the North (Uruphong Raksasad, 2006)
Sunflowers (James Lee, 2000)
The Amber Sexalogy (Azharr Rudin, 2006)
The Beautiful Washing Machine (James Lee, 2004)
The Bird House (Naio Wu, Eng Yow, 2007)
The Year of Living Vicariously (Amir Muhammad, 2005)
Things We Do When We Fall in Love (James Lee, 2007)
Todo Todo Tero (John Torres, 2006)
Tokyo Magic Hour (Amir Muhammad, 2004)
Wind Chimes (Deepak Kumaran Menon, 2005)

CONTRIBUTORS

Benedict R. O'G. Anderson is Aaron L. Binenkorb Professor of International Studies, Emeritus, Cornell University. A specialist on Southeast Asia, his works include *Imagined Communities: Reflections on the Origin and Spread of Nationalism; Spectre of Comparisons: Nationalism, Southeast Asia, and the World; Under Three Flags: Anarchism and the Anti-Colonial Imagination;* and *In the Mirror: Literature and Politics in Siam in the American Era* (editor).

Tilman Baumgärtel is a Visiting Professor at the Department of Media and Communication at the Royal University of Phnom Penh. He has taught at the Film Institute of the University of the Philippines in Manila. Tilman has a blog on Southeast Asian Cinema at http://southeastasiancinema.wordpress.com/ and is the editor of the publications *KINO-SINE: Philippine-German Cinema Relations* and *KON. The Cinema of Cambodia.*

Angie Bexley is based at the Department of Anthropology, School of Culture, History, and Language, College of Asia and the Pacific, Australian National University.

Chris Chong Chan Fui is an independent film director working on fiction and non-fiction stories. His film *Kolam* (Pool) was voted best Canadian short film at the 2007 Toronto International Film Festival. His debut feature, *Karaoke,* was selected for the Directors' Fortnight program of the 2009 Cannes International Film Festival. Chris is currently based in Malaysia.

Hassan Abd Muthalib is a self-taught artist, writer, and film director who wrote and directed Malaysia's first animated feature. His writings on film and animation appear in local and international publications. Hassan is currently researching early Malaysian cinema as Senior Resident Artist at the Faculty of Artistic and Creative Technology, Universiti Teknologi MARA Malaysia. He can be reached at hassan.muthalib@gmail.com.

Eloisa May P. Hernandez is Associate Professor in the Department of Art Studies, College of Arts and Letters, University of the Philippines, in Diliman. She completed her PhD dissertation, entitled "The Political Economy of Digital Cinema in the Philippines: 1999-2009," at the same university. Eloisa is the author of the book *Homebound: Women Visual Artists in Nineteenth-Century Philippines,* and is a member of the Young Critics Circle Film Desk in the Philippines.

May Adadol Ingawanij is a senior research fellow at the Centre for Research and Education in Arts and Media, University of Westminster. May has published articles on Thai and Southeast Asian cinema across a range of academic and general publications, including *Inter-Asia Cultural Studies, Representing the Rural, The Ambiguous Allure of the West, Criticine, Vertigo, Aan Journal, Z Filmtidsskrift,* and *Segnocinema.*

Gaik Cheng Khoo lectures in cultural studies, gender, and Southeast Asian cinema at the Australian National University. Her publications include *Reclaiming Adat: Contemporary Malaysian Film and Literature,* and she has edited special issues on Southeast Asian Cinema in *Inter-Asia Cultural Studies* and *Asian Cinema* (coedited with Sophia Siddique Harvey).

Mariam B. Lam is an associate professor of literature, media, and cultural studies, and Southeast Asian studies at University of California–Riverside. Her forthcoming book, *Not Coming to Terms: Viet Nam, Post-Trauma, and Cultural Politics,* analyzes cultural production and community politics within and across Vietnam, France, and the United States. Mariam is founding coeditor of the *Journal of Vietnamese Studies.*

Benjamin McKay was a writer, critic, and academic based in Kuala Lumpur. On July 18, 2010, he died of cardiac arrest. Benjamin had just completed his doctoral research on 1950s and 1960s Malay cinema. As a lecturer in Film Studies at Monash University, Malaysia, he was much loved by his students. As a critic, Benjamin wrote a monthly column for the Malaysian magazine *Off The Edge* and was a regular contributor to *Kakiseni* and the Southeast Asian cinema online journal *Criticine.*

Vinita Ramani Mohan is the co-founder of Access to Justice Asia LLP, a nonprofit organization dedicated to assisting victims of conflict and genocide in Asia. Her writing and research stemming from her work focuses on memory, trauma, and the ways in which photography, film, and archives are used in memory-making. Vinita has previously worked as a journalist and as the publicist and writer for the Singapore International Film Festival in 2002, 2004, and 2005. She was also the Asian Cinema Publicist for the Toronto International Film Festival in 2004.

Alexis A. Tioseco was a film critic, curator, and lecturer from the Philippines. He regularly contributed to its oldest weekly magazine, *The Philippines Free Press,* and had his articles on cinema published internationally in publications such as *Cahiers du Cinema, Sight & Sound,* and *Cinema Scope.* In 2005, he founded *Criticine,* an online journal dedicated to encouraging intelligent discourse on Southeast Asian cinema. Alexis and his partner, the Slovenian film writer and programmer Nika Bohinc, were killed in their Manila home on September 1, 2009.

John Torres is a musician and experimental filmmaker based in the Philippines. His films include a trio of shorts known together as *The Otros Trilogy,* and the features *Todo Todo Teros, Years When I Was A Child Outside,* and *Refrains Happen Like Revolutions in a Song.*

Chalida Uabumrungjit studied film at Thammasat University, Thailand, and film archiving at the University of East Anglia, UK. She is the project director of the Thai Film Foundation and has been serving as the festival director of the foundation's Thai Short Film and Video Festival since 1997.

Jan Uhde is Professor of Film Studies at the University of Waterloo, Ontario, Canada, where he established the Film Studies program at the Fine Arts Department. His publications include: *Latent Images: Film in Singapore*, book and CD-Rom both co-authored with Yvonne Ng Uhde; *Vision and Persistence: Twenty Years of the Ontario Film Institute*; and *Ontario Film Institute Programming Activities Index 1969–1989*. Jan Uhde is the founding editor of *KINEMA, a Journal for Film and Audiovisual Media*.

Yvonne Ng Uhde is on the editorial board of *KINEMA*. She is the co-author of *Latent Images: Film in Singapore*. Yvonne has contributed to books and periodicals in the United States, the United Kingdom, and Italy, and she also writes the Singapore section of the *International Film Guide*.

SOUTHEAST ASIA PROGRAM PUBLICATIONS
Cornell University

Studies on Southeast Asia

Number 55 *Glimpses of Freedom: Independent Cinema in Southeast Asia*, ed. May Adadol Ingawanij and Benjamin McKay. 2012. ISBN 978-0-87727-755-2 (pb.)

Number 54 *Student Activism in Malaysia: Crucible, Mirror, Sideshow*, Meredith L. Weiss. 2011. ISBN 978-0-87727-754-5 (pb.)

Number 53 *Political Authority and Provincial Identity in Thailand: The Making of Banharn-buri*, Yoshinori Nishizaki. 2011. ISBN 978-0-87727-753-8 (pb.)

Number 52 *Vietnam and the West: New Approaches*, ed. Wynn Wilcox. 2010. ISBN 978-0-87727-752-1 (pb.)

Number 51 *Cultures at War: The Cold War and Cultural Expression in Southeast Asia*, ed. Tony Day and Maya H. T. Liem. 2010. ISBN 978-0-87727-751-4 (pb.)

Number 50 *State of Authority: The State in Society in Indonesia*, ed. Gerry van Klinken and Joshua Barker. 2009. ISBN 978-0-87727-750-7 (pb.)

Number 49 *Phan Châu Trinh and His Political Writings*, Phan Châu Trinh, ed. and trans. Vinh Sinh. 2009. ISBN 978-0-87727-749-1 (pb.)

Number 48 *Dependent Communities: Aid and Politics in Cambodia and East Timor*, Caroline Hughes. 2009. ISBN 978-0-87727-748-4 (pb.)

Number 47 *A Man Like Him: Portrait of the Burmese Journalist, Journal Kyaw U Chit Maung*, Journal Kyaw Ma Ma Lay, trans. Ma Thanegi, 2008. ISBN 978-0-87727-747-7 (pb.)

Number 46 *At the Edge of the Forest: Essays on Cambodia, History, and Narrative in Honor of David Chandler*, ed. Anne Ruth Hansen and Judy Ledgerwood. 2008. ISBN 978-0-87727-746-0 (pb).

Number 45 *Conflict, Violence, and Displacement in Indonesia*, ed. Eva-Lotta E. Hedman. 2008. ISBN 978-0-87727-745-3 (pb.)

Number 44 *Friends and Exiles: A Memoir of the Nutmeg Isles and the Indonesian Nationalist Movement*, Des Alwi, ed. Barbara S. Harvey. 2008. ISBN 978-0-877277-44-6 (pb.)

Number 43 *Early Southeast Asia: Selected Essays*, O. W. Wolters, ed. Craig J. Reynolds. 2008. 255 pp. ISBN 978-0-877277-43-9 (pb.)

Number 42 *Thailand: The Politics of Despotic Paternalism* (revised edition), Thak Chaloemtiarana. 2007. 284 pp. ISBN 0-8772-7742-7 (pb.)

Number 41 *Views of Seventeenth-Century Vietnam: Christoforo Borri on Cochinchina and Samuel Baron on Tonkin*, ed. Olga Dror and K. W. Taylor. 2006. 290 pp. ISBN 0-8772-7741-9 (pb.)

Number 40 *Laskar Jihad: Islam, Militancy, and the Quest for Identity in Post-New Order Indonesia*, Noorhaidi Hasan. 2006. 266 pp. ISBN 0-877277-40-0 (pb.)

Number 39 *The Indonesian Supreme Court: A Study of Institutional Collapse*, Sebastiaan Pompe. 2005. 494 pp. ISBN 0-877277-38-9 (pb.)

Number 38   *Spirited Politics: Religion and Public Life in Contemporary Southeast Asia*, ed. Andrew C. Willford and Kenneth M. George. 2005. 210 pp. ISBN 0-87727-737-0.

Number 37   *Sumatran Sultanate and Colonial State: Jambi and the Rise of Dutch Imperialism, 1830-1907*, Elsbeth Locher-Scholten, trans. Beverley Jackson. 2004. 332 pp. ISBN 0-87727-736-2.

Number 36   *Southeast Asia over Three Generations: Essays Presented to Benedict R. O'G. Anderson*, ed. James T. Siegel and Audrey R. Kahin. 2003. 398 pp. ISBN 0-87727-735-4.

Number 35   *Nationalism and Revolution in Indonesia*, George McTurnan Kahin, intro. Benedict R. O'G. Anderson (reprinted from 1952 edition, Cornell University Press, with permission). 2003. 530 pp. ISBN 0-87727-734-6.

Number 34   *Golddiggers, Farmers, and Traders in the "Chinese Districts" of West Kalimantan, Indonesia*, Mary Somers Heidhues. 2003. 316 pp. ISBN 0-87727-733-8.

Number 33   *Opusculum de Sectis apud Sinenses et Tunkinenses (A Small Treatise on the Sects among the Chinese and Tonkinese): A Study of Religion in China and North Vietnam in the Eighteenth Century*, Father Adriano de St. Thecla, trans. Olga Dror, with Mariya Berezovska. 2002. 363 pp. ISBN 0-87727-732-X.

Number 32   *Fear and Sanctuary: Burmese Refugees in Thailand*, Hazel J. Lang. 2002. 204 pp. ISBN 0-87727-731-1.

Number 31   *Modern Dreams: An Inquiry into Power, Cultural Production, and the Cityscape in Contemporary Urban Penang, Malaysia*, Beng-Lan Goh. 2002. 225 pp. ISBN 0-87727-730-3.

Number 30   *Violence and the State in Suharto's Indonesia*, ed. Benedict R. O'G. Anderson. 2001. Second printing, 2002. 247 pp. ISBN 0-87727-729-X.

Number 29   *Studies in Southeast Asian Art: Essays in Honor of Stanley J. O'Connor*, ed. Nora A. Taylor. 2000. 243 pp. Illustrations. ISBN 0-87727-728-1.

Number 28   *The Hadrami Awakening: Community and Identity in the Netherlands East Indies, 1900-1942*, Natalie Mobini-Kesheh. 1999. 174 pp. ISBN 0-87727-727-3.

Number 27   *Tales from Djakarta: Caricatures of Circumstances and their Human Beings*, Pramoedya Ananta Toer. 1999. 145 pp. ISBN 0-87727-726-5.

Number 26   *History, Culture, and Region in Southeast Asian Perspectives*, rev. ed., O. W. Wolters. 1999. Second printing, 2004. 275 pp. ISBN 0-87727-725-7.

Number 25   *Figures of Criminality in Indonesia, the Philippines, and Colonial Vietnam*, ed. Vicente L. Rafael. 1999. 259 pp. ISBN 0-87727-724-9.

Number 24   *Paths to Conflagration: Fifty Years of Diplomacy and Warfare in Laos, Thailand, and Vietnam, 1778-1828*, Mayoury Ngaosyvathn and Pheuiphanh Ngaosyvathn. 1998. 268 pp. ISBN 0-87727-723-0.

Number 23   *Nguyễn Cochinchina: Southern Vietnam in the Seventeenth and Eighteenth Centuries*, Li Tana. 1998. Second printing, 2002. 194 pp. ISBN 0-87727-722-2.

Number 22   *Young Heroes: The Indonesian Family in Politics*, Saya S. Shiraishi. 1997. 183 pp. ISBN 0-87727-721-4.

Number 21 *Interpreting Development: Capitalism, Democracy, and the Middle Class in Thailand*, John Girling. 1996. 95 pp. ISBN 0-87727-720-6.

Number 20 *Making Indonesia*, ed. Daniel S. Lev, Ruth McVey. 1996. 201 pp. ISBN 0-87727-719-2.

Number 19 *Essays into Vietnamese Pasts*, ed. K. W. Taylor, John K. Whitmore. 1995. 288 pp. ISBN 0-87727-718-4.

Number 18 *In the Land of Lady White Blood: Southern Thailand and the Meaning of History*, Lorraine M. Gesick. 1995. 106 pp. ISBN 0-87727-717-6.

Number 17 *The Vernacular Press and the Emergence of Modern Indonesian Consciousness*, Ahmat Adam. 1995. 220 pp. ISBN 0-87727-716-8.

Number 16 *The Nan Chronicle*, trans., ed. David K. Wyatt. 1994. 158 pp. ISBN 0-87727-715-X.

Number 15 *Selective Judicial Competence: The Cirebon-Priangan Legal Administration, 1680–1792*, Mason C. Hoadley. 1994. 185 pp. ISBN 0-87727-714-1.

Number 14 *Sjahrir: Politics and Exile in Indonesia*, Rudolf Mrázek. 1994. 536 pp. ISBN 0-87727-713-3.

Number 13 *Fair Land Sarawak: Some Recollections of an Expatriate Officer*, Alastair Morrison. 1993. 196 pp. ISBN 0-87727-712-5.

Number 12 *Fields from the Sea: Chinese Junk Trade with Siam during the Late Eighteenth and Early Nineteenth Centuries*, Jennifer Cushman. 1993. 206 pp. ISBN 0-87727-711-7.

Number 11 *Money, Markets, and Trade in Early Southeast Asia: The Development of Indigenous Monetary Systems to AD 1400*, Robert S. Wicks. 1992. 2nd printing 1996. 354 pp., 78 tables, illus., maps. ISBN 0-87727-710-9.

Number 10 *Tai Ahoms and the Stars: Three Ritual Texts to Ward Off Danger*, trans., ed. B. J. Terwiel, Ranoo Wichasin. 1992. 170 pp. ISBN 0-87727-709-5.

Number 9 *Southeast Asian Capitalists*, ed. Ruth McVey. 1992. 2nd printing 1993. 220 pp. ISBN 0-87727-708-7.

Number 8 *The Politics of Colonial Exploitation: Java, the Dutch, and the Cultivation System*, Cornelis Fasseur, ed. R. E. Elson, trans. R. E. Elson, Ary Kraal. 1992. 2nd printing 1994. 266 pp. ISBN 0-87727-707-9.

Number 7 *A Malay Frontier: Unity and Duality in a Sumatran Kingdom*, Jane Drakard. 1990. 2nd printing 2003. 215 pp. ISBN 0-87727-706-0.

Number 6 *Trends in Khmer Art*, Jean Boisselier, ed. Natasha Eilenberg, trans. Natasha Eilenberg, Melvin Elliott. 1989. 124 pp., 24 plates. ISBN 0-87727-705-2.

Number 5 *Southeast Asian Ephemeris: Solar and Planetary Positions, A.D. 638–2000*, J. C. Eade. 1989. 175 pp. ISBN 0-87727-704-4.

Number 3 *Thai Radical Discourse: The Real Face of Thai Feudalism Today*, Craig J. Reynolds. 1987. 2nd printing 1994. 186 pp. ISBN 0-87727-702-8.

Number 1 *The Symbolism of the Stupa*, Adrian Snodgrass. 1985. Revised with index, 1988. 3rd printing 1998. 469 pp. ISBN 0-87727-700-1.

SEAP Series

Number 23   *Possessed by the Spirits: Mediumship in Contemporary Vietnamese Communities*. 2006. 186 pp. ISBN 0-877271-41-0 (pb).

Number 22   *The Industry of Marrying Europeans*, Vũ Trọng Phụng, trans. Thúy Tranviet. 2006. 66 pp. ISBN 0-877271-40-2 (pb).

Number 21   *Securing a Place: Small-Scale Artisans in Modern Indonesia*, Elizabeth Morrell. 2005. 220 pp. ISBN 0-877271-39-9.

Number 20   *Southern Vietnam under the Reign of Minh Mạng (1820-1841): Central Policies and Local Response*, Choi Byung Wook. 2004. 226pp. ISBN 0-0-877271-40-2.

Number 19   *Gender, Household, State: Đổi Mới in Việt Nam,* ed. Jayne Werner and Danièle Bélanger. 2002. 151 pp. ISBN 0-87727-137-2.

Number 18   *Culture and Power in Traditional Siamese Government*, Neil A. Englehart. 2001. 130 pp. ISBN 0-87727-135-6.

Number 17   *Gangsters, Democracy, and the State*, ed. Carl A. Trocki. 1998. Second printing, 2002. 94 pp. ISBN 0-87727-134-8.

Number 16   *Cutting across the Lands: An Annotated Bibliography on Natural Resource Management and Community Development in Indonesia, the Philippines, and Malaysia*, ed. Eveline Ferretti. 1997. 329 pp. ISBN 0-87727-133-X.

Number 15   *The Revolution Falters: The Left in Philippine Politics after 1986*, ed. Patricio N. Abinales. 1996. Second printing, 2002. 182 pp. ISBN 0-87727-132-1.

Number 14   *Being Kammu: My Village, My Life*, Damrong Tayanin. 1994. 138 pp., 22 tables, illus., maps. ISBN 0-87727-130-5.

Number 13   *The American War in Vietnam*, ed. Jayne Werner, David Hunt. 1993. 132 pp. ISBN 0-87727-131-3.

Number 12   *The Voice of Young Burma*, Aye Kyaw. 1993. 92 pp. ISBN 0-87727-129-1.

Number 11   *The Political Legacy of Aung San,* ed. Josef Silverstein. Revised edition 1993. 169 pp. ISBN 0-87727-128-3.

Number 10   *Studies on Vietnamese Language and Literature: A Preliminary Bibliography*, Nguyen Dinh Tham. 1992. 227 pp. ISBN 0-87727-127-5.

Number 8   *From PKI to the Comintern, 1924–1941: The Apprenticeship of the Malayan Communist Party*, Cheah Boon Kheng. 1992. 147 pp. ISBN 0-87727-125-9.

Number 7   *Intellectual Property and US Relations with Indonesia, Malaysia, Singapore, and Thailand*, Elisabeth Uphoff. 1991. 67 pp. ISBN 0-87727-124-0.

Number 6   *The Rise and Fall of the Communist Party of Burma (CPB)*, Bertil Lintner. 1990. 124 pp. 26 illus., 14 maps. ISBN 0-87727-123-2.

Number 5   *Japanese Relations with Vietnam: 1951–1987*, Masaya Shiraishi. 1990. 174 pp. ISBN 0-87727-122-4.

Number 3   *Postwar Vietnam: Dilemmas in Socialist Development,* ed. Christine White, David Marr. 1988. 2nd printing 1993. 260 pp. ISBN 0-87727-120-8.

Number 2   *The Dobama Movement in Burma (1930–1938)*, Khin Yi. 1988. 160 pp. ISBN 0-87727-118-6.

Cornell Modern Indonesia Project Publications

All CMIP titles available at http://cmip.library.cornell.edu

Number 75 *A Tour of Duty: Changing Patterns of Military Politics in Indonesia in the 1990s.* Douglas Kammen and Siddharth Chandra. 1999. 99 pp. ISBN 0-87763-049-6.

Number 74 *The Roots of Acehnese Rebellion 1989–1992*, Tim Kell. 1995. 103 pp. ISBN 0-87763-040-2.

Number 72 *Popular Indonesian Literature of the Qur'an*, Howard M. Federspiel. 1994. 170 pp. ISBN 0-87763-038-0.

Number 71 *A Javanese Memoir of Sumatra, 1945–1946: Love and Hatred in the Liberation War*, Takao Fusayama. 1993. 150 pp. ISBN 0-87763-037-2.

Number 69 *The Road to Madiun: The Indonesian Communist Uprising of 1948*, Elizabeth Ann Swift. 1989. 120 pp. ISBN 0-87763-035-6.

Number 68 *Intellectuals and Nationalism in Indonesia: A Study of the Following Recruited by Sutan Sjahrir in Occupation Jakarta*, J. D. Legge. 1988. 159 pp. ISBN 0-87763-034-8.

Number 67 *Indonesia Free: A Biography of Mohammad Hatta*, Mavis Rose. 1987. 252 pp. ISBN 0-87763-033-X.

Number 66 *Prisoners at Kota Cane*, Leon Salim, trans. Audrey Kahin. 1986. 112 pp. ISBN 0-87763-032-1.

Number 64 *Suharto and His Generals: Indonesia's Military Politics, 1975–1983*, David Jenkins. 1984. 4th printing 1997. 300 pp. ISBN 0-87763-030-5.

Number 62 *Interpreting Indonesian Politics: Thirteen Contributions to the Debate, 1964–1981*, ed. Benedict Anderson, Audrey Kahin, intro. Daniel S. Lev. 1982. 3rd printing 1991. 172 pp. ISBN 0-87763-028-3.

Number 60 *The Minangkabau Response to Dutch Colonial Rule in the Nineteenth Century*, Elizabeth E. Graves. 1981. 157 pp. ISBN 0-87763-000-3.

Number 57 *Permesta: Half a Rebellion*, Barbara S. Harvey. 1977. 174 pp. ISBN 0-87763-003-8.

Number 52 *A Preliminary Analysis of the October 1 1965, Coup in Indonesia (Prepared in January 1966)*, Benedict R. Anderson, Ruth T. McVey, assist. Frederick P. Bunnell. 1971. 3rd printing 1990. 174 pp. ISBN 0-87763-008-9.

Number 48 *Nationalism, Islam and Marxism*, Soekarno, intro. Ruth T. McVey. 1970.

Number 37 *Mythology and the Tolerance of the Javanese*, Benedict R. O'G. Anderson. 2nd edition, 1996. Reprinted 2004. 104 pp., 65 illus. ISBN 0-87763-041-0.

Copublished Titles

The Ambiguous Allure of the West: Traces of the Colonial in Thailand, ed. Rachel V. Harrison and Peter A. Jackson. Copublished with Hong Kong University Press. 2010. ISBN 978-0-87727-608-1 (pb.)

The Many Ways of Being Muslim: Fiction by Muslim Filipinos, ed. Coeli Barry. Copublished with Anvil Publishing, Inc., the Philippines. 2008. ISBN 978-0-87727-605-0 (pb.)

Language Texts

INDONESIAN

Beginning Indonesian through Self-Instruction, John U. Wolff, Dédé Oetomo, Daniel Fietkiewicz. 3rd revised edition 1992. Vol. 1. 115 pp. ISBN 0-87727-529-7. Vol. 2. 434 pp. ISBN 0-87727-530-0. Vol. 3. 473 pp. ISBN 0-87727-531-9.

Indonesian Readings, John U. Wolff. 1978. 4th printing 1992. 480 pp. ISBN 0-87727-517-3

Indonesian Conversations, John U. Wolff. 1978. 3rd printing 1991. 297 pp. ISBN 0-87727-516-5

Formal Indonesian, John U. Wolff. 2nd revised edition 1986. 446 pp. ISBN 0-87727-515-7

TAGALOG

Pilipino through Self-Instruction, John U. Wolff, Maria Theresa C. Centeno, Der-Hwa V. Rau. 1991. Vol. 1. 342 pp. ISBN 0-87727—525-4. Vol. 2., revised 2005, 378 pp. ISBN 0-87727-526-2. Vol 3., revised 2005, 431 pp. ISBN 0-87727-527-0. Vol. 4. 306 pp. ISBN 0-87727-528-9.

THAI

A. U. A. Language Center Thai Course, J. Marvin Brown. Originally published by the American University Alumni Association Language Center, 1974. Reissued by Cornell Southeast Asia Program, 1991, 1992. Book 1. 267 pp. ISBN 0-87727-506-8. Book 2. 288 pp. ISBN 0-87727-507-6. Book 3. 247 pp. ISBN 0-87727-508-4.

A. U. A. Language Center Thai Course, Reading and Writing Text (mostly reading), 1979. Reissued 1997. 164 pp. ISBN 0-87727-511-4.

A. U. A. Language Center Thai Course, Reading and Writing Workbook (mostly writing), 1979. Reissued 1997. 99 pp. ISBN 0-87727-512-2.

KHMER

Cambodian System of Writing and Beginning Reader, Franklin E. Huffman. Originally published by Yale University Press, 1970. Reissued by Cornell Southeast Asia Program, 4th printing 2002. 365 pp. ISBN 0-300-01314-0.

Modern Spoken Cambodian, Franklin E. Huffman, assist. Charan Promchan, Chhom-Rak Thong Lambert. Originally published by Yale University Press, 1970. Reissued by Cornell Southeast Asia Program, 3rd printing 1991. 451 pp. ISBN 0-300-01316-7.

Intermediate Cambodian Reader, ed. Franklin E. Huffman, assist. Im Proum. Originally published by Yale University Press, 1972. Reissued by Cornell Southeast Asia Program, 1988. 499 pp. ISBN 0-300-01552-6.

Cambodian Literary Reader and Glossary, Franklin E. Huffman, Im Proum. Originally published by Yale University Press, 1977. Reissued by Cornell Southeast Asia Program, 1988. 494 pp. ISBN 0-300-02069-4.

HMONG

White Hmong-English Dictionary, Ernest E. Heimbach. 1969. 8th printing, 2002. 523 pp. ISBN 0-87727-075-9.

VIETNAMESE

Intermediate Spoken Vietnamese, Franklin E. Huffman, Tran Trong Hai. 1980. 3rd printing 1994. ISBN 0-87727-500-9.

Proto-Austronesian Phonology with Glossary, John U. Wolff, 2 volumes, 2011.
ISBN vol. I, 978-0-87727-532-9. ISBN vol. II, 978-0-87727-533-6.

To order, please contact:
Mail:
Cornell University Press Services
750 Cascadilla Street
PO Box 6525
Ithaca, NY 14851 USA

E-mail: orderbook@cupserv.org

Phone/Fax, Monday–Friday, 8 am – 5 pm (Eastern US):
Phone: 607 277 2211 or 800 666 2211 (US, Canada)
Fax: 607 277 6292 or 800 688 2877 (US, Canada)

Order through our online bookstore at:
www.einaudi.cornell.edu/southeastasia/publications/